P9-EDH-256

# POETHICS: AND OTHER STRATEGIES
# OF LAW AND LITERATURE

# POETHICS
## AND OTHER STRATEGIES OF
## LAW AND LITERATURE

RICHARD WEISBERG

*Columbia University Press*
*New York*

*Columbia University Press*
*New York      Oxford*

Copyright © 1992   Columbia University Press
All rights reserved
Library of Congress Cataloging-in-Publication Data

Weisberg, Richard H., 1944–
    Poethics, and other strategies of law and literature / Richard
  Weisberg.
        p.   cm.
    Includes bibliographical references and index.
    ISBN 0-231-07454-9
    1. Law and literature.   2. Law in literature.   3. Literature—
  History and criticism.   4. Lawyers as authors.   I. Title.
  PN56.L33W4   1992
  809'.93355—dc20                                                  91-28548
                                                                      CIP

⊗

Casebound editions of Columbia University Press books are Smyth-sewn and printed on
permanent and durable acid-free paper.

Printed in the United States of America

c  10  9  8  7  6  5  4  3  2  1

*For my lifelong friends:*
*Peter Alscher, Richard Danzig, Stephen Dell,*
*Barry Fox, Eric Freedman, Joel Gressel,*
*Bruce Kogan, Joseph Korff, Richard Neugebauer,*
*and Charles Siegel*

# Contents

CONTENTS

# Preface

I AM going to involve my reader in the delightful task of associating two major human enterprises: establishing justice and telling stories. To what fruitful ends may these seemingly different activities be linked? We will answer that question over the course of this book, reading together along the way a rich variety of narratives and learning also of the myths, fabrications, and occasional verbal violence of the law.

This inquiry, although perhaps more systematically engaged here than elsewhere, has already provoked considerable interest among writers. Indeed, Law and Literature now provides fertile soil to many teachers and thinkers. Offered at a majority of American law schools and countless undergraduate institutions,[1] Law and Literature (or one of its variants) has gained in definition, in ambition, and in controversy. If the 1970s could claim only one book and a score of articles for the field, the 1980s saw a tenfold increase in both categories.[2] Two new scholarly journals were created and are continuing to devote exclusive attention to this interrelation.[3] The language of deconstruction, of textual analysis, and of the crisis in Western values pervades the legal academic's world;[4] fiction writers as well as literary critics continue to exhibit an often grudging fascination with the law—its courtroom reconstruction of reality, its rhetoric, its violence.[5]

What has so far been lacking—a void the present volume seeks to fill—is a guidebook to Law and Literature theory and practice, one that will help student and teacher, amateur and specialist alike to understand and participate in this novel area of thought. Part one establishes the theoretical basis for an ambitious interdisciplinary enterprise. Parts two and three then employ many of the prevalent strategies that give Law and Literature its unique analytical strength—from the careful reading of law-related fiction to the social critique of narrative itself, to the emphasis on common interests in ethics, rhetoric, structure, and form. Here my reader may find some evidence that Law and Literature joins a renewed interest in "ethical criticism."[6]

On one level, as I will show in part two, Law and Literature simply seeks to understand the disproportionate interest of fictional works in legal themes, lawyer figures, and the process of legal investigation and ratiocination. For literature's interest in law should not be generalized into an amorphous, quasi-metaphoric blur, as Judge Richard A. Posner attempted to do in *Law and Literature*. The literary treatment of law, moreover, while specific and highly detailed, is usually exhibited only periodically; in fact, whenever law becomes the dominant cultural and political force, literary art tends to immerse itself in matters legal. The way lawyers talk, the way they rule, the way they figure out what has occurred—these pursuits represent for the literary artist an analogue on the level of coercive reality to their own more private but equally verbal pursuits. Thus, in fifth-century Greek tragedy, the Icelandic family sagas, twelfth- to fourteenth-century medieval poetry, Elizabethan theater, and, finally, the modern novel, law has taken a prominent position among the subjects of literary discourse. These have been the epochs, at least in Western culture, in which legality has sprung up, competing successfully with other cultural influences for the attention of storytellers.

But serious fiction has never used law as merely a source of satire or even of social criticism. In each period, law has drawn the attention of the literary artist because of its similarities to narrative art, not its differences. Law's manner of recreating and discussing reality strikes the artist as close (and where misguided or erroneous, threateningly close) to what storytellers themselves are in the business of doing.

Lawyer and writer stand together, the former differing only in his coercive power, not in his technique or value system. Thus, in these essays, I write about such authors as Dickens and Faulkner, two of modern fiction's most prominent "legalistic" writers; and I discuss them less as satirists than as writers fundamentally incapable of expressing their darker vision without the mediation of legal characters, themes, and structures.

In these writers, comedy—even hilarity—has its place. But we must recognize that the lighter side of law-related fiction often serves to emphasize the slightly askew, always self-critical stance of the writer to writing. For it is of course writing, not law, that essentially interests literary artists. And legal writing—legal communication generally—strikes some generations of storytellers as metaphorically useful for their own narrative pursuits. Through law, as through no other medium, the writer's own enterprise of public communication can best be explored—self-consciously perhaps, but with an eye toward drawing the average reader into the sheer drama of legalistic conflict.

It is thus also a mistake (the second of Posner's errors) to assume that the usually scrupulous and sometimes technical treatment of law in fiction will not attract the lay audience. On the contrary, Dickens, Twain, Kafka, Camus, and Faulkner (among many others) perceived that people felt so dominated by law, so mystified yet so involved, that the more legalistic they made the subject matter, the more compelling would be the work.

The model for this seductive use of technical legal detail (as he is the model for so much else in recent literature) is that law-ensconced poet and playwright, William Shakespeare. Although the lawyerlike reasoning of his Danish prince will attract our attention in due time, it is one of his comedies, *The Merchant of Venice*, that will occupy us centrally in several of the following chapters. I will try to show that the play—second to none in the interest it has inspired among lawyer-critics—is neither anti-Semitic nor Shylock's "tragedy." It must be understood as a comedy, with Shylock's defeat in the trial scene perceived as the necessary victory of the comic elements in the play. But by stressing the almost always overlooked Act V, a brilliant denouement that cannot be understood without some attention to Shakespeare's legalistic imagery, I endeavor to show that the playwright strongly doubted the efficacy and the ethics of his own comic medium. Somewhat anticipating the full-fledged modern novelist, he presented legal imagery to undermine his own enterprise. The play's troubling climax, as we shall see, disturbs its comic essence.

Part two of this volume also provides fresh readings of other well-known fictional works. The reader will emerge from the Shakespeare–Dickens–Faulkner essays (and others on Melville and on Barth) with a good sense of the storyteller's legalistic obsession and with a firm grasp, too, of Law-and-Literature methodology. The essays should inspire (if so employed) avid debate and discussion in the classroom as well.

I have chosen in this book not only to challenge traditional readings of well-worked literary texts but also to engage the debate about *what* texts we should read when "doing" Law and Literature. Criticism, all of it implicitly friendly, has been leveled at the seeming indifference of the field to the attack upon "the canon." And, indeed, most of the texts I treat in detail here are to be found on the standard "Great Books" curriculum. Yet I argue that there are excellent reasons, pedagogical and otherwise, for the field's early focus on the traditional canon. When, in *The Failure of the Word*, I treated the ressentient legal narrator in Flaubert, Melville, Dostoevski, and Camus, it was not to exclude lesser-known voices but to prepare for their full integration. The choice of establishment male authors hardly denotes acceptance of the traditional canon when the male narrative enterprise itself is being criticized for its violence and its twisting of the truth. Yet there is value in a more positive sense in emphasizing the Great Books. We cannot, as literary people, and even less as lawyers, afford to lose an entire generation of readers. The disastrous hermeticism of poststructural literary criticism—its turning away from the text—has disserved the general population of potential readers. There can be no principled evasion of excellent literature, no matter how worthy the claims of lesser-known artists, in an environment in which few people are being exposed to the traditional texts.[7]

But my argument for the Great Books is at heart a radical one. Law and Literature rightly attempts to preserve the canon, but only until it is understood that such mainstream texts of literary art themselves undermine virtually every sacred belief of Western culture. Shakespeare may have been a bourgeois white Christian male, but he stands as model and precursor for those whose art signifies iconoclasm, not reverence—rebellion, not acceptance. Our task in reading such superb standard texts is to identify and emphasize within them those fruitful ethical offshoots that have been nipped in the bud, first by the traditionalist literary critics who misconstrued these works as being somehow reassuring and now by "postmodern" literature professors who ignore or denigrate them. Thus the title here of one brief but trenchant chapter, "The Self-Imploding Canon," denotes the self-destructive, autosubverting nature of mainstream nineteenth- and twentieth-century fiction. Through the various law-related subjects they treat (and because of the *manner* in which they treat them), these works undermine most of our culture's sacred beliefs. It would be wrongheaded as well as ironic to scrap the central canon for supposedly progressive purposes before we have located the canon's true target: itself. The narrative perspective on law (and on the act of writing, too, especially in the midst of the repressive violence of the past century and a half) becomes an attack on *all* Christian practices.

The Nietzschean "Umwertung der Werte" (overturning of the table of values) is shown here to illuminate more than the literary canon alone, however. In part three of this volume, the rhetoric of law itself is examined. For if the storyteller's fascination with law has occupied some practitioners of the new interrelation, the narrative, structural, and ethical aspects of law have concerned others. Theoreticians have been applying some of the more sophisticated techniques of reading employed by academic literary thinkers to such foundational legal texts as the American Constitution. Indeterminacy of meaning and other deconstructive notions have unsettled many in the legal establishment: some of this apprehension emerged during the Senate Judiciary Committee's inquiry into (failed) Supreme Court candidate Robert Bork and his "originalist" brand of interpretive theory. Although lawyers and judges have never really been constrained by strict notions of "plain textual meaning" or intentionalism, the "deconstructive turn" in law has for the first time posited that such radical strategies are *theoretically respectable*; in my view, this contribution is fairly modest, and I do not stress it here.

Nonetheless, the move to theory in Law and Literature is represented in part three by several essays grouped under the rubric "Legal Rhetoric, or the Stories Lawyers Tell." The first two deal with the practice of law in Vichy France during World War II: "Avoiding Central Realities" traces the idea of terror from the pages of literature to the halls of Vichy government; and "Legal Rhetoric Under Stress" questions so-called postmodernist theories (particularly as applied to law) by placing them side by side with the awful "deconstructionism" used by Vichy lawyers to distort the normative texts of French egalitarianism and racial tolerance. In that essay, I challenge those who assert the absence of text and referent—the disequilibrium of structure—to answer the ramifications of their theories for Holocaustic professional practice.

While the essays in part three contain a good deal more technical law than do the earlier sections of the book, I believe that the general reader's attention will be sustained throughout. Indeed, as I move westward again (from France back to our own shores), the most topical debate within Law and Literature is joined. Here I answer the often ill-conceived—but surprisingly well received—arguments of the newly literary Judge Posner. His early work, while wrongheaded, has been moderated in subsequent efforts published just as this preface was being completed. Harbingers of a move in the direction of some literary maturity on Posner's part are the nonstatistical sections of his new book on Benjamin N. Cardozo[8] and a libertarian free-speech opinion he has written about nude dancing in *Miller v. Civil City of South Bend*.[9] I could not include in this volume any sustained analysis of these efforts, but they indicate Posner's substantial sensitivity to the literary necessities of the judicial function.

In my two final essays, I address the state of contemporary legal rhetoric. The essay on legal writing skills asserts that a more forceful rhetoric will produce not only a more successful but also a happier practitioner. The essay on James Boyd White sadly reports my estimation that this widely read rhetorician—whose early efforts helped to establish the field of Law and Literature—has not fulfilled his promise. His last few efforts have seemed repetitive, his response to suggestions and criticisms (unlike Posner's) almost nonexistent.[10]

Interdisciplinary approaches come and go, but to my mind Law and Literature (already, in its modern incarnation, more than fifteen years old) deserves the tremendous influx of talent and attention it has attracted. The merging of our two most influential narrative enterprises is bringing about not just a refreshing but indeed an enduring opportunity to understand our cultural life.

Locked in their hermetic caskets, law and literary studies have proceeded somewhat as though nothing outside themselves had occurred in this tumultuous and belief-destroying century. Postmodernist criticism, shunning at some extremes text in favor of theory, has been matched in law by the insurgency of "free market" microeconomics, a disgracefully self-serving system of ethical reductionism and human evasion. Both systems have attracted masses of practitioners away from the essence of their fields, away from the passions, the hopes, the reality of the world around them.

Law and Literature, as it has been practiced (as it is practiced here), embraces the world to which narrative traditionally has been linked, the world of stories. Whether we read fictional law or lawful fiction, it is our imagination, our fears, and our deepest aspirations that will be touched by this effort to link our culture's two most central narrative endeavors. Changes—drastic and needed changes—are in the air. The interrelation of law and literature, freed from unidisciplinary constraints, continues its struggle to understand and to lead. Bearing this in mind, let us begin with the programmatic essay that provides this volume its title.

# Acknowledgments

I THANK the copyright holders for permission to reprint portions of my articles, as follows: "The Quest for Silence: Faulkner's Lawyer in a Comparative Setting," *Mississippi College Law Review* (1984), 4:193; "Accepting the Inside Narrator's Challenge: *Billy Budd* and the 'Legalistic' Reader," *Cardozo Studies in Law and Literature* (1989), 1:27; "Avoiding Central Realities: Narrative Terror and the Failure of French Culture Under the Occupation," *Human Rights Quarterly* (1983), 5:151; "Legal Rhetoric Under Stress: The Example of Vichy," *Cardozo Law Review* (1991), 12:1371; Entering with a Vengeance: Posner on Law and Literature," *Stanford Law Review* (1989), 41:1597; "Review of J. B. White's *The Legal Imagination*," *Columbia Law Review* (1974), 74:327; and "Review of J. B. White's *Heracles' Bow*," *Michigan Law Review* (1985), 85:920.

I would like to thank, for their responsive suggestions, the audiences to earlier versions of the material in this book. "Toward a Literary Jurisprudence" was delivered in May 1990 to the Department of European Literature, University of California/Riverside, and at the Law School, Boalt Hall, University of California/Berkeley; "Narrative Aspects of Judicial Opinions" was first delivered in Phoenix in 1980 to the Law and Humanities Section of the American Association of Law Schools, at its annual meeting; the essay on Mr. Jaggers was first delivered to the Dickens

Project annual meeting (cosponsored by the Law and Humanities Institute) in 1988 at the University of California/Santa Cruz; the sections on *Bleak House* derive from a series of lectures to my Law and Literature classes at the Cardozo Law School (fall 1990), whom I thank for their questions and evaluative comments; "John Barth's Todd Andrews" was originally delivered to the South Atlantic Modern Language Association's meeting in Atlanta, 1980; Essay 16, on legal writing, is taken from remarks to "Friends of the University of Virginia Law Library," in Charlottesville, 1991, and to a session of a Continuing Legal Education program for government lawyers sponsored by the Ohio Legislative Service Commission and Supreme Court, Columbus, Ohio.

Special thanks are offered to the participants in the Law and Literature workshop at the University of California/Irvine (under the direction of Murray Krieger), who in 1989 first heard what is now the essay "Legal Rhetoric Under Stress"; I should also note that the latter essay was assisted to fruition by generous grants from the American Council of Learned Societies, the Vidal Sassoon Center for the Study of Antisemitism (Hebrew University, Jerusalem), and from the Jacob Burns Institute for Advanced Legal Research of the Cardozo Law School and its sponsoring institution, Yeshiva University; and to the English faculty at the Bar Ilan University in Tel Aviv, whose comments on the essay "Then You Shall Be His Surety" were invaluable.

Finally, I express my affectionate gratitude to Frances Olsen, who introduced me to Toni Morrison's *The Bluest Eye* as part of a Faculty Reading Group at the University of California/Los Angeles in spring 1990; to Richard Neugebauer, who greatly helped me with "The Self-Imploding Canon" essay; to Peter Alscher, whose decade-long dialogue with me on *The Merchant of Venice* has been both provocative and influential; and to my wife Cheryl and sons Dan, Benno, and Sam, for their support as this volume took shape.

POETHICS: AND OTHER STRATEGIES
OF LAW AND LITERATURE

# 1

## Paving the Way

CHAPTER ONE

# *Poethics*: Toward a
# Literary Jurisprudence

WHILE LAW and Literature now commands the attention of a growing number of academics and practitioners, no unifying manifesto or program has as yet been announced. This chapter aims to set down one plank of such a program, the one that links Law and Literature to jurisprudence, the study of legal norms. For however the field may have progressed over the lively decade of the 1980s, Law and Literature actually began as a subcategory of jurisprudence.[1] The thought was—and remains—that literature provides unique insights into the underpinnings of law and that stories and poems stand as sources of law, richer and certainly more accessible than those others in legal philosophy that have dominated jurisprudence for many years.

## 1. Filling the Void

The twin conceptions of literature as a source of law, and literary methods and approaches as an analogue to law are not new. John Wigmore at the turn of the century and Benjamin Cardozo in the 1920s cited novelists and poets as our predominant teachers of law.[2] In their way, they were rehearsing the intuitively felt unities of law and literature that informed our national rhetoric in the infancy of the Republic.[3] And when, in the

3

1980s, John Rawls yielded to Ronald Dworkin in many quarters, the jurisprudential square had again been circled—for Dworkin, speaking as a legal philosopher, was confessing in *Law's Empire* that the norms of law are those of literary criticism.[4] His call to literary methodology and the sources of narrative technique surprised only those who had been locked into some version or another of positivistic or idealistic philosophy and who now were being urged to perceive, again, the stronger humanity of literature as the best source of law.

Wonderfully equipped for the task, literature teaches about law in two discrete if related ways. First, by the *how* of literature—or how literature means, to paraphrase John Ciardi[5]—and second, by the *what* of literature—the rationalized rearticulation of its "lessons" for law. As I have consistently suggested, when a novel represents a legal process, or a lawyer in action, it "teaches" about law in both of these ways. First, the manner of the representation (the *"discours,"* in Roland Barthes' sense)[6] evokes uniquely the thing represented.[7] And, at the same time, the matter (Barthes' *"histoire"*) uniquely conveys deep structural insights about many legal practices.

Lawyer and novelist stand as one in the compelled merger of style and substance, of form and function, in each of their various professional utterances. As Cardozo noted years ago, and as every poet and storyteller understands, the carefully crafted utterance (in law *and* literature) unites the message with the medium—indeed, is so constituted that the medium of linguistic expression *is* the meaning. He put it so strongly that it bears repeating:

> The strength that is born of form and the feebleness that is born of the lack of form are in truth qualities of the substance.[8]

The notion that form and substance are one in law reverberates in the present essay and throughout this volume. In my literary jurisprudence, that idea forms the first plank, which I call the "poetic method" for law.

Just as pressing, perhaps, to a literary jurisprudence is the second element, which I call here "poetic ethics," or (neologistically, but with thanks to Aristotle), *poethics*. Poethics, as we shall see, endeavors nothing less than to fill the ethical void in which legal thought and practice now exist. We find in this current environment the extremes of economic pseudosciencism and postmodernist nihilism. The middle ground of standard jurisprudence (the struggle, say, between Kant and Hegel, or Austin and Hart, or Fuller and Kelsen), while rich and important, has never involved more than a handful of legal academics and has never caught the interest of the practicing lawyer.[9] More superficially attractive, legal economics yields a universe of cost-benefit analysis, a demand-curve metaphor that (unlike traditional jurisprudence) often dictates both judicial and advocacy behavior. And postmodernist thought, at an extreme of nihilism, has trickled down at least to the practitioner (if not yet the judiciary)[10], suggesting the absence of ethical constraints in law. Legal academics, for their part, have increasingly entered the interdisciplinary worlds of economics, continental philosophy, and, happily, literary art and criticism.

Literature provides a lively and accessible medium for learning about law in an ethical way. This essay will first elucidate the twinned approach of the literary jurisprudence: a poetic method for law and a poethics of reading. It will then apply the poetic method to four judicial opinions and proceed to a discussion of a half dozen poethical texts, texts that help to explore, teach, and develop further the values of a literary jurisprudence. First, however, we return to the poetic method for law, to the claim that form and substance, sound and sense, merge inevitably in the expression of a just legal system.

# 2. The Poetic Method for Law, or How the Law Means

No great poem, and surely no novel or play, can be reduced without impoverishment to the expression of some logical, linear idea. Storytellers move us *in* and not *by* their language. So the "meaning" of a story does exist, but it lies in the words, in the unity of sound and sense that typifies the successful piece of literature. Think of the exhilarating opening lines in Gerard Manley Hopkins' "The Windhover":

> I caught this morning morning's minion, king-
> dom of daylight's dauphin, dapple-dawn-drawn Falcon, in his riding

or of Hamlet's Act I expression of outraged grief:

> O, most wicked speed, to post
> With such dexterity to incestuous sheets!

We can rearticulate these words to state their meaning, but we know that not only their beauty is thereby impoverished; the *meaning itself* is lessened through each restatement. Hopkins has swept us into the ecstatic heavens long before his sensible noun "Falcon" situates us there with logical certainty. Those heavens and that Falcon have been defined *in* the

5

poetry; we cannot extract them from the words that have given them life (although this does not mean that we should not try). Hamlet's bereavement, his amazement at the overhasty marriage of his mother to his uncle, find expression as something different—something more—than the words I just used at the beginning of this sentence to describe them. In the pervasive sound "s", for example, this emotion is created *as Hamlet's own*. That emotion never existed before, and it cannot be recreated in any form other than its original one. It is a unique feeling, unbounded by standard expressions of what it evokes apart from its own language.

The poetic method always insists on the unity of the words used with the sense expressed by those words. When applied to law, it thus captures something essential that otherwise goes unexpressed. Consider these expressions of judicial sense:

> The risk reasonably to be perceived defines the duty to be obeyed, and risk imports relation.[11]
> ... with all deliberate speed.[12]
> We must never forget, that it is a *constitution* we are expounding.[13]
> Three generations of idiots are enough.[14]

As Cardozo put it, judicial language is always more than the mere translation of a "holding" into words. For law, also, *means* a certain way, and logic rarely prevails in law over what Oliver Wendell Holmes called experience and what Cardozo has called "the transfiguration of the thought." In "The Growth of the Law," he tells us:

> We find a kindred phenomenon in literature, alike in poetry and prose. The search is for the just word, the happy phrase, that will give expression to the thought, but somehow the thought itself is transfigured by the phrase when found. There is emancipation in our very bonds. The restraints of rhyme or metre, the exigencies of period or balance, liberate at times the thought which they confine, and in imprisoning release.[15]

Words create law, for Cardozo. They neither distort it nor stand in its way. Words do not translate the thought of justice, words *are* justice, and words can be the absence of justice. Using the metaphor of a cracknel biscuit, he put it this way to a group of lawyers some sixty years ago:

> We may tell judges till doomsday that they are to love logic more than justice; as in affairs of the heart generally it is easier to give the command than to cause it to be heeded. ... I know the stock distinctions between morals and law. ... But with it all I like to believe that law has the qualities of a cracknel biscuit, and that however solid and dry it seems when we bite into its crust, there is a fluid mixed with the solid and forming the better part.[16]

The fluid, for Cardozo, for all lawyers, conscious of it or no, is the medium of language. How an opinion means, how a negotiating session or an argument to a jury means, is more important than what it means. And so, when Cardozo wrote in *Meinhard v. Salmon* that the fiduciary stands not for the morals of the marketplace but for "the punctilio of an honor the most sensitive," he was replicating the method of the Yeats and the Arnold he loved so much.[17] The formulation of this highest standard of conduct *has become* that standard—no one need even try to paraphrase it, for any rearticulation would be not only an impoverishment *but a change in the standard.*

Cardozo's opinion, all opinions, stand or fall on their language, but also on the appropriateness of the fit—the fluid harmony—between the words used and the aspiration toward justice that every legal pronouncement should embody. In our system, as Cardozo in particular would note, judicial power in the long run is linguistically grounded:

> The opinion will need persuasive force, or the impressive virtue of sincerity and fire, or the mnemonic power of alliteration and antithesis, or the terseness and tang of the proverb, and the maxim. Neglect the help of these allies, and it may never win its way.[18]

At this point, standard legal methodology might still intercede and suggest that the *outcome* in a given Supreme Court case (or other legal situation) surely predominates over the linguistic "form" in which the outcome is justified (or produced). An opinion may be "well crafted," but what consolation does that bring if, finally, we feel that the result in the case is somehow wrong, unjust, misguided?

Standard jurisprudence, thus articulated, sharply distinguishes—as Cardozo never did—between the form of a legal utterance and its substance. Difficult though it may be to grasp, however, Cardozo's insistent unification of legal form and substance makes more sense. The poetic method for law challenges the standard bifurcation in the following three ways:

1. The "holding" in a case cannot without some alteration be abstracted from the words used to express it.
2. No opinion with a misguided outcome has ever in fact been "well crafted."
3. Even opinions that have had salutary effects and are widely applauded will lose power as time goes on if they fail to harmonize sound and sense in working their outcome.

As to point one, of course a court has the immediate power to render a decision, and it need not even give any reasons justifying it. But we would not think of this as an opinion with a "holding." It would be a holding-less, raw act of power (effected these days even by some appellate courts),[19] but our system discourages such procedures except in a small category of "easy" cases. Once the judge begins to write, his use of power automatically is bound up in the words he uses. I analyze the inevitable interrelation of holding to words used in the next essay, where I demonstrate that all judges, conscious or no of their crafting powers, must match language to outcome in order to produce a coherent result. Although, again, even gobbledygook (if followed by a decree for or against a given party in the case) will have some transitory effect, such a text will reveal its own unjustness and will be overturned almost immediately. Judges do not consciously put themselves in such a position, of course; but the step from gobbledygook to sloppiness to unconvincingness to subtle error is a move by degree, not a move from one *kind* of opinion to another. In other words, the language that produces a marginally incorrect opinion reveals itself as certainly—if somewhat more belatedly—as the gibberish that marks a clearly unacceptable piece of legal prose. In any event, it is the language used in the opinion, and only that language, that perfectly constitutes the "doing"—the holding—of the opinion. Rearticulation using other words constitutes, inevitably, a recasting of the opinion's deed.

Point two argues that there can be no dichotomy between craft and result in law. This point should strike the reader as somewhat more controversial than the first. Law professors in particular seem to exult in admitting that they admire the craftsmanship of judicial opinions with which they disagree. But how can this be? The very statement implies that an outcome wrong on the law, and even unjust, can be rendered pleasing and fully acceptable by elegant rhetoric or close logic. In a kind of Pascalian manner, this approach bifurcates the craft of law from law's purpose: the doing of justice. On its face, this credo cannot stand. Recalling Cardozo's powerful antidote to such beliefs ("the strength that is born of form and the feebleness that is born of the lack of form are in truth qualities of the substance"; see note 8), I would assert that an opinion wrong in its outcome may not at the same time be excellent in its craftsmanship. Or, to put it differently, admiration for the craft of an opinion probably carries with it a measure of esteem for the outcome that the analyst may not be willing to reveal.

Point three speaks to the converse of point two and is equally, or possibly more, controversial. Here I argue that even a salutary outcome cannot endure if its narrative craft does not embody its admirable action. This is true even if we are dealing with the ultimate arbiter, over whose decision there will be no review. An opinion that fails to achieve justice through (and not despite) language will not "win its way." Each generation teaches lawyers this lesson, yet only the poetic method for law brings it to the fore. Thus, it is clear that a poorly crafted opinion by, say, the Supreme Court, might have currency temporarily. In the case of a decision such as *Plessy v. Ferguson* (holding that separate but equal facilities satisfy the Fourteenth Amendment), the stretch of authoritative time might be frustratingly long.[20] In other cases, such as the recent *National League of Cities v. Ussery*[21] (holding that the Tenth Amendment affirmatively limits congressional power that invades state and local interests), the disjunction of form and substance in the opinion brings a relatively quick reversal (*Garcia v. San Antonio Metropolitan Transit Authority*[22] a mere nine years later). The lesson is that poor craftsmanship even on the Supreme Court ultimately brings an opinion down.

Do these shifts possibly occur for other than literary reasons, however? Common wisdom might first cite changes in the personnel of the Court. But a moment's thought reveals the inadequacy of that explanation. If a move from liberal to conservative majorities on the present Supreme Court, for example, were conjured to explain certain shifts that we are about to flag—those in the areas of desegregation and abortion—how can we rationalize the continuing allegiance of that same majority to other liberal programs of their predecessors in areas such as gender discrimination and libel law? The court of the Reagan-Bush years has retained the *Craig v. Boren* rule[23] and many of its progeny, for example; and it has unanimously reaffirmed the expansive First Amendment protections of *New York Times v. Sullivan* as well.[24]

Yet weaker authorities—less well reasoned, less well crafted, less well unifying the urge to justice with the language employed to effectuate that urge—do not survive. Thus, my third point, and perhaps the most distressing, might lead one to expect that even *Brown v. Board of Education*[25] (overruling *Plessy*), or *Roe v. Wade*[26] (prohibiting the states from criminalizing abortions in the first trimester) will not survive.

These opinions produced moments of almost incomparable joy in many oppressed communities. But neither opinion fully expressed its central core of justice. Neither speaks fully its only-implicit correctness. The result is not a trivial observation about the aesthetics of the decisions. Rather, the absence of "the mnemonic power of alliteration and antithesis" (or any other powerfully expressive medium) is having the tangible effect of limiting their durability and authoritative scope. While a detailed analysis of *Brown* and *Roe* in this regard awaits another forum, it should be obvious that neither opinion captured in its writing the essence of the human situations they so courageously attempted to alleviate.

*Brown*'s strange reliance on social scientific data robbed the opinion of the poignant focus on the historical and legal fate of individual black people, a focus that might have prevented so much of current affirmative-action backlash. After all, a nonminority individual might say, after *Brown*: if some social scientists find a stigma in one group that is being disadvantaged, it is not difficult to find another who will say that *anyone* (including me) forced to yield some advantage to a minority competitor also is wronged.

*Brown* had to enter, humanistically, into the specific, directly conveyed experience of disadvantaged black people. In large measure, it failed to do so. The justices instead gave their narrative heart to the social scientists. Similarly, *Roe* failed to enter specifically the world of a woman privately struggling with a decision that is intensely personal and often agonizing. *Roe* did not couch its outcome in terms of human autonomy; too much attention is again paid to science, and the opinion reads like a less-than-convincing medical text aimed more at doctors than at women (or even lawyers). To focus on the safety of abortions and the so-called viability of the fetus was to blur—I would argue fatally—the central reality of the situation: a woman's right to choose among distressing but highly personal alternatives.

I have chosen two of our most widely revered opinions to demonstrate the claim of the poetic method that the law *means*; it does not simply exist. Political battles for the survival of mere "outcomes" have their place; but as the phenomenon of the conservative Supreme Court's allegiance to *Boren* and to *New York Times v. Sullivan* indicates, the whittling away by the same Court of the less successfully written *Brown* and *Roe* redeems Cardozo's truth that justice and words must be linked at the generative moment of the decision. Otherwise, even if rendered by the highest authority, it "may never win its way."

So the poetic method already provokes us, as customary learning does not, to highlight the linguistic, sensory aspects of every part of our craft. The years have not changed the reality of law: for better or worse, it is utterly dependent on language; better, it *is*, utterly, language. I now elaborate with greater specificity, turning my attention to the narrative elements of four common-law appellate opinions.

# 3. Narrative Aspects of Judicial Opinions

The proposition that the style of an appellate opinion has an effect on the legal meaning of the opinion should need little in the way of proof.

To some extent style's relationship to function is axiomatic: in the classroom law professors seek everyday not only to understand what an appellate opinion does but also what it means; they ask students to look beneath the overt rationale of the court's argument in order to perceive what is really being said. Particularly when sociological, economic, philosophical, or other extrinsic modes are applied to an opinion do we begin to prick the surface and start to delve into the true substance of the matter. That surface consists, of course, of language. No matter how unconscious an adjudicator may be of his rhetorical abilities, no matter even that he delegates the writing of the opinion to someone else, what analysts are left with is a grouping of words endeavoring to express the court's thinking and its action in a given dispute.

## STYLE AND "PRECEDENTIAL VALUE"

To some extent the dynamism of our Anglo-American legal system derives from the necessity for style in the appellate opinion. Language may be used elegantly or carelessly, but it *is* the judge's medium. The opinion may be effectively organized or it may be haphazard in its explanation of the facts and issues, but it must have a form, and form, a part of style, also contributes to the opinion's present and ultimate meaning.

Although style's relationship to substance has been axiomatic, this does not mean that it will always be (at least, not to the point that scholars have moved beyond axiom to theorems predicated on the axiom). Literary analyses of opinions, as I have suggested, are only now being proferred in a context meaningful to legal scholars. Yet the recent successes of Law and Literature still pale when contrasted with the pervasiveness of less kindred interdisciplinary approaches. Perhaps the intrusion of economics can be explained on the familiarity principle. The fact that lawyers and judges intuit the importance of style to their function has made them loath to investigate the relation systematically. I have met otherwise masterful law teachers who, for example, admit to "never reading fiction." (They ignore thereby, among other things, the inevitable fictional aspects of the judicial opinion.) Social scientific tracts, analyses heaped with empirical data, jargon-filled but modish articles, all of these commonly achieve acceptance; yet, perhaps for being too close to us, the material most clearly relating to the law's meaning is viewed with suspicion.

Beyond this, we now have courts of high authority who, in certain situations, refuse to verbalize. I refer, as just one example, to the Federal Circuit's "Rule 18" and its progeny. This rule states that:

> Opinions which do not add significantly or usefully to the body of law or
> would not have precedential value will not be published. (Rule 18, United
> States Court of Appeals, Federal Circuit)

Happily, the rule has inspired a great deal of comment, and I am far
from being alone in my especial fascination for the phrase "would not
have precedential value." Whatever the merits (and they are many) of the
court's desire to reduce its circuit's workload, the notion of a court
deciding in advance that whatever it might write about a decision would
fail to produce precedential effect stimulates my jurisprudential hor-
mones. Language generates precedential effect; the need to articulate
automatically produces the problems of communication on which our
system of law has thrived.

Cardozo's essays, as we have seen, articulate a consistent theme: the
appellate judge, consciously or no, works within a linguistic medium that
contributes a creative element to his everyday task of decision making.
On this view of things, the decision, a priori, that a dispute *cannot*
generate language later used to resolve a slightly different dispute in a
way that the adjudicator of the first dispute could not predict, is itself a
value determination that requires explanation. As I specified, Cardozo's
own phrase, "the punctilio of an honor the most sensitive,"[27] used countless times since to describe the fiduciary duty, arose from a case that had
little to do with fiduciaries. Its holding's precedential value (if any) pales
next to its dictum's longevity. Had the opinion not been written, the
law today would be different, but different for reasons Cardozo himself
could never have predicted from the issues at hand. His thought was
liberated and "transfigured" (like a poet's) by the necessity to put it into
words.

Appellate judges are not all named Cardozo (and there may be comfort
in the fact for many reasons). But to the extent that appellate judges are
all *writers* (or at least managers of writers), we have all gained comfort.
By "we" I mean here not only law professors and litigators; I mean the
public generally, whose interest in judicial articulation has been explained
for jurisprudential and aesthetic reasons.

I begin an in-depth exploration of the poetic method for law with
the case that appears here as appendix 3.1 (see page 22). *Osterlind v.
Hill*[28] was written by a judge of little renown in a style that would be
eminently forgettable were it not for the inevitable identity of style and
substance in law. The tort issue is a perennial and a fascinating one: is
there an affirmative duty to rescue in our law? The court's answer is no,
but the *way* it puts it colors the meaning of its negative response. In this

case the defendant rented a canoe to Osterlind and another man, both of whom may have been drunk at the time. The vessel overturned (my way of stating the facts, like any court's, subtly alters those facts), and Osterlind clung to it for half an hour screaming for help. The defendant noted the incident from the shore, heard the screams, and although neither life nor limb would have been risked, failed to act.

Osterlind's relatives, suing on his behalf, were to have no recourse. Judge Braley affirmed the lower court's sustaining of the defendant's demurrer. In doing so, he thought his choices to be restricted by the clear message of the precedents: absent some special relationship between the parties, our system imposes no duty to rescue. Cardozo once spoke of this rule as follows:

> For years there has been a dogma of the books that in the absence of a special duty of protection, one may stand by with indifference and see another perish, by drowning, say, or fire, though there would be no peril in a rescue. A rule so divorced from morals was sure to breed misgivings. We need not be surprised to find that in cases of recent date, a tendency is manifest to narrow it or even whittle it away. We cannot say today that the old rule has been supplanted. The rulings are too meager. Sown, however, are the seeds of skepticism, the precursor often of decay. Some day we may awake to find that the old tissues are dissolved. Then will come a new generalization, and with it a new law.[29]

Judge Braley may not have known he was affecting the law, but in the act of writing the opinion he was. He chose not to dissolve "the old tissues" of the rule. He might have reached the same decision using different language and reasoning. But in using the fact that Osterlind clung screaming to the overturned canoe for thirty minutes to show that he must not have been so drunk as to have placed defendant on notice at the time of rental, and in then using the same fact to produce the stylistic pinnacle of the opinion, Braley was altering the shape of the law. He might, under Rule 18, have decided to affirm without opinion. But constrained to stylize, he affected the law for better and worse. I quote from the thirteen-word denouement of his opinion (lines 61 and 62): "The failure of the defendant to respond to the intestate's outcries is immaterial."

Of the many ways the affirming judge could have responded to these facts, this manner seems most designed to prevent the planting of Cardozo's "seeds of skepticism" about the rule. Braley's rhetorical (if not his legal) options were limitless, as immense as the language itself, even within his choice of sustaining the demurrer. Had he wished to assist in a future alteration of the rule, he could have drawn the facts in their most dramatic form; this alone might have affected precedent. He might have emphasized, rather than dismissed, the moral dilemma inherent in the legal rule. He might even have cited continental precedent, which *does* impose an affirmative duty to rescue. Any of these rhetorical choices might have convinced a future judge, on a slightly different set of facts, to make sure that the rule's "tissues are dissolved." Instead, the opinion's climax deliberately shoves to the periphery what seems to most readers to be the heart of the matter in dispute. And by the very weirdness of that displacement, the judge's words survive and influence us.

Braley's thirteen-word stylistic apogee lends his apparent endorsement to the rule. Yet his stark rhetoric may, in the way of our narratively based law, work to give the opinion a quite different "precedential effect" than he intended. That the law will occasionally respond so blandly to a factual situation's essential human element is a phenomenon that screams forth (like the drowning Osterlind himself). Scholars and future judges will note it; in this way, too, the law gains understanding, and the "seeds of skepticism" are further sown.

To this extent, even the Braley opinion establishes an essential point about the appellate opinion: within it, willy-nilly, style serves the function of the law and is not separate from it. An opinion matching a "correct" legal outcome with a weird supporting narrative indicates on its face that the law must be changed.

As Karl Llewellyn puts it in his essay, "The Good, the True, the Beautiful, in Law":

> Thus the only esthetic rule which I recognize about adornment in relation to function is that adornment is best when it can be made to serve function, and is bad when it interferes with function; beyond that, the quest for richness of beauty and meaning seems to me a right quest. You may call these prejudices; to me they are considered values. But whether you like them or not, in general, you will have difficulty in dodging their applicability to things of law.
>
> Consider the single legal rule. Its esthetics are functional, in the strictest sense. It has room for not one jot of ornament; and the measure of its beauty is the measure of its sweetness of effect. [English philosopher Herbert] Spencer's approach to style in terms purely of economy and efficiency seems to me to have application to one sole type of literature: to wit, stripped technical discourse. That is the rule of law. In it, a wasted word is not waste only; it is peril.
>
> But Spencer's approach does not exhaust the esthetics of the individual rule of law. Besides economy and efficiency, the rule of law requires rightness.[30]

Form serves function in the appellate opinion. Rightness emerges because the judge must speak. When we think of judges who were conscious of style's effect upon substance (or "adornment" upon "function," to use Llewellyn's phrase), we think of John Marshall, of Holmes, Brandeis, Learned Hand, and of Cardozo himself "whose writings, like those of Holmes, give meaning to [the] dictum that the judges of our highest courts should have the poetic touch, and that the two callings of law and letters can be joined."[31] But while many analysts equate effective writing with effective adjudicating, realizing that the art of prose affects our understanding of an opinion's meaning, others appear to disagree. Thus a critic of Cardozo has stated that his "facile rhetoric hides many an argument that does not click or marches to a wrong conclusion."[32] The criticism is premised on a severe distinction between form and substance in the legal opinion. The comment assumes there is a legally "right" conclusion in every case that can be perceived objectively even within an opinion that goes the other way. Substance, the critic says, has nothing to do with form; stylistic, rhetorical, and structural elements in an opinion are at best incidental and at worst counterfunctional.

Upon reflection, this not uncommon observation loses its apparent validity. For one thing, we have the empirical datum (in Cardozo's case) that he usually took a unanimous court with him in his great common-law decisions. His dazzling style certainly played a role in this. Furthermore, his opinions have continuing authority, particularly in the nonstatutory areas of tort, contract, and property law. Do these factors exist in spite of or because of his brilliant use of style and what he calls the opinion's "architectonics"?[33]

Reflection further indicates that Cardozo's great opinions do not leave the law where he found it. To say there is a "right" conclusion in any case, existing a priori on only the legal precedent was for Cardozo a nonsense:

> The judge or advocate is expounding a science or a body of truth which he seeks to assimilate to a science, but in the process of exposition he is practicing an art. The Muses look at him a bit impatiently and wearily at times. He has done a good deal to alienate them, and sometimes they refuse to listen and are seen to stop their ears. They have a strange capacity, however, for the discernment of strains of harmony and beauty, no matter how diffused and scattered through the ether. So at times when work is finally done, one sees their faces change; and they take the worker by the hand. They know that by the lever of art the subject the most lowly can be lifted to the heights.[34]

## THE JUDICIAL OPINION AS CREATIVE NARRATION

Cardozo's method articulates the reality for judges far less conscious of their craft than he: rightness in a legal decision derives from an imaginative and intuitive *process* within the adjudicator. This process results in the opinion, and the way in which the adjudicator explains the case *determines* the rightness or wrongness of the decision. Rhetoric, in other words, does not assist an argument to march to a conclusion; rhetoric *is* the argument, and the perceived rightness or wrongness of the conclusion may be as much based on the style and form of the argument as on the extrinsic application to it of the observer's notion of what the law of the case "should have been."

That the critic of Cardozo takes a position on form and substance shared by many judges is indicated by recent circuit-court approaches like Rule 18. Cardozo would have blanched at these rules. How can any judge know in advance the uses to which his language will eventually be put? The dispute between the parties needs merely a resolution (arguably); but our larger system of law requires *form*: a narrative discourse about the dispute whose eventual legal (precedential) effect can only be determined after it has come into existence.

To this extent, and to some others, the effective judicial opinion shares the qualities of a good short story. Enduring novellas, like *Notes From Underground* or *Billy Budd*, remain with us not because they say something new, but because they synthesize the already-there and articulate it in a new way. Fiction's attraction to law, another of this volume's concerns, is in part predicated on the artist's recognition of the common medium of lawyer and novelist: narrative and linguistic structure. As Dr. Johnson put it long ago, "Lawyers have what the writers want." Like the artist, too, the judge achieves a narrative synthesis of his surrounding reality only through observation of other people's actions. Upon the real (or, as we shall see, only nearly real) controversies of the litigating parties, the adjudicator casts his eye, and then writes about the controversy as he resolves it. Far less constrained by precedent and rule than he may think, the judge in almost any case must regard the situation before him from an essentially personal perspective and must then write about that situation in terms that have legal validity and authority. Again, Cardozo:

> There is in each of us a stream of tendency, whether you choose to call it philosophy or not, which gives coherence and direction to thought and action. Judges cannot escape that current any more than other mortals. All their lives,

forces which they do not recognize and cannot name, have been tugging at them—inherited instincts, traditional beliefs, acquired convictions; and the resultant is an outlook on life, a conception of social needs, a sense of [William] James' phrase of "the total push and pressure of the cosmos," which, when reasons are nicely balanced, must determine where choice shall fall.[35]

Adjudication brings forth subjectivity. When the judge is made aware of the facts of the case, he has a response to them. If he is an appellate judge, he may be responding to a factual situation somewhat divorced from the parties' pristine realities, and, indeed, his own opinion may serve to fictionalize the event even more; but he is still responding to at least the shadow of an actual event. As soon as he begins to write, he colors the event with his own subjective approach to it. His articulation of the facts generates a perspective on the law that can never be identical to any earlier perspective.

As Cardozo put it about legal rules and judicial precedents, "If they are plain and to the point, there *may* be need of nothing more" in the case at hand. But, given the idiosyncratic nature of each slice of life that comes before the appellate judge, and given the linguistic ambiguities of the precedential cases, how rarely this inevitability occurs! Imagination and narrative creativity, present even in *Osterlind v. Hill*, where the judge narrows his options to the preexisting rules, dramatically come to the fore when the precedents lack unambiguous control over the operative facts.

I will now refer to two Cardozo opinions (appendixes 3.2 and 3.3) (see pages 24–34), opinions authored by a judicial craftsman conscious of his creative powers. My focus is particularly on *Hynes v. New York Central Railroad*,[36] but I will note parallel effects in *Palsgraf v. Long Island Railroad* (see note 11).[37] Then I will discuss the opinion in *Hollaris v. Jankowski*[38] (appendix 3.4), which was written by an unknown Illinois appellate judge. All these together may serve to indicate that narrative creativity emerges from the act of adjudication itself, generically.

We would do well to consider the two Cardozo opinions somewhat in tandem. They indicate that Cardozo was interested in the *just* outcome in both cases, not in protecting injured people generally or in pursuing strictly logical rules to inevitable ends. In the *Hynes* case, Cardozo finds for the plaintiff; in Palsgraf, he finds *against* the plaintiff, whose suit he dismisses. We will see that the judge's style (or form) admirably parallels (and is indistinguishable from) these differing substantive conclusions.

Hynes' relatives sued on behalf of the deceased boy, who was killed by defendant railroad company's falling electric wires as he was about to dive off a board extending from the railroad's property. Mrs. Palsgraf, also suing a railroad company, was evidently also struck by a piece of the railroad's equipment, but the origin of her injury was such that the outcome could not be the same. The strange incident had commenced some distance away, when the railroad's employees carelessly dislodged a newspaper-wrapped package from another passenger's grip. Weirdly, the package turned out to contain fireworks; the ensuing explosion seems to have dislodged the equipment, which then hit the unfortunate plaintiff.

Turning first to *Hynes*, the reader sensitive to narrative and style will note the use of the phrase "a lad of 16" (see line 1 of appendix 3.2). With these words, Cardozo consciously enters the realm of creative narration. Harvey Hynes is *personalized*: a "lad of 16," he and his "companions" (line 2) as well as other "boys of the neighborhood used to dive" (line 8) off defendant's board into the "navigable stream" below. (Conversely, Mrs. Palsgraf, the losing plaintiff in the second opinion, is referred to throughout by the impersonal term "plaintiff"; her name, family situation, and the other human dimensions of the case are never mentioned.) The *Hynes* narrative quickly projects Cardozo's reader into the familiar world of innocent boyish fun; the imperfect tense in line 9 reminds us that we all "used to" act this way; for "more than five years swimmers had used it as a diving board without protest or obstruction" (lines 17–19). That pluperfect continues the stylistic implication that only the defendant railroad's behavior has interfered with a more idyllic past to which (if we do not find the railroad culpable) we may all never again return.

"On this day," continues Cardozo (line 20), drawing our imaginations not only to a specific human being but now also to a specific moment in history. (Contrast *Palsgraf*'s nontemporal tone: no mention of the weather, the plaintiff's companions or destination, etc. The case exists for the text-books only.) Cardozo reminds us that one of Harvey Hynes' companions had already plunged safely from the diving board. The scene is readied for the fatal moment: "Hynes followed to the front of the springboard, and stood poised for his dive" (lines 22–23). We have before us not only a lawsuit, a dry series of issues, but necessarily a living lad, perhaps a future Olympian, about to be snuffed out by electrical wires falling from defendant railroad's pole.

Twenty-seven lines of factual narrative (compared with only 16 in *Palsgraf*) now give way to Cardozo's equally creative description of the second implied enemy of Harvey Hynes: "the courts" below (lines 27–47). As much as Harvey gains tangibility in the opinion, "the courts" and the law they have used to deny liability here become *depersonalized*.

The pronoun "they" is superimposed on these opponents of Harvey Hynes: "They have thought it immaterial" (line 29); indeed, "they have said" (line 33) that legal technicalities override human realities. Furthermore, "they" have said this to "us"—the opinion's author and its reader have instantly become allies. "But to bathers diving from the springboard, there was no duty, we are told" (38–39); "we are to ignore the public ownership of the water and of air" (line 59). *They* use "much subtlety of reasoning" (line 45) and find against Hynes; *we* see the larger picture, which surpasses logic and attains to justice, and the railroad must pay.

Cardozo's opening gambits in *Hynes* (paralleled, but to opposite effect, in *Palsgraf*) are not aberrational. They are but exceptional examples of what all appellate judges do: frame the facts and legal arguments in the manner most supportive of the court's view. Rhetoric and style are made to march along with legalisms. Precedents contra are denigrated (through style) in this factual situation: form and language will assist the correct result not only to emerge, but to gain authority. As Cardozo put it in his famous "Law and Literature" essay: "The opinion will need persuasive force, or the impressive virtue of sincerity and fire, or the mnemonic power of alliteration and antithesis, or the terseness and tang of the proverb, and the maxim. Neglect the help of these allies, and it may never win its way."[39]

When Cardozo speaks of an opinion's ability to "win its way," he is referring to its chances first of convincing the other judges on the case and second of gaining *authority* within the larger interested community. Much the same statement, of course, can be made about any piece of literature or criticism. In all narrative pursuits, the effective use of style achieves more than mere adornment. As the only way in which the author's message can be conveyed, style determines the stature of the utterance.

Thus when Cardozo (starting at appendix 3.3 lines 52–53 of *Palsgraf*) speaks of the "maze of contradictions" to which a finding for Mrs. Palsgraf would lead, he conjures for his reader an atmosphere of absurd complexity, one that will be avoided only by finding against her. Just as the *Hynes* case's straightforward path led Cardozo to find that the boy was never "beyond the pale of the defendant's duty" (lines 111–12), so the style of the later case finds (and expresses) simplicity in its finding of *no* duty. In that long second paragraph of *Palsgraf*, a series of relatively short sentences matches Cardozo's style to his legal point: simple justice requires limiting liability short of the complex "maze" of this case's facts.

So, too, *Hynes* had concluded with a series of visual images perfectly in harmony with the legal point being made. This was ever Cardozo's technique, and it dazzles us today much as it must have moved the three judicial colleagues who went with him in the case. Thus, the master stylist matches metaphor to law in explaining why "the truth is" (line 91) on the side of the plaintiff. For, with all the defendant's "logic," ratified by the courts below,

> Rights and duties in systems of living law are not built upon such quicksands. (lines 64–65)

These lines, a paragraph unto themselves, cast our imaginations into a spatial sphere deliberately evocative of Hynes' last moments on earth. The railroad's arguments, based on the "quicksands" of ancient property-law concepts, are equated imagistically with the sad end of the lad's life on the sands adjacent to the Harlem River. There commences a unified stream of imagery, continuous until the end of the opinion, where, in its brilliant climax, the poet-judge seals his argument:

> Rules appropriate to spheres which are conceived of as separate and distinct cannot both be enforced when the spheres become concentric. There must then be readjustment or collision. . . . We think that considerations of analogy, of convenience, of policy, and of justice, exclude him from the field of the defendant's immunity and exemption, and place him in the field of liability and duty. (lines 130–41)

Just as the electric wires collided with Harvey Hynes, sending him to the baroque spiral of his death, so the "spheres" of law supporting the railroad are sent to their death by that simple, realistic justice with which they collide in this particular case.

Harvey Hynes, excluded forever from "the field" of mature human development, at least can be posthumously situated by the poet-judge "in the field of [the defendant's] liability and duty." Justice, and "the lad of 16" prevail, through style—that is to say—the style that is justice itself.

*Hollaris v. Jankowski* suffers from a lack of "alliteration and antithesis," but no lack of creative "fire." I include it here as an essential plank in my argument for a legal "poetic method"; *Hollaris*, which has neither the factual drama of *Osterland* nor the hand of a craftsman like Cardozo to edify it, nonetheless (like all appellate opinions) links style to substance in its quest for significance. In *Hollaris*, too, a "lad" was involved, to wit an eight-year-old whose competence to testify about an accident that injured him several years before is being adjudicated on appeal. But Presiding Justice Scanlan does not refer to him as a "lad"; the dominant stylistic treatment accorded the plaintiff here is the sobriquet "minor" (lines 2, 15, 29, 50, 71, 76, and 82 of appendix 3.4). Just as Cardozo prepares his readers for the Hynes lad's (posthumous) victory, so Scanlan brings about Clyde Hollaris' defeat by his relegation of the plaintiff to a purely legalistic status. By the end of the opinion (or at least until two lines from its end) Clyde Hollaris' existence has been limited to only one of its aspects—the fact that he is a "minor."

Victorious on the trial of his case, when a jury found the defendant truck drivers who had run him over liable, the "minor" now finds *himself* under intense scrutiny, as the appellate court examines his maturity and intelligence. Should Clyde have been permitted to testify at the trial? Should the judge there have allowed the jury to hear the "minor's" account of the incident? No, says Scanlan: the matter will be remanded for yet another trial, at which time the "minor" will not be allowed to testify at all. Why? Not absolutely because of his age, but rather because "the testimony of the minor does not show that he is a very intelligent boy" (lines 50–51); in fact, the appellate judge has deduced that "the minor in this case was not a very smart, precocious child" (lines 76–77).

Divorced from the actual proceedings (at which the trial judge and the jury seemed to value the minor's testimony), Scanlan has perused the trial transcript with the creative eye of the appellate interpreter. Scanlan takes from the stuff of that proceeding a Clyde Hollaris capable only of parroting words, of remembering nothing.

But if the "minor" was so slow, why did his lawyer allow him to testify? And why did the judge and jury at the trial conclude that his story made sense? They, unlike Scanlan, actually saw and heard the boy and all the other witnesses to the harrowing event. They awarded him $20,000. With a stroke of the pen, Scanlan obliterates that judgment, replacing it with the following violent narrative:

> Defendants argue, and with some force, that the minor was placed upon the stand not because it was expected that his testimony would have any material probative force, but solely for the emotional effect that the one-legged boy would have upon the jury. (lines 81–85)

Buried in a subordinate clause of this text, Scanlan's entire world view lies available to the careful reader. The jury might well have felt that Clyde's lack of brilliance probably *derived from* the injury caused by the defendant's truck. But the appellate arbiter, waiting until the penultimate moment in his opinion to reveal the extent of that injury, makes of the boy's slowness only an object of blame and derision. Clyde should not have been permitted to speak at all. He was not bright enough; his injury only incited the too-sympathetic jury to an irrational finding in his favor.

Scanlan's narrative (written, as it happens, in the same year Camus created another inarticulate victim of the legal system—*The Stranger*'s Meursault) endures, testimony to the inevitability of narrative elements as contributory forces in appellate decision making. Scanlan's "holding" emerges only from the complete text of this bizarre opinion, which cruelly renders Clyde's injury irrelevant to the question of his "competence" as a witness. Compelled to articulate, Scanlan makes a caricature of *himself*, not of the injured boy he so distrusts. His opinion, because it had to be written out, finally "holds" that judges who lack sensitivity to the human agencies on whom they must rule may also lack the "competence" to gain authoritative status.

While the appellate opinion serves the immediate goal of resolving a dispute between various parties through an analysis and application of one or more legal points, it is also a piece of narrative discourse. Unless the decision is consciously reduced to the mere articulation of its judgment (and even there), the opinion speaks as much through its prose and its structure as through its affirmation or dismissal of a lower court's decision.

Even when the opinion is not written with a conscious appreciation of this fact (or even when it is written by a law clerk), style still affects the decision's meaning. Superb judicial decisions are only those crafted superbly; poor decisions reveal their weaknesses through the analysis of style and may not stand the test of time.

In this essay, I have explored the use or misuse, and the significance, of style in several opinions of greater or lesser legal and literary worth. The essay exemplifies the force of the first element in my literary jurisprudence: the poetic method for law. In essay 4, I will return to the second half of our jurisprudence—poetic substance, or the "poethics" of legal narrative.

## APPENDIX 3.1

### Osterlind v. Hill (1928)

1    Braley, J[udge], delivered the opinion of the court:

2    This is an action of tort, brought by the plaintiff as administrator

3  of the estate of Albert T. Osterlind to recover damages for the

4  conscious suffering and death of his intestate. There are four counts

5  in the original declaration and five counts in the amended decla-

6  ration, to each of which the defendant demurred. The first count

7 of the original declaration alleges that, on or about July 4, 1925,
8 the defendant was engaged in the business of letting for hire pleasure
9 boats and canoes to be used on Lake Quannapowitt in the town
10 of Wakefield; that it was the duty of the defendant to have a rea-
11 sonable regard for the safety of the persons to whom he let boats
12 and canoes; that the defendant, in the early morning of July 4, 1925,
13 in willful, wanton, or reckless disregard of the natural and probable
14 consequences, let for hire, to the intestate and one Ryan, a frail and
15 dangerous canoe, well knowing that the intestate and Ryan were
16 then intoxicated, and were then manifestly unfit to go upon the lake
17 in the canoe; that, in disregard of his duties, the intestate and Ryan
18 went out in the canoe, which shortly afterwards was overturned,
19 and the intestate, after hanging to it for approximately one-half hour,
20 and making loud calls for assistance, which calls the defendant heard
21 and utterly ignored, was obliged to release his hold, and was
22 drowned; that in consequence of the defendant's willful, wanton,
23 or reckless conduct the intestate endured great conscious mental
24 anguish and great conscious physical suffering from suffocation and
25 drowning. . . .
26    The trial court sustained demurrers to both the original and
27 amended declarations and reported the case for the determination
28 of this court. . . .
29    The declaration must set forth facts which, if proved, establish
30 the breach of a legal duty owed by the defendant to the intestate.
31 *Sweeney v. Old Colony & N[orth] R[ailroad] Co.,* 10 Allen, 368,
32 372, 87 Am. Dec. 644. The plaintiff relies on *Black v. New York,*
33 N.H. & H.R. Co. 193 Mass. 448, 7 L.R.A. (N.S.) 148, 79 N. E.
34 797, 9 Ann. Cas. 485, as establishing such a duty on the part of
35 the defendant. In that case the jury would have been justified in
36 finding that the plaintiff was "so intoxicated as to be incapable of
37 standing or walking or caring for himself in any way." There was
38 testimony to the effect that, "when he fell, he did not seize hold
39 of anything, his arms were at his side." The defendant's employees
40 placed a helpless man, a man impotent to protect himself, in a
41 dangerous position.
42    In the case at bar, however, it is alleged in every count of the
43 original and amended declaration that after the canoe was over-
44 turned the intestate hung to the canoe for approximately one-half
45 hour and made loud calls for assistance. On the facts stated in the
46 declaration the intestate was not in a helpless condition. The alle-
47 gation appearing in each count of the amended declaration that the

48 intestate was incapacitated to enter into any valid contract states
49 merely a legal conclusion. *Hollis v. Richardson*, 13 Gray, 392, 294;
50 *Lothrop Pub. Co. v. Lothrop*, L. & S. Co. 191 Mass. 353, 356, 5
51 L.R.A. (N.S.) 1077, 77 N.E. 841. The allegations, therefore in the
52 counts of the amended declaration to the effect that the intestate
53 was incapable of exercising any care for his own safety is controlled
54 by the allegation in the same counts that he hung to the side of the
55 canoe for approximately one-half hour, calling for assistance.
56    In view of the absence of any duty to refrain from renting a canoe
57 to a person in the condition of the intestate, the allegations of
58 involuntary intoxication relating as they do to the issues of con-
59 tributory negligence become immaterial. The allegations of willful,
60 wanton, or reckless conduct also add nothing to the plaintiff's case.
61 The failure of the defendant to respond to the intestate's outcries
62 is immaterial. No legal right of the intestate was infringed. *Griswold*
63 *v. Boston & M. R. Co.*, 183 Mass. 434, 67 N. E. 354, 14 Am.
64 Neg. Rep. 78; *Taft v. Bridgeton Worsted Co.*, 237 Mass. 385, 387,
65 388, 13 A.L.R. 928, 130 N.E. 48, and cases cited. The allegation
66 common to both declarations that the canoe was "frail and dan-
67 gerous" appears to be a general characterization of canoes. It is not
68 alleged that the canoe was out of repair and unsafe.
69    It follows that the order sustaining each demurrer is affirmed.
70 [Case dismissed.]


## APPENDIX 3.2

### Hynes v. New York Central Railroad Co. (1921)

1    Cardozo, J[udge]. On July 8, 1916, Harvey Hynes, a lad of 16,
2 swam with two companions from the Manhattan to the Bronx side
3 of the Harlem River, or United States ship Canal, a navigable stream.
4 Along the Bronx side of the river was the right of way of the de-
5 fendant, the New York Central Railroad, which operated its trains
6 at that point by high-tension wires, strung on poles and cross-arms.
7 Projecting from the defendant's bulkhead above the waters of the
8 river was a plank or springboard, from which boys of the neigh-
9 borhood used to dive. One end of the board had been placed under
10 a rock on the defendant's land, and nails had been driven at its point
11 of contact with the bulkhead. Measured from this point of contact
12 the length behind was 5 feet; the length in front 11. The bulkhead
13 itself was about 3½ feet back of the pier line as located by the

14 government. From this it follows that for 7½ feet the springboard
15 was beyond the line of the defendant's property and above the public
16 waterway. Its height measured from the stream was 3 feet at the
17 bulkhead, and 5 feet at its outer most extremity. For more than five
18 years swimmers had used it as a diving board without protest or
19 obstruction.
20    On this day Hynes and his companions climbed on top of the
21 bulkhead, intending to leap into the water. One of them made the
22 plunge in safety. Hynes followed to the front of the springboard,
23 and stood poised for his dive. At that moment a cross-arm with
24 electric wires fell from the defendant's pole. The wires struck the
25 diver, flung him from the shattered board, and plunged him to his
26 death below. His mother, suing as administratrix, brings this action
27 for her damages. Thus far the courts have held that Hynes at the
28 end of the springboard above the public waters was a trespasser on
29 the defendant's land. They have thought it immaterial that the board
30 itself was a trespass, an encroachment to the public ways. They have
31 thought it of no significance that Hynes would have met the same
32 fate if he had been below the board and not above it. The board,
33 they have said, was annexed to the defendant's bulkhead. By force
34 of such annexation, it was to be reckoned as a fixture, and thus
35 constructively, if not actually, an extension of the land. The de-
36 fendant was under a duty to use reasonable care that bathers swim-
37 ming or standing in the water should not be electrocuted by wires
38 falling from its right of way. But to bathers diving from the spring-
39 board, there was no duty, we are told, unless the injury was the
40 product of mere willfulness or wantonness—no duty of active vig-
41 ilance to safeguard the impending structure. Without wrong to them,
42 cross-arms might be left to rot; wires highly charged with electricity
43 might sweep them from their stand and bury them in the adjacent
44 waters. In climbing on the board, they became trespassers and out-
45 laws. The conclusion is defended with much subtlety of reasoning,
46 with much insistence upon its inevitableness as a merely logical
47 deduction. A majority of the court are unable to accept it as the
48 conclusion of the law.
49    We assume, without deciding, that the springboard was a fixture,
50 a permanent improvement of the defendant's right of way. Much
51 might be said in favor of another view. We do not press the inquiry
52 for we are persuaded that the rights of bathers do not depend upon
53 these nice distinctions. Liability would not be doubtful, we are told,
54 had the boy been diving from a pole, if the pole had been vertical.

55 The diver in such a situation would have been separated from the
56 defendant's freehold. Liability, it is said, has been escaped because
57 the pole was horizontal. The plank when projected lengthwise was
58 an extension of the soil. We are to concentrate our gaze on the
59 private ownership of the board. We are to ignore the public own-
60 ership of the circumambient spaces of water and of air. Jumping
61 from a boat or a barrel, the boy would have been a bather in the
62 river. Jumping from the end of a springboard he was no longer, it
63 is said, a bather, but a trespasser on a right of way.
64     Rights and duties in systems of living law are not built upon such
65 quicksands.
66     Bathers in the Harlem River on the day of this disaster were in
67 the enjoyment of a public highway, entitled to reasonable protection
68 against destruction by the defendant's wires. They did not cease to
69 be bathers entitled to the same protection while they were diving
70 from encroaching objects or engaging in the sports that are common
71 among swimmers. Such acts were not equivalent to an abandonment
72 of the highway, a departure from its proper uses, a withdrawal from
73 the waters, and an entry upon land. A plane of private right had
74 been interposed between the river and the air, but public ownership
75 was unchanged in the space below it and above. The defendant does
76 not deny that it would have owed a duty to this boy if he had been
77 leaning against the springboard with his feet upon the ground. He
78 is said to have forfeited protection as he put his feet upon the plank.
79 Presumably the same result would follow if the plank had been a
80 few inches above the surface of the water instead of a few feet.
81 Duties are thus supposed to arise and to be extinguished in alternate
82 zones or strata. Two boys walking in the country or swimming in
83 a river stop to rest for a moment along the side of the road or the
84 margin of the stream. One of them throws himself beneath the
85 overhanging branches of a tree. The other perches himself on a
86 bough a foot or so above the ground. Both are killed by falling
87 wires. The defendant would have us say that there is a remedy for
88 the representatives of one and none for the representatives of the
89 other. We may be permitted to distrust the logic that leads to such
90 conclusions.
91     The truth is that every act of Hynes from his first plunge into
92 the river until the moment of his death was in the enjoyment of
93 the public waters, and under cover of the protection which his
94 presence in those waters gave him. The use of the springboard was

95 not an abandonment of his rights as bather. It was a mere by-play,
96 an incident [and] not the cause of the disaster. Hynes would have
97 gone to his death if he had been below the springboard or beside
98 it. The wires were not stayed by the presence of the plank. They
99 followed the boy in his fall, and overwhelmed him in the waters.
100     The defendant assumes that the identification of ownership of
101 land is complete in every incident. But there are important elements
102 of difference. Title to the fixture, unlike title to the land, does not
103 carry with it rights of ownership *usque ad coelum*. There will hardly
104 be denial that a course of action would have arisen if the wires had
105 fallen on an aeroplane proceeding above the springboard. The most
106 that the defendant can fairly ask is exemption from liability where
107 the use of the fixture is itself the efficient peril. That would be the
108 situation, for example, if the weight of the boy upon the board had
109 caused it to break and thereby thrown him into the river. There is
110 not such causal connection here between his position and his in-
111 juries. We think there was no moment when he was beyond the
112 pale of the defendant's duty—the duty of care and vigilance in the
113 storage of destructive forces.
114     This case is a striking instance of the dangers of "a jurisprudence
115 of conceptions" (Pound, "Mechanical Jurisprudence," *Columbia*
116 *Law Review* 8:605, 608, 610), the extension of a maxim or a def-
117 inition with relentless disregard of consequences to "a dryly logical
118 extreme." The approximate and relative become the definite and
119 absolute. Landowners are not bound to regulate their conduct in
120 contemplation of the presence of trespassers intruding upon private
121 structures. Landowners are bound to regulate their conduct in con-
122 templation of the presence of travelers upon the adjacent public
123 ways. There are times when there is little trouble in marking off the
124 field of exemption and immunity from that of liability and duty.
125 Here structures and ways are so united and commingled, superim-
126 posed upon each other, that the fields are brought together. In such
127 circumstances, there is little help in pursuing general maxims to
128 ultimate conclusions. They have been framed *alio intuitu*. They
129 must be reformulated and readapted to meet exceptional conditions.
130 Rules appropriate to spheres which are conceived of as separate and
131 distinct cannot both be enforced when the spheres become con-
132 centric. There must then be readjustment or collision. In one sense,
133 and that a highly technical and artificial one, the diver at the end
134 of the springboard is an intruder on the adjoining lands. In another

135 sense, and one that realists will accept more readily, he is still on
136 public waters in the exercise of public rights. The law must say
137 whether it will subject him to the rule of the one field or of the
138 other, of this sphere or of that. We think that considerations of
139 analogy, of convenience, of policy, and of justice, exclude him from
140 the field of the defendant's immunity and exemption, and place him
141 in the field of liability and duty.
142   The judgment of the Appellate Division and that of the trial
143 Term should be reversed, and a new trial granted, with costs to
144 abide the event. [Action permitted.]


## APPENDIX 3.3

### Palsgraf v. Long Island Railroad Co. (1928)

1    [Appeal from a judgment entered on a plaintiff's verdict. The
2 lower appellate court affirmed, 3–2.]
3    Cardozo, Ch[ief] J[udge]. Plaintiff was standing on a platform of
4 defendant's railroad after buying a ticket to go to Rockaway Beach.
5 A train stopped at the station, bound for another place. Two men
6 ran forward to catch it. One of the men reached the platform of
7 the car without mishap, though the train was already moving. The
8 other man, carrying a package, jumped aboard the car, but seemed
9 unsteady as if about to fall. A guard on the car, who had held the
10 door open, reached forward to help him in, and another guard of
11 the platform pushed him from behind. In this act, the package was
12 dislodged, and fell upon the rails. It was a package of small size,
13 about fifteen inches long, and was covered by a newspaper. In fact
14 it contained fireworks, but there was nothing in its appearance to
15 give notice of its contents. The shock of the explosion threw down
16 some scales at the other end of the platform, many feet away. The
17 scales struck the plaintiff, causing injuries for which she sues.
18    The conduct of the defendant's guard, if a wrong in its relation
19 to the holder of the package, was not a wrong in its relation to the
20 plaintiff, standing far away. Relatively to her it was not negligence
21 at all. Nothing in the situation gave notice that the falling package
22 had in it the potency of peril to persons thus removed. Negligence
23 is not actionable unless it involves the invasion of a legally protected
24 interest, the violation of a right. "Proof of negligence in the air, so
25 to speak, will not do" (Pollock, *Torts* [11th ed.], p. 455;). "Neg-
26 ligence is the absence of care, according to the circumstances"

27 (Willes, J., in *Vaughan v. Taff Vale*, Ry. Co., 5 H.&N. 679, 688;
28 *Adams v. Bullock*, 227 N.Y. 298, 211; *Parrott v. Wells-Fargo Co.*
29 [the Nitro-Glycerine case], 15 Wall. [U.S.] 524). The plaintiff as she
30 stood upon the platform of the station might claim to be protected
31 against intentional invasion of her bodily security. Such invasion is
32 not charged. She might claim to be protected against unintentional
33 invasion by conduct involving in the thought of reasonable men an
34 unreasonable hazard that such invasion would ensue. These, from
35 the point of view of the law, were the bounds of her immunity,
36 with perhaps some rare exceptions, survivals for the most part of
37 ancient forms of liability, where conduct is held to be at the peril
38 of the actor (*Sullivan v. Dunham*, 161 N.Y. 290). If no hazard was
39 apparent to the eye of ordinary vigilance, an act innocent and harm-
40 less, at least to outward seeming, with reference to her, did not take
41 to itself the quality of a tort because it happened to be a wrong,
42 though apparently not one involving the risk of bodily insecurity,
43 with reference to some one else. "In every instance, before negli-
44 gence can be predicated of a given act, back of the act must be
45 sought and found a duty to the individual complaining, the ob-
46 servance of which would have averted or avoided the injury"
47 (McSherry, C. J., in *W. Va. Central RR. Co. v. State*, 96 Md. 652,
48 666). "The ideas of negligence and duty are strictly correlative"
49 (Bowen, L. J., in *Thomas v. Quartermaine*, 18 Q.B.D. 685, 694).
50 The plaintiff sues in her own right for a wrong personal to her, and
51 not as the vicarious beneficiary of a breach of duty to another.
52     A different conclusion will involve us, and swiftly too, in a maze
53 of contradictions. A guard stumbles over a package which has been
54 left upon a platform. It seems to be a bundle of newspaper. It turns
55 out to be a can of dynamite. To the eye of ordinary vigilance, the
56 bundle is abandoned waste, which may be kicked or trod on with
57 impunity. Is a passenger at the other end of the platform protected
58 by the law against the unsuspected hazard concealed beneath the
59 waste? If not, is the result to be any different, so far as the distant
60 passenger is concerned, when the guard stumbles over a valise which
61 a truckman or a porter has left upon the walk? The passenger far
62 away, if the victim of a wrong at all, has a course of action, not
63 derivative, but original and primary. His claim to be protected against
64 invasion of his bodily security is neither greater nor less because the
65 act resulting in the invasion is a wrong to another far removed. In
66 this case, the rights that are said to have been violated, the interests

67 said to have been invaded, are not even of the same order. The man
68 was not injured in his person nor even put in danger. The purpose
69 of the act, as well as its effect, was to make his person safe. If there
70 was a wrong to him at all, which may very well be doubted, it was
71 a wrong to a property interest only, the safety of his package. Out
72 of this wrong to property, which threatened injury to nothing else,
73 there has passed, we are told, to the plaintiff by derivation or succes-
74 sion a right of action for the invasion of an interest of another order,
75 the right to bodily security. The diversity of interests emphasizes the
76 futility of the effort to build the plaintiff's right upon the basis of
77 a wrong to some one else. The gain is one of emphasis, for a like
78 result would follow if the interests were the same. Even then, the
79 orbit of the danger as disclosed to the eye of reasonable vigilance
80 would be the orbit of the duty. One who jostles one's neighbor in
81 a crowd does not invade the rights of others standing at the outer
82 fringe when the unintended contact casts a bomb upon the ground.
83 The wrongdoer as to them is the man who carries the bomb, not
84 the one who explodes it without suspicion of the danger. Life will
85 have to be made over, and human nature transformed, before pro-
86 visions so extravagant can be accepted as the norm of conduct, the
87 customary standard to which behavior must conform.
88    The argument for the plaintiff is built upon the shifting meanings
89 of such words as "wrong" and "wrongful," and shares their insta-
90 bility. What the plaintiff must show is "a wrong" to herself, i.e., a
91 violation of her own right, and not merely a wrong to some one
92 else, nor conduct "wrongful" because unsocial, but not "a wrong"
93 to any one. We are told that one who drives at reckless speed through
94 a crowded city street is guilty of a negligent act and, therefore, of
95 a wrongful one irrespective of the consequences. Negligent the act
96 is, and wrongful in the sense that it is unsocial, but wrongful and
97 unsocial in relation to other travelers, only because the eye of vig-
98 ilance perceives the risk of damage. If the same act were to be
99 committed on a speedway or a race course, it would lose its wrongful
100 quality. The risk reasonably to be perceived defines the duty to be
101 obeyed, and risk imports relation; it is risk to another or to others
102 within the range of apprehension. This does not mean, of course,
103 that one who launches a destructive force is always relieved of li-
104 ability if the force, though known to be destructive, pursues an
105 unexpected path. "It was not necessary that the defendant should
106 have had notice of the particular method in which an accident would

107 occur, if the possibility of an accident was clear to the ordinarily
108 prudent eye" (*Munsey v. Webb*, 231 U.S. 150, 156.). Some acts,
109 such as shooting, are so imminently dangerous to any one who may
110 come within reach of the missile, however unexpectedly, as to im-
111 pose a duty of prevision not far from that of an insurer. Even today,
112 and much oftener in earlier stages of the law, one acts sometimes
113 at one's peril. Under this head, it may be, fall certain cases of what
114 is known as transferred intent, an act willfully dangerous to A re-
115 sulting by misadventure in injury to B (*Talmage v. Smith*, 101 Mich.
116 370, 374). These cases aside, wrong is defined in terms of the natural
117 or probable, at least when unintentional (*Parrot v. Wells-Fargo Co.*
118 15 Wall. [U.S.] 524). The range of reasonable apprehensions is at
119 times a question for the court, and at times, if varying inferences
120 are possible, a question for the jury. Here by concession, there was
121 nothing in the situation to suggest to the most cautious mind that
122 the parcel wrapped in newspaper would spread wreckage through
123 the station. If the guard had thrown it down knowingly and willfully,
124 he would not have threatened the plaintiff's safety, so far as ap-
125 pearances could warn him. His conduct would not have involved,
126 even then, an unreasonable probability of invasion of her bodily
127 security. Liability can be no greater where the act is inadvertent.
128     Negligence, like risk, is thus a term of relation. Negligence in
129 the abstract, apart from things related, is surely not a tort, if indeed
130 it is understandable at all. . . .
131     The law of causation, remote or proximate, is thus foreign to
132 the case before us. The question of liability is always anterior to
133 the question of the measure of the consequences that go with lia-
134 bility. If there is no tort to be redressed, there is no occasion to
135 consider what damage might be recovered if there were a finding of
136 a tort. We may assume, without deciding, that negligence, not at
137 large or in the abstract, but in relation to the plaintiff, would entail
138 liability for any and all consequences, however novel or extraor-
139 dinary. There is room for argument that a distinction is to be drawn
140 according to the diversity of interests invaded by the act, as where
141 conduct negligent in that it threatens an insignificant invasion of an
142 interest in property results in an unforeseeable invasion of an interest
143 of another order, as, e.g., one of bodily security. Perhaps other
144 distinctions may be necessary. We do not go into the question now.
145 The consequences to be followed must first be rooted in a wrong.
146 [Case dismissed].

## APPENDIX 3.4

### Hollaris v. Jankowski (1942)

1    Scanlan, Presiding Justice. A suit for damages for personal injuries
2  sustained by the minor. A jury returned a verdict finding defendants
3  guilty and assessing plaintiff's damages at $20,000. Defendants ap-
4  peal from a judgment entered upon the verdict. . . .
5    The complaint charges that defendants were driving a truck in
6  an alley and carelessly and negligently drove it so as to injure the
7  plaintiff, a boy four years of age; . . . Defendants filed a general
8  denial to the allegations of the complaint. . . .
9    Defendants strenuously contend that the manifest weight of the
10  evidence is in favor of defendants. After carefully reading the entire
11  evidence that bears upon the instant contention we are satisfied that
12  the contention must be sustained. As this case may be tried again
13  we refrain from commenting upon the evidence.
14    Defendants contend that the trial court erred in permitting Clyde
15  Hollaris, the minor, to testify; that a child of eight years of age
16  should not be permitted to testify to an accident that happened to
17  him when he was between four and five years of age. Defendants
18  argue that the child would not have been competent to testify as
19  to the accident if he had been called as a witness directly after it
20  occurred, and that the mere fact that he has now reached the age
21  of eight years does not now make him competent to tell what
22  happened when he was between four and five years of age, and
23  counsel argues that "many children do not walk until they are two
24  years of age and do not talk until they are three. At four a child is
25  very apt to be in the prattling age in which impressions are nebulous
26  and conversations vague." Counsel for plaintiff argues that "it is the
27  intelligence and understanding of the witness, and not his age, that
28  determines his competency." Upon the first trial of the case the
29  court refused to allow the minor to testify. Neither the Legislature
30  of this State nor our Supreme court has laid down a hard and fast
31  rule with respect to the minimum age at which a minor is permitted
32  to testify. . . .
33    We find no case in this State wherein the competency of a child
34  under six years of age to testify has been passed upon.
35    In *State v. Michael,* 37 W. Va. 565, 16 S.E. 803, 19 L.R.A. 605,
36  the complaining witness was five years of age at the time of the
37  alleged criminal offense. The opinion in that case states at page 569

38 of 37 W. Va., at page 803 of 16 S.E.: "Under the age of 6, pre-
39 sumption of incompetency would arise, and at the age of 5 the
40 utmost limit would be ordinarily reached, unless extraordinary de-
41 velopment of the mental and religious faculties should be shown
42 to take the case out of the ordinary course of nature." The court
43 held that the child should not have been permitted to testify.

44    In *Macale v. Lynch*, 110 Wash. 444, 188 Pl. 517, the plaintiff
45 was five years of age at the time of the accident. Fourteen months
46 later he was allowed to testify in his case over the objection of the
47 defendant. The child had often discussed the facts of the accident
48 with the members of his family and the lawyers. It was held that
49 the child should not have been allowed to testify.

50    In the instant case the testimony of the minor does not show
51 that he is a very intelligent boy. Moreover, his testimony shows that
52 he had little, if any, memory of what actually occurred at the time
53 of the accident. He testified that "the lawyers have talked about it
54 to me, I don't know how many lawyers"; that he remembered the
55 facts better at the time of the first trial; that "My memory isn't so
56 good about it now, because it was so long. I mean it is so long ago
57 that I don't remember much about it"; that "My memory is not
58 very good about what happened at that time so long a time has
59 gone by. After I heard my brother and other people talk about it,
60 I didn't remember so much more about it."

61    "Q. In other words, the more they talked about it, the less you
62 knew about it, is that what you mean? A. Yes, sir.

63    "Q. Do you really remember about it Clyde? A. No, not so well.

64    "Q. You said something about the truck turning over to you?
65 Did you see that truck turn over to you at that time? A. Well, my
66 brother told me.

67    "Q. Your brother told you, and that is the reason you thought
68 the truck kept turning over to you? A. Yes, sir.

69    "Q. Did you see the truck come out of the garage? A. No, that
70 is the only time when my brother yelled."

71    We are not obliged to hold, however, that the minor was an
72 incompetent witness solely because of his age. Undoubtedly there
73 are some very smart, precocious children, who, at eight years of age,
74 can remember the details of an accident that happened to them
75 when they were between four and five years of age, but the record
76 shows that the minor in this case was not a very smart, precocious
77 child. Moreover, it affirmatively appears that he had been talked to
78 so much about the accident by members of his family and lawyers

79  that the child had little, if any, independent recollection as to the
80  facts and circumstances surrounding the accident. In any future trial
81  he should not be allowed to testify. Defendants argue, and with
82  some force, that the minor was placed upon the stand not because
83  it was expected that his testimony would have any material probative
84  force, but solely for the emotional effect that the one-legged boy
85  would have upon the jury.
86      The judgment of the Circuit court of Cook county is reversed,
87  and the cause is remanded for a new trial.

## 4. Poetic Substance: The Poethics of Legal Narrative

It is only a short step from the poetic method to the subject matter of
law within fiction. What does literature have to tell us about law? This
second unique source of learning for lawyers I have called poetic substance or, because of its deeply ethical aspects, *poethics*. Here we can
see the literary text as a potential gold mine of knowledge about law;
yet our first insight—that sound and sense, form and substance, are united
in legal language—continues to stand as the preeminent contribution of
literature to our substantive vision of law.

This essay proceeds to join together, for the purpose of detecting
literature's substantive vision of law, several well-known works, some of
which will surely be familiar to most readers. Part two of the larger
volume then proceeds to a detailed analysis of the poethical vision introduced through these texts. The latter include several modern novels
and a play by Shakespeare.

All these works are in a sense "about" law, but any well-crafted story—
whatever its subject matter—uncovers for the lawyer the inevitable primacy of the poetic method to law. Still, when the distinguished legal
scholar John Wigmore at the beginning of this century proposed a reading
list for lawyers of "100 Legal Novels,"I think he was right to focus on
books that had law as their central theme. His aim was both to attract
that professional audience to the delights of reading and to help lawyers
find "those features of their profession which have been taken up into
general thought and literature."[40]

The stories I will discuss here include Charles Dickens' *Bleak House*
and *Great Expectations*, John Barth's *The Floating Opera*, Herman Melville's *Billy Budd*, William Faulkner's *Intruder in the Dust*, Toni Morrison's *The Bluest Eye*, and Shakespeare's *The Merchant of Venice*. As I

go along, I hope to provide, in more or less detail as appropriate, plot summaries of these masterpieces. The poethical vision yielded by these texts is especially important today when law seems to be moving away from its humane roots and toward a variety of formalisms. Taken collectively, I believe they teach us about at least four basic elements of law otherwise either ignored, unstressed, or misperceived in traditional approaches to jurisprudence. These four elements are:

1. *How a lawyer communicates.* Here, again, the poetic method merges into poetic substance. Stories about law always are stories about how people in power tell their stories to interested audiences.

2. *How a lawyer treats people and groups outside the power structure.* That is, how lawyers deal with those whose "otherness" makes them challenging—and sometimes threatening—to the law.

3. *How a lawyer reasons.* Although much time is given to this factor in law schools, I claim here that literary portraits of lawyers in action provide an emphasis missing in traditional sources of learning.

4. *How a lawyer feels.* Fiction about law continues to uncover better than any other medium what might be called the private lives of lawyers. But it does so in a manner that—unlike most television or film treatments—encourages long-range thinking about law. For, as we shall see, fiction about lawyers compels us to recognize that lawyers' private lives directly affect their public performance.

These four points constitute a literary jurisprudence; the seven works featured to exemplify them (plus a few other texts that will be mentioned more briefly along the way) also offer to prospective teachers of Law and Literature a veritable core syllabus that I highly recommend, whatever the instructor's own individual approach to the specific texts may be. (For a discussion and defense of the predominantly traditionalist nature of this "core," see essay 12 in this volume.)

The remainder of this chapter spells out in greater detail the first two elements of our literary jurisprudence. The third and fourth elements (legal reasoning and how lawyers feel) will be addressed via Dickens, Barth, and Faulkner in the next chapter. There, too, I offer fully formulated analyses of many of these texts. Each analysis stands on its own; and a reader who is less interested in jurisprudence but who might want, for example, to see how Dickens treats his lawyer figures, or how Act V of *The Merchant of Venice* unbinds Portia from her previous declarations and binds her to the values of Shylock, may of course turn immediately to those later essays.

## How Lawyers Communicate

When storytellers evoke our first substantive category, *legal communication*, they do so with gusto. Think of Dickens' various lawyers. In two of Dickens' texts (which receive fuller treatment in the next chapter), how lawyers speak and write becomes a central narrative focus. In *Great Expectations* we find the immortal Mr. Jaggers, a brilliantly successful lawyer who "cross-examined his very wine when he had nothing else in hand." Mr. Jaggers' refusal to speak naturally and forthrightly, even to use the first-person-singular pronoun, stands as a paradigm for the fictional satire of legal language. In *Bleak House*, the account of the generations-long case of *Jarndyce v. Jarndyce*, Dickens reveals the full spectrum of lawyerlike communication. While the dark "superlawyer," Mr. Tulkinghorn, will be discussed in detail in essay 7, *Bleak House* also provides a panoply of lesser lawyers and clerks whose approach to language can inform and delight any self-aware reader. Here Dickens gives us the unforgettable law clerk, Mr. Guppy, who proposes marriage to Esther Summerson, " 'without prejudice . . . one of our law terms. . . . In short, it's in total confidence.' "[41] He insists on calling in a witness when, later, he withdraws his offer. Guppy typifies the unreflective lawyer, so lost in his own peculiar language that he fails to acknowledge the needs of his listener. (I will address the fully contemporary relevance of this Dickensian portrait for legal writing in essay 16.[42])

Meanwhile, the *Jarndyce* case drones on without resolution, and its befogged path seems epitomized by the lawyer Vholes, who represents the hapless Richard Carstone in the matter. Poor Richard! A youthful and pleasant fellow, he is utterly undone by the lawsuit, to which he fatally decides to devote his life. Instrumental in his downfall is Mr. Vholes, a far more effective communicator than Guppy. Vholes sucks Richard in, subtly implying that Richard's interests are being served when, in fact, only the lawyers stand to gain. For, as Dickens tells us through the story of Vholes, "the one great principle of the English law is, to make business for itself" (2:39). Vholes, whose name means a short-tailed rat or field mouse, communicates like a rodent, his words trapped within himself and emerging as though in a gasp. "So slow, so eager, so bloodless and gaunt," remarks the concerned Esther, as she listens to Vholes lure her friend Richard to his doom. Vholes' discussions with Richard brilliantly evoke the subtle manipulation—marginally ethical at best—that articulate lawyers can impose on their clients. Realizing that Carstone's chances of winning a farthing from the estate are meager,

Vholes finds the words to bait his client with a misleading (yet never factually false) sense of optimism. Finally, when the estate is eviscerated by legal costs, Vholes "gave one gasp as if he had swallowed the last morsel of his client" (2:65) and vanishes. However, the lawyer is here portrayed not as mere caricature; the behavior of Vholes in hewing a fine line of professional communication to his client—never explicitly lying but again never really being forthright—stands as a realistic lesson to late-20th-century lawyers.[43] If Guppy represents lawyerlike speech at its most ridiculous (totally untuned to the feelings and needs of the audience), Vholes' manner of speaking is altogether respectable and highly effective for his self-interested purposes.

At a stroke, then, *Bleak House* conveys to lawyers the extremes of lawyerlike speech: from Mr. Guppy's bizarre and insensitive formalism to Mr. Vholes' more devious and finally unethical verbal stratagems. Somewhat in between is Mr. Kenge (nicknamed "Conversation Kenge"), who is portrayed with a measure of humanity but whose absurd way of talking and writing emerges as early as the novel's third chapter. There he writes the naive Esther of his unnamed client's plans to have her move to a new situation; his letter to her, full of legalistic jargon and obscurity, is featured in its entirety by the satiric Dickens. But Kenge is no Guppy; as Mr. Jarndyce's lawyer, he pursues various professional goals effectively throughout the novel. Although far less demonic than Tulkinghorn and less unctuously self-interested than Vholes, Kenge shows his true colors in chapter 62, when he and Vholes are confronted with a "new will" that might (if inserted into *Jarndyce*) give Richard Carstone a greater "share." In fact, as Dickens implies by having Vholes and Kenge distance themselves from the laymen in the room and, "at some length," discuss the situation between themselves, the lawyers already know that the estate is bankrupt. Esther (narrating) picks up from her excluded vantage point only a few words: " 'Receiver-General,' 'Accountant-General,' 'Report,' 'Estate,' and 'Costs.' "

Yet, true to the portrait of clever lawyers as communicating hermetically when among themselves but as otherwise obfuscating when speaking with the laity, neither Kenge nor Vholes discloses the estate's condition to their clients. Instead, returning to the others, they engage in the following dialogue:

"Well! But this is a very remarkable document, Mr. Vholes?" said Mr. Kenge.
Mr. Vholes said, "Very much so."
"And a very important document, Mr. Vholes?" said Mr. Kenge.

37

Again Mr. Vholes said, "Very much so."

"And as you say, Mr. Vholes, when the Cause is in the paper next Term, this document will be an unexpected and interesting feature in it," said Mr. Kenge, looking loftily at my guardian.

Mr. Vholes was gratified, as a smaller practitioner striving to keep respectable, to be confirmed in any opinion of his own by such an authority.

"And when," asked my guardian, rising after a pause, during which Mr. Kenge had rattled his money, and Mr. Vholes had picked his pimples, "when is next Term?"

"Next Term, Mr. Jarndyce, will be next month," said Mr. Kenge. "Of course we shall at once proceed to do what is necessary with this document, and to collect the necessary evidence concerning it; and of course you will receive our usual notification of the Cause being in the paper."

"To which I shall pay, of course, my usual attention."

"Still bent, my dear sir," said Mr. Kenge, showing us through the outer office to the door, "still bent, even with your enlarged mind, on echoing a popular prejudice? We are a prosperous community, Mr. Jarndyce, a very prosperous community. We are a great country, Mr. Jarndyce, we are a very great country. This is a great system, Mr. Jarndyce, and would you wish a great country to have a little system? Now, really, really!"

He said this at the stair-head, gently moving his right hand as if it were a silver trowel, with which to spread the cement of his words on the structure of the system, and consolidate it for a thousand ages. (2:62)

When artful lawyers like Vholes, Kenge, and, as we shall see, Tulkinghorn, are shown to succeed in their profession, writers throw up a red flag to all aspiring lawyers. Today's lawyers need to learn the pitfalls of manipulative communication, particularly when dealing with the laity. The very skill of articulate, self-interested rhetoric can wreak havoc with the fates of those less skilled clients with whom the lawyer inevitably must deal. Stories like *Bleak House* evoke the need for great sensitivity to those vulnerable enough to need legal counsel, a comprehensive understanding that is both technical and humane and that can only be conveyed through a language of pragmatic caring.

Ironically, however, literature's successful lawyers, far more than the caricatured buffoons like Guppy, often provide a seductive model for a merely self-interested professional discourse. Fiction's great practitioners—ethical or not, sympathetic or not—are all masterful communicators. In this important regard, storytellers allow such (professionally) successful lawyers to stand as colleagues in the craft of communicating; these lawyers are thus far more than caricatures whose social power makes them objects of ridicule, fear, and envy. Stories about lawyers often convey at least as much attraction to them as repulsion. To this extent, the close reading of law-related novels reveals an identification between articulate lawyer and artful storyteller that is both aesthetically fascinating and ethically troubling.

No better example exists in fiction for the irony of brilliant speech working questionable ethical ends than Melville's Captain Vere, whose stunning use in *Billy Budd* of the naval law and the mutinous times manages to convince an unwilling audience that the morally innocent Billy Budd has to hang. The winning lawyer, or lawyer figure, knows exactly what the interested audience needs to hear. Melville lets us know that neither law nor politics really compels Billy's execution; rather it is brought on by Vere's stunning rhetoric, in the service of his earlier intuitive reaction when he sees Billy lash out and kill the evil John Claggart: "Struck dead by an angel of God! Yet the angel must hang!" Vere privately decides the outcome that he—not the law—requires. He then surrounds this subjective prophesy with the cool outer form of legal discourse. The law *is* his discourse to the jury, neither more nor less.[44]

*The Merchant of Venice*'s Portia, too, another of literature's most persuasive and successful lawyer figures, finds just the right words to undo Shylock's case against the merchant, Antonio, even though the "objective" law seems to work in Shylock's favor. With the strict commercial precedents of Venice seemingly on his side, Shylock demands judgment in the peculiar but contractually driven form of a pound of Antonio's flesh. Like Vere, Portia must work with a set of laws that operates against her interests; like Vere, too, she nonetheless finds the words to overwhelm her audience and to bring about the legal outcome she most desires. She prevails, as many modern lawyers prevail, by finding precisely the right *words*. The "law," again, *is* those words, and no specific contract or statute, except as her words re-create those otherwise empty forms.

Our poetic method once again joins with the poethical treatment of legal language. Sound and sense work to the careful communicator's benefit, because they are linked in every display of effective legal discourse. Portia strikingly invokes the music of the word *mercy* in her most famous speech, though she intends no merciful treatment of Shylock; Vere manages to insert the word *mutiny* at a key point in his argument, though Billy of course is not being tried for mutiny. Shakespeare and Melville here show us that effective arguments are as sensuous as they are logical, that audiences respond to the music and the confluence of words perhaps more than to their merely rational sense. These sounds deliberately appeal to the values and interests of the given audience. John Barth's fictional lawyer Todd Andrews puts it well (in the midst of a legalistic text that will occupy us in detail shortly); struck with admiration by opposing counsel's stunning choice of rhetoric in an estate case that is central to the story, Andrews reflects: "How could mere justice cope with poetry? Men I think are ever attracted to the *bon mot* rather than the *mot juste*, and judges, no less than other men, are often moved by considerations more aesthetic than judicial."[45]

Yet Andrews, along with Vere and even Portia, are challenged by their storytellers to conform to a somewhat higher standard. As we shall pervasively examine through poethics, the standard is the *linkage of justice to beautiful speech*, not their cynical or merely self-serving dissociation.

However complex this challenge to match ethics and aesthetics in legal rhetoric, one observation of storytellers about legal discourse is considerably less ambiguous: *verbosity* serves lawyers poorly. Gavin Stevens, Faulkner's favorite lawyer, moves through four decades of novels from wordy philosopher to pithy advocate. *Intruder in the Dust* exemplifies this progression. It deals with a community's crazed hunger for revenge against an innocent black man who stands accused of murder. Gavin is a right-minded fellow, but his tendency to pontificate outpaces his common sense. His nephew, Chick Mallison, and a feisty old lady, Miss Havesham, do the literal dirty work of uncovering the accused man's innocence. Only then does Gavin gear up, employing his linguistic skills carefully and effectively in the service of justice.

The good lawyer is the skillful communicator, and for literary artists whose everyday work also involves communication, the essence of the skill is awareness of audience. Yet lawyers rarely learn much about their audiences in school. Nor are they trained well in the collateral skill of listening. (It is ironic, for example, that only the storyteller can convey to lawyers the power of silence and the strength of the nonverbal moment.)[46] What law professors do teach is thoroughness, but that is less than half the battle and has little to do with effective speech.

Legal communication, as portrayed in literature, stands also as a warning to disinterested audiences. (This is a separate question from that of lawyer-client communication, raised earlier.) Shakespeare, Dickens, Melville, and Faulkner remind us that we, as informed members of a citizenry, must be on our guard against effective speech that subtly misleads. They require us, as readers of their texts, to be scrupulously careful and to work hard at seeing what the story is about. Their mode of discussing justice is thus never by a logical demonstration of what justice means. Rather these artists link the act of communication to the given outcome in the case at hand, powerfully conveying (rather than merely showing) how eloquence can either serve or distort justice. Shylock's annihilation (not, as we shall discuss, his mere defeat in the contractual quibble) stands with the destruction through "law" of Richard Carstone, Billy Budd, and a variety of Faulknerian victims[47] to urge upon poethical readers justice through language and not articulateness shorn of ethics.

## LAW'S TREATMENT OF THE "OUTSIDER"

Cardozo's "cracknel biscuit," and its fluid that places justice in our mouths, is the language that convinces an audience of the *correct*, not merely the desired, outcome. And in the same stories that most feature skillful communication, the correct outcome is conveyed by the law's treatment of the outsider, the "other." Literature's second contribution to jurisprudence, this sensitivity to the needs of the disempowered, also finds, sadly, no analogue in today's world of law and economics and little even in the shifting world of liberal constitutional theory.

Think of the articulate, considerate, and hence successful lawyers or lawyer figures we have already mentioned. In whose service is their eloquence placed? Universally, in the service of the powerful, ensconced interests—the "fat cats," as Justice Thurgood Marshall sometimes likes to call them.[48] Mr. Tulkinghorn's sole passion—with one telling exception, to be explained shortly—is the good of his aristocratic clients in *Bleak House*; Portia supports the Venetian merchant class; Vere is a bulwark for what he perceives to be the values of the British Crown, its navy and its empire; and Gavin Stevens, before his nephew finally shows him the truth, stands ready to gab and hence tacitly to accept the verdict of the majoritarian lynch mob. To this list we can add Dostoevski's brilliant lawyer, Porfiry Petrovich, who destroys Raskolnikov's superman theory in *Crime and Punishment* (a theory certain to be quite unsettling to mainstream Russia), and Albert Camus' tactically clever examining magistrate in *The Stranger*, who analogously defends Christian values against what he sees as the amorality of Meursault.

Why should not legal talent be used to support the power structure? Storytellers have an answer that traditional legal reasoning and ethics do not offer: all too often the advocacy of mainstream values seems to carry with it the destruction of exogenous, nonconformist values. Sometimes, storytellers do create idealist lawyers to defend the nonpowerful. But usually, as with Fetyukovitch in Dostoevski's *The Brothers Karamazov*, Atticus Finch in Harper Lee's *To Kill A Mockingbird*, Horace Benbow (another Faulknerian lawyer) in *Sanctuary*, or Bibikov in Bernard Malamud's *The Fixer*, those lawyers cannot save their innocent clients. These "outsiders" are all convicted wrongly.

Even where the defendant is guilty, too severe a penalty is often inflicted, given what the reader knows to be as the complex reality of the crime and the prejudices of the jury or judge. This is true of Bigger Thomas in Richard Wright's *Native Son*, of the Isaacsons (modeled on the Rosenbergs) in E. L. Doctorow's *The Book of Daniel*, of Meursault in Camus' *The Stranger*, or of Billy Budd himself.

Furthermore, fiction dealing with the persecution of disfavored others goes beyond the portrait of the convicted innocent or the excessively punished defendant. Instead, lawyers like Tulkinghorn and lawyer figures like Portia and Vere are described as *subjectively seeking* the destruction of the outsider. As I shall emphasize in the next chapter (essay 7), *Bleak House*'s Tulkinghorn sets himself the task of uncovering the past sins of his client's beautiful wife, Lady Dedlock. With the acute powers of observation typical of the excellent lawyer, Tulkinghorn notices a momentary change in her impassive exterior, as she glances at the handwriting on a legal document in *Jarndyce v. Jarndyce*. He seizes upon that one indiscretion, obsessively probes Lady Dedlock's past association with the law-writer, and discovers finally that the writer was her lover and the father of her out-of-wedlock child. Tulkinghorn's motives for all this unpaid detective work are unclear. Why would he pursue, in his clever and taciturn way, Lady Dedlock's past? Will it serve any conceivable interest of his client, her husband, to reveal these secrets, as he eventually is ready to do? Does even the most zealous advocate go this far, unbidden by his client, into the mystery of things?

Mr. Tulkinghorn, that unopenable oyster, has been pried open just a bit. And it turns out that he is a resentful, sharply repressed misogynist. His secrecy he imputes to all women; his deviousness to them, too. But he despises them because they are "other," because they bring chaos to what should be an ordered world, because they feel, because they love.

The careful legal communicator stands accused by the only force in the novel stronger than himself when it comes to words—Dickens' third-person narrator, who helps us to see that Tulkinghorn's ability with language serves not only the needs of his rich clients but also his own deepest, darkest subjectivity. This much and more will be elaborated in the next chapter.

What a lesson for lawyers, and how appropriately literary! No other medium can so expose the inevitable mix of professionalism and personal bias that motivates the socially powerful lawyer. Perhaps what we learn here is that professional success in law necessitates a kind of resonance between the lawyer's private biases and those of the wider power structure he serves. For there is reason to believe that Victorian society as a whole may have shared Tulkinghorn's repressions. So Tulkinghorn, even with the meter not ticking—for he gains nothing in a pecuniary sense from the pursuit of Lady Dedlock and is eventually destroyed himself in the process—single-mindedly brings her down.

Again, this is not to assert that there are no idealistic lawyers in fiction. But they rarely prevail. Perhaps the storyteller wishes to criticize the ensconced social structure by demystifying its advocates; or perhaps, more subtly, storytellers mistrust artful language—even their own—and hence refuse to link its usage with the worthy cause of justice.

Take, again, the case of Portia. While no one wants to see Shylock win his pound of flesh, most audiences nevertheless have some doubts about the draconian nature of Shylock's punishment at the end of the trial scene. Why does the character who has spoken so effectively of mercy now force Shylock to the loss of his wealth and, more seriously still, of his beloved religion? Is it that Shylock, too, is one of literature's outsiders, victimized beyond the needs of law, destroyed by a classic insider exhibiting her own private animus?

What do we know about Portia that might explain such harshness? Does Shakespeare give us a glimpse into her character similar to the one provided by Dickens into Tulkinghorn's? One hint lies in Portia's manner of dismissing her Moroccan suitor in Act II: "A gentle riddance. Draw the curtains, go," she says, "Let all of his complexion choose me so" (II.vii.79–80).

The Venetians are anti-Semites; they are also, we learn here, indifferently racist. Yet the essential Portia is a wonderfully expansive woman, alive to the nuances of language and to the variety of human passions. She is too attractive, too much the mouthpiece of Shakespeare in untying the Gordian knot by foiling Shylock, to be held in our low esteem. And by defeating Shylock, she saves *love*. Perhaps the answer lies elsewhere.

Indeed, if Shylock is an outsider, harshly treated because his firm sense of ethics, of oaths, and of marriage vows differs from the casual breaches and easygoing relativism of the Venetian world, Portia, too, is an outsider. As a woman, she cannot, until Act V, speak in her own voice. First held hostage to her dead father's literal Will, then forced to appear disguised as a man at the trial, she is not yet ready at the trial to announce her own, self-willed, sense of justice. She is at worst complicit, for she allows Antonio to wreak the legalistic havoc; it is the merchant, not Portia, who devises every punishment that Shylock suffers in the cruel resolution of the Act IV trial scene.

Shorn of her disguise, Portia displays in the often overlooked Act V the same allegiance to law, to oaths, and to wedding rings that we earlier associated with Shylock. (It is Act V particularly that will concern us later in the expanded essay on *The Merchant of Venice*). There the liberated Portia affectionately but firmly insists of her husband, Bassanio, that he forever more respect their vows, epitomized in the ring. She thus follows Shylock, who, several acts earlier, learning of his daughter's obscene sale (for a monkey) of the ring he received from his wife, has said, "I would not have sold it for a wilderness of monkeys." Shakespeare links Portia's values in Act V to those of Shylock. As a woman and hence an outsider, Portia can display these inner beliefs only in the world of her domestic island, Belmont. Previously disguised as a man during the trial scene, she has been constrained to further the commercial interests and casual values of the Venetian Christians.

In Camus' *The Stranger*, too, a kind of "other" is destroyed by the law. Meursault *had* killed and surely deserves punishment. But the measure of punishment is caused less by Meursault's intent at the time of the homicide than by his morality in general. He has shown insensitivity at his mother's burial, begun a liaison that very day, and generally demonstrated a pattern of behavior that the prosecutors later label "bizarre." Under the legalistic microscope, a series of fairly benign earlier acts becomes negatively colored. But beyond this nonconformity, and immensely more threatening to law, is Meursault's way of *communicating*. Meursault must die because he will not speak as the law demands.

When asked at trial why he shot his victim five times, Meursault replies: "It was—the sun." This spontaneity, so typical of Meursault, offends the law not because it is false; it is offensive because it is forthright, it lacks "logic," it is antilegal. The law requires from those over whom it has power a *form* of communication that replicates the values of the law. Like Billy Budd or Dimitri Karamazov, whose cases are analogous, Meursault is punished with the utmost severity because he does not "speak the law," because he honestly conveys, and declines to distort, his inner drives and convictions.[49]

As a final example having to do with the law's persecution of the outsider, I would like to look all too briefly at a work that belongs on any Law and Literature syllabus, Toni Morrison's masterful *The Bluest Eye*. Although this short novel does not deal explicitly with law, I have indicated that poethics can be conveyed by any effective narrative, because it asks the lawyer to recall always the vital centrality of narrative and language to law. But *The Bluest Eye* speaks feelingly to the exclusion, even the annihilation in the eyes of authority, of the outsider. To this degree, it is as much about law as any of the earlier stories.[50]

Pecola is coming to maturity as a black girl in the Ohio of the early 1940s. Destabilized by a violent father, she is often sent to live with other families. At school, and in the neighborhood, her poverty and her

# 4. Poetic Substance

lack of roots make her prey to the cruelties of the environment. She begins to understand the world in terms of the blue eyes she sees both on her doll and on some of the white girls who seem to have things so easy. If only she could have those blue eyes . . .

The fascination with eyes becomes, in the hands of this storyteller, the reader's own. We are asked to understand Pecola *through our own eyes*, despite the differences in time, place, race, and sex that may exist. But we are constantly reminded how hard that task is, however right-minded ("wide-eyed"?) we think we are.

In a central passage, the tendency of those in authority to avoid seeing those who are "other" becomes explicit. Pecola wants to purchase some penny candies at Yacobowski's grocery store. In the following paragraphs, the tone of Morrison's prose challenges us both to criticize the middle-class white grocery-store owner and (which is so much more difficult) *to see* that we run the risk of treating others just as he does:

> She pulls off her shoe and takes out three pennies. The gray head of Mr. Yacobowski looms up over the counter. He urges his eyes out of his thoughts to encounter her. Blue eyes. Blear-dropped. Slowly, like Indian summer moving imperceptibly toward fall, he looks toward her. Somewhere between retina and object, between vision and view, his eyes draw back, hesitate, and hover. At some fixed point in time and space he senses that he need not waste the effort of a glance. He does not see her, because for him there is nothing to see. How can a fifty-two-year-old white immigrant storekeeper with the taste of potatoes and beer in his mouth, his mind honed on the doe-eyed Virgin Mary, his sensibilities blunted by a permanent awareness of loss, *see* a little black girl? Nothing in his life even suggested that the feat was possible, not to say desirable or necessary.
>
> "Yeah?"
>
> She looks up at him and sees the vacuum where curiosity ought to lodge. And something more. The total absence of human recognition—the glazed separateness. She does not know what keeps his glance suspended. Perhaps because he is grown, or a man, and she a little girl. But she has seen interest, disgust, even anger in grown male eyes. Yet this vacuum is not new to her. It has an edge; somewhere in the bottom lid is distaste. She has seen it lurking in the eyes of all white people. So. The distaste must be for her, her blackness. All things in her are flux and anticipation. But her blackness is static and dread. And it is the blackness that accounts for, that creates, the vacuum edged with distaste in white eyes.[51]

Now, we have not before met nor will we again "see" this Yacobowski. Yet it is enough, through this passage, to understand that he is not "other" from us—he *is* (or, at best, always risks being) us, in the sense that any reader risks his kind of myopia. Whatever his "loss" (and we are not told it), he has allowed it to desensitize him to the losses of others. His eyes are glazed with inner-directed resentment; they exclude from their field almost everyone. They cannot help because they do not see.

No lawyer reading this passage—and the rest of *The Bluest Eye*—will perceive in quite the same way as before his professional responsibility to the countless, needful "others" with whom he will be dealing. Indeed, we are challenged here to recognize that each person deserves the caring, fully involved look that seeks to include, not to dismiss.

I mentioned earlier in this section that *Brown v. Board of Education* and *Roe v. Wade* are as impoverished as texts as they are inspiring to people's hopes. I noted that the chipping away of those decisions derives from their failure to tell the real story at the heart of the conflicts they were resolving. Had the justices read *The Bluest Eye*, they could not have written a social-scientific treatise to try to affect race relations for generations to come (*Brown*); nor could they have centered their vision on medical science (instead of on women) in deciding that abortions should be permitted during the first trimester of pregnancy (*Roe*).

Stories about the "other" induce us to *see* the other, and once we do so, we endeavor consistently to understand the world from within the other's optic. Our own urge to organize things exclusively according to our experiences (an especial risk run by lawyers) diminishes. We may then work to create a legal system truly responsive to all those it serves.

In a society that seems to be moving back to a cycle of racism and repression, lawyers must once again read these stories, and many others like them. They reveal, through the law's only medium—language—at least three lessons about justice. These are, in *ascending* order of difficulty to the empowered practitioner or judge, that:

1. The law cannot *do* justice without fathoming the inner worlds, aspirations, and values of those who are different from itself;
2. The law cannot *speak* justice unless its practitioners continuously scrutinize their *own* values to strive for what is most fair and least hostile in them;
3. The striving for justice can finally be accomplished only through an act of communication with an audience whose own prejudices and values must be engaged, without sacrificing or even compromising the speaker's informed sense of fairness.

Poethics, in its attention to legal communication and to the plight of those who are "other," seeks to revitalize the ethical component of law. As all of part two will now proceed to elaborate, the literary vision of law goes beyond even this, for it aspires to a unique scrutiny of legal reasoning and indeed of the lawyer's inner self. This volume's developing jurisprudence, always grounded in narrative, will then (in part three) en-gage actual legal situations ranging from legal rhetoric in Nazified France to the seemingly more benign discourse of late-twentieth-century Amer-ican lawyers. On the way, we will take a brief look at the "canon" and examine why my preponderantly traditional choices actually serve as the most value-shattering and forward-looking sources for a just society.

# 2

## Legalistic Storytellers

CHAPTER TWO

# Let's Not Kill *All* the Lawyers: Anglo-American Fiction's Equivocal Approach to the Lawyer Figure

IN *The Failure of the Word*, I examined the gloomy portrait of law in three continental novelists, Flaubert, Dostoevski, and Camus.[1] Prescient to an almost depressing extreme (but is this not the special function of the novelist?), the continental writer integrated the theme of legal investigation into the two-dimensional framework of artistic self-criticism and cultural re-valuation. Franz Kafka, himself a lawyer, chose as his dominant metaphor of personal and social integration the nightmarish forms of continental criminal procedure (see essay 13 in this volume).

Contemporaneously, however, novelists in England and America were taking a somewhat more benign, if no less serious position on their legal subjects. (An exception is Herman Melville, whose dark view of contemporary legality in *Billy Budd* aligns him with the continental vision, as I have elsewhere suggested.[2]) In this chapter we will examine that gentler novelistic tradition and its particular subject: the practicing lawyer. Among the central fictional lawyer figures to be elaborated on here are Charles Dickens' remarkable twosome of Jaggers in *Great Expectations* and Tulkinghorn in *Bleak House*, Todd Andrews in John Barth's *The Floating Opera*, and lawyer Gavin Stevens (from the beginning to the end of William Faulkner's oeuvre).

The word gentler may surprise those readers who recall, accurately, the more glaringly pejorative portraits of the profession, particularly those to be found in English literature. Indeed, lawyers themselves take an almost masochistic delight in reciting to each other the many literary passages critical of their guild. From Shakespeare's "let's kill all the lawyers" and Samuel Johnson's "I would be loath to speak ill of any person who I do not know deserves it, but I am afraid he is an attorney," through such nineteenth-century remarks as Keats' "I think we may class the lawyer in the natural history of monsters" and Dickens' own uncharacteristically pithy "The law is a ass," to various twentieth-century observations, such as the American poetic vision of Carl Sandburg: "When the lawyers are through, what is there left? Can a mouse nibble at it and find enough to fasten a tooth in?" or, "Why is there always a secret singing / When a lawyer cashes in? / Why does a hearse horse snicker / Hauling a lawyer away?"

Such passages reflect Anglo-American literature's less equivocal lines of approach to the law. Whole portraits, or rather caricatures, come to mind, fictional conveyances of the public's feelings about the legal profession. The nineteenth century, perhaps particularly, took an almost definitional stance toward lawyers, so that even disinterested descriptions often managed to be implicitly derogatory. Thus, George Eliot, in *Felix Holt, Radical*, describes a character's perspective: ". . . he would not have been disgraced, if, on a valid legal claim being urged, he had got his lawyers to fight it out for him on the chance of eluding the claim by some adroit technical management."

Images such as these might leave one surmising that narrative fiction in English at least matched the vituperation toward lawyers of the continental artists. Surely, the sheer obsession with law as a fictional subject has extended beyond the nineteenth-century English precedents, perhaps particularly to the American storyteller. As we shall see, the Anglo-American novelists' fascination with law carries with it an intriguing blend of social satire and subtle admiration.

## 5. The Literary Lawyer's Six Compelling Traits

Since World War II alone, major fictional portraits of lawyers have been rendered by William Faulkner, Richard Wright, Bernard Malamud, E. L. Doctorow, John Barth, Louis Auchincloss, Gore Vidal, Truman Capote, Tom Wolfe, and many others (without mentioning the fascinating categories of detective and popular fiction, films, or television). Yet, despite the tyrannic, often "lawful" repression practiced by various regimes during this period, the image of the lawyer in twentieth-century fiction somewhat modifies the pejorative view of the nineteenth-century novelist, while perhaps increasing, through narrative technique as much as theme, the sense of bewilderment before the law itself that typifies the modern alienated layman.

Indeed, American literary culture specifically, in a manner perhaps harmonious with its idealistic and constitutional strain, has managed to produce fully sympathetic lawyers, a statement impossible to support from the stuff of English or continental fiction. Such humanly likable figures go some way at least to offset the purely negative image previously mentioned. The film or television version of the crusading lawyer derives in part from this novelistic strain, but in serious fiction these individuals rarely achieve their professional goals. One simply does not find Perry Mason figures—consistent winners—among the good guys. Instead, sympathetic fictional lawyers all fall into one of three categories: they have no law practice worth mentioning; or they lose the cases on which they are working in the novel; or they lose their lives altogether without solving anything.

Examples of the three unfortunate types of "nice" lawyers come readily to mind. Pudd'nhead Wilson stands as the nineteenth-century model for the first: Mark Twain's protagonist has to wait twenty years to get a case. Interestingly, he fails to attract clients because, soon after arriving in town, he gains a reputation for simple-minded directness, and people seek cleverness (even deceitfulness) in their lawyers. Only Wilson's lifelong hobby of fingerprinting eventually places him in the legal limelight.

The category of nice lawyers who lose their cases is larger. Wright's Max misconceives the jury's interests, and Bigger Thomas, his client, dies (*Native Son*). Doctorow's Ascher bestows care upon his client's *children*, but the parents are convicted and electrocuted (*The Book of Daniel*). Horace Benbow, in Faulkner's *Sanctuary*, transposes most of his personal life's ineffectiveness to the courtroom; "the fundamental Benbowish failure" extends to his defense of Lee Goodwin, which breaks down because of Horace's fatal inability to see the connivance of his adversaries. More poignantly yet, the sympathetic family man Atticus Finch does not have the necessary skills (admittedly Herculean in nature) to prevent a jury from convicting his innocent client, Tom Robinson, in Harper Lee's *To Kill A Mockingbird*. And among those right-thinking lawyers who lose more than their cases is Robert Bolt's Sir Thomas More (*A Man For All Seasons*), whose dilemma powerfully represents the discrepancy between a lawyer's sense of justice and that of his surrounding society. More refuses to compromise that sense, which he equates with law, and he perishes. Similarly, Malamud's Bibikov, the sole lawyer willing to see Yakov Bok's position in *The Fixer*, dies for his insistence on elevating justice above pragmatism. Indeed, Yakov Bok stands as one of legalistic fiction's most poignant "outsiders"; Malamud's superb story indicates that some righteous lawyers find the poethical strength to join with, even to give their all to, the "other."

Strikingly, some of the fictional cases alluded to here are based on real legal situations; these include *The Fixer*, whose realistic origins I will describe shortly. In fact, as in fiction, many good men and women practice law but find themselves at peril of professional failure or even worse. While it need not be so, it is significant that serious fiction cannot perceive justice or personal merit as coterminous with legal success.

But if so much of law is pilloried and if fiction's nice-guy lawyers are doomed to professional failure, where do we find the shades of gray emerging from the extreme tones of black or white thus far identified? Clearly, humor, satire, bitter parody, mystification, and outright hostility to lawyers have their place; so, too, do sympathetic protagonists whose law degrees get them nowhere. But the very writers who most effectively vilify the lawyers they have created also produce brilliantly subtle figures whose legal training redounds to their benefit and renders them, if not lovable, at least fascinating. Indeed, the Anglo-American novelist's complex attraction to legal figures finally can be explained better by the *identity*, more than the antipathy, between lawyer and literary artist. Like the literary protagonist confronted with his doppelgänger ("double," another preoccupying theme of modern fiction), the mainstream English or American novelist feels both self-interested attraction and satiric repulsion in the face of his legal characters.

The most compelling features of legal power, it turns out, also delineate the strengths (and potential weakness) of the novelist! Thus the greatest lawyers in modern fiction cannot be portrayed simplistically. Too much of their creators goes with them into the story. And if professionally successful lawyers have in common (as they do) a package of novelistically endowed traits, these reflect some of the storyteller's own deepest self-critical concerns. Indeed, I believe that successful literary lawyers can be placed invariably under the sign of six remarkably consistent characteristics:

1. *Verbal manipulation.* All great literary lawyers have mastered the art of verbal communication. Storytellers may have otherwise satirized legal jargon, but when they portray successful lawyers, they endow these figures with the ability to control situations through language.

2. *Apartness.* Literary lawyers are separate from the mass of humanity. They are compulsive professionals and shine more in isolation than in groups. They seek sociability, if at all, in the company of their fellow craftsmen.

3. *Distrustfulness.* Most successful novelistic lawyers suffer from an unhealthy skepticism bordering on misanthropy. (Think of Dickens' Mr. Jaggers, who washes his hands after each client leaves.)

4. *Professional ethical relativism.* Rigorously loyal to their clients' interests, these lawyers may not always appear to act with a keen eye toward the strictures of ethical legal behavior. The traditional professional dilemma in the English and American adversary system—do we serve, ultimately, the client or the court?—seems by most successful literary lawyers to be resolved for the former.

5. *Frugality (and bachelorhood).* While literary lawyers like to earn large fees, they rarely expend much on self-gratifying extravagances. Jagger's clerk Wemmick tells Pip, for example, that Jaggers never purchases silver; "Britannia metal" will do. In a less material sense, the fictional lawyer's lack of interest in personal comforts frequently extends to his remaining a bachelor; storytellers do not permit accomplished lawyers to have personally fulfilling lives.

6. *Passivity.* A paradox to be elaborated shortly, all the earlier traits contrive to produce an individual not totally at the center of things but rather on the fringes, directing the fates of others and not participating fully in life.

Throughout the remaining pages of this chapter, I will exemplify in some detail these features and their relevance to novelistic meanings. The paradigm is Mr. Jaggers (the subject of essay 6), but many English and American characters vary only slightly on his theme. Jaggers is verbally acute, tyrannical, and distant. Yet he has an underlying humanity, revealed both in his actions (saving Estella and her mother; allowing Pip to benefit from his financial wisdom) and in his occasional moments of insecurity, as when he and Wemmick *almost* enter into a discussion of feelings in the marvelous chapter 51 of *Great Expectations* that will concern us presently.

No wonder that Dickens alludes to a sympathetic side of Jaggers, for Jaggers' combined traits of keen intelligence, observation, and articulateness make of him a true "author figure." Like many another novelistic lawyer, he possesses qualities shared only by the novelist who has created him. Thus Jaggers catalyzes the legal and economic relationships among characters who are more passionate and spontaneous than he, but less intelligent, verbal and perceptive. If Dickens in part meant Jaggers to represent himself within the action of the book, he surely wanted him to possess more than craftsmanship, admirable though that is; he needed some likable personal traits as well. Otherwise the novel's most author-like character would be a mere empty shell. Dickens did not want this.

Twain's Pudd'nhead Wilson, surprisingly, shares many of Jaggers' traits (at least after he begins to practice law), and forms almost as significant a nineteenth-century model for subsequent *American* depictions of the profession. Incapable of attracting clients because he is considered a simpleton, he leads a frugal bachelor's life until he finally earns fame and a fee during his defense of the Italian twins who stand accused of murdering old Judge Driscoll. Wilson proves his nickname false by using the courtroom (as powerfully and cleverly as Jaggers) both to exonerate his client and to gain personal renown. Pragmatism, hard work, personal magnetism, verbal acumen, and, above all, the appearance of superior knowledge—the tools of Jaggers himself—allow Pudd'nhead, a "nice" lawyer, to win.[3]

Faulkner's Gavin Stevens, in *Intruder in the Dust*, replicates Jaggers' model to the letter, but with a soupçon of Twain's folksy lawyer. So significant for the collectivity of literary lawyers is Gavin that he also will deserve more detailed attention shortly (essay 9). For my purposes here, several resemblances between Gavin and Mr. Jaggers should be noted. First, like all professionally successful literary lawyers, both are bachelors whose lives are devoted mostly to their craft. For another, *Intruder in the Dust*, like *Great Expectations*, employs an adolescent voice or perspective as the dominant narrative technique. *Intruder*'s adolescent narrator is emblematic of society's less powerful elements and responds to the lawyer figure with a mixture of fear, admiration, and gradual skepticism. Having apparently derived a basic approach to experience from Uncle Gavin, rather than his own parents, the novel's youthful Chick Mallison finally comes to see that his uncle's words may not lead to actions. Gavin's long allocutions about social institutions and justice seem to mask a basic passivity; if the story's wrongly accused black man is to be exonerated, then he, Chick, must do the legwork.

Still, for all his faults, Gavin is a man of substantial vision. So Faulkner, always attracted to lawyers,[4] cedes to Gavin a considerable amount of narrative space as the novel draws to a close. Gavin expounds subjects as diverse as the white southerner's racism, the American's love of his automobile, and the European's response to Nazi and Communist totalitarianism. Why does Faulkner choose to cede so much of his own authorial voice to the lawyer, particularly as the novel draws to an end?

Because, like Jaggers, Gavin has become one with the novelist who has created him.

Chick Mallison's view of the powerful lawyer, like Pip's, is paralleled in Daniel Isaacson, the young protagonist and narrator in *The Book of Daniel*, E. L. Doctorow's fictionalized version of the Rosenberg spy case. Gazing with frightened eyes at an impending orphanhood, Daniel relies on the idealistic attorney Ascher to defend his parents in court and, more, to protect his younger sister and himself. Ascher matches Jaggers' physical bulk and uses it to try to convey security to his doomed clients' children. Through Ascher's failures as a lawyer (for he is the more typical nice guy who loses), Daniel's Kafkaesque terror in the face of the American legal system increases. No more than Pip or Chick can Daniel find personal security or identity through law.

We have seen a veriety of storytellers place adolescent protagonists before the power of the law. The idea that legal systems can treat their subjects with the callous disregard of adults toward children is furthered in *The Fixer*, which is also based on an actual criminal trial. The infamous Beiliss case,[5] one of the last of a horrific line of "blood libels" against Jews in tsarist Russia, afforded Malamud the opportunity to portray two kinds of lawyers and to have their contrasting destinies observed by his alienated protagonist, Yakov Bok. While Bok (Beiliss) is not in fact an adolescent, his distance from the prevailing legal culture could be no more pronounced if he were, indeed, a babe-in-arms. Recently arrived in the metropolis, Kiev, from the Jewish shtetl of his youth, Bok finds himself arrested and (like Mitya Karamazov) the subject of a preliminary investigation.[6] Innocent of the charge, the murder of a Christian child and use of Christian blood to prepare the ritual matzoh on Passover, Bok is bounced between two lawyers, one benevolent, one anti-Semitic and malicious. How can Bok detect "law" in this morass? And on whom or what is he to pin his hopes? Yakov Bok's quest for self-definition, like that of Pip, Chick, and Daniel, reveals to him the limits of the law and forces him finally to turn to his own inner strengths, unreliant on what has proved to be too fickle an institution.

Perhaps most effectively of all, through a lawyer created contemporaneously with Camus' equivocal Clamence,[7] John Barth's *The Floating Opera* sharply modernizes the Anglo-American portrait of the lawyer, without substantially altering it. The narrator and protagonist, bachelor Todd Andrews, a seemingly successful Maryland practitioner, attempts to explore the unsettling regions of his personal past, proceeding in a humorous but somewhat deceitful manner reminiscent of Clamence. His highly literary investigation (which he calls his "Inquiry") fills his sleepless nights while during the day his law practice brings him success through means not always the most ethical. Todd Andrews stands, in his verbal manipulation, his ethics, and his overall philosophy, as a fine successor-in-interest to the puzzling Jaggers. Andrews, too, shall return shortly to these pages (essay 8).

Thus the Anglo-American lawyer in shades of gray wears the suit both of his creator and of his real-life colleagues and engages in a substantially similar enterprise. The buffoons and villains of the clichés have softened into figures perhaps even more portentous by virtue of their subtlety. Four detailed portraits now follow, beginning with Dickens' two most memorable lawyers and then elaborating upon Barth's and Faulkner's.

# 6. "I'll have no feelings here!": More on Mr. Jaggers

Dickens, who like Dostoevski excelled in his portraits of lawyers,[8] created no subtler or finer character (and certainly no more representative lawyer) than Jaggers. A total professional, Jaggers strikes us also as a contemporary; few English or American lawyers of the present day would fail to perceive similarities to the fictional lawyer created in the 1860s.

Yet Jaggers is a prototypical Victorian, whose manners and mores not only fit into the surrounding environment (from which he draws his clientele) but actually are vital to its perpetuation. For the lowliest criminal in his office and the wealthiest benefactor whom he serves, Jaggers uses his talents to further a social structure. If he seems completely modern to us today, it must be that our sense of the lawyer has not really altered: someone who uses his peculiar outlook and talents not so much for his own power as for the perpetuation of his clients' well-being.

But Jaggers, to this extent a mere surrogate, also subtly manipulates and controls the destinies of his various clients. From Molly, his first celebrated criminal defendant, to Magwitch, whose estate he secretively manages on Pip's behalf, Jaggers thrives on the surrogate's position and, without really participating in life, comes to control the lives of others. This, too, is a modern irony, explaining in part the resentment lawyers sometimes both feel and evoke.

Despite his central place in *Great Expectations*, Jaggers has inspired for the most part only secondary treatment among book-length critics.[9] J. Hillis Miller, in his fine work, nevertheless disposes of Jaggers in two or three sentences.[10] Perhaps this is because, in the words of Humphrey House, critics rightly show a deference to Dickens' "treatment of the law [which] cannot safely be discussed by anyone who is not a trained lawer."[11] In any event, Jaggers' role in this brilliant novel has yet to be fully analyzed.

As we have been suggesting throughout, wherever a lawyer appears as more than a purely ephemeral figure in nineteenth- and twentieth-century fiction, he is likely to carry a disproportionate weight of structural significance. As a kind of *porte-parole*—or spokesman—for the author of the text, and as a figure whose interest in language and form is (professionally) second only to that of the novelist, the lawyer deserves a reader's scrupulous attention. It follows, too, that the aim of this essay—to elaborate on the identifiable traits that make of Jaggers a paradigm for all subsequent Anglo-American fictional lawyers—has as a modest concomitant the search for meaning within the single Dickensian masterpiece itself. Let us see whether these great expectations can be fulfilled.

The novel recounts the growth into physical and social maturity of a boy, Pip, whose status as a country blacksmith's apprentice is sharply altered by the appearance of two powerful strangers, the criminal Magwitch (whose life Pip saves on the marsh) and the lawyer Jaggers (who, several years later, arrives to tell Pip that an unknown benefactor intends to make him a London gentleman). That the anonymous author of Pip's expectations is in fact Magwitch, since grown rich during his Australian banishment, remains a secret hidden behind Jaggers' professional armor. Instead, Pip mistakenly pursues the theory that the money gradually changing him from provincial to elitist comes from old Miss Havisham (another of Jaggers' clients), whose beautiful ward Estella remains confused in his imagination with this future life of blissful comfort. The house of cards tumbles when Magwitch returns to London, at mortal risk, to dote upon his young creation transformed into a gentleman: there Pip discovers that his hopes were both baseless and base, as the escaped criminal is apprehended, executed, and his (Pip's) wealth escheated to the Crown. Pip goes to work for his dear friend, Herbert Pocket; his great expectations as to wealth and love ended,[12] he emerges a reflective and sympathetic man.

Through it all, from entrance to ending, Jaggers' presence is felt, replacing that of the almost saintly blacksmith, Joe Gargery, as the sole older man guiding Pip into the intricacies of mature life. In recognizing Jaggers' lawyerlike traits, we may therefore also come to see Dickens' complex view of contemporary English manhood more generally, for Jaggers is as much Pip's social role model as Magwitch is his economic benefactor.

Pip's first glimpse of Jaggers, as they cross paths at Miss Havisham's, reminds us of the seminal quality of Dickens' portrait for all subsequent lawyers in modern fiction; it combines the most universal of the six traits lawyers usually possess in novels (see essay 5) with the adolescent narrative perspective from which these seemingly masterful professionals are often viewed:

> He was a burly man of an exceedingly dark complexion, with an exceedingly large head and a corresponding large hand. He took my chin in his large hand and turned up my face to have a look at me by the light of the candle. He was prematurely bald on the top of his head, and had bushy black eyebrows that wouldn't lie down, but stood up bristling. His eyes were set very deep in his head, and were disagreeably sharp and suspicious. He had a large watch-chain, and strong black dots where his beard and whiskers would have been if he had let them. He was nothing to me, and I could have had no foresight then that he ever would be anything to me, but it happened that I had this opportunity of observing him well.
>
> "Boy of the neighbourhood? Hey?" said he.
>
> "Yes, sir," said I.
>
> "How do *you* come here?"
>
> "Miss Havisham sent for me, sir," I explained.
>
> "Well, behave yourself. I have a pretty large experience of boys, and you're a bad set of fellows. Now mind!" said he, biting the side of his great forefinger as he frowned at me, "You behave yourself!"
>
> With these words he released me—which I was glad of for his hand smelt of scented soap—and went his way downstairs.[13]

Dickens quickly impresses both Pip and the reader, in this early passage, with Jaggers' powers of verbal and social manipulation. The youngster, not yet knowing the place this "burly" man will retain in his future development, experiences almost the degree of fear in this confrontation as he had felt with Magwitch on the heath, and the parallel is all the more striking considering the relative safety of Miss Havisham's staircase. Mr. Jaggers *seizes* Pip, physically and mentally, and if he does not turn him upside down as Magwitch did, he nonetheless looks into the lad's soul and begins to capture it with professional as well as brute strength. As in a later scene, when Pip observes Jaggers grabbing the wrist of his maidservant, Molly (his first client, and Estella's mother), this grasping of Pip's physical person emblematizes the total comprehension brought by the lawyer to every thing or individual he is called upon to know.

Jaggers, with prototypical lawyerlike distrustfulness, burdens this boy whom he has just met with the brand of "a bad set of fellows." From Jaggers' perspective, the brand fits: Pip is not yet civilized (or rather socialized, for Jaggers would surely admit that the two are different). It will fall to the lawyer to take the adolescent and make him mature, but he will accomplish that task as fictional lawyers often do, by exposing him to reality and letting him make his own choices.

And here the comparison of Pip and Molly ends, for although both fall into Jaggers' sphere, Molly belongs to that single class for which the lawyer's social power becomes totally defining: the class of criminal defendants. In all other professional relationships the lawyer is an *option-definer*; sometimes the only figure with the training and intelligence to see the way a given situation is really developing, he still leaves the decisions to his clients. In the relationship of lawyer to prosecuted suspect, however, he becomes also the *decision maker*. Thus Jaggers' *verbal manipulation* (lawyerlike trait number one) gains full prominence in his guise of criminal lawyer; defendants, opposing lawyers, and even the judges themselves "dread him" (to use Wemmick's phrase; 224). Jaggers' stance, quite to the contrary, is one of a "determined reticence" (263) toward everyone involved in the system.

Indeed, the second and third paradigmatic qualities in this lawyer—*apartness* and *distrustfulness*—reflect Jaggers' response to a severely flawed criminal justice system. He might seem just as unhappy today, and more recent novels are abundantly rich in cynical defense lawyers.[14] Thus there is much to Edgar Johnson's brief but generally sensitive appraisal of Jaggers on this point:

> Mr. Jaggers specializes in representing accused criminals, whose unsavory cases he handles with the most unscrupulous and triumphant skill. But with the departure of every felonious visitor he goes to a closet and cleans his hands with scented soap, as if he were washing off the client. On one occasion, Pip remarks, "he seemed to have been engaged on a case of a darker complexion than usual, for we found him with his head butted into this closet, not only washing his hands, but laving his face and gargling his throat. And even when he had done all that, and had gone all around the jack-towel, he took out his penknife and scraped the case out of his nails before he put his coat on."
>
> Though Mr. Jaggers is a highly successful and respected professional man, his own sense of the necessities his life imposes on him is one of degradation and pollution. Could there be a clearer symbolic suggestion that much of the business of such a society is dirty business? ... Both for Wemmick and for Mr. Jaggers, then, their office in Little Britain is a kind of prison in which they lock up their better selves and subdue them to the world of venality.[15]

Yet Jaggers is not perfectly true to Johnson's analysis. First and foremost, he cannot be compared to the delightfully schizophrenic Wemmick, who (like some modern-day weekend barhopping lawyers) loses his joie de vivre only upon entering the office.[16] Jaggers, like most fine lawyers in our system, expresses (not represses) his essential self in every professional act he performs. "A wise and disillusioned Olympian," as John H. Hagan has put it,[17] Jaggers passionately protects his clients, knowing too well the harshness of the social system that has otherwise left them friendless. The compulsive washing of hands, beloved by the critics, might indicate repulsion not for his job, or his clients, or the law itself, but rather for the disordered and unjust society that has produced Magwitch and Molly, Miss Havisham and Estella. Mystery and silence cloak his faithful assertiveness on behalf of those clients, civil *and* criminal, who have paid for his professional expertise. So too his distrustfulness, born of daily contact with people not likely to match what Wemmick calls his "constant height [which] is of a piece with his immense abilities" (285), cloaks an almost idealistic commitment to certain legal values.

Jaggers' manipulative powers, secretiveness, and distrustfulness come with the territory of his professionalism, but they are not necessarily a Dickensian indication of monomania or egocentricity. Jaggers' traits are shown to serve not only his clients (important, after all, though that service is) but also a professional perspective that incorporates (in Dickens's England and our America) some intrinsically noble concepts. This ironic mixture of less than sympathetic human qualities and fundamentally worthwhile legal safeguards typifies Anglo-American literature's equivocal approach to lawyers and truly defines Jaggers' place in *Great Expectations*.

To understand this, we must recall that Dickens, by the mature period that produced *Great Expectations*, was beyond the youthful radicalism (Johnson and Jackson to the contrary)[18] that condemned all institutions out of hand. Law in this novel, like Jaggers, is treated evenhandedly.[19] Yes, Jaggers' own imagination has been shocked by that part of the system in which, as he tells Pip during their strikingly intimate conversation in chapter 51, " 'he often saw children solemnly tried at a criminal bar . . . whipped, transported, neglected, cast out, qualified in all ways for the hangman, and growing up to be hanged.' " (444). Yet Jaggers essentially condones the legal system within which he operates, and on far from cynical grounds. Much earlier in the novel (the second time we meet him), Jaggers contradicts Mr. Wopsle at the Jolly Bargeman on a fundamental point of law (chapter 18). Mr Wopsle, the talkative but sloppy-thinking clerk at the provincial church of Pip's childhood, is holding forth on what he views is the clear guilt of an accused murderer soon to be on trial. Pip notices a "strange gentleman" taking in the oration with "an expression of contempt" (149). Not yet recognizing the stranger as his "burly" interlocutor from years before, Pip hears him humiliate

Wopsle in the name of a legal concept dear to us all:

"... Do you know, or do you not know, that the law of England supposes every man to be innocent, until he is proved—proved—to be guilty?"

"Sir," Mr. Wopsle began to reply," as an Englishman myself, I—"

"Come!" said the stranger, biting his forefinger at him. "Don't evade the question. Either you know it or you don't know it. Which is it to be?"

He stood with his head on one side and himself on one side, in a bullying interrogative manner, and threw his forefinger at Mr. Wopsle—as it were to mark him out—before biting it again.

"Now!" said he. "Do you know it, or don't you know it?"

"Certainly I know it," replied Mr. Wopsle....

"Yes," repeated the stranger, looking round at the rest of the company with his right hand extended towards the witness, Wopsle. "And now I ask you what you say to the conscience of that man who, with that passage before his eyes, can lay his head upon his pillow after having pronounced a fellow-creature guilty, unheard?"...

The strange gentleman, with an air of authority not to be disputed, and with a manner expressive of knowing something secret about every one of us that would effectually do for each individual if he chose to disclose it, left the back of the settle, and came into the space between the two settles, in front of the fire, where he remained standing—his left hand in his pocket, and biting the forefinger of his right. (150–52).

All of Jaggers' traits merge here (it is not the only time Pip sees his manipulation as "bullying"),[20] but to no selfish or cynical end. He "bullies" for us all, refusing to let the precious presumption of innocence be devalued by sloppy thinkers, even in the "moot court" of a country inn. Dickens thus proposes the lawyer as a professional wedded not only to his clients but also to the superb traditions of a remarkable system admittedly flawed but potentially fine.

In this way, what we have earlier called (as the fourth lawyerlike trait) Jaggers' *professional ethical relativism* also comes into focus.[21] Responsive to modern philosophical trends (as we shall emphasize more fully in reference to Barth's Todd Andrews), the literary lawyer's seeming ethical relativism turns out to mask an almost anachronistic allegiance to absolute values. Thus, if the English and American lawyer's adversarial protection of criminally suspect clients sometimes seems either mystifying or self-serving to the average layman, literary art tends to indicate that it is noble either in its own right (for who else would be the champion of the Magwitches, the Mollies, and the other impoverished of this world?) or as a reflection of a system that (unlike the European's) sees the primacy of value of each single individual.

This claim is not made, Wopsle-like, without weighing its words, for consider: Dickens indicates, through the subtlety of his portrait, that Jaggers is essentially a worthwhile and even sensitive individual not despite, but because of, his profession. His *frugality* (the fifth characteristic typical of literary lawyers) further marks the disinterested passion ("the determined reticence") of his craft; yes, he insists on being paid, but even that, considering the spare nature of his dress and furnishings, seems more out of respect for his profession than for himself specifically. And when he invites Pip to the dinner party in chapter 26, he characteristically insists on "No ceremony . . . and no dinner dress" (229).

Yet Jaggers' characteristics, even when placed by Dickens in a largely favorable light, do not add up to a whole human being. Indeed, no lawyer in Dickens (Sydney Carton, remember, is merely a law student and a clerk)[22] enjoys the full humanity of even the most flawed client; and the novel ever since (American "sympathetic losers" aside) has followed this lead. Why does the same writer who recognizes the value of a given professional existence refuse to grant it integration into a harmonious personal whole? Why must the lawyer who preserves a positive life out of the office, like Wemmick, utterly repress that side when at work (so that, incredibly, Jaggers only learns of Wemmick's "old father [and] pleasant and playful ways" (443) through Pip's careful mediation in chapter 51, where Jaggers' rule ("I'll have no feelings here"; 446) is briefly relaxed?

Dickens, with a sensitivity to lawyers born of personal experience and professional comity,[23] puts his finger on a dilemma perhaps more interesting to legal than to lay readers of such works. The very traits that make lawyers so useful both to clients and society rob the lawyers themselves of a certain holistic, passionate existence. This we have summed up earlier in the chapter as the sixth characteristic of novelistic lawyers, and easily the most complex: *passivity*.

Again Jaggers establishes the firm literary precedent. His way of speaking partly indicates the almost enforced passivity of his social role: he rigorously abjures personal admissions (442) or direct communication of information. "I don't recommend him, observe," Jaggers says to Pip of Mr. Pocket; "because I never recommend anybody" (156). And (of Magwitch's whereabouts), "Don't tell me anything; I don't want to know anything; I am not curious" (359). It is not only that, as Pip says of him at Miss Havisham's table, "He cross-examined his very wine when he had nothing else in hand" (263) or that all conversations with Jaggers (save chapter 51's) are "strictly regulated by the rules of evidence" (440); his careful use of language is part of a trained, effective, professional stance toward life. Several times he corrects Pip's speech[24] (and indeed what we today would call Pip's communication skills improve dramatically under the lawyer's tutelage), but the meticulousness has a pathetic aspect to it, negating Jaggers' individuality.

The astounding chapter 51 again conveys this best. There, even though Pip has learned enough from Jaggers about communication to manipulate the lawyer's omnipresent handkerchief back into his pocket and to force some feelings out of him instead (442), Jaggers cannot speak forthrightly. Heed how he reveals Estella's parentage:

> Mr. Jaggers nodded his head retrospectively two or three times, and actually drew a sigh. "Pip," said he, "we won't talk about 'poor dreams;' you know more about such things than I, having much fresher experience of that kind. But now about this other matter. I'll put a case to you. Mind! I admit nothing."
>
> He waited for me to declare that I quite understood that he expressly said that he admitted nothing. . . .
>
> "Put the case, Pip, that there was one pretty little child out of the heap who could be saved; whom the father believed dead, and dared make no stir about; as to whom, over the mother, the legal adviser had this power: 'I know what you did, and how you did it. You came so and so, you did such and such things to divert suspicion. I have tracked you through it all. Part with the child, unless it should be necessary to produce it to clear you, and then it shall be produced. Give the child into my hands, and I will do my best to bring you off. If you are saved.' Put the case that this was done, and that the woman was cleared."
>
> "I understand you perfectly."
>
> "But that I make no admissions?"
>
> "That you make no admissions." And Wemmick repeated, "No admissions." . . .
>
> "Put the case that the child grew up, and was married for money. That the mother was still living. That the father was still living. That the mother and father, unknown to one another, were dwelling within so many miles, furlongs, yards if you like, of one another. That the secret was still a secret, except that you had got wind of it. Put that last case to yourself very carefully."
>
> "I do."
>
> "I ask Wemmick to put it to *himself* very carefully."
>
> And Wemmick said, "I do."
>
> "For whose sake would you reveal the secret? For the father's? I think he would not be much the better for the mother. For the mother's? I think if she had done such a deed, she would be safer where she was. For the daughter's? I think it would hardly serve her to establish her parentage for the information of her husband, and to drag her back to disgrace, after an escape of twenty years, pretty secure to last for life. But, add the case that you had loved her, Pip, and had made her the subject of those 'poor dreams' which have, at one time or another, been in the heads of more men than you think likely, then I tell you that you had better—and would much sooner when you

had thought well of it—chop off that bandaged left hand of yours with your bandaged right hand, and then pass the chopper on to Wemmick there, to cut *that* off, too." (443–45)

Jaggers, even at his most human, cannot be totally direct with his audience. Having set in motion—on behalf of the storyteller—all of the actions that produce the novel's plot (the other being his unsuccessful defense of Magwitch and later willingness to manage the trust for Pip), may he not be evoking the novelist's own dilemma of communication? Yet he cannot express his feelings directly. "The case" must always be put impersonally, or at least incompletely, leaving it up to each listener (or reader) to draw his own conclusions.

To the extent, precisely, that Jaggers has become a fine lawyer, so he has lost his capacity for direct speech and even for spontaneous interaction with others. Thus, perhaps associated also with his frugality—and in common with many another literary lawyer—Jaggers has chosen to remain a bachelor. So he displaces, in a typically passive way, any remaining romantic impulse; for example, he takes an abnormally keen interest in the rivalry of Bentley Drummel and Pip for the hand of Estella.

Jaggers' role is both powerful and *reactive*; generally speaking, as Pip puts it, "my guardian seemed to follow rather than originate subjects" (232). At work, when a client retains his services, Jaggers swoops in on the problem, and the effects of his intervention devolve upon the client. This will ever be the lawyer's destiny: to control, briefly, the lives of others, to bring order to those lives where possible, and then to leave the true joy (or despair), drama, and passion to be experienced in his absence.

Finally, even where the increasingly successful lawyer has time for a personal life, the exigencies of his craft come to dominate it. Jaggers' constant flirtation with unethical behavior, as where he "refuses to hear" compromising information about a needed witness (184–85), is made by Dickens almost a natural concomitant of a successful career at the criminal bar; but this selective approach to what others say and do finally infects a man's personal side. Jaggers' nobility lies in this double-edged awareness: he may no longer experience others' "poor dreams," for his intense professionalism *requires* the abnegation of any active personal life.

Pip, thanks largely to Jaggers, learns how to behave—how, indeed, to speak. His redemption ironically lies in his rejecting his mentor and in seeking a more direct, harmonious life. Chapter 51 (in which Pip becomes Jaggers' peer in the skill of manipulative communication, squeezing from him the truth of Estella's parentage) equally marks the protagonist's narrow escape from the impersonality and repression of modern professionalism more generally. Earlier Pip had lamented that "coming of age ... seemed hardly worth-while in such a guarded and suspicious world as he [Jaggers] made of it" (315); but here, through a mature act of will, Pip liberates himself from Jaggers' skepticism and prepares—liberated also from the criminal wealth behind his false expectations—to comfort the dying Magwitch and enter the world of reflective adulthood.

Dickens' novel, through the lawyer who has been rendered both idiosyncratic and symbolic, thus both indicts and commends the social order. Portrayed as quintessentially conservative, the lawyer superbly safeguards (without necessarily condoning) the interests of his various clients. But whatever strong objections to the social structure Dickens preserved while writing *Great Expectations*, he surely did not at that point see the law itself solely in pejorative terms. For, unlike the deep-rooted iconoclasm of the continental novelists, or the overly harsh caricatures of his own earlier novels, such as *Bleak House*, Dickens' art here expresses some appreciation of the legal institutions of his day, while also identifying the terrible effects of professional excellence upon the practitioner's personal development.

Law, like literary art, Dickens seems to be saying, has much to commend it as an English institution; but lawyers (like their confreres in the careful use of language, novelists) pay a heavy personal price for the privilege of entering its temple. Before turning to two American writers, it is worth exploring that latter observation further via an analysis of Dickens' darkest lawyer: Mr. Tulkinghorn.

# 7. Law's Oppression of the Feminine Other: Mr. Tulkinghorn v. Lady Dedlock

Some of the equivocation about law otherwise typical of English and American fiction is clarified in Dickens' best-known "law-related" novel, *Bleak House*. It is through the dark portrait of that work's Mr. Tulkinghorn that Dickens seems to speak for all novelists in undermining the strong outer conventions of the law. Somewhat akin (as we shall see) to Faulkner, whose critique of law softened considerably as his novels progressed, so in Dickens we must await the Jaggers of the early 1860s, who is a saint compared with the demonic Tulkinghorn, created in the early 1850s.[25] For those who might wish to link Anglo-American to continental fiction in an unambiguous portrait of legal malevolence, Mr. Tulkinghorn and *Bleak House* undoubtedly provide Exhibit Number One for the prosecution.

Yet *Bleak House* is still best known for its unredeeming description of a single English legal institution and a single instance of its many cases: the court of Chancery and the case of *Jarndyce v. Jarndyce*. No thorough analysis of Mr. Tulkinghorn himself has been essayed that might refocus the attention of the interpreter upon *lawyers*, as opposed to the Chancery jurisdiction itself. While Dickens quite obviously detested Chancery (he was publishing contemporaneously in his own journal periodic descriptions of Chancery's "real-life" excesses),[26] the reader's attention to Chancery alone risks minimizing the broader-scale attack upon law that *Bleak House* best mounts through its sinister depiction of Mr. Tulkinghorn. Furthermore, if Chancery is to be solely emphasized, we must in fairness recall that *other* legal institutions provide reasonably benign outlets for *Bleak House*'s characters.[27] Finally, if the reader emphasizes Dickens' attack on legal institutions—as opposed to lawyers themselves—then he or she must also reckon with the narrative's similar disdain for competing Victorian enterprises (the aristocracy, philanthropy, altruism, and amateurism, as represented by, respectively, Sir Leicester, Mrs. Jellyby, Mrs. Pardiggle, and Skimpole).

No, what distinguishes the attack upon law from *Bleak House*'s other pet peeves is not the force of its thrusts at Chancery;[28] it is, rather, the more subtle but utterly incomparable negativity of a single legal character—Mr. Tulkinghorn (whose practice, by the way, is hardly limited to Chancery jurisdiction). Tulkinghorn generates the novel's plot; indeed, an argument can be made that he even collaborates in some of its narration.[29] Above all, he expresses in his carefully chosen words and deeds the repressed violence of his time and place, the single-minded destructiveness that Dickens, here unequivocally, associates with the law.

When, in chapter 2, Mr. Tulkinghorn observes Lady Dedlock's uncharacteristic emotion in detecting the handwriting on an ordinary specimen of legal documentation, the action of the novel begins. It will not end until, with the lawyer's compulsive skills to guide his investigation, Lady Dedlock's past is unraveled, and she is brought down. But in the process, Tulkinghorn himself will be destroyed, for it is as much the annihilation of this dark force as it is the end of *Jarndyce v. Jarndyce* in chapter 65 that permits the optimistic prediction of that chapter's title, "Beginning the World."

As readers will recall, Mr. Tulkinghorn monomaniacally pursues the secret that Lady Dedlock's swooning response has suggested. The good lawyer misses nothing, leaves nothing unexplored, and stops at nothing to find the answer he is seeking. Why would this beautiful lady, utterly bored by the law (although she, and not her husband, is the party in interest in *Jarndyce*), suddenly manifest such excitement? To the end of answering that question, Mr. Tulkinghorn immediately turns all his impressive skills. The process—legalistic in nature—of ferreting out Lady Dedlock's past takes the reader through almost two-thirds of the novel; undoing Tulkinghorn's malice (to the extent possible, in at least absolving Lady Dedlock from suspicion of his murder) takes us to its conclusion.

Indeed, the careful reader will structure his understanding of Dickens' attack on law by organizing a reading of the story around Tulkinghorn's pursuit of Lady Dedlock.[30] Implicated in the lawyer's surreptitious inquiry will be many of the story's main and incidental characters: the street-sweeper Jo, located by Tulkinghorn as the key witness to Lady Dedlock's indiscretions and then pathetically, but of course indirectly, destroyed by the lawyer; the noble George Rouncewell, whom Tulkinghorn coerces into cooperating by threatening George's friends, the Bagnets, on a debt to the demented Smallweed family; the rag-shop owner, Krook, whose "spontaneous combustion" is linked to the inquiry; Lady Dedlock's envious French maid, Hortense, who willingly offers Tulkinghorn both information and her own person to assist his quest; the detective Bucket, who only can reveal his basic goodness after Tulkinghorn dies, but who nonetheless rigorously does the lawyer's investigative bidding beforehand; and a whole host of minor lawyers, hangers-on, and flunkies, who are all in awe of the lawyer's sheer power.

Now, Mr. Tulkinghorn's power, like that of all great and successful fictional lawyers, lies in his mastery over the channels of information and communication. He knows all, tells little. This "unopenable oyster of the old school" (an epithet used twice in chapter 10) sucks in the knowledge that will, if kept unrevealed, render him an enigmatic necessity to his aristocratic clients. Like Sir Leicester, these latter find comfort in the otherwise unappealing and unglamorous Tulkinghorn, whose very intelligence, lack of family ties (he is, of course, a bachelor), and single-minded devotion deserve a generous annual retainer. As "the steward of the legal mysteries" (chapter 2), Tulkinghorn allows his clients to feel that at all times their interests are being protected. As much in Victorian England as today, lawyers commanded high fees (although their frugality required much less) through a combination of apparent omniscience and very real loyalty.

But this by now familiar portrait begs the question that to my mind is central in the novel: *why* does Tulkinghorn pursue Lady Dedlock's fleeting emotion to its extreme conclusion? Is it because his client, Sir

Leicester, may stand to benefit from any revelation about his wife's past? Or is Mr. Tulkinghorn himself personally or professionally likely to gain from the considerable expense of time he begins to put into the inquiry? Why, in short, does this sophisticated professional devote such resources to an unprofessional matter when, to use the jargon, the meter is not even running for him?

Now it might be argued that Tulkinghorn feels so committed to Sir Leicester that he is duty bound to uncover any and all facts relating to his client's wife. But why? Tulkinghorn knows that Sir Leicester lives and dies by his wife's presence. Nor is the Dedlock name or interest likely to be helped by the inquiry: quite the contrary. And no one else is remotely on the scent of Lady Dedlock's indiscretions. At the very least, when Tulkinghorn does find out the whole truth, he surely has no reason connected to his professional duties to torture Lady Dedlock with this knowledge or to threaten to reveal it to her husband.

We have arrived at one of those great moments in Law and Literature when the professional veil of the successful lawyer is about to be pierced—a rare occurrence, for the essence of the portrait lies in its emphasis on the lawyer's indifference to humanity, his aversion to passion in any form. When, as in Captain Vere's outburst[31] or in the matter of Tulkinghorn's motive, literary lawyer figures are deconstructed, the basic values of institutional authority are finally revealed. And these are shown by the storyteller to be subjective, value-oriented, and qualitative, not (as we might expect from the rational-seeming lawyer) objective, neutral, and merely procedural.

The revelation in Dickens comes early. Yet the lawyerlike narrator prefers to drop it in, between the lines as it were. In the brilliant chapter 16 ("Tom-All-Alone's"), Tulkinghorn hardly plays a major role. It is the chapter in which an increasingly distraught Lady Dedlock imprudently rushes to meet Jo in a seedy part of London. But Dickens gives us, briefly, the lawyer, sitting in his frugal chambers, pondering developments in his inquiry. If he *would*, at a certain point, look out the window, he would see his client's wife at her nocturnal ramblings and thus discover, rather sooner than later, her fatal mystery. But,

> what would it be to see a woman going by? There are women enough in the world, Mr. Tulkinghorn thinks—too many; they are at the bottom of all that goes wrong in it, though, for the matter of that, they create business for lawyers. What would it be to see a woman going by, even though she were going secretly? They are all secret. Mr. Tulkinghorn knows that, very well.[32]

This remarkable and pithy passage identifies Tulkinghorn's covert passion.

He wishes not the enhancement of his client's well-being, nor the furtherance of his own professional reputation. He wishes the destruction of Woman, and Lady Dedlock's unintentional momentary show of feeling will lead him to his goal, whatever the cost to him.

Misogyny. The repressed Victorian man, here epitomized in the lawyer—the one professional whose very job it is to quash the emotional, the sensate, the disordered, the passionate, from the world of authoritative power; the lawyer stands revealed. In his hatred of Woman as troublemaker, Tulkinghorn—thus demystified by the narrator, who shares most of his traits—gives Dickens' readers the key to the legal system. Then (and perhaps still now?), the law single-mindedly aimed to reduce human passion to a process, to impose a formalized linguistic system mastered only by its practitioners upon the chaotic world of the laity. Woman resists, by her very being, the reductive process.

Ironically, Tulkinghorn also sees Woman as secretive; we have already of course associated *him* with secrecy. But the difference is precisely this: that whereas his secrecy is stripped of all emotion and directed toward others' power, Woman's is based on love and directed toward others' well-being. The lawyer tries to make formal everything that gives life meaning, and in the process he represses love, sexuality, affection. Woman relishes these, but she must often seek them in secret, for the male-dominated forms will not permit such overt behavior.

For Lady Dedlock's secret is, of course, her love affair with Captain Hawdon and the out-of-wedlock fruit of that affair. It is the nature of the secret, rather than the fact of the secret, that leads the woman-hater to pursue her, to her destruction. In scenes fraught with sexual innuendo, Tulkinghorn and Lady Dedlock finally play out their battle of mighty opposites. Tulkinghorn, now fully informed, recites her secret as hypothetical fact (names removed) in public. Frightened, she takes an unprecedented step across Tulkinghorn's threshold as he spends the night at the Dedlocks'. He relishes her agitated incursion into his lonely chambers, then tortures her, telling her that he may never reveal her secret but that, then again, circumstances may compel him to do so. He berates her, berates in fact all those who choose to get married: " 'My experience teaches me, Lady Dedlock, that most of the people I know would do far better to leave marriage alone' " (2:41; and spoken like a true lawyer-bachelor!). He then leaves her hanging.

Yet Lady Dedlock is never stronger than in this scene. Learning of the hold that the lawyer (law generally) has on her life, and understanding how her passions have always in fact been regulated by law (why else give away her "illegitimate" daughter, Esther, or refuse to see Esther again after their brief reunion?), she magnificently holds her raging emotions in check. Dickens presents her almost as a blueprint for a more humane and understanding law, as one who can give order to what is *good*; the contrast with Tulkinghorn, who establishes order on a misogynistic base of repressed violence, heightens as this scene progresses. And the third-person narrator, much more like Tulkinghorn than Lady Dedlock, becomes one with the lawyer in their mutual, grudging respect for just that part of Woman that must be (mutually) brought down: "So! Anger, and fear, and shame. All three contending. What power this woman has to keep these raging passions down! Mr. Tulkinghorn's thoughts take such form as he looks at her" (2:41).

The narrative admiration for Lady Dedlock continues as she graciously (but at some personal risk) allows her pretty attendant, Rosa, to leave her service; again, in the name of love, Lady Dedlock will not keep back Rosa's engagement to the youthful Rouncewell. This gesture, more on its merits than on its procedural aspects (although Tulkinghorn emphasizes only the latter), gives the lawyer what he needs to defeat Lady Dedlock utterly. This time he goes to *her* room (his dominance complete, or so he thinks) and tells her, in chapter 48, that her actions in dismissing Rosa threaten to arouse rumors that might lead others to find out her secret. Improbable at best, this argument is then joined by the procedural one: Lady Dedlock has breached their earlier understanding that she would make no basic change in her general pattern of life. Tulkinghorn declares himself free, without further notice to her, to reveal her secret.

The scene in Lady Dedlock's room temporarily marks the victory of legalistic repression over affective, vital, compassionate humanity. The arid formality of law seems to have vanquished the superb formality of Lady Dedlock's always generous self-control. But the sheer force of the feminine (really, the feminist) perspective impresses the lawyer even at his moment of apparent victory: " 'This woman,' thinks Mr. Tulkinghorn, standing on the hearth, again a dark object closing up her view, 'is a study.' " And, in fact, his victory is short-lived. His obsessive quest to destroy her will lead, within an hour, to his own death. Although Lady Dedlock has little time left herself, it is her noble approach to life that ultimately prevails, through the generosity of the novel's surviving characters—Esther, Ada, Woodcourt, and Mr. Jarndyce.

For the law, then, *Bleak House* leaves hope not so much in the reform of any single institution (such as Chancery) as in the reform of those who practice it and who achieve success in their profession. Far from suggesting that the law should abandon its function as an ordering system (for no other such system stands out positively in *Bleak House*, and anarchy such as Skimpole's is even more brutal), Dickens asks for the system to accommodate (rather than repress) the spontaneous, the passionate, and the empathetic in the behavior of those whose lives it regulates.

The portrait of Tulkinghorn is at an extreme of darkness, of monomania, of perversity. But even here, Dickens—typically among those writers in England and America who realize that there is much good in their country's laws—provides the glimmer of optimism that, as we saw in *Great Expectations*, would spark a mitigating and even a redeeming conception.

# 8. John Barth's Todd Andrews: Inductive Reasoning, Relative Values

> I considered too whether, in the real absence of absolutes, values less than absolute mightn't be regarded as in no way inferior and even be lived by.          John Barth, *The Floating Opera*

As noted earlier in this chapter, most major portraits of lawyers in the modern American novel have been influenced by the strong precedents from Dickensian fiction; of lesser importance, but still to be reckoned with, Twain's Pudd'nhead Wilson has contributed the folksy humor and grass-roots pragmatism peculiarly indigenous to American lawyers, real or imagined. The mix both compels and puzzles.

What are we to do, for example, with a successful mid-twentieth-century Maryland lawyer who charms us with his seeming nihilism and disingenuous self-abasement, but who also toys with his clients and the law and seems to be planning the murder of almost seven hundred people (including himself)? Todd Andrews, the protagonist of John Barth's early (1956) novel, *The Floating Opera*,[33] has been described as "a roguish lawyer who contemplates suicide as the logical outcome of his absurdist philosophy of life."[34] Critics generally peg him as a "nihilist"[35] or at least an "existentialist," usually underestimating the narrative importance Barth allows Todd's totally conventional life and career. As with Camus' Clamence (a character created at almost exactly the same point, in the mid-1950s), we will discover in Todd more the lawyer than the iconoclast, more the prosaic middle-aged man than the "absurdist philosopher," more the playful planter of lowly puns than of high explosives.[36]

Each of fiction's mainstream lawyerlike traits (essay 5) Todd possesses in abundance, but with a modern American twist of acerbic humor thrown in. The six chacteristics also serve both to indicate the conservatism of Todd's actions, appropriate for his craft, and to review the novel's deceptively straightforward "plot."[37]

Todd Andrews, a successful fifty-four-year-old general practitioner in the smalltown Maryland firm of Andrews, Bishop & Andrews, has set out (in 1954) to trace events that transpired on a single day in June 1937. While he is, as we shall see, abundantly precise about many of the events of that day (and still possesses several letters and legal documents containing its date), Todd claims he cannot remember whether it was June 21 or June 22.[38] This absolutely incredible declaration (2–3) must place the reader on his guard about the protagonist; as with most lawyers in literature, "imperfect communication" (216) abounds, and the reader is possibly more likely than Todd's fellow characters to be manipulated into a too-facile acceptance of the protagonist's statements. In any case, Todd is fixated on June 21 (or 22) because, on that day, he *almost* consummated a suicide and *did* complete a years-long private document entitled "Inquiry." The "Inquiry" was also concerned with suicide, since it represented Todd's attempt to understand his father's suicide in 1930.

The narrative comes to a climax when Todd prepares to test his more "nihilistic" theories by destroying himself and hundreds of others. As dusk descends, he brings Jeannine, his best friends' little daughter (possibly his own) to "Capt. Adam's Floating Opera," an itinerant showboat that happens to be in town. During the riotous final act of that night's show, Todd slips below decks and ignites the acetylene gas-jets that provide power to the footlights. (Lawyerlike, he has carefully retained information about the acetylene pipes under the stage from a chance conversation earlier with the "Floating Opera's" Capt. Adam.) Todd expects—perhaps not with much certainty, since Capt. Adam told him he had provided for the ship's safety even in the case of a leak (198)—to cause an explosion that will destroy the showboat and everyone on board.

As readers who by now know that literary lawyers are essentially passive outside their practice, we should not be surprised that nothing happens. Todd later surmises that the safety system must have worked or that a crew member may have come by and turned the jets off. In any event, his pathetic incursion into nihilism and potential criminality remains as unknown to others as was Clamence's theft of the Ghent Cathedral altarpiece in *The Fall*. These be our modern adventurers.

Todd's life and career appear perfectly conventional; the only aberrations any biography might evince are the usual eccentricities of his profession—no less, no more. One must observe then, that whatever his assertions about himself, Todd in fact typifies, rather than violates, standard middle-class ideas and values.[39] Born in 1900, he has faithfully followed the patterns of experience of that period:[40] loss of virginity during an awkward teenage grope (and pervasive use of brothels for the next decade or so);[41] service in World War I (where, after an overnight foxhole struggle between his fear and his conscience, he kills a German soldier); fulfillment of paternal expectations as to college and profession as he is dutifully graduated from Johns Hopkins, receives a law degree, and enters his father's practice; loss of father, when (classically) the latter chooses suicide over rebounding from the Depression; and achievement of professional success—"I am perhaps the best lawyer on the Eastern Shore" Todd tells us (71), and the punctilious ensuing descriptions of his practice seem to confirm the boast. No nonconformist he.[42]

As noted, the only mildly unconventional aspects of his life reflect those qualities literature usually associates with successful lawyers anyway: bachelorhood and residence in a modest hotel (frugality); friendships in which either he becomes the medium for chic sexual experimentation (passivity with the Macks) or he exploits others to do what he will not (manipulation of Mister Haecker to commit suicide).

The critics have perhaps taken Barth too much at his word, therefore (or perhaps not literally enough), when he said "I thought I was writing about philosophy, about Nihilism."[43] In the same conversations Barth actually twice declared, "I'm not a philosopher," and this absence of any overriding system of belief or action more faithfully describes the Todd Andrews we have detected. If Todd does a bit more thinking than the average person, it is always in a lawyerlike manner, not a nihilistic or even an abstract one. Like that first true literary lawyer (Hamlet, who is mentioned frequently in the novel), Todd moves slowly and thoroughly through an experience, rejecting received generalizations in favor of empirical learning. Yet the refusal to follow absolutes leads (as it did in Hamlet) to a purely inductive approach to reality (reasoning from facts to generalizations), which is neither nihilistic nor even "existential": it is simply lawyerlike. This idea merits some brief elaboration.

In the Anglo-American legal system, reasoning generally moves from the particular case to the generalization, not vice versa. Unlike their continental colleagues, who must apply the text of the written code to the specific case, lawyers like the ones I am analyzing in this chapter are trained to seize a case, digest it, and only tentatively to move to the existing legal authorities (often unwritten) that might control the case. I cite Hamlet (obviously not a lawyer by training), as does Todd Andrews, because Hamlet epitomizes the careful, empirical, inductive method of English and American law. He rejects the ghost's ruling demand and allows the shifting proofs of his environment to lead him. Throughout the novel, Todd—excellent lawyer that he is—displays the inductive tendency: "But I am not a thinker, nor have I ever been. My thinking is always after the fact, the effect of my circumstances, never the other way round" (43).

Only once does Todd say the opposite (typical of both his Clamence-like equivocation and his lack of philosophical consistency), but it has impressed the critics overly much: "I tend, I'm afraid," he tells us early, "to attribute to abstract ideas a life-or-death significance" (15). As a philosophical imperative taken to explain his half-hearted decision to commit suicide, this statement would be unlawyerlike and is, indeed, contradicted throughout the novel by everything else Todd says and does.

Todd's life, both personal and professional, does typify an age, but it is *the age of the lawyer*, not of the abstract philosopher. Barth thus began his storytelling career by stressing the predominance of inductive reasoning, the intuitive individual response that has replaced all overriding abstractions. So it turns out that Todd's ephemeral decision to commit suicide, like every other decision he makes, reflects the mood of the moment, not the carefully reasoned nihilism of the "Inquiry":

> There remained still no small measure of the excitement which had attended my first realization that I was ready to destroy myself; but, like all my major decisions of policy, that resolution had been a rapid one, the effect of external impingement upon whatever was my current mask—and as in those other cases, the resolution itself was only afterwards rationalized into some kind of coherent and arguable position. (201)

As in Clamence's rationalization (in *The Fall*) for his decision to leave his Parisian practice, so in Todd's explanation of the suicide attempt there is a self-admitted lawyerlike inclination to impose a post-hoc system on what has really been a rapid response to certain stimuli.

For Todd in his law practice, the power to work from a confused set of facts *toward* an ordered (post-hoc) generalization favorable to his client has been a staple of his success.[44] In the verbal recasting of his personal life, however, the same weltanschauung leads to deception. Todd's flirtation with self-destruction, like that of the Hamlet he is always citing, derives from several directly experienced personal failures. This he fairly admits about the "Inquiry" toward the end of the book: "I called these ideas rationalizing, and so they were: the post facto justification, on logical grounds, of what had been an entirely personal, unlogical resolve.

Such, you remember, had been the case with all my major mind-changes. My masks were each first assumed, then justified" (219).

The "unlogical" impetus for Todd's death wish, when all the novelistic evidence is examined, is sexual rejection (another allusion to Hamlet's condition in Act I vis à vis Gertrude?). In the wee hours of that day in June 1937, his mistress, Jane Mack, had called his fingers "ugly," occasioning Todd's defensive failure during sex with her; later that day, she and her husband inform Todd that the sexual experimentation among them is at an end. Todd's pervasively ironic tone should not hide from us the sympathetic half of the prosaic coin: he has feelings. For a brief moment, he considers ending it all; but *chance* (in one Barth version) or *choice* (in another) prevents the wished-for consummation.[45] Todd leaves the self-slaughter to Mister Haecker, the truly desperate old man whom he has manipulated to that end in his brilliantly cold rejoinder to Haecker's insistence on the nobility of old age (chapter 23).

Like all literary lawyers, Todd reacts, he does not act. He eagerly joins the Floating Opera mob's vilification of T. Wallace Whitaker's "To be or not to be," giving full vent to his prosaic nature. Symbolically, Todd simultaneously rejects Hamlet's idea of suicide. Instead, Mister Haecker, Ophelia-like, performs the suicide that the lawyer-figure can merely conceptualize.

"There's no final reason for living (or for suicide)" (245) becomes Todd's ultimate abstraction. That day in June 1937 is over. He resumes the routine life of the literary lawyer, now bereft even of its few eccentricities. Like all of us, perhaps, he lives from moment to moment. If, because of his professional training, he is better prepared than most for a life without absolute beliefs, yet he also is more conscious of the effect of such a life. His "inquiry" completed (on the false note of a poorly rationalized abstraction), he is doomed to play out the role of a Hamlet deprived of meaningful soliloquies.

For Todd Andrews, the Maryland lawyer whose humorously organized ramblings fill the pages of Barth's novel, Hamlet stands as fellow equivocator and professional colleague. Ultimately, both characters consider and reject the option of suicide (allowing others, nay, inspiring them, to take that road for them); rather they drift, like Barth's titular entertainment, from experience to experience, controlled by the ephemeral tolerance of others for their formalized artistry. But if Hamlet's weaknesses reflect on Todd Andrews, so do his strengths. Foremost among these is his lawyerlike capacity to elevate mere proceduralism to the level of nobility and verbal art. Absolute guidelines (or, to put it another way, such substantive ends as the quick killing of Claudius) may be rejected, but the power to explore a given situation meticulously and to delay its consummation until all its possible meanings have been explored and articulated, this is the literary lawyer's true inheritance from the Danish prince.

Indirection, Hamlet's mode, becomes that of most legalistically inclined modern figures, real or fictional. Todd, of course, is no exception. He promises no direct information, preferring secrecy or at least Jaggers-like covertness when discussing vital matters. But for every absence of needed data, there is a plethora of *seemingly* needless detail, much of it legal in nature. Thus Todd "briefs" us on two endless pieces of litigation: the will contest involving Harrison Mack Senior (his best friend's father) and the tort action of *Morton v. Butler*. The crapulous Mack's seventeen wills and the proponents and contestants thereunder are described to the reader as completely as they would be to another lawyer in the case (85–94); and *Morton v. Butler*'s procedural maneuvering fills narrative paragraphs precisely as they would a law journal's technical reporting of the matter (170–76). For example:

> 1937: Now I had never agreed with the two lower courts that what they thought was the question was really the question. And so, on April 26, I argued to the Supreme Court that the *real* issue was whether a defendant in a tort action who, like Butler, was barred by the statute of limitations from joining an additional defendant (to whom he was also liable, you see) on the grounds of sole liability, might yet preserve his right of contribution by pleading joint or several liability without alleging facts admitting his own liability to the plaintiff (Col. and Mrs. Morton). My position was that if Butler, in order to establish Allan's joint liability, were obliged, in addition to averring facts showing Allan's negligence, to admit his *own* negligence, it amounted to denying Butler's right to bring Allan on the record at all, since any such admissions could be placed in evidence and exploited by Col. Morton when the case came to trial. Now, since in our amended complaint we alleged facts establishing Allan's negligence, all we were pleading, actually, was that if, when the thing ever came to trial, the jury should find Butler to be negligent as the plaintiffs charged, then Allan's negligence, as described in our complaint, was also a contributing cause of the collision. The Supreme Bench, reasonable fellows all, saw no justification for not allowing such a plea, especially in the case of an automobile collision, where it is always possible that both drivers were at fault. On May 24, they rendered their opinion, which reversed the order of the Court of Appeals affirming the order of the Circuit Court dismissing our second amended complaint against the additional defendant, and remanded the record to the Circuit Court with a procedendo. (174–75)

As with so many of Western literature's greatest novels since the early nineteenth century, we are faced here with the question of why the most attuned contemporary fiction writers of their day employ such legalistic detail. Are we in a cultural period similar to the medieval, in which law struck the epic writer as fully evocative of his surroundings? Or has the Icelandic *Njal's Saga*, replete with legal forms, become a model for our own century's fiction?

John Barth fills his pages with the stuff of Todd Andrew's law practice, thus responding (through the additional mediation of other novelists we have discussed in these pages) to the modern-day fiction-reader's craving for the soothing language of form and procedure. The literary lawyer claims detachment from the goal of his enterprise: "Winning or losing litigations is of no concern to me," confesses Todd (83). Yet he revels in its procedural minutiae. The average reader of modern novels is no different. Thus when Todd admits that "the truth is that my interest in *Morton v. Butler* ended with the Supreme Court's ruling, for that terminated the procedural dispute" (175), he becomes the champion of a contemporary worldview that recognizes both the futility of absolutes and the potential of procedures.

"I'm interested in any number of things, enthusiastic about nothing," says Todd (4). Small wonder, for where "Everything, I'm afraid, is significant, and nothing is finally important" (6), detail tends to dominate, and lawyers achieve mass power. For Todd's stance is typical of lawyers and not a product of a nihilistic or even a particularly idiosyncratic worldview. Trained to view phenomena in an ordered manner, the lawyer seeks significance (somewhat like the novelist) in the tiniest aspect of a given situation. But the lawyer possesses no magical power to endow that situation with any ultimate importance. He therefore seems to reveal, with a perceptive precision unavailable to others, both the essence of reality and—at least in certain cultural periods—reality's total meaninglessness.

Small wonder that lawyers in the "real world" provoke lay resentment. Professionally trained to capitalize on behalf of their clients on "everything," lawyers outwardly epitomize that obsession with procedure that defines a meaningless age. As writers like Dickens and Barth show, however, this outward display and concomitant resentment are doubly deceptive. First, the Anglo-American lawyer (unlike his continental counterpart) in fact stands for the closest thing to absolute values still available to us; second, the resentment he provokes derives from the average *layman's* incapacity to discover *for himself* anything that "is finally important."

People believe, for example, that murderers and rapists may be let free because of a myriad of complex legal procedures. To some extent, they are right. Their sense that the defense lawyer and the criminal are two edges of the same frightening sword has been picked up in some of the fiction analyzed in *The Failure of the Word*.[46] On the civil side, aggrieved plaintiffs rail against rich corporate or individual defendants who can pay their lawyers to concoct endless procedural delays. Again, there is in such resentment a measure of truth.

But the fiction we have been studying (continental and Anglo-American) renders a more subtle judgment about modern lawyers, and perhaps truer still than the lay observer's. Lawyers see reality as a procedural game, yes; but *they are right*. Certain cultural periods do lack absolute guidelines, even though people's need to have beliefs and goals continues unabated. In such periods, the lawyer steps in, master of the case at hand, craftsman of proceduralism, the one who finds an end-in-itself in what is meant to be merely process. We must address ourselves to such professionals when we have a problem (or even when we seek an aesthetic experience such as the reading of a novel), for only they understand *how things work*. We may complain about these modern-day shamans and manipulators, but we will pay top dollar for their sophistication.

Only in America and England is the cynical recognition about lawyers quite rightly mitigated, however. These lawyers' penchant for procedure masks their commitment to deeper values inaccessible to others. Even Jaggers would not countenance Mr. Wopsle's Jolly Bargeman attack on the presumption of innocence; few other professions would take uncompensated delight in vehemently exercising their craft for a principle. American lawyers, while manipulative and secretive, also follow this model into rigorous defenses of the United States Constitution. The very procedures that sometimes place criminals back on the streets derive from what Todd might call the "values less than absolute" of that fundamental text. People finally realize that those values deserve safeguarding, and that lawyers perform a noble function in so doing.

To the twin satisfactions of mastering a procedural environment and standing for the last discernible (if still relative) values, the lawyer can add the quiet reward of an artistic job well done. Procedural jousts, Todd teaches us in *Morton v. Butler*, can finally produce substantive ends, even if these sometimes relate only to the lawyer's own sense of personal accomplishment. But often, the procedural morass of cases such as the two Todd garrulously describes throughout *The Floating Opera* does redound to the client's (and society's) substantive benefit.

Summarizing this truly gray area of Anglo-American fiction's attraction to law, Todd Andrews speaks of the virtue of strong relative values in an age without absolutes. Perhaps what we have called the lawyer's "professional ethical relativism" also captures this somewhat elusive notion. Within the proceduralisms that mark our contemporary legal system lies, somehow, the only foundation available to modern relativistic man. English and American fiction evoke the struggle between client loyalty and absolute truthfulness most penetratingly, probably because the legal systems of those countries (unlike Europe's) have always overwhelmingly favored the individual over the State. As champions of such a tradition, lawyers and their six peculiar traits somehow seem less threatening. Like Jaggers and Todd Andrews, the real-life lawyer's "coldness may be a sign of the strength of his real attachments."[47]

## 9. Gavin Stevens' Quest for Silence: Faulkner's Developing Lawyer Figure

One thing can be said for William Faulkner's choice of a lawyer in his novels: he remained loyal to that choice over many years of hardship, ambiguity, embarrassment, and even public displeasure. Few real-life attorneys could ask for a more faithful client, one who calls on us for almost all his complex problems and always forgives us our minor faults. So it was between Faulkner and his favorite fictional lawyer, Gavin Stevens. Not content with retaining his services over a thirty-year span for matters ranging from racial politics to real estate conveyancing and from criminal litigation to college admissions counseling, Faulkner would occasionally go so far as to substitute Gavin, quite brutally, for other lawyers with whom he occasionally flirted. So, in *Requiem for a Nun*, Gavin steps into the shoes of Horace Benbow and picks up Temple Drake's sordid perjuries as though poor Horace had never dealt with them before, had never even existed, for that matter. Seemingly confident of Gavin's abilities and substantive support, Faulkner also lends him out to many characters, so that at one time or another Gavin assists the whole county of Yoknapatawpha, including, severally, a falsely accused black man, a woman whose house has been burned to the ground and (at the same time) the family that did the burning, various bank presidents (against two of whom he also brings a fruitless lawsuit), a Snopesian hog-owner (and immediately thereafter the family that Snopes is trying to blackmail), and even a man Gavin knows full well has just committed premeditated murder.[48]

## The Critics' Surprising Distaste for Gavin Stevens

If Faulkner's career-long confidence in Gavin Stevens led in part to some of these fictional conflicts of interest, his allotting Gavin reams of narrative space has also produced confusion, if not distaste, among the literary critics. Although Gavin was created with all the embellishments of a liberal, even literary, education, he has ultimately failed to win the hearts and minds of similarly educated and verbally gifted Faulknerians. For whatever the artistic motives behind Faulkner's loyalty to Gavin, the critics have finally rejected his favorite lawyer and sought counsel among other Faulknerian speakers.

Now it is well known that educated and articulate protagonists since Hamlet have fared well with the critics, and, as we have shown, lawyer figures far less ethical or sympathetic than Gavin Stevens have also won their way. Yet soon after the publication of the work in which he plays most centrally, *The Town*, mainstream Faulknerians started to turn against Gavin. Cleanth Brooks, in part because he thought so little of Gavin, seemed to suggest that *The Town* should be skipped over as an uninteresting and repetitive bridge between *The Hamlet* and *The Mansion*. For Brooks, Gavin was never meant to be Faulkner's mouthpiece; the lawyer's "sophomoric posturings and high-minded silliness" could grant him "no privileged position in Faulkner's novels,"[49] not in *Intruder in the Dust* nor even this later, less doctrinaire novel. And Irving Howe, rarely in agreement with Brooks about Faulkner, was himself pointing out Gavin's "passion for rant" and hoping that no one would associate the lawyer's "frantic verbal outpourings"[50] with Faulkner's own point of view.

While other critics were eventually granting *The Town* its rightful place among Faulkner's worthy efforts, they too had little good to say about Gavin.[51] Steven Marcus, writing soon after the novel appeared in 1957, called it "the most interesting work Faulkner had published in 15 years."[52] More accepting of Flem and Eula Snopes' place in the text than Brooks appears to be, Marcus, however, forcefully and incredibly applies the word "monster"[53] (which Brooks had always used for Flem)[54] to the mild-mannered, if all too garrulous lawyer.

Poor Gavin! What a distance in critical perception he had traveled, from being the well-received, clever detective and trial lawyer of the early stories (and, later, the spokesman for Faulkner himself)[55] to earning the disapproval or outright hostility of thoughtful critics such as Cleanth

Brooks and Steven Marcus. The best he could hope for, it seemed, was benign neglect by critics such as Warren Beck, who refused (at least in his longest book about Faulkner) to list the seemingly reflective intellectual as one of Faulkner's "compassionate troubled observers."[56] (Even the Beck of *Man in Motion*, who eloquently supports Gavin as an ethical "intervenor," provides an analysis stressing Gavin's "chivalric"—almost Benbowish—"desperation."[57])

Now one might think that Gavin Stevens, graduate of Harvard, Heidelberg, and the University Law School, exceptionally well-read and selflessly eager to convey his poetic and rhetorical wisdom to the young, would be placed on any list of the compassionate, the idealistic and the humane. One might think this even without fully endorsing the view that those sentiments could also represent Faulkner's true voice in these novels. Yet Gavin, a respectably unhappy and reflecting intellectual, usually is ranked below apparently less humane observers, sometimes losing out to fellow lawyer Horace Benbow, or to the suicidal Quentin Compson but more typically ranking below V. K. Ratliff (whom Steven Marcus adores), the older Bayard Sartoris, the Reverend Gail Hightower, or even his own protégé and nephew, Chick Mallison.

Something about Gavin clearly bothers the critics, paradoxically even those (like Beck) who try to answer what they call a "nihilist, Frankensteinian" approach to Faulkner's meanings. Originally admiring of his courtroom brilliance in *Knight's Gambit*, the critics resented his didacticism in *Intruder in the Dust*, and wrote him off as a "high-minded egghead" in *The Town*.[58] Brooks finally claimed that Faulkner treated Gavin "as a figure of fun—almost as the butt of the author's jokes," and Howe suggested darkly that Faulkner "will someday have to answer for the creation of Gavin Stevens."[59] To the extent that enlightened American literary culture—north or south—was seeking ratification of its values in Faulkner, it apparently needed to reject the most articulate and well-read of his characters, Lawyer Gavin Stevens.

It might have been the kind of dilemma to bring a grin to Faulkner's lips, the kind of story about which Phil Stone would have shared "half the laughing."[60] To see the adjective "monstrous" applied (by Brooks) to the arriviste Flem Snopes might have seemed appropriate enough; to find it transposed (by Marcus) onto the Harvard-educated country lawyer would surely have struck a comical chord.

My purpose here is not necessarily to revive Gavin's reputation, but to reassociate it with the most pressing difficulties in approaching Faulkner's meanings. I argue that we can no more shunt Gavin aside or perceive him as monstrous than we can ignore Flem and Eula or utterly despise their behavior.[61] Whatever shortcomings those characters have, they are central to Faulkner; they do not stand at either of his moral antipodes—as do the despicable Jason Compson and Popeye, at one end, or the perfectly sound Byron Bunch and the admirable Dilsey, at the other. It follows that we cannot ignore *The Town*, the text in which the portrait of Gavin admittedly gains focus, and in which (not coincidentally) the fates of Flem and Eula reach their denouement. We must return to "the Snopes Trilogy" in general, and to *The Town* in particular, to approach Faulkner's implied system of meaning and values. Ultimately we may find that Gavin Stevens, although Faulkner's finest lawyer, was never meant to be Faulkner himself but rather modern literate culture as a whole—not Faulkner, in other words, but ourselves. Concomitantly, we may perceive that Flem and Eula, both of whom retain Gavin's professional services, are closer to Faulkner and his values than we might have surmised.

These claims will best be supported by seeing Gavin Stevens as he has, oddly enough, not yet been seen—as a contribution to the development of the lawyer figure in Anglo-American fiction. Similar (in *Knight's Gambit* and *Intruder in the Dust*) to fictional lawyers created elsewhere, he finally departs from those models (and from those of other Faulknerian lawyer figures like Horace Benbow) in one key respect: Gavin Stevens becomes the first major literary lawyer to develop positively as a human being *in the direction of*, and not in rebellion against, his professional strengths. As part of this growth, Gavin gradually learns the primacy of *silence over language* in all vital human affairs, an easier conclusion for a lawyer to draw than one might think; as another part, he finally extends to his personal life his greatest virtue as a lawyer in *Knight's Gambit*: a willingness to take risks (even to the point of personal embarrassment) in the service of what he considers right.

These are remarkable virtues and ones not usually granted lawyer figures by their creators; when added to Gavin's other qualities and faults more typical of novelistic lawyers, they produce a rich, if highly flawed, character but a truer index of Faulknerian meaning than is to be found in Ratliff, Hightower, or anyone else (Flem, Eula, and Linda Snopes perhaps excepted).

## THE EARLY GAVIN STEVENS IN A COMPARATIVE CONTEXT

When Faulkner created Gavin Stevens (and Horace Benbow and his many other fictional lawyers), he was writing under the sway not only of biographical but also of literary influences.[62] Anglo-American fiction, as we have seen, had already produced a fair sampling of important characters who practice, or try to practice, law. Sensitive, as older values waned, to the growing importance of legal substance and procedure, nineteenth- and twentieth-century novelists delighted in creating lawyers. These writers were known to Faulkner. The lighter note in the English-language portraits contrasted with the harsh assessment of lawyers among continental writers. From the latter (from Balzac and Dostoevski to the more contemporary Camus), Faulkner seems to have developed a preliminary view that successful careers in law undermined a practitioner's personal development.

By the same token, Faulkner concurs with the mainstream in declining to permit sympathetic characters any success at legal careers. His other central lawyer, Horace Benbow, is paradigmatic of the nice-guy legal loser.[63] In *Sanctuary*, for example, Horace botches the defense of Lee Goodwin, and his failure is connected by Faulkner to his empathetic human qualities. On the other hand, in that same novel (and elsewhere in Faulkner) conniving, unsympathetic lawyers manage to prevail. This less-than-mature approach to lawyers in Faulkner replicates the use of the other nice-guy legal failures in American fiction that we noted earlier in this chapter.

But, as we saw, equivocation epitomizes the greatest fiction concerned with lawyer figures, and this is surely truer of Faulkner's novels about Gavin than those about Benbow. As lawyer Stevens gradually comes into his maturity as a character, Faulkner fits him more closely to the gray tradition of lawyer figures. As an almost lifelong bachelor and an obsessive practitioner, Gavin begins to glimmer with the brilliance and, finally, the humanity of Mr. Jaggers and Pudd'nhead Wilson at their best.[64] It is worth tracking the transition in Gavin from brilliance to maturity. The younger Gavin Stevens of *Knight's Gambit* and *Intruder in the Dust* clearly evokes both Jaggers and Wilson, although he has been explicitly compared by critics only with the latter.[65] As noted earlier, all three, like Todd Andrews, are bachelors; all are compulsive when professionally engaged;[66] all excel in the tricky, witty atmosphere of the courtroom; and all occasionally philosophize at length about many social issues besides the law. But they are still basically *reactive*, needing the actions of others to generate their own, basically verbal responses.

But Faulkner's portrait of Gavin Stevens displays over time a three-dimensional progression, ultimately producing a fascinating variation on this strong literary tradition. In the *Knight's Gambit* stories, Gavin is the purely clever, somewhat tricky and manipulative courtroom investigator.

While the relationship with his nephew Chick does show signs of an underlying warmth, Gavin is mostly (as in "Smoke") indistinguishable from the other alert and aggressive professional "winners" who are not above using unethical tactics and mystifying speeches to prevail in their chosen career. *Intruder in the Dust* sharply modifies this aggressive tendency in Gavin as he slips toward reflection and passivity while still maintaining his love of clever, even voluminous and somewhat mystifying, speech. But with *The Town*, we begin to see a development in Gavin beyond these Dickensian qualities. We will discover (perhaps because the narrative voice of Chick Mallison has itself matured and become influenced by the gently skeptical Ratliff) that this later Gavin seems far more vulnerable, less Jaggers-like than in *Knight's Gambit* or *Intruder in the Dust*. As some of his traditional lawyer-figure traits become softened, while others develop positively, Gavin's human qualities emerge fully. We must explore this sharpening Faulknerian portrait of Gavin as a variation on the traditional of fictional lawyer and at the same time try to understand why this seemingly less manipulative, more humane Gavin has become so unpopular with mainstream critics.

## SILENCE AS THE WAY TO UNDERSTANDING

As I suggested earlier, those critics who have disliked *The Town* tend to consider Gavin Stevens an embarrassment; those who see merit in the text do so despite Gavin, either enjoying Faulkner's renewed interest in narrative perspective,[67] or singling out the portrait of Ratliff as indicative of what Steven Marcus has called Faulkner's "impulse to discover the condition [of] achievement."[68] Those few critics, like Beck, who have come to see some merit both in the novel and in Gavin Stevens, stress Gavin's idealistic and inflexible nature, admitting its quixotic excesses and practical failings. As Beck puts it, "Horace Benbow, also lawyer and interventionist, seems Gavin's prototype."[69]

Surely Faulkner did not intend, however, for the lawyer who obliterated Benbow's presence in *Requiem for a Nun* several years earlier to retreat to a Benbowish stance of pathetic ineffectiveness. Indeed, Gavin is simply not accurately grasped as "a moral idealist," bound up in "quixotic . . . absolutes."[70] He stands, first and foremost, as a highly successful lawyer, the one whom the eminently pragmatic Flem Snopes himself engages twice during the midsection of *The Town*, first to help rid Jefferson of Montgomery Ward Snopes and his "French postcards," then to act as witness to Flem's reconveyancing of a mortgage on Mrs. Hait's burned house.

"Why did you come to me?" Uncle Gavin said.

"For the same reason I would hunt up the best carpenter if I wanted to build a house, or the best farmer if I wanted to share-crop some land," Mr. Snopes said. (246)

Now Flem Snopes may be "monstrous" in certain contexts, but his rare articulateness in answering Gavin's question, combined with his willingness to plunk a ten-dollar bill down on his lawyer's desk, clearly indicate the town's continuing professional esteem for Gavin. No Benbow he, no perennial loser, but a lawyer who, throughout *Knight's Gambit*[71] and even *Intruder in the Dust*, generally succeeds at his craft. And the daily practice of law in a small but savvy community demands, as Flem knows best, not idealism but cleverness, not moral absolutism but studied flexibility and a keen knowledge of the human animal.

Thus, of the various traits earlier associated with novelistic depictions of *successful* lawyers, Gavin has exhibited all six. In the earliest story Faulkner wrote about him, "Smoke" (1929–1930, later part of *Knight's Gambit*), Gavin solves the mystery of Judge Dukenfield's murder and elicits a courtroom confession in the grand tradition of modern literature's cleverest lawyers—Twain's Pudd'nhead, Dickens' Jaggers, and let us add here, Dostoevski's Porfiry Petrovitch.[72] Gavin's keen insight into the nature of reality, his knowledge that facts and truth are disjoined, and above all his advanced powers of sight, hearing, even smell, and, of course, speech help garner him the reputation on which Flem Snopes continues to rely in the novel written years later.

If Faulkner's lawyer is in some ways an idealist, his moral abstractions thus seem to cloud only his personal development (never a forte of literary lawyers anyway), not his professional career. Unlike Benbow, Gavin does not confuse the hard-boiled exigencies of the adversarial system with the softer yolk of philosophical romanticism. He mixes his ingredients only once, when (in *The Town*) he sues Manfred de Spain and Flem Snopes regarding the brass fixtures, masking through litigation a fierce jealousy about these men's relationship with Eula Snopes. But Gavin is no more a Captain Vere[73] than he is a Benbow; the litigation ends quickly, and (through the mediation of his father, Judge Stevens) somewhat successfully: Manfred resigns his post as Mayor of Jefferson.

For all the emotional turmoil he experiences in *The Town*, Gavin never repeats that error. Idealism is confined to the personal; its place in legal professionalism, as Gavin has always known (the Pudd'nhead Wilson in him) is restricted to the *ends one chooses to seek* through the highly practical, often marginally ethical, medium of litigation. Gavin's admitted tendentiousness, which reaches its height in the closing half of *Intruder in the Dust*, usually descends not on his clients or juries but on his nephew and protégé, Chick Mallison. It serves a pedagogical, not a practical, function.

Yet, for all this, Gavin begins to change as the pages of *The Town* take us intimately through his sentimental education. There is no doubt, as Volpe observes, that Gavin's "moral development . . . has become the main story of the novel," and it may be the critical intuition that Gavin is changing that leads even Volpe to consider *The Town* "one of Faulkner's weakest novels."[74] For if Gavin's professional skills remain a constant in *The Town* we are forced, perhaps for the first time, to look closely at the *personal* dimension of this complex, highly verbal, and reasonably sensitive protagonist. The task is unpleasant, for it is risky: Gavin's personal traits are too close to our own. Better to see these virtues rigorously devoted to professional success, however manipulative or even unethical the tactics;[75] for once they are tested against others in the unregulated domain of financial, political, martial, and sexual power, they may come up wanting.

Thus Faulkner's relentless exploration of the enlightened, verbal, bourgeois personality (particularly during the middle pages, when Gavin plots and schemes to communicate surreptitiously with the teenaged Linda Snopes) strikes much too close to home. Admiring always of the Faulkner who fathoms states ranging from idiocy to courage, from suicidal depression to Snopesian deviousness, we grow restless when the genial novelist turns his attention to a figure akin to ourselves. Gavin's fatuous pursuit of a cause we probably endorse (education of the young) and his role as mediator between an intelligent girl and her ignorant foster father make us squirm.

Faulkner relentlessly associates the sillier aspects of Gavin's behavior in *The Town* with various verbal acts. Gavin's note-passing to Linda and his laborious and totally misguided lecture to Eula on the eve of her suicide force us to recognize that the professional strengths of great literary lawyers—but also their personal failings—have always derived from their dependency on language. Gavin knows better even than Chick that his presumptive condition is that of a talker—"(I presume I was; I usually am) speaking"—and that a man who almost always talks is one who is also "incapable of harm" (216) in any domain, perhaps, except law and literature.

Thus chinks in Gavin's professional armor threaten all readers—including literate intellectual lawyers—who gather behind his ornate shield. But before Faulkner (and excepting the nice-guy loser type), literary lawyers had been distinguished from their fellow verbalizers (the intellectuals) through their effective use of language for a practical purpose. Constrained to sharpen their use of speech and hone it to the exigencies of their craft, literary lawyers (whatever their personal problems) disciplined themselves to talk only after they had observed, to fill the air with sounds only after they had listened to the sounds of others.

For the great literary lawyers like Jaggers, the use of the observational senses always precedes speech; for intellectuals, speech comes before everything. It takes the highly verbal Lambert Strether at least his long physical and spiritual voyage to the Paris Opera to learn, at the single visual moment when Chad makes his entrance, of the primacy of the visual over the oral, and he still resists the evidence of his eyes and ears beyond that incident. Faulkner did not like Henry James and was not using *The Ambassadors* as a model, but he had ample opportunity to refine his insights about the dichotomy between lawyers and intellectuals through his reading of *Crime and Punishment* and *The Brothers Karamazov.*

Lawyers seem to learn right away—at least the good ones who fill literary texts—that their gift of gab must be tempered and disciplined by the superior power of silent observation. To some extent, I believe, we tend to respect successful lawyer figures, whatever their personal failings, because of this capacity to channel articulate speech into meaningful, practical pursuits. As a disinterested courtroom winner, Gavin is thus almost universally admired; but as human passion threatens to degrade his professional speech—witness his total discursive breakdown in open court trying to explain the aim of his suit against Manfred de Spain (86)—he upsets the equilibrium of all verbalizers and hence stands indicted as ridiculous.

From this nadir of professional inarticulateness, Gavin gradually recovers. He must first relearn, however, through his dealings with the Snopes women and their various men, what he always knew as an excellent lawyer: the most vital elements of human behavior are tied up in silence, not speech. This process is painful, but it is, as we shall see, the structuring principle in *The Town,* and one of the most central themes in Faulkner as well.

Two generations of Varner–Snopes women first force this difficult realization upon him. He discovers at the Cotillion Ball that sentimentality and speech do not even approximate love. Observing Manfred and Eula, he perceives that love ennobles a couple to a state of epic being, not consistent and self-conscious becoming. In Eula's well-earned phrase to the Gavin who later refuses to take the gift she unambiguously offers him, "You spend too much time expecting. . . . You just are, that's all" (94). From Linda Snopes he learns the magical yearnings, allegiances, and fears of the as yet unformed and unformulated spirit. He tries hard to listen to her plans about college, but at the climax of their relationship, he is still so steeped in verbal preconceptions that he fails to grasp her final message to him, through her mother: Marry me! (217).

Gavin cannot make silence supreme in his personal life until he ends his relationship with Eula and then Flem. This takes a structurally effective series of three exchanges with each, a double-tripartite structure that Faulkner may have first observed in *The Brothers Karamazov*.[76] The lawyer is finally touched by Eula—not physically, for he rejects such simple modes of communication—but spiritually. Few sections in all of Faulkner's writing since *The Sound and The Fury* are as moving as the three dialogues Gavin has with Eula in *The Town*. Her increasingly mature and gentle tone, her elliptical use of language, her loving incapacity for bitterness, these reveal her as more than a magnificent sexual being. She has softened into a radiant understanding of human love that surpasses in its effect her merely physical impact on Yoknapatawpha's men (including Gavin); and his elegy for her recapitulates the professional lesson of observation over speech:

> "Thank you," she said. "Good night," and I watched her, through the gate and up the walk, losing dimension now, onto or rather into the shadow of the little gallery and losing even substance now. And then I heard the door and it was as if she had not been. No, not that; not not been, but rather no more is, since was remains always and forever, inexplicable and immune, which is its grief. That's what I mean: a dimension less, then a substance less, then the sound of a door and then, not never been but simply no more is since always and forever that was remains, as if what is going to happen to one tomorrow already gleams faintly visible now if the watcher were only wise enough to discern it or maybe just brave enough. (334)

Perhaps for the first time in his mature life,[77] Gavin in this passage applies professional technique to a personal experience. The senses of sight and sound are finally allowed to predominate, in love, over random speech. And, most importantly for Faulkner's reader, the resulting language is ordered, poetic, beautiful. As the excruciatingly aware (because totally non-verbal) Benjy Compson might say about this hierarchy of the senses: each, finally here, is "in its ordered place."[78]

But Gavin also gains this knowledge from an even more surprising teacher: Flem Snopes. Ratliff says of his own fateful ride with Flem to the Varner house late in *The Town*:

And we had the conversation, too, provided you can call the monologue you have with Flem Snopes a conversation. But you keep on trying. It's because you hope to learn. You know silence is valuable because it must be, there's so little of it. So each time you think Here's my chance to find out how an expert uses it. Of course you won't this time and never will the next neither, that's how come he's an expert. (297)

The same power to observe that triggered Flem's ascendancy over Jody Varner in *The Hamlet* now comes full circle in *The Town*; the stakes are higher—several lives and the bank presidency itself—but Flem's tactic is the same: knowledge precedes speech.

For Gavin, whose three dealings with Flem in *The Town* parallel the tripartite relationship with Eula, the awareness of how closely Flem's methods replicate his own professional approach gradually leads him to a foreboding of the Snopes within himself. Faulkner subtly and silently hints at a growing alliance that lies beneath the superficial (because highly articulated) *opposition* between these two characters. In the first interview in Gavin's office, the lawyer and the banker covertly agree that Montgomery Ward Snopes' transgression should be legally transmogrified from pornography to bootlegging, all this "for the good of Jefferson." In their second face-to-face meeting, Flem retains Gavin to act as his "witness" in returning Mrs. Hait's mortgage. Their third transaction, by far the most important, requires no physical meeting, no exchange whatsoever of words: Gavin goes about completing Flem's plan for the cemetery monument to Eula. "It was Flem's monument," reported Ratliff, protesting somewhat too much. "Don't make no mistake about that. It was Flem that paid for it." But the unspoken unity of Gavin and Snopes ("like that one between a feller out in a big open field and a storm of rain: there ain't no being give nor accepting to it: he's already got it"; 348–49) induces the lawyer to complete the project and also to take full charge of sending Linda Snopes to pursue her life in Greenwich Village.

The structural care with which Faulkner brings the novel to closure emphasizes Gavin's growth, through the surprising mediation of Flem and Eula Snopes, into a lawyerlike person. In all things human, he has learned, language plays a subordinate role. Silent observation or nonverbal action takes precedence over all uses of speech and finally colors the effectiveness of such speech. Gavin has merged with Flem and Eula in this crucial respect and now is ready at last for the overt social action, and the unspoken conjugal happiness, that await him in the pages of *The Mansion*.

## THE AMERICAN LITERARY LAWYER AS SUCCESSFUL AND SYMPATHETIC

Among the already mixed group of Anglo-American fictional lawyers, Gavin Stevens surely stands as one of contemporary literature's more sympathetic evocations. While the literary lawyer's method of looking and listening before speaking occasionally seems manipulative, in Gavin's case (since as early as the *Knight's Gambit* stories) it is placed in the service of justice—the fitting resolution of the given legal case. Even in *Intruder in the Dust*, where Gavin's tendency to wait and watch almost costs Lucas Beauchamp his life, the lawyer finally takes his clue from young Chick Mallison and forcefully sees to Lucas' safe release from prison.

As to Gavin's personal side, Faulkner also paints the equivocal portrait normatively offered by great novelists depicting complex lawyers. Again, *Intruder in the Dust* tests our tolerance for Gavin's personal passivity, a tendency to inaction that colors most negatively the now-obtrusive verbal gift. However we try to understand his long lectures on southern race relations in that text, we cannot admire endless speech dissociated from professional or personal commitment.

My argument here has been that the structure of *The Town* allows Faulkner finally to extend the traditional portrait of fictional lawyers to encompass *personal* growth through professional methods. Whereas most successful lawyers in fiction fail to grow personally, or do so *in reaction against* their legal skills, Gavin Stevens ultimately recognizes that a unified approach will enhance his personal as well as his professional life. A generous quest for silence must override the articulate individual's impulse to talk. While Gavin never totally overcomes this proclivity, his assimilation of Eula Varner Snopes' suicide and of Flem Snopes' successes moves him closer to the norms of human communication in areas previously foreign to him: sexual love, the will to power, and the demands of human empathy. Given his coextensive capacity, in *The Town*, to exchange personal comfort for what he deems right (another trait he takes from his practice of law), there is every indication of ultimate soundness, after all, both in Gavin Stevens and in the American lawyer figure he embodies.

CHAPTER THREE

# Christianity's Ends

THIS CHAPTER continues our exploration of the literary jurisprudence by exploring the theme of Christian oppression in two masterpieces of the Law and Literature syllabus, *The Merchant of Venice* and *Billy Budd, Sailor*. In the first, I treat a classical "outsider," Shylock, whose infamous lawsuit against the merchant Antonio is defeated through the legalistic brilliance of the disguised Portia. I argue not that Shylock is a kind of victimized hero—indeed, there can be no doubt that he is the comedic villain—but rather that he is depicted with a fully formed set of ethical values that stands in noble and noncomedic contradistinction to the more ephemeral, playful, and musical standards of the Venetian majority. Portia implicitly redeems Shylock's ethical system in Act V, the first sustained period in the play in which she speaks in her own voice, unmediated by male influences. In so doing, she challenges the comic values and reactions of the audience, one reason many viewers feel a touch of anxiety about what should be a fully redemptive fifth act.

Portia's values (like Shylock's) are those of direct commitment and the keeping of promises, including of course the marriage vow. Like Shylock, she thus believes in the symbolism of the ring, and for her—as for Shylock—the careful use of language as another symbolic "system of commmitment" comes to rival the witty turns of phrase typical of the oath-breaking circle of Bassanio and his friends.

Portia rejects, in my view, everything that Antonio, in particular, seems to her to represent. In so doing, Portia first casts out the various structures of Christian mediation that have led to disaster (and great cruelty) throughout the play; and she then throws back at the audience its own casual acceptance of that cruelty. Ultimately, she reinvigorates Shylock's Jewish ethics, but in a context more forgiving and less somber than the audience for comedy would otherwise be willing to abide.

In the chapter's second essay, I answer a number of critics who had difficulties with *The Failure of the Word*'s treatment of Melville's *Billy Budd*. Here, too, the destruction of an "outsider" is linked, through the tale's hermetic (or, as I call it, "considerate") system of communication, with the repressive cruelty of Christianity.

Poethics, we are discovering, involves more than meets the eye. The literary jurisprudence asks each reader to challenge constantly his or her own deepest beliefs and to test them in the world against patterns of behavior that have wrought havoc on innocent "others" throughout history. Both of these masterpieces deal with systems in opposition, and they challenge us to choose which of the latter is more likely to lead to true justice on this earth.

## 10. "Then you shall be his surety": Oaths and Mediating Breaches in *The Merchant of Venice*

Legal commentary on *The Merchant of Venice*, by both Shakespeare scholars and lawyer-critics, has centered upon the trial scene. There, of course, Shylock seeks in a Venetian civil court to redeem the penalty provision of a single bond sealed by his adversary, Antonio, that grants Shylock a pound of the merchant's flesh if payment on a loan has not been timely tendered. Portia, appearing in disguise as a kind of *amicus curiae*, really the envoy[1] of a learned legal scholar, foils Shylock by construing the penalty provision extremely narrowly (no jot of blood, not one ounce more or less than a fair pound); she proceeds to invoke a statute rendering criminal Shylock's own behavior and, through the mediation of the suddenly victorious Antonio, Shylock becomes subject to a complex series of *inter vivos* and testamentary constraints on his wealth.[2] He must also convert to Christianity.

To understand the bond, the curious reader needs to return to Act I, scene iii, where its terms are defined and where, somewhat more ambiguously, the intent of the parties is revealed. Scrupulous discussion, primarily among lawyers, has correctly concluded that the bond is a *simplex obligatio*, or single bond.[3] Thus it is unconditional: if Antonio fails to repay the 3,000-ducat loan by a date certain, the penalty is automatically forfeit.[4] The cash tender in open court—too late by the bond's terms—cannot, as a matter either of English common law (the "single money bond") or Roman civil law, save Antonio if Shylock insists on the penalty. Readers have also noted that, although there is some playfulness in Shylock's Act I conjuration of the penalty, Antonio takes it seriously, understands it fully, wards off his friend Bassanio's doubts, and reduces all prior negotiation to a sealed legal document, penalty clause emphasized. Neither at this point in the comedy nor during the trial scene itself does any character even implicitly raise the nonenforceability of such a seemingly unconscionable clause. As the distinguished natural lawyer Von Ihering wrote in the late nineteenth century, with that issue ruled out by the terms of the play, the trial scene must be scrutinized as to the relative merits and methods of Portia's courtroom strategy.[5] Others have noted that in fact such a provision might have been enforceable under Roman law;[6] common lawyers note that Shakespeare may have been indicating the cruelty of English law and its necessary mitigation by the new courts of equity.[7]

For the purposes of this essay, however, I enter less into these well-worked areas than into still largely untrod Law and Literature territory, by emphasizing another promise made in Act I, scene iii, that is ignored by most critics (although it is invoked several times in the trial scene); then I will attend to Act V, which although replete with legal imagery and thoughts of oaths and promises, is usually overlooked even by legal analyses of the play. I will argue that the legal aspects of the play illuminate what I here call the structure of mediation in *The Merchant of Venice*. "Mediation," as used in this essay, means the decisive intervention by a party originally unengaged in an earlier relation; the intervention is designed to resolve indecision (or stasis) in that relation and to make it either progress or terminate.

Throughout the comedy, paired characters who have a direct bond to each other are portrayed as unable to conclude their affairs without the mediation of a third character. Often the irresolution of the paired characters revolves around a written text.

The mediator facilitates each such situation by unbinding the two parties from the problematic association. Increasingly, the role of the mediator is associated with that of interpreter, his or her hermeneutic function that of freeing an interested audience from its too-threatening relationship with an authoritative text. Furthermore, the mediating act or declaration is equated with the genre of comedy itself, which reassuringly prevails over the threat of tragedy or ethics as Shylock's lawsuit against Antonio is utterly negated through a series of climactic interventions. In Act V, however, the structure of mediation is rejected and the keeping of promises equated with the preservation of both direct ethical commitment and precise textual responsibility.

Each of the first four acts contains a structurally central example of mediation. In Act I, scene iii, Shylock and Bassanio are depicted as irresolutely awaiting the arrival of the commercial middleman and surety,[8] Antonio. The merchant, who is the most pervasive mediator in the play, stands between the creditor and the debtor to secure funds for the latter by promise of his own wealth. In the midst of Act II, the parental-filial relation of Shylock and Jessica is shown as equally fruitless until Lorenzo arrives to "save" the Jewess and steal some of her father's wealth in the bargain. Act II also introduces, and Act III fulfills, the casket subplot, in which Portia remains stymied by the text of her father's last Will and Testatment until Bassanio—himself under the mediation of Antonio's venture capitalism—fulfills the will's requirement by correctly "reading" the casket. Portia (completely mediated in her choice of spouse by the text of her father's will) is saved by the mediation of an already-mediated character, one whose appearance and winning chances derive from another's credit and yet another's ready cash. The commercially necessitated suretyship has by now developed into a series of mediations affecting personal commitments (filial and spousal). No one seems ready to act in direct obligation to another. In Act IV, this phenomenon finally envelopes law, and here there is a most damning statement made about legal systems incapable of resolving disputes forthrightly. The Duke, who is ostensibly the presiding legal officer in the court of Venice, must await the arrival of Portia (mediated by her disguise) to read the law successfully. As the trial scene ends, Portia's mediation is joined to that of Antonio (who is asked by Portia to provide the final reading of the Alien Statute), and Shylock is removed—violently but temporarily—from the hermeneutic circle of the lawsuit and the play as a whole.

Shylock's removal constitutes the necessary public defeat of his alternative, unmediated pattern of ethical conduct. But Act V reverses the hitherto dominant drive to mediation and reinvokes Shylock at the expense of Antonio, the play's most influential middleman. To fathom this, we must return in more detail to the very beginnings of the comedy.

The structure of mediation actually precedes somewhat its first principal evocation in Act I, scene iii, although the example is relatively insignificant. In scene i, Bassanio is shown replacing several of Antonio's other friends, who have been incapable of cheering the merchant. While Bassanio's mediation at that point also fails directly to enliven the doleful Antonio, the younger man's scheme to win Portia's wealth at least generates Antonio's willingness to use his credit in the service of the venture. Thus the comic plot has already been associated with mediation as Act I, scene iii commences. Yet the setting is less the traditional critic's idealized one of generosity than it is one of a troubling irresponsibility.

Paradigmatic of the inability of directly paired characters even to communicate with each other, the scene begins with Bassanio aimlessly addressing Shylock (I.iii). Although it is the latter's liquid wealth that will bring him everything his heart (and pocketbook) desires, Bassanio literally cannot deal with the moneylender. Shylock, realizing this, manages to say nothing whatever of real substance until Antonio arrives. Experience has taught Shylock—and he shows throughout the play—an acute awareness of how mediated the Christians are. So only on the mediator's entrance will Shylock display his customary attentiveness and verbal force. His keen and direct intelligence will vie with the elegance and world-weariness of the Christian merchant. He has done this many times before; although he cannot know it now, he will have to compete like this again soon in open court against a far worthier intervenor, Portia herself.

In his typically straightforward way, Shylock tells us how he feels about Antonio's brand of Christian mediation, and he concludes his aside with a self-directed oath:

> He hates our sacred Nation, and he rails,
> Even there where merchants most do congregate,
> On me, my bargains, and my well-won thrift,
> Which he calls interest. Cursèd be my tribe
> If I forgive him. (I.iii.45–49)

For Shylock, words constitute an unmediated pipeline to his thoughts: unlike any (male) Christian character, his speech is usually direct, literal, precise. Such an oath—pledged upon the credit of his entire nation—would not be lightly taken. Although the oath precedes by some hundred lines the articulation of Antonio's single bond, it is inextricably linked to it. Indeed, it is the sole oath taken by Shylock in this scene; only *Antonio* need seal to the single bond (lines 141, 149, 167), since Shylock's role at the notary is completed upon transfer of the 3,000-ducat loan. But through this earlier oath, Shylock commits himself and his tribe to Antonio's downfall, and it is the single bond that gives Shylock his weapon.

Shylock later ratifies and reaffirms his personal oath not to forgive

Antonio. In Act III, scene iii, when the merchant's ships have all failed and when Jessica has sold (for a monkey) the ring given her father by her mother, Shylock puts Antonio on notice: "I have sworn an oath that I will have my bond," he tells the merchant. This statement indicates literally that Shylock has sworn to see the penalty through; and he again confirms this twice in open court, using the sacred imagery of that first vow:

> And by our holy Sabbath have I sworn
> To have the due and forfeit of my bond. (IV.i.36–37)

> An oath, an oath! I have an oath in heaven;
> Shall I lay perjury upon my soul? (IV.i.227–28)

Act I thus generates two covenants: Antonio's sealed, single bond and Shylock's separate oath not to forgive the merchant. When the latter's ships all fail and no one produces the 3,000 ducats in a timely manner, Shylock reasserts his oath: Antonio's bond, with its penalty provision, must not be forgiven. Unwilling to forgo a promise that, on its very terms, implicates both Shylock and his people, the moneylender stands in open court for the sanctity of verbal expressions of commitment.

Everyone else in court wants Shylock to forgive the penalty. But then, no one else there whose behavior has been tested believes with Shylock in the durability of verbal obligations. Bassanio, for example, gleefully borrows as much from Antonio as the latter's mediation-prone friendship will permit and then fails to pay back his debts; during the trial itself, he and Gratiano seem quite willing to barter their new brides for Antonio's freedom; and not present at the trial but waiting in Belmont— and surely unfriendly to Shylock's bond—is Lorenzo, whose mediation has already relieved his new bride of her filial obligations and his new father-in-law of a part of his wealth.

I have noted that the structure of the play involves intercessions by third persons between parties who stand close to each other but are seemingly powerless to conduct business without such mediation. The Venetian characters' dependence on mediation is reflected in their equivocal stance toward oaths. For the oath marks off that moment at which mediation ceases and the single individual becomes responsible—directly—to another. The attack upon Shylock in court thus constitutes also an attack upon verbal obligation, upon, in short, the unmediated approach to human commitments. And Portia's victory there, marking also the triumph of Antonio and the Venetians, demarcates the ascendency of the casual breach of promise, the lighthearted breaking of the sacred oath.

There is no better symbol of this mediation than the trial's victor, Antonio. In Act I, his mediation permitted Bassanio to use Shylock's capital, which Bassanio's credit otherwise could never have attracted. During the trial, he offers himself as "a tainted wether of the flock / Meetest for death." (114–15) His mediating victimization, compared to that of a sacrificial lamb, will bolster others. But the outcome of the trial preserves both Antonio's life and what it symbolizes: the victory of mediation over obligation. For it is he (and not Portia) who insists at the remedy stage of the proceedings that Shylock perish as a committed Jew and thus as a believer in direct dealing and in oath keeping.

Part of the mediator's mode is the devaluation of language. In court, this comes out through the Venetian's sloppy talk, which I shall discuss in a moment. But Shylock chooses not to cheapen his own words, for an economy of sentiment is typical of the committed promisor. His refusal to answer the Duke's questions—his insistence on the bond, on law, on justice—eventually undoes Shylock, but the costs of mediated prose are made evident, too. Thus, as I have noted, Bassanio and Gratiano provoke each other in court by offering up their wives to have Antonio saved. Supposedly at the height of his vengeful malice, Shylock takes a moment to note this rhetoric, and observes in a wonderful aside, "These be the Christian husbands!" (IV.i.294). He is less violent and obsessive here than we would expect; rather his clear-eyed analysis of Bassanio and Gratiano indicates that sloppy words, connected particularly to sacred obligations, epitomize the mediated world view and threaten the sanctity of precious relationships.

On marriage vows generally, Shylock has already indicated his commitment. Jessica's Christian husband and she have absconded with Shylock's property; but the loss that hits him hardest is that of Leah's ring: "I would not have given it for a wilderness of monkeys," says the supposedly avaricious moneylender on hearing of the couple's casual sale (III.i.108). There, as in court, Shylock indicates his allegiance to marriage and its sacred symbol, the ring. Of the Christian husbands' and their use of wedding rings, we are to learn even more after the trial.

Meanwhile, Shylock's allegiance must be undone in open court. But whereas the attentive Shylock knows that Gratiano's hysterical anti-Semitism cannot harm him ("Till thou canst rail the seal from off my bond / Thou but offend'st thy lungs to speak so loud"; IV.i.139–40), Portia's eloquence overpowers his oath and Antonio's bond. She wins on the contractual quibble, then takes his property in equitable remainder and his soul in fee simple absolute.

Of Portia's mercy, or her cruelty, much has been said. I am convinced by Von Ihering that she is wrong on the law (see note 5); I am convinced by René Girard that at the least Shakespeare wants his audience to detect the similarities between the Christians' vengeful behavior and that of their victim.[9] But I believe also that Shakespeare desired the audience's pleasurable response that always comes when Portia defeats Shylock.

Act IV must provide the defeat of Shylock, whatever the audience's justified doubts about his vanquishers. This is true not because Shakespeare was anti-Semitic: his attraction to Jewish ethical dialogue is too clear, and the dignity of his villain too great. Nor is the trial's outcome necessitated by any Christian virtue. Portia herself, an exquisite heroine, behaves excessively in invoking the horrors of the Alien Statute even after defeating Shylock on the contractual quibble;[10] she also allows her curiosity about Antonio to get the better of her and—as we have seen— wrongly leaves Shylock's ultimate fate to the merchant's mediation. The other Venetian characters, again as we have seen, are systematic oath-breakers, or outright racists. Shylock's defeat is, rather, mandated by the play's comedic essence, which is the very world of mediation sustained in open court by Portia. Her attack on Shylock is literally an attack on the anticomedic qualities Shylock represents. She stands as Shakespeare's eloquent mouthpiece in keeping her (and his) audience free of any taint of seriousness or even irony.

Comedy craves breaches of promise, and the casualness of language that goes with them. Molière's misanthrope stands so clearly apart from his comic milieu that he must leave the stage at the play's end—somewhat like Shylock —seeking a place where a man of honor can live by his own high standards. Shylock, too, must be banished from the comedic universe. Banished not merely because he may be a stock comic villain but more because he embodies everything that opposes comedy itself. Portia takes on the task of banishment, although this neither ends the play (as in Molière) nor represents her own true position. But, at least in Act IV, she is willing to advocate the mediating, comedic qualities of disguise, equity, soothing eloquence, stinging wit, moral relativism, and even re-directed sexual energy.

For let us not forget that Portia's main interest in the proceedings is to end the litigious business and finally to consummate her marriage with the preoccupied Bassanio. Here, too, the defeat of Shylock is synonymous with the victory of comedy, which cannot bring itself off without completed marriages. In the process, Portia manages to demonstrate to her husband her own verbal power and personal force; when the disguise is eventually lifted, these lessons will not be wasted upon Bassanio.

First, however, she tests him. Responding just after the trial to Bassanio's zealous wish to give the legal genius a token of his gratitude, Portia asks for his newly fitted wedding ring. Goaded by the omnipresent mediation of Antonio, Bassanio gives in. Gratiano, meanwhile, devolves his wedding ring upon Nerissa—also, of course, in disguise.

Now, all this sets the stage for the often forgotten final act. Here Shakespeare continues to use Portia as his own voice; yet he contrives through that voice to reverse the comedic victory hard won in Act IV, and he again does so by legal imagery. The brilliance of the play's conclusion lies in the subtle ascendancy of ethics over comedy, of law over equity, of oaths over breaches, of commitment over mediation. This may be the reason that few thoughtful viewers have ever left the theater untroubled by at least a bit of the comedy they have just witnessed.[11]

Act V, with its single scene set entirely on the island of Belmont, begins with Jessica and Lorenzo. They toy with each other, setting a mood of quarrelsomeness that pervades the action thenceforth. They compare themselves to classical couples (all of whom were unhappy in love). A messenger enters—again interrupting a direct transaction—with news that Portia is about to return to the island. Portia and Nerissa take center stage and together sustain the somewhat jarring tone established by Jessica and Lorenzo. Jessica had remarked: "I am never merry when I hear sweet music," and Portia now adds, "The crow doth sing as sweetly as the lark / When neither is attended." Disharmonies abound, as does a sense of ironic perspectivism. Portia calls the night "the daylight sick." Everything we expect in a comic ending—love, music, moonlight–is being undermined. But this is not yet ironic, because we must recall that Act IV precisely condoned constant change. Steadfastness, even to comic values, has been defeated with the defeat of Shylock.

We might still leave the theater in high spirits if the play ended with these disharmonies. But immediately, Portia's sensitive ear picks up a real quarrel, this one between Nerissa and Gratiano. The latter resents Nerissa's anger at the fact that he has given away his wedding ring. Gratiano, the loosest figure in the Venetian circle, wonders why she is so upset "About a hoop of gold, a paltry ring" (146). Exemplifying the confusion of appearance and reality that informs his approach throughout the play, Gratiano observes that he has given the ring to a deserving *boy*, the law clerk who was, of course, Nerissa in disguise. But Nerissa, knowing the truth (for here absolutes begin subtly to prevail over mediation), invokes some of Shylock's language in declaring: "Gave it a judge's clerk! No, God's my judge / The clerk will ne'er wear hair on's face that had it!" (157–58).

Portia sees her opportunity and lectures Gratiano (the last of the play's suble mediations) with words aimed exclusively at Bassanio. Her language again indicates the strong shift that Nerissa's words have introduced into the atmosphere of this scene:

> You were to blame—I must be plain with you—
> To part so slightly with your wife's first gift,
> A thing stuck on with oaths upon your finger,
> And so riveted with faith upon your flesh. (167–70)

This induces the never-prudent Gratiano to reveal that Bassanio, too, gave his ring away. There follows the marvelous dialogue between Bassanio and Portia, both playing on the phrase "the ring."

Oaths and their physical representation, rings, have taken center stage as the play winds toward its end. Shylock may be gone, but his unmediated approach to commitment lingers on. Of course, Portia and Nerissa are about to forgive their husbands, although we have the sense that they are serious about their subject, too. Portia demands "an oath of credit" from her oath-breaking husband. Comedy lives in her demand; but comedy dies with the enforced reentry of Antonio at this point:

> I once did lend my body for his wealth,
> Which but for him that had your husband's ring
> Had quite miscarried. I dare be bound again,
> My soul upon the forfeit, that your lord
> Will never more break faith advisedly. (249–52)

There should always be at least fifteen seconds of complete, uncomedic silence at this point, as Portia looks Antonio up and down with wonder. How can he dare once again to interpose himself between Bassanio and those to whom Bassanio is obliged? How can Portia not grasp the hideous move Antonio now is making from the commercial level on which he first protected his friend to the intensely personal level of mediation between Bassanio and herself? This is too much for her, and, after those fifteen seconds or so, she at last utters the play's most ironic words:

> Then you shall be his surety. (273)

The legal relationship adopted as a commercial matter by Antonio as the play began now threatens to mediate the most personal of human relationships. Portia, exhausted by her own courtroom tactics on behalf of the mediators, will have none of it. It is time for Bassanio to stand for himself; it is time for the couple, unhindered by third-person intervention, to consummate their marriage.

Commitment has replaced comedy on the island of Belmont. Portia, still Shakespeare's *porte-parole*, has laid claim to the unmediated posture through her twin defense of oaths and rings and her rejection of Antonio and everything he stands for. The trial scene and its immediate aftermath (in which the disguised Portia observes the interventionist Antonio's doleful influence on her husband's sense of fidelity) have not endeared Antonio to Portia. But, perhaps until this moment, she cannot make her distaste for Antonio overt, nor give voice to her increasing recognition that his brand of mediation threatens everything she desires, everything she holds dear. Indeed, her observations of Antonio at trial's end and at his goading of Bassanio to give his wedding ring away combine here—with this last, almost mortal insult to her marriage—to clarify in Portia's spirited intelligence a complete abhorrence for mediation. Finally shorn of the male mediations of paternal marriage making and courtroom disguise, Portia speaks in her own voice and makes her beliefs known.

I think we can envision a world on Belmont in which Antonio plays no further role. Portia is prepared, as the play ends, to rule her domain with all the force of Shylock's directness and in the service of Shylock's world view. For Portia, mediation, equity, oathbreaking—these have been mere diversions. What she wants is immediacy—time alone with her husband, and the assurance of his allegiance to her, that he will eternally safeguard their marriage oath and that oath's symbol, the ring.

To put it epistemologically, Jewish commitment finally prevails over Christian mediation in *The Merchant of Venice*. To put it imagistically, the circle of marital allegiance thrusts out the cross of constant sin and forgiveness. To put it legally, law conquers equity, and the covenant regains its ascendancy.

Act V carries with it, of course, considerable risk to the audience's comic response. Our sense of irony has been reawakened, as has comedy's nemesis, our ethical perception. Portia's behavior guides us away from the anterior, comedic values of play, mediation, music, and ethical ease. Portia's rejection of suretyship, her ban on oathbreaking, these sound too much like a ratification of the views of the just-defeated villain.

But rather than smooth out these ambiguities, Shakespeare deepens them at the very close of the work. Portia tells Lorenzo of his windfall from Shylock, a piece of news greeted as "manna in the way / Of starved people" by Jessica's new husband. That Shylock's wealth be construed as an edible to these Christians reenforces the ironic association of them and the supposedly avaricious Jew. Not only does Jewish biblical imagery furnish forth Christian rhetoric; Jewish substance feeds Christian hungers. The "quality of mercy" is in fact wolfish. Portia's mediation at the trial saved Antonio's flesh but in the process transformed Shylock into manna.

The metaphysics of the play, seemingly so clear as Act IV ends, are now reversed.

In the end, everyone has become just as legalistic as the Jew whose legalism they had sought to banish. Portia ends her role by suggesting that the group answer "inter'gatories" about the trial; Gratiano concludes by providing the "first inter'gatory" to Nerissa: will she come to bed with him now or, given the imminence of dawn, does she prefer to await tomorrow?

Shylock is gone but not forgotten. And we are left to ponder whether his values are not somehow better, more direct, more forceful. I doubt that *The Merchant of Venice* convinced Elizabethan viewers to convert to Judaism, or even to honor better their oaths and promises. But I would be willing to wager—my soul upon the forfeit—that most of these theatergoers avoided comedy for at least a few nights thereafter.

# 11. Accepting the Inside Narrator's Challenge: More on the Christ Figure in *Billy Budd, Sailor*

Billy Budd, organically incapable of producing rational discourse at times of keen personal and moral crisis, has lashed out. The foretopman of the British man-o'-war *Bellipotent*, he has just struck down and killed the duplicitous master-at-arms, John Claggart. Before their captain, Edward Fairfax Vere, Claggart has paid the price for falsely accusing Billy of mutiny. Passionately moved by what he has witnessed, the usually calm and prudent Vere calls for an immediate drumhead legal proceeding against Billy. "Struck dead by an angel of God!" he exclaims, "Yet the angel must hang!"

Summoned to declare Claggart dead, the *Bellipotent*'s surgeon wonders about Vere's behavior, both the irrational and prejudicial outbursts and the very idea of calling a drumhead court into session.

At the very onset of the famous drumhead trial scene itself, the story's narrator associates himself with the surgeon, asking the reader to use "such light as this narrative may afford" to illuminate the question not of Billy's guilt but rather of *Vere's* "sanity or insanity." The narrative gambit provokes us to regard the ensuing trial as a piece of key evidence in the captain's case; it asks us to be alert, to read carefully, and to synthesize what the narrative has already taught us about the captain-turned-adjudicator.

In the early decades of reader response to the tale, most commentators politely declined the narrator's invitation. For many years, it was unthinkable to criticize Vere at all, much less to ponder his alleged "insanity"; his was the unenviable and tragic task of preserving the whole at the expense of the innocent one. He did his best. Who among us could have done better? An intellectual, like ourselves, he saw his duty as a leader facing a complex and a trying situation. He talked openly and even endlessly about his dilemma, and he proceeded to have Billy hanged under the constraints of formalized law and political order. Vere, like the author who created him, was testimony to the "fearful symmetries" of life and the mature acceptance of them.[12]

Starting in the early 1960s, pioneers such as Merlin Bowen and C. B. Ives tentatively began to suggest that the forms were not as Vere perceived them and that his words and actions in the trial scene had to be analyzed rather than meekly accepted.[13] During the 1970s, the reader's judgmental move—her or his responsiveness to the narrative invitation—became fully overt. In an important article, Barbara Johnson noted that "judgment, however difficult, is clearly the central preoccupation of Melville's text, whether it be the judgment pronounced *by* [Vere] or *upon* him."[14] And, for the legal audience, Robert Cover perceived Melville as "astonishingly successful in making his readers ask dreadful questions, of Vere and his behavior."[15] Both Johnson and Cover reached equivocal verdicts in Vere's case. Johnson called him "sagacious and responsible" yet ultimately willing to see an innocent man hang; Cover spoke of Vere's "dilemma of righteousness." But their mutual task was to impel Melville's readers to weigh each bit of evidence on Vere offered by the narrator. Simple admiration and bland acceptance could not do for a story so rich and complex.

At the present critical juncture, defenders of Vere, like the "scared white doe in the woodlands" Melville was fond of citing, reveal themselves rarely and then usually "covertly and by snatches"—for the decade of the 1980s was not kind to Captain Vere.

Thus I set about to demonstrate Vere's hypocrisy in cloaking his rush to hang Billy under the mantle of law. In fact, I suggested that he deliberately violates the clear-cut procedures of the very statute by which he claims to be constrained. I demonstrated from the text of the tale itself (and from some widely known facts about Melville's life and other works) that the storyteller knew his naval law and wanted his reader to recognize that Vere was disobeying it. I elaborated by suggesting the motivation for Vere's manipulation and deceit: the opportunity he saw to remove from his ship the very symbol of spontaneous and heroic life.[16]

Vere seeks to destroy Billy not because the lad's fatal blow required such capital retribution; instead Billy is eliminated for what he evocatively represents: the simple, affectionate, organically just man of the sea. On this view, Vere makes Billy a surrogate for that incomparable naval figure whom the story has elaborately posited as Vere's colleague and rival, Admiral Horatio Nelson. Nelson and Billy share a native sympathy for the life of the sailor and exhibit a kind of natural authority binding their shipmates to duty and to heroism, traits that the bookish Vere can emulate only through the needless violence of this sham trial. Vere thus contrives through an unlawful proceeding to dampen the Billy–Nelson heroic impulse and to install forever a regime of repression, covertness, and citified artificiality.

Yet, while lawless (indeed insane), the execution of Billy Budd is inscribed for generations in the books as a benign restoration of order. Melville, whose pervasive theme in this story is the mode of communication of men in authority, carefully depicts this postexecution behavior. Vere, ever mindful of the response of *audiences* to his various acts, continues to create "forms, measured forms" to follow quickly upon the warped formalism that led to Billy's death. First, the awestruck witnesses to the hanging are mustered back to work before they can rebel; then an authoritative naval journal (the *News From the Mediterranean*) falsely colors the execution, depicting it as a vindication of the "loyal" John Claggart. But Melville's "inside narrative" tells a story different from the one recounted by Vere and the authoritative naval reporters: Claggart is a villain; Billy is a moral innocent and legally unworthy of a capital sentence; Captain Vere is less a tragic adjudicator than an eloquent outlaw. Melville freezes Vere's behavior in time: we will dispute it for generations. It is nothing less than mankind's awful "vere-ing" from the glory of Nelson and times past to the repressed wordiness and pragmatic utilitarianism of the present age.

For this response to the story, I have been praised by some,[17] made to walk the plank by others. Among those who would see me if not hanged at the yardarm then at least roundly rattaned is Judge Richard Posner. For Posner, "there is no hint in the text of *Billy Budd*, nor could the reader be assumed to know from other sources, that there is anything illegal about Vere's mode of proceeding—harsh, perhaps horrible, but not illegal."[18] Although Posner's prose here seems responsive to the narrative hope that readers will be fully attentive in judging Vere's "aberration," his own span of attention seems to have flagged. In a passage inserted by Melville late in the development of the text, the narrator explicitly articulates the disquieted surgeon's belief that

> The thing to do ... was to place Billy Budd in confinement, and in a way *dictated by usage*, and postpone further action in so extraordinary a case to such time as they should rejoin the squadron, and then refer it to the admiral.[19]

To pin the point down, the narrator adds that all the surgeon's fellow officers who came to learn of Vere's uncharacteristic agitation and inappropriate contemporaneous call for judgment "fully shared his surprise and concern. Like him, too, they seemed to think that such a matter should be referred to the admiral" (102).

Since, as it turns out, the Articles of War that Melville (after all) knew so well[20] precisely affirm the officers' analysis of what should have been done, it is for the alert reader (if not for the overly deferential officers and crew) to challenge Vere's statements at the trial and afterward. Indeed, so distorted is Vere's approach to the law that it colors much of what the narrator has already told us about him. If he is "honest," as we have been informed earlier, why does he act this way now? Could it be that Vere's evenhanded appearance masks a passion that only certain situations will ignite? That against his bookish and overly pragmatic veneer must be set an aura of intense desire detectable to only a few and then only at moments of keenly felt crisis? That the shipboard "crisis" endlessly discussed by Vere and the narrator in chapter 21 is of Vere's unique making and can be resolved only by an unlawful rush to judgment?

If so involved a reader as Judge Posner insists on ignoring the officers' skepticism, indeed insists on minimizing the obvious confusion of substantive arguments proffered by Vere at the procedurally unauthorized trial itself, it must be that certain readers' investigations will be restricted by their own insistence upon a given outcome. So the narrator's explicit questioning, just prior to the trial scene, of the lawfulness and the rationality of Vere's behavior must be deflected, nay, disregarded by the captain's advocates. A general "feel" for the story's larger meanings must trump, so to speak, the evidence of the most relevant specific passages in the text.

But how is a text's "general" atmosphere and approach to be gleaned? This question is implicitly posed by another critic who has found fault with my approach. For Brook Thomas, one of the critics who has no stomach for Vere, my approach is nevertheless overly "legalistic."[21] Like Posner, but without wishing to defend the captain, Thomas suggests that the "emphasis on procedural technicalities often diverts people from questioning the assumptions of the entire legal system," and he challenges me to ask whether, even if the case had been referred to the admiral, "Billy's fate would have been any different."[22]

From different sides, therefore, these readers of the novella seem to me to be missing the essential point of its narrator's invitation. We must, after all, use "such light as this narrative may afford" to understand Captain Vere. Now there is much in that narrative (pace Posner) impugning Vere's procedures and even his honesty; and there is nothing in the narrative (pace Thomas) attacking law generally, or even (as in Melville's earlier story, *White-Jacket*) the Articles of War themselves. The narration finally disarms Captain Vere, but it does so without shooting a broadside at the institution of law generally. If readers such as these fear the process of thoroughly ransacking the narrative as a whole (if, in other words, they fear being "legalistic"), they strike me therefore as violating both the methodology and the thematics of this amazing story.

As in other law-related texts I have examined, the narrator here seems to ask—nay, demand—a rigorous, minutely detailed approach to the narrative; for in a story this complex and whose message is conveyed this covertly, detail alone creates an atmosphere, or a "sense," of meaning. We are asked—nay, implored—to avoid imposing on this text (as Vere imposes upon the Articles) a subjective gloss that merely reinforces our own needs and beliefs as interpreters.

Now, as I have discussed elsewhere, the urging of such law-related stories (procedural narratives, as I call them)[23] goes against the grain of ultramodernist literary theory. If Vere is to be judged for imposing his authoritative interpretation on others, then *all* unconstrained acts of "reader response" subjectivism are equally called into question, no matter how eloquent or acceptable to an "interpretive community" (such as the jurors handpicked by Vere); here at last we have a text that explicitly constrains us to look at it (although the path is winding and full of traps) before, during, and after our act of judging its meanings. Not to do so is to be guilty of Vere's crime: to destroy the innocent text in favor of the clever but aberrational reading.

Yet, given Judge Posner's position, the novella also challenges more traditional approaches to textual meaning. In the mid-1980s, Posner took a stand neither for deconstruction nor reader response; instead, at least in matters literary, he calls himself a "new critic."[24] "Close readings" of texts delight him, and he is uninterested in so-called "extrinsic" data, such as my use of the Articles of War and Melville's obvious knowledge of naval law.

I believe that our inquiry into Captain Vere finally leads us to challenge new critical as much as postmodernist interpretive methodologies. Melville, after all, depicts Vere first as a "close reader" of the Articles and only then as one who must deconstruct them. Vere begins, like Posner, with a self-styled attention to text alone. Like Posner's reading, too, there is a superficial attractiveness to Vere's interpretation that may entice the unwary.[25] For, indeed, those Articles do contain a provision calling for the death penalty for striking an officer in time of war. But by isolating that single provision, Vere deliberately avoids other operative parts of the same text. Standing dominant on the "weather side" of his cabin, he hopes to impress his selective reading upon the jury. And how close his handpicked "interpretive community" comes to such impressment! But one of them—as courageous as the Duke of Cornwall's servant in *King Lear*—speaks up to challenge the interpretation. "May we not convict and mitigate the penalty," he asks, displaying at once a sensitivity to the complexity of the matter and an awareness of the proper procedures under the Articles. Only this parry forces Vere from an erroneous emphasis on part of a document to a "policy" argument based on the supposed needs of the ship and its "people."

If Melville's reader is to avoid interpretive error during the mandated inquest into Vere's sanity, then the trial scene teaches a methodology neither ultramodern nor fully traditional. To deconstruct a text is to avoid its material existence as a text; but to isolate and emphasize parts at the expense of the whole, or of the operative context identified as "includable" within the text's meaning, is to be almost equally as subjective. In both cases, Melville implies, erroneous readings may prevail for a time because of the relevant audience's willingness to be ensnared. Many must follow, but in interpretive communities (as in the navy), only a few shall lead.

The story as a whole reenforces the methodological lessons of its trial scene. An "inside narrative," it endeavors (as we shall see) to reverse the falsehoods of the *News From the Mediterranean*, the prior authoritative interpreter of "what manner of men" sailed on the *Bellipotent* that fateful summer. This attempt to right that wrong, to replace that erroneous text with a better one, provides us with all the information we need to know— but with frustratingly few direct answers. We are enjoined, however, to employ a structural method: to engage the text in its fullness, avoiding no hint, embracing each nuance. Melville's message, both about Vere and about our world on land, must be provocative to require such subtlety of narrative technique, but it must also be universal in its implications. To discover that message, we must be legalistic in our attention to detail and awareness of structure.[26]

The structural method seems particularly appropriate for a text that *explicitly* asks us to use all of it to understand each part of it. Deliberately leaving us unanchored, *Billy Budd* avoids direct information about its seemingly most central subjects. Of John Claggart, the narrator almost proudly tells us straightaway: "His portrait I essay, but shall never hit it" (64). And of Vere, as we have noted, little is given and much must be gleaned. Like some puzzling but vital provisions of a constitution, a statute, or a contract, central aspects of this tale require a sensitivity to structure; but unlike most of these legal texts, *Billy Budd, Sailor* becomes most overt precisely when it is discussing how to understand itself.

As I have argued at length, the central passage for entering into the mysteries of this story comes, as we might expect from any carefully wrought structure, early. The narrator, as aware as any communicator of the importance of what comes first, fills our ears with handsome sailors, Admiral Nelson, and British history *before* introducing us to Claggart or Vere. And in the midst of these seemingly digressive beginnings, the narrator offers us a central insight into the storytelling technique itself. Although I have tried to bring this insight to center stage, curiously enough, no critic of my work—at least until Steven Mailloux—has yet focused on it. Since it so clearly and early contributes to "such light as this narrative may afford," that passage from chapter 3 in the novella merits renewed citation here. It comes as the narrator, hoping to educate us on theories of communication before he has even begun his "story,"[27] tells us how the British public has been told of the Nore Mutiny:

> Such an episode in the Island's grand naval story her naval historians naturally abridge, one of them (William James) candidly acknowledging that fain would he pass it over did not "impartiality forbid fastidiousness." And yet his mention is less a narration than a reference, having to do hardly at all with details. Nor are these readily to be found in the libraries. Like some other events in every age befalling states everywhere, including America, the Great Mutiny was of such character that national pride along with views of policy would fain shade it off into the historical background. Such events cannot be ignored, but there is a considerate way of historically treating them.
>
> If a well-constituted individual refrains from blazoning aught amiss or calamitous in his family, a nation in the like circumstance may without reproach be equally discreet. (55)

This important, almost foundational[28] paragraph implies that knowledgeable, hermetic groups do communicate *something* about vital situations to outsiders; silence alone would risk encouraging the curious to probe further. But the communication is deliberately arranged to deceive most listeners, by omitting most facts and rearranging others.

The passage further suggests that misleading communication may occasionally be necessitated by what we today would call "national security." The more dramatic or passionate the circumstances being described, the more likely it is that the "discreet" communicator will adopt the mode of covertness.

So the narrator takes careful, even deceptive communication to be a fact of modern life; no judgment is made as yet as to the moral implications of this mode of behavior. Indeed, in the principal example given, the Nore historians were "considerate" in their manner of describing the mutiny. The paucity of information both comforted their immediate audience and also hinted at enough of the truth to permit future analysts of the event (as, in this case, the narrator himself) to achieve an understanding of it. Furthermore, the narrator at the end of the passage suggests that some *private* events are also best communicated with consideration both for speaker and for audience.

Every time an act of "considerate" communication runs up against Billy Budd, however, it is negatively imbued. As an example of the "handsome sailor" type, Billy reflects the essential harmony of outer form and inner nature that utterly negates covertness. In the very first chapter, a more sophisticated type erroneously assumes that one of Billy's utterances has a covert tinge; the scene involves the lieutenant who has impressed him onto the *Bellipotent* and who reacts harshly to the sailor's "good-bye" to the *Rights of Man*:

> This he rather took as meant to convey a covert sally on the new recruit's part, a sly slur at impressment in general, and that of himself in especial. And yet, more likely, if satire it was in effect, it was hardly so by intention, for Billy, though happily endowed with the gaiety of high health, youth, and a free heart, was yet by no means of a satirical turn. The will to it and the sinister dexterity were alike wanting. To deal in double meanings and insinuations of any sort was quite foreign to his nature. (49)

Billy's joyful, "genial, happy-go-lucky" nature instinctively prefers direct dealings with others. Like most sailors, but unlike Claggart and Vere,[29] Billy has never learned the British historians' tactic of keeping interested audiences both contented and misinformed. In fact, Billy is unself-consciously disregarding of others' opinions and suffers from this directness only when his fate falls into the hands of the "considerate" ones on the *Bellipotent*. Thus Billy's lack of verbal sophistication does not signify that he is innocent or passive. Like Billy's job as foretopman, his personality is both active and observant. Billy and his fellows, "spinning yarns like the lazy gods," usually adopt an attitude of "amusement" toward the "busy world" below, but their number is not to be tampered with lightly. Billy exhibits childlike responses to complex verbal stimuli, but his occasional physical ferociousness (as with Red Whiskers on the

*Rights of Man*) and his zestful taste for all the activities engaged in by sailors hardly denote excessive naiveté.

Indeed, the almost automatic critical formula contrasting Billy's innocence with everyone else's consciousness of evil[30] may be less accurate than the narratively sanctioned contrast of overt to covert modes of behavior. Of the five direct narrative applications of "innocence" to Billy, two occur in the face of, and three in the eyes of, covert men (86 and 88; 70, 78, and 121). Confronted with deviousness, overtness must temporarily flounder; but Billy fails only once to recover his natural self-containment and to lash out against covertness with all the justified wrath of an open nature wronged. Billy's little-remarked "dance house" adventures while on shore leave (52),[31] Red Whiskers' "drubbing" (47), and John Claggart's corpse all testify poorly to the workings of innocence, passivity, or childlike purity.

Billy is neither a serpent nor a dove but, as the narrator puts it, "a sound human creature" (52). Further, whatever innocence he does possess comes neither from idiosyncratic ingenuousness nor metaphysical sinlessness. Billy epitomizes the "unconscious simplicity" (131) of most people who spend their lives on boats:

> And what could Billy know of man except of man as a mere sailor? And the old-fashioned sailor, the veritable man before the mast, the sailor from boyhood up, he, though indeed of the same species as a landsman, is in some respects singularly distinct from him. The sailor is frankness, the landsman is finesse. Life is not a game with the sailor, demanding the long head—no intricate game of chess where few moves are made in straightforwardness and ends are attained by indirection, an oblique, tedious, barren game hardly worth that poor candle burnt out in playing it.
>
> Yes, as a class, sailors are in character a juvenile race. (86-87)

Billy's approach to life marvelously embodies the prevalent, overt values of the pre-Vere sailor. The story at its very heart is about what happens to joyful life when attacked by repressed, overly complex, and highly verbal outsiders. Before this attack is mounted, Billy happily represents the sailors as a group, because he is "a superior figure of their own class" (43).

Shorn of any metaphysical overtones wholly out of keeping with his basic nature, Billy might perhaps best be classified as "overt man." Organically incapable of masking his true feelings at precisely those passionate moments when cleverer types always use deceptive communication, Billy stands in sailorlike contradistinction both to his "ferreting" opponent, John Claggart, and to the complex, deeply repressed captain who will ultimately seal his fate.

Indeed, as Merlin Bowen first indicated, Claggart and Vere share a variety of characteristics that contrast with the usual "straightforwardness" of men on ships.[32] Instead of a more sailorlike frankness, Claggart and Vere tend toward prudence, and "an uncommon prudence is habitual with the subtle depravity, for it has everything to hide" (80). Claggart and Vere have aims that are "never declared" (76; 96, 112); if Claggart's personality is "hidden" (76), Vere's is "undemonstrative," "not conspicuous" and "discreet" (60); if Claggart "has shown considerable tact in his function" (94), so Vere tends to "guard as much as possible against publicity" (103). And while the captain at one point orders Claggart to "be direct, man" (92), the uncharacteristic rashness of the remark bespeaks less a man who opposes verbal dissimulation in general than one who recognizes and is impatient with the covert tendencies of a fellow deceiver.

Once alert to "considerate" communication, the reader tends to grasp such connections in a text that otherwise pridefully exposes its own "ragged edges." This method of structuring the tale both unifies it and identifies its largest concerns. "Legalism" in this sense, far from narrowing the story's scope, finally encompasses the fullness of the text. Close readings of passages connected by tone and content, but not by physical proximity within the text, reveal a kind of "principle of parallel overtness": the narrator—and his verbally adroit characters—will often use one subject to speak of another, closely connected one that they are otherwise reluctant to discuss.

"Parallel overtness" helps to explain Vere's behavior at trial, once that has been shown to be unlawful and irrational. What "special object" inspires his passion? Certainly it is not Billy himself, any more than it was the drummer boy himself who had earlier inspired Claggart to lash out covertly after Billy accidentally spilled soup in his direction. Rather, just as Billy is the source of Claggart's violent attack on the drummer boy, *another* is the source of Vere's orchestrated destruction of Billy. As I have demonstrated at length elsewhere, the real object of Vere's repressed legalistic violence is none other than his incomparable colleague and rival, Admiral Horatio Nelson, a major heroic figure throughout this novella.[33]

Vere acts at the trial to destroy Nelson (with whom he is unfavorably compared not only implicitly by the narrator but explicitly by his fellow naval officers), but he can do so only symbolically. No law compels what he is about to do.[34] He must move from a moment of inspiration ("Struck dead by an angel of God! Yet the angel must hang!") to the creative, formalistic implementation of that prophecy. His essential contributions to posterity are Billy's trial and death, not any naval accomplishment. But to achieve immortality and to destroy his rival (although in effigy), he must defy the law.

Melville thus does not counsel here that the law is inevitably evil; rather he urges his audience to scrutinize continuously the discourse and the values of those who practice and adjudicate that law. Would Nelson in Vere's place have done aught than follow the procedures of the statute? Would he, who found no reason to shed blood on a ship (chapter 4's *Theseus*) where the threat of mutiny was real, have unlawfully hastened to execute a nonmutineer who was the favorite of a docile, nonmutineering crew?[35]

Nelson, of course, survives Vere's disappearance from this story just as he had preceded Vere into the narrative. The victories at the Nile and Trafalgar lie ahead. For Vere, whose death is more pathetic than tragic, the sole lasting accomplishment of a life spent mustering sailors to an alien formalism was to have been the story of Billy's death. But it fell to that other survivor—Melville himself—to upset forever the distorted tale left behind by the naval authorities. Melville meets his creation in the awful space between their parallel functions: scriptwriters and authoritative reporters of the sea. Perhaps the ultimate parallelism—or, as we shall see, the penultimate—is the one that couples Vere and his creator.

The mysterious chapter 4 passage on Nelson at Trafalgar reveals that overt heroism and eloquent literary form can, indeed, coexist. Nelson's Last Will and Testament perfectly articulates his forceful personality. Yet the author of this tale, through his very style, indicates his rejection of the overt option. Ultimately critical of Vere's tortured formalism, the narrator seems to adopt it. "I too have a hand here," as he has told us regarding his alliance with "the envious marplot of Eden" in endowing the heroic Billy with a fatal stutter. No truth is reported directly; we must seek through a legalistic rigor to find answers to the tale's most provocative questions.

As a late nineteenth-century writer, Melville seems constrained to adopt the "considerate" way of communicating, a culturally compelled choice that allies him with Vere and Claggart and opposes him to Nelson and Billy. But if Vere's covertness lay in the service of a vendetta against the naval heroic mode, Melville's is poignantly self-conscious and immensely courageous. His implied sense of failure finds expression in the narrative as a covert attack upon Christianity, whose antiheroic compulsion the modern writer must unwillingly accept. Melville's lifelong struggle with this tension points to the ultimate level of meaning in the tale, a message far too delicate to reveal in any but a "considerate" way.

As we have just seen in *The Merchant of Venice*, here, too, a "mainstream" master sets his sights on nothing less than the Christian religion itself. Vere's destruction of the best we have merely hints at Melville's wider themes, which go beyond law to the source of human belief itself. And he begins by tracing the origins of what "hitherto has stood in human record to attest what manner of men respectively were John Claggart and Billy Budd." His text is the authoritative naval account of these events in the *News From the Mediterranean*, set forth at chapter 29.

In that report, John Claggart was made the hero and Billy Budd the villain. Many facts were distorted or even falsely inserted to color a story obviously designed to keep the reader blissfully ignorant, passively controlled by the journal's subjective biases. But what really is this Mediterranean news? Consider, as I first asked readers to do some years ago,[36] that Melville here "considerately" alludes to that first authoritative account from the Mediterranean—the Gospels. Note next that there, too, we find a hero and a force that dispatches him. Recall that that text also artfully expresses strong personal beliefs and that for many years it has authoritatively controlled the mass of its readers.

But then, what further link can we make between Melville's story, which has in chapter 29 included a diametrically opposed version of itself, and the Gospels? Consider, by being "considerate," that the *News From the Mediterranean* has a hero whose initials, like those of the Gospel's hero, are "J.C." Note that Claggart has earlier been called "the man of sorrows" (88), a Biblical epithet for Christ. Recall, too, the association of Claggart with a certain "X" (74), whom the narrator explicitly uses "through indirection" to explain his ungraspable master-at-arms.[37] Not only are these latter three references patently evocative of a Claggart-Christ connection, but they are furthered by the narrative tone in dealing with Claggart. After all, the narrator begins his description of the master-at-arms by admitting his failure in the face of such a subject (again, "His portrait I essay, but shall never hit it"; 64).

This formula, used by Milton and Dante about the divine—not the satanic—figures in their works, emphasizes the need for covertness, especially in a "non-Biblical" age. The narrator must communicate subtly about his difficult subject and is enjoined against overtly citing any authority "tinctured with the Biblical element" (75). Hence, he will explain the Biblically central Claggart through indirect means.

Claggart's age at death is around thirty-five, as was Christ's; there is "a dearth of exact knowledge" (65) about his "antecedents" (a fact that lends grist to his enemies' mill). Claggart's position and his success in achieving it have been, like Christ's, those of a hard-working upstart.

Both men attain the ultimate vindication of their "passion" posthumously, with the help of sympathetic governmental officials; and, finally, both are transformed into heroes by authoritative accounts favoring their roles in the central events of their lives, accounts that originate as "news from the Mediterranean."

Considering Claggart's part in the tale, that of a figure who attempts to undermine the dominant values of his day (which are Billy's essentially overt ones)—the evidence implicating him as a Christ figure is not necessarily shocking. Into the marvelous pagan spontaneity of Billy's world steps the moral antipode, the figure who generates through his perhaps misunderstood words and actions a new and covert mode of behavior in the world. The purveyor of these new values uses his verbal skills (the "too fair-spoken man" of page 88 and the Bible) to bring himself to the attention of a skeptical world. But pagan man, in his declining and somewhat tarnished form, strikes out at the new force in a last effort to preserve the heroic integrity of the dying, outmoded world he epitomizes. The pagan slays the newcomer, but the latter will gain his victory nonetheless. For humanity literally "veers." An authority figure—perhaps understanding the social benefits of the new values—institutionalizes them by destroying the old. As testament to this change, a text—the Mediterranean news—makes the rounds. Claggart becomes its hero, Billy its villain. Order is restored, but the world will never be the same.

Never again the same, that is, until the arrival of this "inside narrative." For Melville here sets aright the order of values inverted by the covert upstart and his governmental ally. Here Melville's covertness serves a necessary end (given the modern environment of "considerate" communication). We have for too long lived in a world characterized by indirectness; threatening messages will not be received if communicated directly. We refrain "from blazoning aught amiss," but there comes a time when a cultural SOS must be sent.

Is it ironic that the legalistic method has helped to suggest the tale's most private message? No. Recall that Melville does not here attack the law. The last years of his life were devoted to yet more sacred cows. I believe, at any rate, that he had no problem with law, only with those whose covert, distorted vision gained authority over it from time to time. Indeed, he may have felt that the law, once programmatically sacrificed and internalized, had become the main victim of Christianity, about which he always harbored such doubts. From the Gospels forward, justice has declined, its sole hope of restoration lying within those sensitive enough to heed the "inside narrative" in their midst.

CHAPTER FOUR

# The Self-Imploding Canon

## 12. Law, Literature, and the "Great Books"

The "core" of poethical texts thus far treated in this volume resonates with tradition, although perhaps not unequivocally. If a prospective Law and Literature instructor, for example, were to structure a course around these texts, the syllabus might look like this:

> Weeks 1 and 2: LAWYERS IN FICTION. *Hamlet* as Prototype: Inductive Reasoning and the Obsession for Thoroughness; John Barth, *The Floating Opera*.
> Weeks 3, 4, and 5: THE LAW'S TREATMENT OF THE "OUTSIDER." Captain Vere as Outlaw in the Prosecution of *Billy Budd, Sailor*; the Necessary Defeat (and then the Provisional Reinstatement) of Shylock in *The Merchant of Venice*; Authoritative "Nonseeing" in *The Bluest Eye*. (Also, see *Bleak House*, below.)
> Weeks 6, 7, and 8: DICKENSIAN LAWYERS AND THE PECULIARITIES OF LEGAL COMMUNICATION. Mr. Tulkinghorn and the Lesser Lawyers in *Bleak House*; Mr. Jaggers as Superlawyer in *Great Expectations*.
> Weeks 9 and 10. THE FAULKNERIAN VARIATION ON THE DICKENSIAN VISION. Lawyer Gavin Stevens in *Intruder in the Dust* and *The Town*.

(A longer semester might include, of course, a unit on legal ratiocination, based on some of the readings of continental novelists discussed in my book *The Failure of the Word*: Dostoevski, Flaubert, Camus; or a unit on the poetic method for law, with the stress on "how the law means"— as discussed in chapter 1 of this volume.)

Although rich and varied, and including authors of different genders, tastes, and backgrounds, this syllabus could also form the basis of any "Great Books" course in a core university curriculum; it thus runs the risk of being criticized for just that reason. Indeed, some feminist innovators in the field of Law and Literature have already taken its pioneers to task for their focus on the Great Books. Thus Carolyn Heilbrun:

> Yet when I, a literary critic hiding out in the country of law, discover a whole new area called "law and literature," I learn that feminism has no part in it, that it is again a male domain, and seems in its whole history to have learned nothing from the best of literary criticism in the past two decades.[1]

Jane Maslow Cohen more receptively engages early Law and Literature work, but her discovery of a "Great Books Project" in the field leads her to seek a wider set of sources.[2] And even the pioneering Milner Ball (who has written so eloquently on *Billy Budd*, for example) now counsels the identification of works written "from the bottom," by which he means by those people whose disadvantaged status has kept them from gaining their legitimate recognition.[3]

The thrust of these thinkers has provided movement to a field that itself is just beginning to *destabilize* both the legal and literary establishments. Such prods have been joined with specific suggestions about feminist approaches to Law and Literature, about exogenous writers to add to the syllabus, about new states of mind and sensitivities that belong both in the classroom and in the scholarly pages. I will return in a moment, however, to the irony that Law and Literature—on the traditional syllabus—has been seen (even by some of these internal critics) as unsettling, even "subversive."[4] But first, I need to address briefly the implicit syllogistic logic of some of these thinkers.

For Carolyn Heilbrun, there is the sense that Law and Literature as a new movement automatically needs to engage and even accept much of what is new in literary criticism generally. How can an innovative interdisciplinary approach in the late twentieth century, she seems to ask, not adapt to or at least recognize sister pathbreaking methodologies?

Of course, to begin with, Law and Literature has not avoided either feminism or other schools that—perhaps—constitute "the best of literary criticism in the past two decades." Long before Heilbrun and Resnik's article, feminists such as Judith Koffler and Robin West had been centrally committed to Law and Literature studies, approaching both legal theory and a variety of literary texts (most of them from the traditional canon) from a feminist perspective.[5] And, at least since 1982, Law and Literature has been bound up with such postmodern schools as reader response, deconstructionism, pragmatism, and other ostensibly nontraditional theoretical approaches.[6] Also, The presence of Geoffrey Hartman and Stanley Fish as leaders of the Law and Humanities Institute, founded in 1979 to pursue the interdisciplinary relation, further indicates that Law and Literature has always been at the cutting edge of literary methodologies.[7]

Now suppose that the movement had programatically avoided feminist and postmodernist influences. Would this disqualify it as an interesting, or even progressive movement? This would be to suggest that Freud, in avoiding Marx, was unprogressive; or that, on a unidisciplinary plane, Law and Economics has contributed nothing because it has rarely addressed itself to critical legal studies issues. In other words, it cannot fairly be resented of one progressive line of thinking that it pays scant attention to other contemporaneous innovators. More logically, such movements *compete* with each other for the rare privilege of surviving the enthusiasm that attends their births.

I take Heilbrun to be ignorant of the very strong feminist influences in Law and Literature and to mean, by criticizing it as "a male domain," not so much its cast of characters as its choice of texts. Surely this is the argument of Cohen and Ball, among others. And although here, too, my own syllabus includes Toni Morrison's *The Bluest Eye*, and many instructors feature numerous works of women, minorities, and culturally diverse writers,[8] I believe an important issue has been joined.

For, as certain essays in this volume have already conveyed, the traditional canon hardly yields a traditional perspective, certainly not on the institution of law and decidedly not on the institution of mainstream religion either. If the body of masterpieces we have on hand—works of indisputable narrative brilliance—contains within it the seeds of a radical departure for Western culture, what more than knee-jerk response would lead a progressive movement to jettison it in favor of the unknown?

So it turns out that, even when treating male-authored texts, some of which have no female characters, the Law and Literature syllabus still raises many issues of concern to feminists. Finding in the authoritative male voices of mainstream fiction little but hypocrisy, repressed violence, and covert lawlessness, analysts of works such as *Bleak House* or *Billy Budd, Sailor* (to choose almost at random from recent work on modern fiction) have challenged traditional readings and invoked powerful counterunderstandings. What Judith Koffler (a law professor criticised by Heilbrun for associating literature with law instead of feminist topics!) calls "the feminine presence" in *Billy Budd* evokes central feminist questions in a text without females. "The heart in man" has been too much suppressed, Melville tells us in his tale of the legalistic murder of the spontaneous and the good. Melville's lawless prosecutor, Captain Vere, reminds us of *Bleak House*'s misogynist lawyer, Mr. Tulkinghorn. Here, too, Law and Literature reveals a feminist side to the Great Books not ordinarily discussed; for Tulkinghorn's dark hatred of Lady Dedlock reflects the male-oriented legal world, with all its suspicion of the passionate, the loving, the humane. Whether written by a man or a woman, a masterpiece by its very nature must touch us; whether a victimized character is male or female, first-rate modern fiction implicates central feminist issues.

People of color, too, may take heart from Law and Literature, whether we are discussing Toni Morrison on the insensitivity of authority or Emilia Pardo Bazan on legalistic violence; whether we are reading Richard Wright's *Native Son* or William Faulkner's *Intruder in the Dust*, or for that matter Harper Lee's *To Kill a Mockingbird*. What is going on is a progressivism beyond labels, an attack on the virtues of male-dominated WASP institutions.

Movements, critics, and teachers should not avoid the most widely read worthy fiction just to satisfy some social litmus test. Our must wonderful stories still seek illumination along the lines of a rigorous iconoclasm. So whatever the substantive view of any given critic on any given text, the field of Law and Literature fully accepts responsibility for hewing to the Great Books. It does so not by ignoring (in Heilbrun's facile phrase) "the best of literary criticism in the past two decades," but by defining that "best" quite differently from the current myopic fashion.

Law and Literature furthers the somewhat radical notion that the Great Books need to be read, period. Having been trained in literature myself by Paul de Man and Geoffrey Hartman, I realized early that reading literature was going to be, under their tutelage anyway, a largely self-generated activity. They were—are—themselves "the best" (particularly when they lead us to Wordsworth, to Rousseau, to Hölderlin). But how many of their students have managed to take as their lesson that reading the masters is somehow an impoverishment of their professional calling? Although now teaching literature in universities, many of the offshoots of these superb teachers proudly avoid the Great Books like (and including) *The Plague*, in addition to some of the nonpareil masterworks mentioned in the present volume.

We are losing a generation, not (as in some past ages) because of war or famine or pestilence, but instead because of our own narrow postmodern agenda of value-avoidance and nonjudgmentalism. I do not mean to indict the feminists on this score; the women who have found an ally in Law and Literature revere it partly because of its specificity, because it *does* make judgments. Rather, here, the feminists who might otherwise part company with, say, the deconstructionists, contrive also to downplay the Great Books because they feel threatened by the traditional canon. I believe, as I shall point out presently, that this fear is misplaced.

Law and Literature unabashedly takes responsibility for carrying literary culture across a divide otherwise too broad to bridge. Between the safe but superannuated ethical textualism of the past and the programmatic "antifoundationalism" of the present there may be no alternative. The Great Books, as we understand them, are virtually the sole effective source of postmodern radical thought. No wonder the West's most aggressive rebuilders, from Nietzsche to Foucault, have relied on these masterpieces to structure and inform their own iconoclasm.

On a pedagogical level, Law and Literature teachers often bemoan the loss to fledgling professionals of all contact with the Great Books. Our courses in this field offer these students sources otherwise unexplored even by nominal English majors. Lawyers particularly need Shakespeare and Dickens more—infinitely more—than they need Derrida, Rorty, or de Man. Yet it is often through Law and Literature that those thinkers, too, are revealed to students, who are then more able to respond to them (having finally read the fiction to which they so often refer). Law and Literature renders comprehensible an often relativistic postmodern program. So, in addition to providing what might be called remedial training to people not responsible for having read so little, Law and Literature expands their sensitivity to the more contemporary fads.

Some have asked ask us to use film, an analogous kind of critique of the Great Books. Tony Chase, for one, has argued well the case for popular culture.[9] There, the gain in accessibility is said to offset the loss in richness of source. Television, film, detective stories, these of course cater to the limited attention span of students today. But what in their lives offers them the chance to delve deeper, to feel more deeply, than the Great Books? To see and feel the complexity and scope of the human experience, we must go beyond the sound bite and the two-hour cinematic fix. To fathom the parallel worlds of narrative fiction and narrative law, we must plumb the best of what has been thought and said.

It is also more than faintly demeaning to audiences to assume they can appreciate the creativity only of those who are just like them. The TV generation, we are told, needs a televised message; a woman requires a woman's message, a Jew only that of another Jew. Yet Shakespeare says more in one play than all the rest of us English-speakers combined. We cannot attack or disregard him, or displace him from our first and staunchest vision, simply because he was a bourgeois white Christian male. And when it turns out that he often shows women and Jews and blacks as being *better* than their surroundings, all insistence that we read minority writers solely for the sake of their minority status disappears.

Black students need not feel patronized at finding a work of, say, Toni Morrison on the curriculum with books by Dostoevski and Camus. She appears in my courses because I find *The Bluest Eye* the easy equal of other contemporary works I love, such as John Barth's *The Floating Opera* and Bernard Malamud's *The Fixer*. If that were not so, she would not be taught in my classroom—unless I articulated for myself (and I think I could) reasons to feature surfacing writers intentionally suppressed or disadvantaged by mainline culture. But these latter need not displace traditionalist texts that in fact provide a rich base of understanding for the emerging lines of narrative.

In any case, I am not convinced that female writers in particular *need* affirmative action to rise to the deserved ranks of greatness. I would guess that the canon has been under white male control much less than have other institutional structures. Surely nonminority women have compelled certain *kinds* of creative performance since at least Elizabethan times, as they have formed a substantial audience for fiction. And our canon would not include the names now in it without the active influence of Elizabeth I, Mme. de Lafayette, Mme. de Staël, Catherine the Great, Queen Victoria, Gertrude Stein, Sylvia Beach, Marguerite Duras, Simone de Beauvoir, and Susan Sontag, among countless other authoritative female readers.

So, even if all new movements were constrained to follow "the best" of all other contemporary progressivisms, I do not think the case has been made for Law and Literature's abandoning the canon just because some feminists insist we do so. There is a reason why, these days, lawyers are furthering the return to the Great Books. We feel—perhaps more keenly than do the literature professors—the risk of having another generation lost to these sources of profound personal joy as well as professional and human wisdom.

In short, some of us in the field of Law and Literature have simply not been convinced that there exist any better sources of *radical* understanding. Melville's five-year losing struggle to bring down the Christians with *Billy Budd* still needs to be understood and continued.[10] Camus' indictment of Western culture in *The Fall* still has not been fathomed—particularly in the very France whose Vichy period he discusses, a period still cloaked in the tawdry mythology of "universal French resistance" to the Nazis. And, given the perennial smugness of the standard approach to *The Merchant of Venice*, Shakespeare's stunning defense of his "villain's" noncomedic values still must be articulated.

Law and Literature brings together disciplines of the human mind and spirit that individually would require a lifetime of understanding. So there is a logic in beginning (although surely not in ending) with truly "the best" that both fields have to offer. There are many of us who do not believe, on the present record, that postmodernist criticism has made its case for avoiding, nor feminist criticism its case for restructuring, the canon.

# 3

## Legal Rhetoric,
## or the Stories Lawyers Tell

CHAPTER FIVE

# Lawtalk in France:
# The Challenge to Democrary

THIS CHAPTER contains two related essays on the way intelligent people—particularly lawyers—spoke during the period of French history known as "Vichy," the awful years from 1940 to 1944 in which France gave expression to the darker side of its fascinating culture. The essay that immediately follows situates Vichy legal and literary rhetoric within the ambit of blame for French collaboration. The second essay, written almost a decade later, adds both empirically and theoretically to the findings of the first. The chapter as a whole conjures the special risks to American law represented by Vichy's disregard or distortion of basic constitutional beliefs shared by our two systems.

## 13. Avoiding Central Realities: Narrative Terror and the Failure of French Culture Under the Occupation

Several independent studies have recently examined the responses of French law and literature to the Occupation period of World War II. Works such as Marrus and Paxton's *Vichy France and the Jews* and Lottman's *The Left Bank* have scrutinized French jurisprudence, on the one hand, and the literary community on the other.[1] I may be understating it to say that neither French institution emerges from these studies in a very positive light.

What caused the literary and legal acceptance, or even furtherance, of Nazi policies in occupied France? The question is significant not only because it has not been adequately answered, but also because Americans in those disciplines ought to consider the lessons of that period. I would suggest, in a very tentative way, that there may be some subtle common causes behind the failures of both law and literature in wartime France. Both found it possible, so to speak, to "avoid central realities." Since the very notion of that reality is still being called into question (partially, I think, because of our difficulty in coming to grips with the meaning of the Holocaust), it is necessary at the outset to rediscover the difference between reality and interpretation.

One of many incidents related by Marrus and Paxton illustrates the distinction: A Protestant leader, Marc Boegner, met with the French collaborationist leader Pierre Laval in September 1942 and described to him the horrible fate of the Jews who had been rounded up and sent to the French concentration camp at Drancy. As Boegner recalled later, Laval claimed that the Drancy camp was being used as an agricultural center. "I talked to him about murder . . . he answered me with gardening."[2] The French succeeded in avoiding the obvious, cold realities taking place under their very eyes.

Language is so critical to law and literature that distorted words, employed in those vital disciplines, may have helped people to deny or misunderstand the central reality in their midst. In Günter Grass' *The Tin Drum,* the dwarf Oskar says of German culture during those years: "Sutterlin script is logically indicated for succinct, striking statements . . . certain documents which, though I admit I have never seen them, I can only visualize in Sutterlin script. I have in mind vaccination certificates, sport scrolls, and hand-written death sentences."[3] Accounts of the Vichy years reveal that the French language, too, was capable of sowing atrocities under the guise of merely tending its own garden.

My methodology for this essay, it should be noted, departs from the empirical orientation of historians, biographers, and journalists, and combines both literary criticism and legal analysis. I attempt here only a preliminary step into the kind of approach to the Holocaust that literary and legal scholars in this country are now beginning to offer. With an emphasis on literary techniques and a focus on narrative devices, I hope to bring us closer to the spirit of those horrible years; I seek to add to what Marrus and Paxton call the "archaeology of consciousness"[4] of

Vichy France, to explore the avoidance of central realities through a linguistic demonstration of a distorted spiritual condition.

My texts are legal and literary, and they do not all come from the period in question, or even from France itself. Most are written by non-Jews. Vichy France poignantly symbolizes an *entire* European culture in distress, a culture that had in some ways been indicating the Holocaust mentality for a century before the event. Narrative artists, both Jewish and non-Jewish, had since early in the nineteenth century been hinting at the avoidance of central realities, a denial that finally allowed the actual terror to arise and become institutionalized. Presentiments of atrocity are to be found in many disparate writers; not all invoked *thematic* terror—stories in which characters are actually oppressed and victimized—but almost all created *narrative* terror through the disequilibrating techniques of literary language and form. For literary studies, the "Holocaust period" in Europe begins a century before Hitler.

## LITERARY PRESENTIMENTS

Whatever the subject of the story itself, the most representative strain in modern fiction tended to jar the reader from his everyday notion of reality. As Viktor Shklovski and the Russian formalists of the 1920s observed, no particular thematic content is necessary, only some form of linguistic defamiliarization or distortion:

> And art exists that one may recover the sensation of life; it exists to make one feel things, to make the stone *stony.* The purpose of art is to impart the sensation of things as they are perceived and not as they are known. The technique of art is to make objects "unfamiliar," to make forms difficult, to increase the difficulty and length of perception because the process of perception is an aesthetic end in itself and must be prolonged. *Art is a way of experiencing the artfulness of an object; the object is not important.*[5]

The effect on the reader of such literature arises from the sense of disequilibration that begins all experiences of terror or the sublime. Laughter may predominate at the early stages of such an experience and continue, with increasing anxiety, throughout. But the ultimate effect is terror, as these texts teach us that there is to be no resolution, no path back to the familiar world of objects that grounds our everyday sense of morality and logic.

A grotesque line runs through pre-Holocaust continental narrative fiction from Gogol in Russian to Kafka in German. That line culminates fittingly not only in French wartime literature, but also in the nonfictional but still somehow artistic texts of French law under the German influence. The modern novelist perceived the coming debacle and attempted to convey to his readers through the medium of narrative technique that all was not well in traditional European values. No single storyteller, of course could imagine the exact horrors that were to come; but disorientation (described *and caused* by these stories) prophesied the ultimate anguish of a culture going haywire.

## NARRATIVE TERROR

What do I mean by "narrative terror"? The quest for definition raises some complex issues regarding the relationship of narrator to reader, but we have all probably experienced the phenomenon on some level or another. Our terror in reading certain texts often emerges from preliminary reactions of amazement and laughter. For instance, in the traditional ballad "Sir Patrick Spens," consider the reaction of the title character to the king's letter, in which he is ordered on a perilous voyage:

> The king has written a braid letter,
> And signd it wi his hand,
> And sent it to Sir Patrick Spens,
> Was walking on the sand

> The first line that Sir Patrick red,
> A loud lauch lauched he;
> The next line that Sir Patrick red,
> The teir blinded his ee.

> "O wha is this has don this deid,
> This ill deid don to me,
> To send me out this time o' the yeir,
> To sail upon the se!6

Sir Patrick Spens' reaction to the messenger's text is one of my favorite paradigms for narratively described terror. The disequilibrating tension between laughter and dementia as he passes through disbelief to amazement and then recognition chills his bones. The king's text submits Sir Patrick to a grotesque experience, like the harrowing voyage he must eventually take.

### Nikolai Gogol's "The Nose"

In nineteenth- and twentieth-century narrative, the terror that was merely described in "Sir Patrick Spens" becomes the reader's own unmediated terror. Like Spens' reaction, indeed like every reaction to the grotesque, it often begins in disbelieving laughter.[7] But in this famous passage from the early paragraphs of Gogol's "The Nose," the laughter is ours, not the character's:

> For the sake of propriety Ivan Yakovlevich put a jacket over his shirt, and, sitting down at the table, sprinkled some salt, peeled two onions, took a knife in his hand and, assuming an air of importance, began to cut bread. After dividing the loaf into two halves he looked into the middle of it—and to his amazement saw something there that looked white. Ivan Yakovlevich probed at it carefully with his knife and felt it with his finger: "It's solid," he said to himself. "What in the world is it?"
>
> He thrust in his fingers and pulled it out—it was a nose! . . . Ivan Yakovlevich's hand dropped with astonishment, he rubbed his eyes and felt it: it actually was a nose, and, what's more, it looked to him somehow familiar. A look of horror came into Ivan Yakovlevich's face. But that horror was nothing compared to the indignation with which his wife was overcome.
>
> "Where have you cut that nose off, you monster?" she cried wrathfully. "You scoundrel, you drunkard, I'll go to the police myself to report you! You villain! I have heard from three men that when you are shaving them you pull at their noses till you almost tug them off."
>
> But Ivan Yakovlevich was more dead than alive: he recognized that the nose belonged to none other than Kovaliov, the collegiate assessor whom he shaved every Wednesday and every Sunday.
>
> "Wait, Praskovia Osipovna! I'll wrap it up in a rag and put in a corner. Let it stay there for a while; I'll return it later on."
>
> "I won't hear of it! As though I would allow a stray nose to lie about in my room."[8]

As with much of Gogol, the passage may well leave the reader in tears (and not just because of the onions). But they are, first of all, tears of laughter. Husband and wife sit in their kitchen. The husband, equating "propriety" over a bread and onions breakfast with the wearing of a dress coat, finds something unusual in his bread. "Nos!" says the bald Russian exclamation. A stray nose! So how do he and his wife handle this grotesque occurrence? Each goes off on a self-interested tangent. The barber wonders about the nose's familiarity, without recognizing its ultimate significance. (Similarly, French wartime lawyers suddenly confronted by the new anti-Jewish laws focused, as we shall see, on ancillary details and disregarded the central reality.) The wife, for her part, won't have the nose cluttering her kitchen. Her banal sense of order, and no greater virtue, forces the barber at least to pay some attention to the troubling new reality.

Gogol's paragraphs fill us with the uneasy laughter of the condemned man because the narrative deliberately fails to provide us with a mooring

LAWTALK IN FRANCE

place from which to observe these crazy events calmly. Such laughter can be a presentiment of pure pain, terrorized pain (see also note 7). This pristine narrative circumstance, in all its absurdity, produces in us a laugh that, like Sir Patrick's, hides a deeper reaction of disequilibrating fear. While reading, we realize that continuing our self-inflicted voyage through the rest of Gogol's text may endanger us (just as the stormy seas threatened Sir Patrick). Yet we know that we are somehow bound to proceed with—even to throw ourselves into—the narrative experience. The two characters in the first scene, the barber and his wife, respond to the discovery of the stray nose in a manner deliberately designed to send a tremor through the reader. It is one thing to be confronted by a bizarre circumstance; it is quite another to find that those who have been confronted by the same circumstance are reacting to it differently from the expected norm. Sir Patrick Spens' terror, after all, imitates our own; it is inspired by forces greater than ourselves. But the barber and his wife, more than any external force, inspire our anxiety because of their skewed sense of priorities: the wife won't have stray noses lying about her kitchen, while Ivan Yakovlevich, of course, feels "horror" at the discovery of the nose—but it seems his horror is based on his amazing recognition that the nose belongs to an influential bureaucrat, one of his patrons, and that the police might come "search there for the nose and throw the blame of it on him."

The reader's uneasiness increases as this first chapter comes to a close; Gogol describes the barber and his wife in elaborate detail before revealing that they are not to be central characters in the tale. In his own inimitable way, Gogol thus ends the chapter: "Ivan Yakovlevich turned pale ... but the incident is completely veiled in obscurity, and absolutely nothing is known of what happened next" (477).

In his marvelous lecture on Gogol, Vladimir Nabokov reports that Gogol once reacted to the exotic flowers of Italy with "a fierce desire to be changed into a Nose ... with nostrils the size of two goodly pails so that [he] might inhale all possible vernal perfumes."[9] So after we meet the actual owner of the missing nose, the self-important bureaucrat Kovaliov, we are confronted with the autonomous nose itself, moving about town in full dress. A series of ludicrous details threatens to remove us yet again from the central reality—what does it matter, for instance, that Kovaliov is an excellent cardplayer? Finally, Kovaliov recognizes his nose dressed in a gold-braided uniform emerging from a coach. Gogol's Italian fantasy comes true on the page; Kovaliov finds himself conversing with his own nose, chastising it for ruining his chances with certain elegant

132

ladies. But the nose departs, and Kovaliov begins a chase through the city that brings us as readers to the point of recognizing that narrative terror, even as early as Gogol, prefigures actual terror. No one whom Kovaliov meets seems upset to see him noseless; his own doctor assures him that "even without a nose you will be just as healthy as with one," and life goes on. When Kovaliov's nose mysteriously reappears on his face, he returns to his former acquaintances, even his barber, as though nothing had happened.

In reading Gogol, laughter quickly turns to disequilibration and then amazement. We have nothing to get a grasp on, no rational perspective on the tale from which to make judgments, no sense whatsoever of what is central or merely tangential, or utterly irrelevant. Reality threatens to become nauseating. So in the tale's final two paragraphs the narrator, seeks to assuage his reader's anxiety but fails, ludicrously, to do so:

> So this is the strange event that occurred in the northern capital of our spacious empire! Only now, on thinking it all over, we perceive that there is a great deal that is improbable in it. Apart from the fact that it certainly is strange for a nose supernaturally to leave its place and to appear in various places in the guise of a civil councilor—how was it that Kovaliov did not grasp that he could not advertise about his nose in a newspaper office? I do not mean to say that I should think it too expensive to advertise: that is nonsense, and I am by no means a mercenary person: but it is improper, awkward, not nice! And again: how did the nose get into the loaf, and how about Ivan Yakovlevich himself? . . . [N]o, that I cannot understand, I am absolutely unable to understand it! But what is stranger, what is more incomprehensible than anything is that authors can choose such subjects. I confess that is quite beyond my grasp, it really is. . . . No, no! I cannot understand it at all. In the first place, it is absolutely without profit to our country; in the second place . . . but in the second place, too, there is no profit. I really do not know what to say of it. . . .
>
> And yet, in spite of all, though of course one may admit the first point, the second and the third . . . may even . . . but there, are not absurd things everywhere?—and yet, when you think it over, there really is something in it. Despite what anyone may say, such things do happen—not often but they do happen. (497)

Gogol put an end forever to the safe harbor of a defining narrative perspective. His "explanation" leaves us less secure than ever. Citing Gogol at length, Eikhenbaum, Shklovski, and the Russian formalists of the 1920s noted that the truest narrative art involved the deliberate alienation of the reader from his everyday approach to reality. The literary artist was to shock the reader out of the humdrum, to render as new and as keen as possible the experience of perception itself, but at the same time to diminish the importance of the object of that perception. Art at its essence was capturing the culture's gradual move "off center."

## Franz Kafka's The Trial

In the seventy-five years or so from Gogol's stories to Kafka's, there occurred even further destabilization, and a newer, more disquieting narrative vision that allowed little of Gogol's redeeming comedy, however grotesque. For Kafka's readers the narrative terror merges into a persistent awareness that the center of reality has become permanently displaced, that every futile gesture the protagonist makes can only distance him further from that center.

Like Sir Patrick Spens and like Gogol's barber, Josef K. in *The Trial* is confronted as the narrative begins with a given, externally imposed, reality—on his thirtieth birthday he finds himself arrested at his apartment for an unstated crime. Sir Patrick meets his reality head on, recognizing its horror: his king has commanded, the seas are treacherous, and death is inevitable. For Gogol's lowly, common characters, the reality of terror is deflected; what should have been their terror instead becomes ours in a ludicrous circumstance rendered terrifying by narrative uncertainty. Josef K., however, is the first protagonist to be responsible (like the reader himself) for his own terror. Neither king nor fantasy orchestrates his fate: throughout *The Trial* Josef K. is his own worst enemy, moving with increasing enthusiasm and bewilderment from his arrest into a self-chosen world with no firm grounding. In the process Kafka paints a portrait *of the reader himself,* unmediated, in the act of floundering about, seeking self-definition in an impersonal, threatening world.

As does the reader he represents, Josef K. has the option of escaping the narrative any time he wishes; he is free to turn away from the grotesque world of criminal procedure. "The Court wants nothing from you," a priest who "belongs" to it tells K. late in the book. "It receives you when you come and dismisses you when you go."[10] It is true that K. seems required to go to the first examination (39), but from then on his trips to "the Court" are purely on his initiative (61). K. realizes that his own sense of guilt is the main impetus for his behavior (45).[11]

As Richard Pearce has pointed out, K. is even free to "fight for justice and demonstrate his innocence," but he does neither; perceiving (in Pearce's words) "as does the reader, who shares his perspective—only the discontinuities of the world of random configuration and unreasonable connections,"[12] K. injects himself wholeheartedly into the process. He is like a reader who takes on, more enthusiastically than any author could require, the terrible experience of an unanchored, artistic universe. But is Kafka telling us that the world, the real world, is without anchor? It is true that Kafka's emphasis (like that of the contemporary Russian formalists) is on perspective and not, usually, on the object perceived;[13] it is equally true that, as his biographer Harold Hayman puts it, "he seemed to be living off-centre in relations to his own identity."[14] But, as the following passage from *The Trial* indicates, it may also be possible that Kafka did preserve a notion of the *reality of the object perceived.* Perhaps his detailed daily work as a lawyer for fourteen years or the increasing importance of his Jewish identity led Kafka to believe in a graspable ordering of reality. This belief emerges late in *The Trial*.[15]

Josef K., like the reader he represents, wanders through a darkened cathedral of symbols and images. Suddenly his eyes fall on one of these images, and Kafka's narrative details his perception:

> Away in the distance a large triangle of candle flames glittered on the high altar; K. could not have told with any certainty whether he had noticed them before or not. Perhaps they had been newly kindled. Vergers are by profession stealthy-footed, one never notices them. K. happened to turn round and saw not far behind him the gleam of another candle, a tall thick candle fixed to a pillar. It was lovely to look at, but quite inadequate for illuminating the altarpieces, which mostly hung in the darkness of the side chapels; it actually increased the darkness. The Italian was as sensible as he was discourteous in not coming, for he would have seen nothing, he would have had to content himself with scrutinizing a few pictures piecemeal by the light of K.'s pocket torch. Curious to see what effect it would have, K. went up to a small side chapel near by, mounted a few steps to a low balustrade, and bending over it shone his torch on the altarpiece. The light from a permanent oil-lamp hovered over it like an intruder. The first thing K. perceived, partly by guess, was a huge armored knight on the outermost verge of the picture. He was leaning on his sword, which was stuck into the bare ground, bare except for a stray blade of grass or two. He seemed to be watching attentively some event unfolding itself before his eyes. It was surprising that he should stand so still without approaching nearer to it. Perhaps he had been set there to stand guard. K., who had not seen any pictures for a long time, studied this knight for a good while, although the greenish light of the oil lamp made his eyes blink. When he played the torch over the rest of the altarpiece he discovered that it was a portrayal of Christ being laid in the tomb, conventional in style and a fairly recent painting. He pocketed the torch and returned again to his seat. (256–57).

The passage is one of several in the story evoking Josef K.'s inability to grasp central realities. K. dwells on the soldier, while the true subject of the altarpiece is the burial of Christ. This K. learns, too late, as his flashlight skims past the central figures on the altarpiece at the very end of the experience. Whatever time he had to perceive was wasted on an unimportant figure, a soldier who is merely observing the central theme.[16]

In K.'s skewed ordering, the trifle becomes the central event, and the central figures are virtually overlooked. So it is with the man from the country seeking entrance to "The Law," who becomes so preoccupied with the doorkeeper and the details of his clothes and voice that he dies without having tried the door meant only for him.

Our terror as readers of *The Trial* parallels K.'s terror; his misreadings of reality threaten to become our own. It is we, now, who may observe the noseless face and find it acceptable, who may spend our vision on ancillary objects, who may waste our lives on (and even create new realities out of) meaningless details; all the while, as Kafka strongly hints in most of his stories, the central reality is there to be found, after all.

In each of the texts discussed so far, the experience of terror plays a central role; but there is a progression worth summarizing before I turn to the horrific world of World War II France. Sir Patrick Spens stares death in the face as he reads the king's letter; we watch him read it and, from the safety of our armchairs, we understand his response to the text. Gogol's barber and spouse feel little terror at the discovery of a stray nose amidst their bread and onions; they and the other characters focus not on it but on seemingly extraneous details. When the narration purporting to anchor us goes off on the same irrelevant tangents, our previously secure armchairs become more unsteady and unsettling. Finally, in Kafka, we are deprived even of the mediation of characters reacting to a *clearly* grotesque circumstance. We *are* Josef K., creating our own horror out of realities whose central meanings we seem constantly to misapprehend. At least in Gogol's mad universe, some opening remains for the reader's moral and logical senses to have their way; in Kafka's creation, those senses are barely discoverable amidst the darkened and claustrophobic world of threatening irrelevancies.

## REAL TERROR

French culture's depressing response to the genocidal Nazi occupier in World War II brings to mind a great deal of Gogol's barber and at least some of Kafka's Josef K. An entire nation went about its business successfully ignoring what seems, from the outsider's perspective, to be the central, horrifying reality in its midst. Ours is the terror, not theirs, as we learn of individual and collective attempts to put the Nazi reality (as Gogol's barber attempted) "in a corner for a while." There was shockingly little of Sir Patrick Spens' ability to stare the terrifying reality in the face, much less to battle against it.

Even after the Kristalnacht attack on Jews in Germany, and before the Occupation, the French responded to Nazism by avoiding its central reality. After November 1938, French newspapers demanded an end to the admission of foreign refugees to France, those "whose contradictory ideologies can only create disorder, stimulate violence and make blood flow by expressing themselves on our soil."[17] One newspaper responded to Kristalnacht by fearing that "today synagogues burn; tomorrow it will be our churches."[18] By the time the Nazi beast was actually in their midst, self-interest,[19] coupled with self-deception, allowed the French substantially to look away—or, worse, to look directly and yet see something else. French law, and the executive and police authorities, effectively outdid the Germans at their own racial game.[20]

From this point on in this essay and through the next, I focus on French law and reactions to it under the German influence. The two French Statuts des juifs (dated October 3, 1940, and June 2, 1941) drafted by ministers of the Pétain government in unoccupied Vichy, applied also in occupied France.[21] The laws won ready acceptance from the many bureaucracies and individuals responsible for implementation. While Xavier Vallat, the first commissioner-general for Jewish affairs in Vichy, was dissatisfied with the uncertain definition of Jews in the statutes,[22] most of official France worked comfortably, sometimes enthusiastically, within the new laws.[23] The statute of June 2, 1941, which replaced the earlier statute, defined a Jew as either "he or she, of whatever religion, who is an issue of at least three grandparents of the Jewish race, or two only if his or her spouse is an issue of two grandparents of the Jewish race," or "he or she who is part of the Jewish religion, or who was part of it on 25 June 1940 and who is an issue of two grandparents of the Jewish race." To clarify who was "part of the Jewish religion," the statute went on to provide that "non-affiliation with the Jewish religion is established by proof of adherence to one of the other religions recognized by the State before the law of 9 December 1905."[24] Individuals classified as Jewish in a census employing those definitions became subject to deportation and consequent annihilation.

In addition, the statute's next five articles effectively barred Jews from many government positions. Yet like the grotesque details of a Gogol story, article 7 of the same statute preserves the pension benefits of certain Jewish bureaucrats fired under the law and allows returning Jewish prisoners-of-war two months on the job before being fired; laughable though this largesse appears at first, it merely underscores the horror of the full text.

The bureaucrats managing the professions and services itemized under the statute, however, apparently accepted it with none of our sense of amazement. Many of them at the lower levels looked the other way. Some at or near the top adopted a stance similar to Josef K.'s: responsible for carrying out the statute, but usually left to their own devices, they frequently exceeded the limits the authorities required of them. Just as the French in Vichy out-Nazied the Nazis,[25] so French officials exceeded their own statute's vigorous mandates. Statutory restrictions on Jewish members of the learned professions, for example, led French educators and students to seek a 3 percent quota for university enrollment.[26]

Xavier Vallat himself was not satisfied with the definition of Jew under the June 2, 1941 statute. Did the state or the individual have the burden of proving the individual belonged to one religion or the other? Individuals with two Jewish grandparents but claiming nonaffiliation arguably had to prove baptism and "adherence to [another] religion." Thus Jews who had become nonbelievers did not qualify. Vallat still felt that too many members of the "Jewish race" were escaping the strictures of the law.[27] In their necessarily brief but excellent account of the French legal response, Marrus and Paxton report that Vallat wanted to reverse the traditional burden of proof and place it on the accused in enforcing anti-Jewish statutes.[28]

French lawyers, too, were grappling with the question of this definition. I find a 1943 narrative written for legal consumption by Joseph Haennig, a member of the French appellate bar, strikingly similar to the passage from Kafka cited above. Haennig's title for his discourse was appropriately Kafkaesque: "What Means of Proof Can the Jew of Mixed Blood Offer to Establish His Nonaffiliation with the Jewish Race?" There follows a careful legal analysis of the problem:

> The Commission on the Jewish Laws has been established by the head of State to give its view on the interpretation of Article I of the Law of 2 June 1941 concerning the subject of nonaffiliation with the Jewish race.
> The Commission believes that the statute writers allowed more proof than merely that of belonging to another religion recognized by the Statute prior to the law of 9 December 1905. It has noted that "in each case, the adjudicator must ascertain that the claimant either has never belonged, or has ceased to belong in fact, to the Jewish community."
> We believe that neither good sense nor the law could lead to the view that the statute writers required of an individual having only two Jewish grand-

parents proof of his belonging to the Catholic or Protestant denominations in order to avoid being included on the lists of Jews. . . .

Since the courts must now decide each case on its own merits, we would do well to cite as an example German law, and thus to see how it overcomes any difficulty relating to proof of nonaffiliation with the Jewish race. This exercise reveals a largeness and objectivity of spirit. . . .

A recent case of particular note dealt with the female descendant of two Jewish grandparents, baptized as a Protestant, who, under the Article stipulating the definition of a citizen of the Reich, only would become Jewish if she adhered to the Jewish religion, the same solution incidentally as is reached under the law of 2 June 1941.

This woman of mixed Protestant and Jewish heritage had, for a period of six months, at the express request of her Jewish father and against the wishes of her Protestant mother, attended classes at religious school to learn about the Jewish faith. Once each year until her father's death in 1931, she accompanied him to synagogue on the New Year.

On the other hand, she never contributed to the synagogue, while still retaining her name on the list kept there.

Under these circumstances and facts, the Supreme Court of Leipzig was called on to consider her case. It first noted that, as soon as she learned of the presence of her name on the Jewish lists, she requested its removal, in the spring of 1938.

The Court affirmed the lower court judges' view that she had only attended New Year's services in order to preserve family peace. The view that there was no sufficient tie to the Jewish community in this case was thus deemed correct. [However, the defendant had called herself a Jew in order to obtain employment from a Jewish agency.]

Theoretically, the Court of Leipzig refused to consider the motives leading an individual to certain specific acts apparently linking him to the Jewish community. However, where these links have been merely for pretense, the Court instructed lower courts not to take them into account if it has been established, as in the instant case, that the defendant was merely using the Jewish religion as a means to acquire an advantage by the intermediary. . . .

This analysis of the German law furnishes an interesting contribution to the study of a subject still little understood by the French courts. The analysis indicates a possible route, without risk of distorting the statute writers' intention, and in conformity with the principles that underlie the racial statutes and cases.

Joseph Haennig
Member of the Appellate Bar
Paris[29]

Like Josef K., Joseph Haennig was not necessarily malevolent. Indeed, my discussion of literary and legal terror has so far included no clearly evil characters or individuals. I do not emphasize here rabid anti-Semites such as the Célines or the Bernanos, the Darquiers or the professors of ethnoracism such as Georges Montandon. One need not, perhaps should not, focus upon extremists. The real work of the Holocaust was done by the commonplace "homme moyen." But this is the very point: the phenomenon of avoiding central realities had become so widespread in European culture that it—far more than the instigation of evil leaders— explains the Holocaust. When Joseph Haennig beamed his flashlight, so to speak, on the Franch Statut des juifs, he failed to see—or at least openly would not admit—any of its terroristic racism. Like K.'s attempt to understand the two arresting officers in *The Trial*, Haennig ignored the casual mix of horror and legalism. Rather, he saw in the statute an excuse to exercise his own professional, hermeneutic talents as a legal interpreter of statutory texts.

This ingrained proclivity to throw himself into whatever framework outsiders had built about him, without thought to the rotten nature of the structure itself, characterized the French lawyer's response to gen- ocidal German policies. One of the highest French judicial bodies, the Conseil d'état, established the Commission on the Statut des juifs to which Haennig refers. In purging Jews from the administration, the Con- seil increasingly placed the burden of proof of "nonaffiliation" on the victimized individual; in other cases they put the burden on the state prosecutor. Legal professionalism supported ardent and dispassionate in- terpretation of the racial laws.[30] It is Josef K.'s fatal willingness, nay, eagerness, to allow his "arrest" to define his sense of self and reality, now raised to the level of professional and institutional behavior.

Josef K. barely catches a glimpse of the true subject of the Cathedral altarpiece while dwelling on the huge but trifling figure of the knight. Similarly, Joseph Haennig's response to Parisian police roundups of the Jews in France that led to some seventy thousand deportations to the camps between 1942 and 1944 also missed the most obvious point of the statute he was regarding.[31] Haennig focused on, of all things, the intent of the German legislature in drafting the Nuremberg laws and the behavior of the Nazi courts in construing that legislation. He managed, like K., to find a sense of definition in the object of his analysis, but to find it in the most peculiar place. The "flashlight" of professional training led Haennig to illuminate only the corner of an enormous phenomenon, and to miss its ultimate meaning.

What forces shaping the life of Joseph Haennig—and thousands like him across Europe—could have led to this perhaps well-meaning, but still grotesque, placement of the professional eye? Was it something akin to the response of certain French authors who, however troubled by aspects of the Occupation, happily found their careers thriving under

Nazi rule? Apparently a literary upbringing, as much as a legalistic one, could encourage otherwise decent people to avoid central realities. Simone de Beauvoir actually produced a radio program for Pétain's propagandistic "Radio Nationale,"[32] and Jean-Paul Sartre's plays *Les Mouches* (The Flies, 1943) and *Huis clos* (*No Exit*, 1944) opened to excellent reviews in the controlled Occupation press. Publishing, theatric, literary, and artistic endeavors all proceeded without undue concern for the plainly visible roundups, racial laws, and terrorized victims.

## SOURCES OF DISTORTED VISION

As an outgrowth of my earlier analysis, I now suggest that three elements contributed to this distorted vision of Holocaust terror. None of these three has, in my opinion, received sufficient attention in explaining that terror.

First is the embedded notion of "profesionalism" itself. Those who have recently analyzed Melville's Captain Vere have questioned that character's seemingly cool professionalism during Billy Budd's trial; in the face of a burning moral issue, he appears steadfastly legalistic.[33] "What deep urge," Robert Cover has asked of Vere, "leads a man to embrace, personally, the opportunity to do an impersonal, distasteful task?"[34] French and German lawyers as well as other professionals shared that urge to perform distasteful tasks during the Holocaust. Professionalism became the end in itself of the lawyer's vision; Marrus and Paxton report that Vichy courts "kept on with their job" under the Statut des juifs, "amidst all the horrors of deportation, even through the summer of 1944, reflecting the magistrates' determination to assert control over statutory persecution."[35]

Was it the quest for professionalism, or pride in doing one's job, that was the "deep urge" leading jurists to achieve by pen and parchment what other professionals accomplished with guns and gas? We must not forget that American lawyers and judges have shown a similar capacity to proceed with lawyerlike tools and arguments through a grotesque structure of laws during periods such as slavery or even this same horrible war.[36]

Yet even these flagrant American examples of legal professionalism displacing direct moral observation should not lightly be compared with the way contintental law perceived its function. Kafka's central metaphor in *The Trial* stresses the immutability of codified text and the infinite diversity of interpretation. The French lawyer's way of interpreting the Statut des juifs constituted merely a professionally satisfactory but textually inappropriate acceptance of the lowest level of generalization available to him in reading the new laws. His abandonment of the larger questions, raised (as we shall see in the next essay) by a minority of courageous lawyers, must give us pause. Perhaps it comes down to one literary critic's formulation of Kafka's thematic: "Despite its internal accommodation of an unlimited set of variant readings, the domain of the law is bounded by an absolute barrier proscribing the penetration of the textual by the existential."[37] Again, however, Kafka's characterizations of K. and Block show surrender to the court not as a necessity but as a function of spiritual and linguistic exhaustion.[38]

Thus the second contributing factor, I suggest, is *the distorting capacity of language itself*. Law and literature are both shaped by language. How natural it must have been for lawyers and authors to deflect their deepest urges away from moral revulsion and toward the balming redefinitions of the new language: "non-appartenance à la race juive," "échapper à l'inscription sur les listes juives," "la jurisprudence allemande" (that) "dénote un espirit large et objectif," and so on. Haennig's mellifluous phrases, rendered in the most glorious language ever created, must have reassured those who used them.

Better than any Christian novelist I know, Günter Grass has portrayed the third source of distortion I wish to consider. In the remarkable chapter "Faith, Hope, Love" of *The Tin Drum*, Grass provides a hint of the ultimate "deep urge" that allowed millions of otherwise unexceptional Europeans to avoid the central reality of injustice in their midst; his narrative takes place the morning after the Kristalnacht attack on Jewish synagogues and stores.

> Outside, it was a November morning. Beside the Stadt-Theatre, near the streetcar stop, some pious ladies and strikingly ugly young girls were handing out religious tracts, collecting money in collection boxes, and holding up between two poles, a banner with an inscription quoted from the thirteenth chapter of the First Epistle to the Corinthians. "Faith . . . hope . . . love," Oskar read and played with the three words as a juggler plays with bottles: faith healer, Old Faithful, faithless hope, hope chest, Cape of Good Hope, hopeless love, Love's Labour's Lost, six love. An entire credulous nation believed, there's faith for you, in Santa Claus. But Santa Claus was really the gasman. I believe—such is my faith—that it smells of walnuts and almonds. But it smelled of gas.[39]

The words that helped Europeans to support the beast in their midst were not only legal or literary. They were also the words of Christianity, words of metaphysical support to those whose acts took the lives of millions. Sadly, just as Josef K. overlooked Christ himself to dwell on the authority figure, the Pope condemned neither Vichy France nor even Nazi Germany.[40] Similarly, liberal Protestants, in the courageous words of Franklin H. Littell, were "marked by a 'predisposition toward abstraction' which rejected particularity and repudiated the peculiar history of any religious community."[41] Unlike the Jews, for whom Littell states "a split of the 'spiritual' and 'material' has no place at all" (p. 7), European Protestantism could support what the Nazis accepted in them: "positives Christentum." Littell continues: "Positive Christianity is the same thing in its thought structure as 'non-sectarian religion,' 'spiritual religion,' 'civic religion.' . . . It is religion-in-general, without intellectual discipline or ethical content beyond that imposed by the society at large (p. 35).

The responsibility of the dominant religions of the oppressing culture has perhaps not yet been sufficiently studied vis-à-vis the Holocaust. Marrus and Paxton, with some reserve, devote a few pages to the topic,[42] but its momentousness and complexity discourage widespread scholarly attention. My thought here, simply stated, is that the metaphysics of Christian faith and the technicalities of Christian hermeneutics both helped turn law into terror in Vichy France.

If, as I have suggested, narrative was foreshadowing reality, we cannot then ourselves turn away from the implications of these nineteenth- and twentieth-century literary insights. We can no longer consider the Holocaust to be merely a German, or even predominantly an economic or political, phenomenon. Nor, perhaps, should we focus quite so avidly on the behavior of the *victims* of that terror, those who, in Littell's words "have clung to history, earthiness, concrete events."[43] Instead, those who bifurcated culture and ethics must now come to the center stage of legal and literary inquiry.

# 14. Legal Rhetoric Under Stress: The Example of Vichy

Most of us have a tendency to think of the European disaster of 1933–1945 in terms of physical violence of the worst, previously unimaginable kind. We have, in our mind's eye, masses of bodies. We think of the depersonalization of victimized groups, of the refusal to see certain people as real and specific individuals, and of the resulting elimination of "anonymous, despised hordes." We do not think of language as playing much of a role in this horror—with one exception. We tend to believe that the German people, on whom we almost exclusively lay the blame for the Holocaust, were somehow seduced into the violence by the brilliantly crazed rhetoric of their führer. From Hitler's hysterical words to the death camps sometimes appears to have been one short and horrifying step.

The purpose of this essay is to show that a very different kind of rhetoric, in a very different kind of country, also led to death on a massive scale during the turbulent years of World War II. The rhetoric was generated in France by men and women sitting at their desks; it arose, remarkably enough, with substantial independence from German interference or influence. It was the rhetoric of the law. This was a rhetoric of individual cases, not of mass depersonalization. It isolated out for individual analysis, rather than herded together, the subjects of its discourse. It used reason, not emotion, to identify these subjects.

For several years I have been examining the way in which lawyers spoke during the stressful period of French history known as "Vichy" (1940–1944). Here I will present a variety of empirical data and make a disturbing claim arising from that data: that a loose system of institutionally acceptable professional rhetoric caused (as much as did the terror or influence of German occupation) the definition, identification, and eventual destruction of tens of thousands of Jews—for the majority (but not the entirety) of such legal rhetoric was unchecked by any interpretive model that would have permitted recourse to certain foundational beliefs to evaluate and constrain itself.

There are at least three corollaries of my claim, the first two of which are fully developed here and the third of which is merely introduced in these pages: first, that the French legal community went beyond the demands of the German occupiers and the examples of the German precedents; second, that "interpretive communities" need more than their situational sense of things to avoid catastrophe both to themselves and those their decisions affect; and third, that the Vichy lawyers' ingrained ability to avoid the conflict between the racial laws and the foundational egalitarianism of traditional French constitutional law shows there may well be a cause-and-effect link between an interpretive theory (here, antitextualism) and the behavior of the group of interpreters it purports to describe.

The first corollary flows from the claim itself: German power and coercion cannot alone account for the ills that befell Jews on French soil during 1940–1944, some 75,000 of whom were deported from France to their extermination abroad.[44] By analyzing the sophisticated jurisprudential debate in Vichy France on the issue of "Who is a Jew?," and then by providing an example of an autonomous body of French legal doctrine connected to that definitional discourse (landlord-tenant law), I demonstrate that unconstrained professional discourse *more* than German political pressure led to an excess of French zeal and thus a needless amount of Jewish suffering. My treatment of the first corollary expresses a central risk of professionalism, perhaps most notably *legal* professionalism—that lawyers seek relief from considering the basic premises of their actions by recourse to eloquence, formalism, and the situational realities of the "job." It stands as a lesson to contemporary American lawyers, whatever the constitutional, egalitarian, or procedural principles that appear to protect us from such behavior. For those "foundational" premises also existed in wartime France; yet they were trumped by the community's tolerance for narrower lines of discourse that studiously avoided (for the most part) the challenge of first principles.

The second and third corollaries relate both to the specifics of French legal history and the seemingly far-removed topical phenomenon of Law and Literature theory. In the second corollary, I seek to demonstrate that the popular notion of a protective professional or situational discourse— typified by the phrase "interpretive community"[45]—bends and breaks in the wake of Vichy France's example. By answering Richard Posner's critique of my earlier use of Vichy law,[46] I first show that many of Posner's normative assumptions about professional rhetoric and behavior in fact unwittingly demonstrate the force of the second corollary—that interpretive communities need more than a merely situational sense of things. And by engaging the somewhat-related discourse of Stanley Fish (who has not as yet addressed the implications of his theory for periods of holocaustic professional conduct), I assert that lawyers need recourse to textual standards of conduct and cannot rely on the practices of their profession alone to avoid future catastrophes. Here I willingly concede the difficulty of establishing norms apart from the interpretive practices surrounding them;[47] but my point, embodied in the third corollary, is that the lesson of Vichy demands of our generation a *theoretical* posture in search of such norms. Hence I argue that the prevalent "postmodernist" hermeneutics, itself in radical disarray for reasons connected to my subject,[48] directly risks producing modes of practice that replicate Vichy's text-avoidance, relativism, and ethical debasement.

The historical subject of this essay thus serves both as an example and as a first cause of our contemporary, situational duty to explore the *risks* of professional discourse. Post-Holocaust (a term I prefer to postmodern) theories that appear to liberate legal rhetoric from ethical norms are at best untimely and at worst perverse. No matter how difficult the quest for a "text" that will stand on its own to influence lawyers and others on the meaning of Vichy France, I argue here that the quest should proceed, sanctioned—rather than contradicted—by mainstream interpretive theory.

It is well worth recalling, now some two hundred years after the French Revolution, how little allegiance there was to eighteenth-century revolutionary norms once the rhetorical floodgates were opened by articulate Vichy collaborators. Thus, in 1940, only eighty of almost six hundred French legislators refused on constitutional grounds to grant the Vichy leader, Pétain, virtually total monarchical powers.[49] One of those eighty, the young lawyer Philippe Serre, was to be hounded into exile for his courageous allegiance to text; others in his camp were to be executed by the Vichy regime for their vote. Serre, whom I recently interviewed, recognized at the time that the breach of constitutional norms represented, in his words, "the end of democracy in France."[50]

This same Philippe Serre, a non-Jew and still proud Frenchman, remarked to me of the Vichy-authored anti-Jewish laws of 1940–1944: "The Germans would not have insisted on a racial policy if the French had refused."[51] By the time of our conversation, in late 1988, my research had led me to a similar conclusion, but for different reasons. Serre saw the extensive Vichy racism as the twin result of Pétain's "dictatorship" and the elevation of mediocre and often anti-Semitic ideologues to power under the Maréchal; he excepted his fellow private lawyers, who "se sont bien tenus" (i.e., who "conducted themselves properly"), criticizing instead the magistrates. But I felt, by then, that mixed results had been demonstrated in all areas of legal practice, and that *it was legal practice itself and its discursive elasticity*—and not the anti-Semitism of any one leader or group—that brought about the full extent of the horror.

I focus here on merely two of literally hundreds of areas of Vichy legislation and case law.[52] The first considers the disputes as to burden of proof and admissibility of evidence on the basic question, "Who Is a Jew?" The second exemplifies a discrete body of case law—here concerning landlord and tenant—arising from the new legislation.

## THE DEFINITION OF A JEW

Any analysis of Vichy rhetoric must begin with the law of June 2, 1941, promulgated by Vichy Justice Minister Joseph Barthélemy and other government officials, and known as the Statut des juifs. A sequel to the Vichy law of October 3, 1940,[53] this June 2 statute was designed to eliminate Jewish property ownership and to restrict or even eliminate

Jewish participation in many professions and trades. Eventually it would be supplemented by almost two hundred laws, ordinances, decrees, and rulings authored by French lawyers and officials.[54] The June 2 statute begins, quite logically, with a definition of the word "Jew":

1. A Jew is: He or she, of whatever faith, who is an issue of at least three grandparents of the Jewish race, or of simply two if his/her spouse is an issue herself/himself of two grandparents of the Jewish race.
   A grandparent having belonged to the Jewish religion is considered to be of the Jewish race;
2. He or she who belongs to the Jewish religion, or who belonged to it on 25 June 1940, and who is the issue of two grandparents of the Jewish race.
   Nonaffiliation with the Jewish religion is established by proof of belonging to one of the other faiths recognized by the State before the law of 9 December 1905. The disavowal or annulment of recognition of a child considered to be Jewish is without effect as regards the preceding sections. [There follow the prohibitions for such people on property ownership and some employment; sanctions—including imprisonment—are then declared for engaging in proscribed activities.][55]

When I read the statute for the first time, I asked myself and others these questions: Was this written by the French, with their long history of at least theoretical and constitutional equality before the law and freedom of religion—or was this imposed by the German conqueror? Was this degree of precision and legalistic verbiage really at work in the arrests of Jews on French soil that eventually led to large-scale deportations? Did not the German occupier (rather than the French) simply round up masses of indistinguishable people who lived in Jewish neighborhoods, herding them into trucks or buses, then onto trains to the death camps? Was not depersonalization, rather than specific definition, the method of the terrorizers, as Hannah Arendt seemed to argue?[56] Were even Jews in Vichy itself (the so-called nonoccupied zone administered exclusively by the French) defined and victimized by this law? And did the June 2, 1941, statute become the linchpin for decisions—taken by courts before whom learned counsel would argue—that would then decide the fate of thousands of individuals in both zones?

As I learned more, I came to ask two additional questions: In what ways did the racial policy in France exceed that required by the German conquerors? Was there any rhetorical device or tactic, available situationally to the French lawyer who wrote, interpreted, and applied that social policy, to reverse the fatal flow of events? My research into these basic questions was structured by analyzing the three major domains in which lawyers write and speak: in the government,[57] in the courts,[58] and in the private sector.[59] For each domain, I examined primarily, but by no means exclusively, the means of interpretation and implementation of the Jewish laws; their relationship to legal rhetoric and practice *within* the domains (e.g., the *numerus clausus* on Jewish lawyers and law students; the prohibition against Jewish magistrates) and *without* (e.g., the application of the laws to specific situations).

I quickly found, however, a kind of seamless web of legislation and policy, in which the racial laws became connected, for example, with broader constitutional issues;[60] with problems of conflict of laws or rules of evidence;[61] with traditional values such as the right to counsel and to an attorney-client privilege;[62] with jurisdictional disputes as between administrative courts or agencies, and civil courts; and with various internal issues such as the salaries of lawyers, the explosion of litigation under Vichy,[63] and the way entrance examinations and even law school courses should be conducted. From the earth-shattering to the banal, there was an expansion of legalistic issues connected to that law of June 2, 1941, and its predecessors and progeny.

The June 2 statute indeed gave rise to what was easily the richest and most protracted legal debate of the period: who bore the burden of proof on the question of what the Vichy writers called "belonging to the Jewish race"? The June 2 statute is not explicit on the point, although the language ("is established by proof of belonging to one of the other faiths . . .") might imply that the individual had the burden. The procedural issue, vital (as lawyers know) to the outcome of any piece of litigation, divided lawyers for four long years.

Upon this burden-of-proof question hung careers, fortunes, and lives. For the June 2 statute left another gaping loophole when attempting to deal with the pervasive case of an individual with only two Jewish grandparents. It was here that the law coerced litigation and legal rhetoric. Anyone with three or more Jewish grandparents was irrebuttably Jewish, as a matter of "race"; anyone with one or no Jewish grandparents was an "Aryan" under this racially based approach, even if Jewish under Jewish law (by having a Jewish maternal grandmother) and even if secretly a Jew. Unless married to another Jew, however, the person with exactly two Jewish grandparents provided an ambiguous case.

This is the kind of debatable question that lawyers love to attack. American as well as French lawyers might have found here the tempting kind of statutory void that volumes of verbiage would soon fill. How could (or can) an interpretive community that thrives on such problems resist? What choices do members of that community have? Before returning to these questions, which are central to a discussion of my claim, let me continue empirically by revealing what French lawyers actually did. First, they drew actual diagrams to explain to themselves the various perambulations.[64] Then they began to debate the ambiguous statutory point; within a matter of weeks they were divided, as one observer put it (making it sound more like a young wine than a legal matter of the gravest consequence), on "cette matière fort délicate et nouvelle" (this new and very delicate matter).[65]

Of no small interest was the obvious mistake in the statute, declaring to be Jewish any individual with only two Jewish grandparents but married to someone "of two Jewish grandparents of the Jewish race." This, on its terms, would exclude from Jewishness half-Jews marrying someone with *more* than two Jewish grandparents or himself/herself a practicing Jew. While no private lawyer, to my knowledge, dared to present that argument in favor of a half-Jewish client, the lawyers in government agencies quickly saw the mistake. As the French administrative agency charged with Jewish questions—the Commissariat général aux questions juives (CGQJ)—put it in December 1941:

> We are faced with a defect in the drafting of the law that will soon be corrected. [It never was; it never needed to be.] But good sense requires that it be interpreted as though it said: "if his/her spouse is Jewish," and not "if his/her spouse is an issue of two grandparents of the Jewish race."[66]

Government lawyers, judges, and private attorneys all had much to say about the "delicate" debate. As early as the end of 1940 (construing a similar provision in the law of October 3 of that year), a justice department lawyer wrote to the minister of the interior about

> a yet more delicate case, although admittedly unusual and manageable, that of an individual, presumably of Jewish origins, but the issue of grandparents who practiced no religion or who were married civilly. How can we find the key to this problem? Arduous genealogical research might have to be on an international scale. (*AN* BB30–1714)

For Vallat, the first commissioner of the CGQJ, there was no doubt that the June 2 statute placed this occasionally overwhelming burden on the individual; writing about this problem just after the war, he said:

> But *how could we know* if the grandparents were of the Jewish religion, since Jewish communities in France did not have records like those of the parish churches? It was only possible to determine this by forcing their descendants to furnish the contrary proof, that is evidence establishing that their grand-

parents had belonged to other recognized religions then in France: Catholic, Protestant, Orthodox or Islam.
And what about atheists, some will ask us? The answer is simple. We were dealing with people born in the first half of the 19th century and, in that period, atheism practically did not exist.[67]

As quickly as November 21, 1941, Vallat's CGQJ was busy slapping the wrists of such magistrates as the *procureur* in Toulouse who dared to reverse the burden. Declaring the CGQJ itself to be the best judge of the June 2 statute, "because of the minute study of the texts . . . our position is unattackable. It consists of this affirmation: that the burden of proof, in all contests relating to the quality of Jewishness, must be carried by the individual and not by our Commission."[68]

Not everyone connected with the Vichy government reveled in placing this almost insurmountable burden on the individual rather than the state. But it may be significant that the strongest statement from Vichy against such an interpretation came from a writer, not a lawyer.[69] An essayist who briefly served in Pétain's cabinet, René Gillouin complained directly to the Maréchal on this point:

Il est regrettable . . . que ce soit désormais au présumé juif de faire la preuve de son innocence [!], et non plus à la justice. L'innovation juridique est inquiétante pour tous. La dispersion des biens par dissolution de la communauté sapera la famille. La loi française est plus sévère que la loi allemande.

(It is regrettable . . . that from now on the putative Jew will have to prove her/his innocence [!], and the State no longer needs to prove her/his guilt. This judicial innovation is disquieting for everyone. The dispersion of property by dissolution of the community will sap the family. French law is more severe than German law.)[70]

Gillouin's concluding sentence was prescient and deserves elaboration here. As Robert Aron put it somewhat modestly a decade after the war, the French statutory scheme was "plus sévère que celle de quelques pays satellites du troisième Reich" (harsher than those of a few countries attached to the Third Reich); Aron cites specifically the Vichy imposition of the burden of proof on the individual instead of the state.[71] Certainly Jewish observers at the time concurred as they analyzed the effects of the June 2 statute. The newsletter "Information juives" of November 7, 1941, for example, observed that the statute exceeded even earlier German ordinances for occupied France by adding two substantive factors—the limit of June 25, 1940, for any attempts to convert or otherwise show nonobservance of Judaism; and the stipulation that, with only two Jewish grandparents, one married to a Jew would irrebuttably be deemed a Jew. (The Germans themselves were far less fixed in their approach to this common situation.)

Indeed, on several occasions the Germans had to slap the wrists of French lawyers and bureaucrats whose legalistic zeal carried them beyond the strictness of German legal precedents. Hence, the chief of the Parisian SS, Roethke, felt constrained to write CGQJ to advise them that the testimony of Catholic priests affirming the baptism of an alleged Jew with two Aryan grandparents or otherwise needing to sustain the burden of proof, was definitive from the perspective of German law. He wanted the French, who tended to disallow or devalue such evidence, to follow the more liberal German evidentiary model.[72]

The Germans of course chose to *capitalize* on French legal excesses in most areas. Although the first German ordinance defines Jew (anterior to any Vichy legislation), this was replaced by two later ordinances parroting the then-existing Vichy laws, which were more inclusive.[73] Thus, on July 1, 1942, SS Oberstürmführer Dannecker writes in a memorandum regarding the June 2 statute that, comparing the German and French definitions of Jew, "the French definition, being broader, it will now serve as a basis in all doubtful cases."[74]

As to the overbreadth of the French racial definition, the case of ethnic Georgians living in France is instructive. Here, the French themselves recognized they were breaking new ground, in terms of comparative law with the Nazi courts, yet proceeded anyway. The head of CGQJ's section on these laws thus writes, as late as March 10, 1944, to his subordinate in Toulouse, that Georgians of Mosaic belief on French soil should be considered Jews under Vichy law:

> For the moment, under French law, Georgians of Mosaic belief must be regarded as having issued from three grandparents of Jewish religion and thus covered by the Statut des juifs. . . .
> The German authorities exempt from the wearing of the Star such Georgians, because they consider them not to be of pure Jewish race.
> Still, it does not appear that this exemption must ipso-facto bring about the removal of the Aryan trustees that you have deemed it necessary to place in control of Georgian property. On the contrary, I have decided that, in every case, these Georgians must be made the object of aryanization measures.[75]

In every regard, including the "Final Solution" itself, the French could be fully counted on to provide the legalistic basis and the means to rid France of Jews. The lawyer Pierre Laval begged the Germans to deport Jewish children not previously demanded.[76] No wonder that, in late 1942, Dannecker's office could confidently write the following:

It is desirable that, regarding the Final Solution of Jewish questions, purely French organizations handle this in France. Still, this solution cannot yet be realized 100 percent with the present structure. (CDJC no. XXVI–80)

The Germans soon after this learned that there was still less need for German manpower in the French "final solution." By mid-1943 the Paris *Standartenführer* and head of the Paris police (Dr. Knochen) was asking Berlin for two hundred and fifty SS to help in French-originated roundups of newly denaturalized Jews, and Berlin gently but firmly denied the need for such numbers: "I recognize how hard your work is without sufficient personnel, but one SS-Führer and three subordinates will suffice."[77] Vichy law, and not German demands, created the need for Vichy police enforcement. In May 1942, the chief of police on Jewish questions of the CGQJ observed:

> The rapidity with which Jewish legislation has been established and with which these measures have been applied makes us fear that, from what we see everyday with our own eyes, there may be huge deficiencies in vital personnel [to implement the policies]. (CDJC no. CXI–17)

Thousands of police, guards, bus drivers, railway workers, even construction people, had to be repositioned or newly hired; all of this was accomplished with an absolute minimum—even in the occupied zone—of German personnel or guidance (see below, notes 106 and 107).

On the broadest scale, a preliminary review of the documents makes clear that detention and even deportation (e.g., of children) were largely initiated by French lawyers, with the reactive support (and only later the active insistence) of the Germans. Although my conclusion on this point goes somewhat beyond that of earlier historians such as Marrus and Paxton, they state emphatically that "Any simple [explanation] of German *Diktat* can be dismissed summarily."[78] The following communication illustrates that Vichy legislation originated the policy of detention long before the Germans insisted upon it. In January 1941, Dr. Knochen wrote to the German military:

> Foreign Jews on French soil number one-half of all Jews. The anti-Semitic developments of the past few months indicate that anti-Jewish feelings among the French are mainly directed to these foreign elements. This perspective is indicated by the French regime's legislation, for example the law of 4 October 1940 about French stateless persons of the Jewish race, that gathers them together in concentration camps [*Konzentrationslagern*], as well as makes possible the enforcement of special places of residence.[79]

The debate on burden of proof thus masks an entire underlying reality of French legalistic violence. No wonder government lawyers quickly decided that the individual would have to prove his or her non-Jewishness ("innocence" as even the sympathetic Gillouin put it), a second domain of legalistic rhetoric—the courts—all the more extensively and controversially entered the fray. In the case of *Michel Benaim*, for example, a court in Rabat stated that

> an individual, issued from two Jewish grandparents and two non-Jewish grandparents, who is both baptized according to the Catholic faith and circumcised according to the rites of the Hebraic law, but who has never really belonged to the Catholic religion [must], by reference to Article One, Section Two [of the 2 June statute], be declared Jewish as not having proved his nonadherence to the Jewish religion by an actual membership in one of the other religions recognized by the French state before the law of 9 December 1905.[80]

Elsewhere, a criminal court in Brive decided that two small children had not sufficiently shown their "innocence." Aged two and three, these children had two Jewish and two non-Jewish grandparents; they were both baptized. But the court decided that truly to "belong" to another religion required "une volonté réfléchie et nettement exprimée que ne sauraient posséder des enfants de 2 et 3 ans" (a considered and clearly expressed will that no child of two or three can possess). Their father was thus convicted of not having declared the children to be Jewish.[81]

In contrast to the *Benaim* case—except as to its harsh outcome—was the view of such legal analysts as Dr. Mosse of Perpignan that, at least as regards proof of Jewish ancestry, the personal feelings of the ancestor are irrelevant. Hence, "From the point of view of the Law of 2 June 1941, it is irrelevant to argue the lack of religion or the impurity of race of the Jewish ancestors. The law inquires neither into the religious beliefs nor the greater or lesser racial purity of the ancestors."[82]

More benign civil courts in such jurisdictions as Bergerac, Aix, and Nice were placing the difficult burden of proof on the state.[83] Such insubordination caught the attention both of the CGQJ and its reviewing administrative court, the immensely powerful Conseil d'État; throughout the Vichy period, the Conseil d'État agreed with the CGQJ that the civil courts simply had no jurisdiction over Jewish definitional questions. While, as we shall see, the Conseil d'État gradually broadened the *kinds* of evidence of non-Jewishness it might permit the individual to submit, it rigorously stuck to the views both of its own exclusive jurisdiction and of the individual's bearing the burden of proof.

The Conseil d'État finally seized upon the *Maxudian* case in April 1943, both to illustrate its approach and to declare its sole jurisdiction over this issue. Mme Maxudian had apparently petitioned her local police precinct to remove her name from its list of Jews. When the police failed to respond, and the CGQJ also failed to grant her request, she appealed to the Conseil d'État. That court held as follows, declaring its jurisdiction as an explicit part of its decision:

> Whereas it is stipulated that the petitioner is an issue of two Jewish grand-parents in the maternal line; that, if she produces a document originating from the consistory church of Verdun of the reformed faith from which it appears that her paternal grandparents, Moses and Sarah Lang, received the nuptial benediction in said church, on 14 March 1843, this evidence is not of the sort to establish that neither one nor the other of those people belonged to the Jewish religion, in contrast to the presumption that arises from the entirety of the evidence in the dossier which, apart from such proof, disallows Mme Maxudian from justifying the claim that she cannot be considered a Jewess under the meaning of the law of 2 June 1941.[84]

To cement the point about administrative control over matters of racial definition, the CGQJ several months later insisted that a couple seeking a declaration of their non-Jewishness in order to have removed the Aryan trustee who had been assigned to run their toy store in Béziers be pro-hibited from petitioning the civil tribunal of that town. "It is beyond doubt," said the agency, "that civil judicial tribunals have no competence to declare the Aryan nature of individuals. Only the CGQJ can do that, because only it can issue certificates of non-adherence to the Jewish race.... If the CGQJ should refuse to deliver such a certificate, that person can appeal to the Conseil d'État."[85]

Indeed, on occasion the Conseil d'État *did* overturn a decision of the CGQJ. For an example, consider the case of one *Brigitte Sée* to whose shoe store on the Boulevard Malesherbes in Paris the CGQJ assigned an Aryan administrator ("Administrateur provisoire"); although insisting that Mme Sée had the burden of proof, the Conseil found she satisfied it by showing two non-Jewish grandparents and a third of uncertain religion (the fourth being Jewish), and that she had been baptized at birth.[86] Other frustrations for the CGQJ on this point are exemplified, throughout 1942, by its unavailing attempts to get the minister of justice (Barthélemy) to recognize its claim that ordinary courts did not have the expertise to handle many matters—particularly the aryanization of property—requiring definitions of Jewishness, and so on. The Justice Ministry specifically declined to impose unique jurisdiction on its administrative agency and courts, observing to the CGQJ on February 12, 1942, that, as to at least one of the issues raised, civil tribunals might be especially competent to make decisions:

> I have the honor of informing you that "the judge's belief" on the point of knowing whether a sale transacted before the designation of a provisional administrator eliminates effectively all Jewish influence, comes from an understanding of certain factual and legal elements (the race of the buyer, relationship to the seller, true market value of the property...) about which magistrates and tribunal judges seem specially qualified, as a result of their experience in civil and commercial matters.[87]

The "Certificat de non-appartenance à la race juive" referred to above (at note 85) was the passport to relief from the life-threatening strictures of the racial laws. For hundreds of cases similar to the ones we have noted, the "inside" and "delicate" debate on the meaning of the June 2 statute decided whether the individual would receive such a certificate, exemplified by the one appended here.[88] Such certificates had a near-magical effect, allowing the bearer to avoid the special curfews and travel restrictions imposed on Jews; to fend off Aryan administrators all too eager to take over businesses and real property; to engage in various professions and trades otherwise prohibited to Jews; to avoid, finally, deportation—sometimes at the last minute as lawyers rushed to the internment camp at Drancy with the certificate, thus plucking their clients from the line heading for the bus, heading for the train "to the East."

The CGQJ treasured its monopoly on this jurisdiction, but the civil courts kept finding ways to compete. Throughout 1943, opinions such as the following appeared that at one and the same time claimed civil court jurisdiction over the June 2 statute (infuriating the CGQJ and the Conseil d'État) while also taking a more liberal interpretive approach (thus confusing the jurisprudence and broadening the debate):

> [I]t appears from the [2 June] statute that definition as a Jew is a function of the number and race of the individual's grandparents.
>
> Whereas Charles Touati ... was born on 22 December 1898 in Algiers of Israel and Eugenie Temime, themselves born of unknown fathers and mothers who never acknowledged them;
>
> That there are neither maternal nor paternal grandparents on which his race can be determined;
>
> That thus the law of 2 June 1941 is not applicable to him.
>
> Therefore, it is held that Charles Touati is not Jewish under the meaning of the law of 2 June 1941.[89]

As the war was ending, and even the Conseil d'État could see the handwriting on the wall, it too began opposing the CGQJ. In mid-1944, the latter bitterly attacked its former surest ally for declaring as an Aryan a woman with two Jewish grandparents who had "spontaneously declared herself to be Jewish."[90]

Around the same time, in a CGQJ document ("une perle de la jurisprudence vichyssoise," punned a contemporary observer), the lawyer for a certain M. Élina was advised as follows:

> My dear colleague: In order finally to dispose of this case, which has been pending since 4 February 1943, I would be in your debt if you could have sent to me by a member of the Medical Association a declaration as to whether or not your client benefits from his entire preputial integrity [que votre client jouit de toute son intégrité préputiale].[91]

Sadly, the use of such circumcision data was pervasive, particularly where the state was deemed to have the burden of proof. Civil prosecutors used such data in their rigorous efforts to detect Jews even toward the end of the war. In a case decided as late as May 17, 1944, a Marcel Joseph Weiller narrowly escaped losing his liberty, although he had been hitherto untouched—unlike tens of thousands of other Jews on French soil who had by then been deported. Before the Tribunal civil de première instance of Céret, Weiller was accused of failing to register himself as a Jew, even though the state could not prove that he had at least three Jewish grandparents. Weiller's "crime"? I quote from the opinion of the court:

> [B]eing born of at least two grandparents of that race, he would be Jewish if found to belong himself to the Jewish religion. Weiller's belonging to the Jewish race is apparent from the discovery, in his house, of the Tablets of the Law, and of Hebrew prayers; from the fact that he was circumcised at birth, and, contrary to his allegations, never baptized, the certificate of baptism delivered by the vicar Berges of Toulouse being just an accommodation to him.

Weiller's production of a baptismal certificate, always (as we have seen) less convincing to French courts than to German,[92] availed him little. The court thought it not quite a forgery, but almost so, and they had the evidence of the Jewish sacred objects in Weiller's home, and of a Dr. Cortade that Weiller was indeed circumcised. On the other hand, a maid testified that she had seen Weiller perform certain Catholic rites. Because the state (in this tribunal) had the burden, and because the evidence was equally balanced, Weiller escaped retribution and deportation. On such thin reeds, wispier than the words themselves of which they are made, were fates decided, over and over again, in Vichy France.

The evidence presented in this very late case thus fulfilled the plea of Joseph Haennig, in 1943, that the broadest inquiry be allowed into the Jewishness of the individual: the state should present evidence, and so should the individual, he argued; also, he thought that not only the individual's belonging to a recognized religion should satisfy the courts, but also any other proof that person might be able to mount. This, Haennig advised, using the gentle rhetoric he felt comfortable with at the time, was the approach of the Nazi courts in Germany itself, whose "largeness and objectivity of spirit" he hoped the French would emulate. (For the text of Haennig's article, see pages 138–39).

Haennig's analysis, published in the *Gazette du Palais*, the authoritative reporter of French law, raises dreadful questions, despite its benign aura of liberal, legalistic eloquence. Superficially read, it looks like a well-meaning attempt to limit somewhat the extent of racial oppression. Placed in the context of Vichy rhetoric on Jewish definitional questions, however, it stands as a paradigm for the French legal profession's willingness to abandon allegiance to its textual traditions and to "think the unthinkable, write the unwritable." As I have preliminarily discussed[93] and shall discuss more fully later in this essay, Haennig's statement typifies the immersion in discourse that all too often screens lawyers from the corrupt atmosphere lurking above the surface of their words.

At the turning point of Vichy power, with the Axis armies largely in retreat and the Normandy landing about a year off, Haennig and most of his colleagues were just warming to the jurisprudence of Jewish identity. Gone for the majority of French lawyers were thoughts of the still-existing constitutional guarantees of equal protection, safeguarding of property, and avoidance of ex post facto laws.[94] Instead, considering himself only bound by the internal discourse of the "Jewish question," and not by any external norm, Haennig neatly debated issues that shortly before he would have considered inadmissibly grotesque.

Haennig's apparent lack of viciousness thus makes his case compelling for us today. Scores of lawyers like Haennig—even more than those few who relished the infliction of suffering upon the Jews—made that suffering possible. Once the Nazi state and its courts could be cited *by a main-stream lawyer* as providing any kind of a model on race issues, French law became unanchored—dashing toward its own doom with no one at the helm but the most recently published rhetoricians.[95]

For any lawyer in 1943 who might still have wavered on the professional propriety of debating racial laws in "free" as well as occupied France, Haennig's seeming benevolence must surely have been persuasive. If such a man, trying to narrow the already overly broad French definition of Jew, could discourse freely on such a subject, surely it had now become acceptable practice. And, indeed, the French bar (always remarkably autonomous from governmental control) had by then taken the statute to its bosom, nurtured it, discovered its defects and its strengths, and—like the parents of a still youthful upstart—discussed its future with a combination of wariness and optimism.[96]

## LANDLORD AND TENANT

Another broad body of case law, perhaps less well known to the bar, and apparently of less interest to government lawyers, exemplifies the seamless web of litigation I indicated earlier. In its interweaving of various strands of French legislation, it further indicates how agonizing and unstable Vichy law became once it substituted—Haennig-like—the freedom of the discursive moment for the constraint of constitutional ideals. By a decree of September 26, 1939—predating by a year all racial laws—any tenant who had been mobilized for the war could benefit from a 75 percent reduction in rent during the period of his military service.[97] Furthermore, the decree permitted tenants the right to reductions, even after mobilization, if debilitated, economically or otherwise, by "a circumstance of war" (un fait de guerre).[98]

The question to which dozens of lawyers and judges had to turn was whether Jews disadvantaged by the June 2, 1941, statute could benefit from the rent reduction prescribed by the September 26, 1939, decree. The latter, of course, was silent as to Jews. Lawyers for landlords who might never have seen the racial statutes, and lawyers for Jews who had been living with them on a daily basis, now had to use their skills to harmonize two unrelated statutes and to use them for their clients.

No documents have surfaced indicating any interest by the German occupiers in this jurisprudence, even though most of the cases arose in occupied Paris. Here was a purely internal matter of law, subject (even more so than in the rhetoric we have just examined) only to the usual discourse among lawyers and judges. Many landlords, faced with Jewish tenants unable to pay their rent, went to court to evict. From mid-1941 until the end of the war, before justices of the peace in many of Paris's twenty arrondissements, before other civil courts of original jurisdiction, and before various courts of appeal, lawyers argued the legal niceties of the September 26, 1939, decree on rent reductions.

As developed regarding the June 2 statute, so here (so everywhere that the interpretive community of French lawyers focused its attention) the debate was confined narrowly to several issues. The main question was whether unemployment, detention, or deportation constituted a "circumstance of war," so that victims might claim the rent reduction; or whether the French government had acted quite apart from the war, actions that might constitute a "fait du prince" (act of state). In the latter instance, the tenants or their survivors would not be granted rent reductions. The vicissitudes of legal argument further created a minidebate on whether the results of the anti-Jewish climate might not have been a circumstance of war *prior* to June 2 1941, and an act of state afterward. Because it *was* a Vichy statute, now applicable to the occupied zone as well, the June 2 law marked a reasonable date to infer purely French activity of a racially restrictive nature, arguably unconnected with the war.

Further squabbles arose as to whether detention might be seen as a circumstance of war (whenever arising), while "mere" loss of job an act of state. Also, in the resolution stage of the trials, courts had to decide whether the rent reduction (set by the decree at 75 percent for any period of actual mobilization) should be the same or less when the circumstance of war was forced unemployment, detention, or deportation.

What developed is unique in the jurisprudence of the Vichy years. Courts of first jurisdiction overwhelmingly allowed some rent reduction to the Jewish tenants. Yet the manner in which even favorable decisions were rendered served to promote uncertainty and confusion among similarly situated tenants who could not, chose not to, or would only later litigate the question of their monthly rent. The case law here, like Joseph Haennig's "benign" approach to the June 2 statute, forces on the analyst an inquiry as to the effect of seemingly benign legal discourse that chooses to work with—rather than to challenge centrally—a grotesque superstructure of law.

I will emphasize two courts of original jurisdiction, because they decided more cases than any other on this point. These are the justices of the peace of the 20th and 11th arrondissements of Paris itself. We will see that each court—again quite independently of the Germans, of the French administrative structure, and of much appellate jurisprudence—chose to define the questions before it in fascinating and troubling ways. While each, although arguably contradicted by a Paris appeals court decision that will be analyzed, favored the tenants' claims, they did so in conflicting ways. Their case law finally failed to give heart or even certainty to a Jewish community desperate for anchoring, for solace, and for some sign of resistance by the French legal establishment.

I begin with the 20th arrondissement. In a typical case, the justice of the peace there found for a M. *Bankhelter,* who received the full 75 percent reduction for his army period (four months) and 35 percent for his period in detention, which the court formulaically asserted to be "by order of the Occupying authorities." This court viewed forced detention as a "circumstance of war," and it relieved Bankhelter of that much of his rent from the date of his internment until the date of the decision on December 12, 1942, a period of nineteen months.[99]

The 20th arrondissement had already developed a small body of case law on this issue. On June 19, 1941, in the *Lerman* case, the court allowed a nonveteran a 70 percent reduction for having been fired the year before, leaving him since then without resources.[100] While there is no discussion of the cause of Lerman's unemployment, it seems probable that he demonstrated its link to the racial laws. And in *Baraban,* decided July 30, 1942, a detainee at the camp at Beaunes la Rolande was relieved of 75 percent of his rent obligation during his mobilization and 50 percent since his internment some fourteen months prior to the decision.

*Baraban* begins to demonstrate some of the effect of rhetorical maneuvering on the development of these laws. It is thus worth quoting in part:

> Whereas his incarceration . . . by the Occupying authorities could not flow from the Law of 2 June 1941, since the arrest was prior to that date (14 May 1941) but is in fact a circumstance of war;
> Whereas this arrest has resulted in depriving him of all resources that he might have had as an artisan-tailor, although Jewish,[101] as long as he conformed to the laws concerning Jewish work . . . ;
> [Thus, the court orders the reduction in rent.][102]

The first quoted paragraph is disingenuous. There was already a Vichy-authored racial law of October 3, 1940, in effect when Baraban was arrested and detained;[103] neither it nor the June 2 statute authorized the random arrest and special incarceration inflicted on people like Baraban. On the other hand, other Vichy statutes specifically condoning the detention of Jews, and their placement into special camps, had also long been on the books prior to Baraban's arrest.[104] One of these, the law of October 4, 1940, stated:

> Foreigners of the Jewish race can, as of the promulgation of this law, be interned in special camps by the decision of the prefecture of the Department in which they live.[105]

The *Baraban* court failed to mention any of these statutes, preferring to situate its rhetoric as a legalistic argument distinguishing pre–June 2,

1941, arrests as clear "circumstances of war" from later ones, which might be acts of state. This is not the only time we will see lawyers and judges feeling comfortable when they establish narrow and quite artificial zones within which to structure their discussions. The *Baraban* judges, like many Vichy lawyers, chose a low level of discursive generalization: by focusing on the June 2 statute, they avoided dealing with the earlier October 4, 1940, detention statute that would be more difficult to rationalize. Furthermore, the term "Occupying authorities" begs the question—often begged in these cases—of who actually *did* the arresting of Jews during the Vichy years. We know by now, at least, that the French police did almost all the actual detaining of Jews until mid-1944. The Germans devoted almost no manpower to the process.[106] Indeed, during the month of the *Baraban* decision, judges and other citizens of Paris had observed with their own eyes, or at least heard about, the infamous roundups (or "rafles") of thousands of Parisian Jews by hundreds of Parisian police on July 16–17, 1942. The police, with little or no German backing, herded the terrified Jews into crowded houses in the various neighborhoods, and from there to the Velodrome d'Hiver. It was, for most of them, a matter of days until transfer to Drancy and, ultimately, Auschwitz.[107]

Why did the *Baraban* court, together with most of its colleagues in the other arrondissements, come to use the formula "arretés par les autorités de l'Occupation?"[108] A simple answer would be that it was employing what I have elsewhere called "considerate communication,"[109] that it was hiding from its various audiences the troubling truth that, from the earliest days of Vichy, the French (without German help) were arresting Jews both in the occupied and unoccupied zones, by force of their own statutes.

Whatever the motive, it is worth reflecting for a moment on the *legal effect* of the three cases from the 20th arrondissement so far described—*Bankhelter*, *Lerman*, and *Baraban*. What might the family of a detained Jew, arrested *after* June 2 1941 (eventually the vast majority) argue to that apparently sympathetic court in an effort to gain a rent reduction? Nothing in the jurisprudence so far would allow the argument that post–June 2 1941, arrests constituted "circumstances of war," because the jurisprudence universally involved arrests prior to that date. The court might have taken a stance from the beginning forthrightly recognizing that most of the victimization of Jews was a phenomenon of *Vichy law*, but bearing a cause-and-effect relationship to the war and hence covered by the September 26, 1939, decree. (Such an approach was used in the

*Krouck* case, to be discussed momentarily.) This approach would have empowered *all* suffering Jewish tenants to acquire rent reductions. Instead the court consistently left open the central questions that a lawyer more constrained by constitutional text should have asked.

As we saw with the rhetorical approach taken to the June 2 1941, definitions themselves, the piecemeal, tunnel-vision resolution of specific contests—even if producing a benign outcome in the individual case—had the effect of disempowering vast categories of people who came later. And rarely, even in these unique landlord-tenant cases, did any lawyer or court attempt at the beginning to ask different sets of questions that might more broadly have challenged the legislative scheme altogether.[110]

Indeed, the legalistic distinction (itself based on a fiction) drawn in *Baraban* between arrests made prior to the June 2 statute and those subsequent to it gained authoritative legalistic acceptance.[111] The fiction both ignored Vichy detention and race legislation (from at least October 3 and 4, 1940, until June 2, 1941) and left open whether the latter was a circumstance of war or an act of state. Analogous to the swift tide of rhetoric that made the June 2 statute unchallengeable at its rotten core, this argument deflected attention from the pervasiveness of French anti-Semitic statutory activity long before June 2, 1941.[112] It disabled the families of thousands of Jews, who were arrested *after* June 2, 1941, from arguing with any probability of success in that arrondissement.

The 11th arrondissement, on the other hand, took the bull by the horns in a February 1943 decision that faced more squarely the long history of Jewish incarceration by Vichy law. It adopted, in the *Krouck* case,[113] the rhetorical variation I mentioned earlier. *Krouck* held that, since the first such Vichy law (dated September 3, 1940)[114] stated explicitly that "the effects of this measure, circumscribing individual rights, will end with the war," all subsequent detention laws must—a fortiori—also be connected with the hostilities, by now long since over. The 11th arrondissement, unlike the 20th, thus admitted the Vichy origins of laws detaining Jews (laws that predated the June 2 statute by nine months), but used statutory interpretation to connect those French laws with the war. Thus Krouck, detained for the simple reason of being a stateless Jew,[115] received a rent reduction of 50 percent.[116]

The same court would use this reasoning a month later to help another detainee. In the March 1943 case of *Eisenberg*, again in the 11th arrondissement, the landlord was forced, by the *Krouck* case, to become even more explicit about French influence on anti-Jewish legislation and punishment. He argued, frankly but unsuccessfully, as follows:

> Eisenberg, who was interned for being Jewish, cannot claim a rent reduction [under the Decree of 26 September 1939, etc.]. As an act of state [*fait du prince*], the legislation imposed in occupied and nonoccupied France cannot be causally connected with an Act of War. . . . It applies to all of France and is of unlimited duration; it will remain in effect until the Legislator rescinds it.

Using its earlier reasoning from *Krouck*, the court was now able to admit both the French origins of internment laws *and* their causal connection to the war. It rejected the landlord's argument and ordered a 40 percent rent reduction.

Thus, while the 11th and 20th arrondissements found ways to grant relief to some Jewish tenants, their differing rhetoric created confusion among the families of many other Jews potentially seeking such relief later. The 11th arrondissement, by freely admitting French authorship and activity in anti-Jewish legislation of all kinds, produced a more realistic rhetoric but nonetheless used statutory interpretation to grant rent reductions; the 20th, on the other hand, used a formulaic approach to create less forthright distinctions that kept similarly situated Jews in the dark about their rights. No wonder that the Jewish legal service of the Union générale des Israélites français (UGIF),[117] in advising hundreds of tenants and even their landlords' lawyers, could not rely on this jurisprudence to make legalistic distinctions with any confidence.

In countless such situations, disequilibrated by the jurisprudence, Jews were first advised to ask their landlords to decide the matter "à l'amiable"—without recourse to litigation. Thus for example, in October 1942 the UGIF offered its help to the *Topolanski* family, whose breadwinner had been arrested and deported after the enactment of the June 2, 1941, statute; the UGIF, despite the tenant-favorable cases already on the books, had to write prayerfully to the landlord's lawyer, a certain M. Poisson, as follows:

> May we not try to arrive at a friendly agreement here . . . ?
> Mr. Topolanski, employed before the war in the Commercial Pharmaceutical Office, volunteered at the beginning of hostilities. He always paid his rent fully and on time.
> On 20 August 1941, he was interned at the camp in Drancy, on the order of the Occupation authorities. He was freed on 5 November for reasons of health; but on 16 July 1942, he was again arrested and on the 22d of the same month deported to an unknown place. His wife has had no news of him since then.

Mrs. Topolanski has remained behind with three young children of 7, 5½, and 20 months, and without any source of funds. She has been described to us as particularly worthy of note.

Could you not, under these conditions, ask your client . . . if he could grant these pitiful tenants a reduction of 50 percent. . . .

We ourselves will guarantee that M. Poisson receives the balance of the rents due from these tenants.[118]

Other cases at the level of original jurisdiction might have afforded some consolation—as the horrors of the Jewish experience in both zones increased—to the UGIF and to potential Jewish tenants or their survivors. But they provided no doctrinal anchoring, no sense of predictability. On the contrary, their rhetoric, and even their disposition of cases, showed more variation than we have seen as between the courts in the 11th and 20th arrondissements.

For example, in a suburban case, the justice of the peace reduced the rent of M. *Buch*, who had volunteered for the war, returned, and then found himself arrested. There are two interesting aspects of this case. First, the court, unlike most others even in this area, does not hesitate to characterize vividly the plight of Buch's wife and children since his arrest: "His wife and three children are in a state of total deprivation [*dans le plus grand complet de dénument*], their subsistence available only through charities." Second, the court allows, as a remedy, the full 75 percent reduction, "until the end of the duration of hostilities," a strange but wonderful formulation in view of the cease-fire of June 22, 1940![119]

*Jewish landladies*, who lost their property due to the June 2, 1941, laws were handed back (Kafka-like) some relief of a legalistic sort by this body of cases. Thus, the justice of the peace of the 3d arrondissement, in *Dreyfuss-Pignon*, allowed a 60 percent reduction in the rent of a woman whose *own* real property no longer brought her rentals because it had been aryanized and was now under the control of an administrator.[120]

The related case of hostages—those Jews taken randomly and specially as reprisals for attacks on Germans—was unproblematic, particularly in view of the doctrine that had developed. By May 1942 a justice of the peace of the 13th arrondissement could observe that the case of the hostage was already part of the "Doctrine et de la jurisprudence" of the decree of September 26, 1939.[121] Hostage-taking was, indeed, a German activity, although the Vichy Ministry of Justice under Barthélemy collaborated in the creation of the infamous *sections spéciales* that came to try and often execute such hostages.

Just as troublesome and disequilibrating was the only authoritative appeals court case that seems to have come down on this point of landlord-tenant law. In the case, decided September 29, 1941, the *Chambre des référés* of the Cour de Paris unfortunately decided to construe each of the two doctrines I ascribed to the 11th and 20th arrondissements in a manner detrimental to the Jewish tenant, a doctor. First, the court held (unlike the 20th arrondissement) that even very early legislation was of Vichy origin: the August and September 1940 decrees restricting the practice of medicine by Jews were deemed pure acts of Vichy administrative law. Second (unlike the 11th arrondissement), this court specifically declined to associate that legislation with the necessities of war:

> As to that last order of administrative law [the decree of 16 August 1940 prohibiting such practice[122]], it cannot be said that it bears a cause-and-effect relationship to the war; rather it derives from measures adopted by the Legislator[123] that might have been taken in circumstances having nothing to do with the war.[124]

Thus, the doctor was allowed his 75 percent reduction dating from his mobilization until September 10, 1940, the exact date when he was informed by the French police that he could no longer practice medicine because of the racial laws. But he was not permitted any other reduction in rent under the September 29, 1939, decree.

The appeals court's frank admission that the racial policy of France was unconnected with the war not only again confirms this essay's first corollary, but seems to run counter to the earlier cases discussed.[125] It stood as an authoritative roadblock to any sense of understanding (even under this uniquely benign set of cases) that impoverished and terrified Jewish tenants might bring to the laws that controlled their fate.

Synthesizing these cases, in an official memorandum from its legal department in late 1943 or early 1944, the UGIF parses the law with combined rhetorical considerateness and legalistic opportunism. First, the UGIF deemed it prudent to avoid the central reality of the Vichy years, and the implied holding of the Paris appeals court: that French lawyers and policemen consistently outperformed in their anti-Semitism the fondest wishes—much less demands—of the conqueror.[126] The UGIF construed the cases as follows, drawing an interesting distinction between detention and loss of work:

> In fact, if it cannot be denied that the head of the French state has promulgated a number of laws and decrees about Jews; these texts limit the activity of Jews, either by restricting them in their trades or certain professions, or in creating for them a special Law, but none of these texts involves deprivation

of liberty [sic],[127] none orders the placement in an internment camp of Jews [sic] because of their Jewish origin [sic].

On the other hand, the Occupation authorities have rendered a number of ordinances regarding Jews in the occupied zone (nine to this date),[128] not only measures analogous to those taken by the Head of the French state, but also a certain number of restrictions on their liberty. . . .[129]

Finally, at different times, and for the first time in May 1941 . . . Jewish males were arrested, sometimes with the assistance of lists compiled by the Occupying authorities, sometimes just on the mention of the word "Juif" on identity cards.[130] Soon, Jewish females were made the object of identical measures. . . .

Some categories of Jews have been specially targeted, for example on 21 August 1941: arrests of all [sic] Jewish lawyers.[131]

These are measures taken by the Occupation authority, which have struck all categories of Jews, both French and naturalized. . . .[132] If it cannot be denied that such measures, imposed by the Head of State, restraining or suppressing activity, may not, according to the cases, permit a rent reduction by application of the Decree of 26 September 1939—since "such measures would have been passed in circumstances other than of war (Paris Appeals Court decision of 9/29/41)," the situation is different for internment measures taken by the Occupation authorities solely for reasons of war. . . . It is clear that under these conditions, internment in the camp at Drancy must be considered a consequence of the state of war.[133]

We have no subsequent decisions confirming the UGIF's analysis. We are left with a body of legal rhetoric, racially favorable to a class of Jewish litigants but finally also contributing to the terror as it further legitimated racial jurisprudence. The case law's ambiguities certainly afforded relief to those Jewish tenants—or their families—who might eventually fall within the developing doctrine. But to the many Jews in the 20th arrondissement who were arrested after June 2, 1941; to those advised by lawyers of the appeals court's decision that only job-related loss, and not loss of liberty, could be ascribed to the French state; and to those in the 11th arrondissement who saw the contrary confirmed by the court, which recognized that their own countrymen, and not the Germans, were responsible for the incarceration of men, women, and children—for them these cases created only further confusion and terror.

Landlord-tenant law in the France of 1940–1944 again indicates that professional rhetoric that disregards long traditions of professional behavior is unacceptable even as it appears to be "doing good." The next and final section of this essay analyzes the theoretical implications of this empirical observation.

## LAW AND LITERATURE

Having perused two bodies of French wartime legal doctrine, we are ready to return to my claim about the insufficiency of fluid, situational discourse in moments of crisis. Where, as in Vichy France, legal rhetoric is permitted to float free, it contributes to—perhaps even creates—the most dire consequences. We have seen demonstrated the corollary claim that Vichy legal discourse resulted in activity that far surpassed the racial demands of France's German conquerors.[134] Of this claim, Richard Posner has imprudently written:

> There was indeed much anti-Semitism in France before and during World War II, but the proposition that France would have tried on its own, as it were, to exterminate the Jews, or that it embraced genocide more enthusiastically than Germany did, cannot be taken seriously.[135]

We have not yet reached the point in our own discourse that merely assertive rhetoric such as this will block the clear-eyed analysis, by interested audiences, of historical realities. I have shown that Philippe Serre, a hero of the Vichy years and a man who is very moderate otherwise in his critique of French lawyers, blames on the French the racial policy that brought death to 75,000 Jews from French soil.[136] Contrary to Posner's blithe assertion, the most comprehensive historians of the period agree with at least the part of my conclusion that Vichy racism, in many key respects, outdid that of Germany (see note 53). Also, the legal documentation gathered for this essay considerably expands upon earlier findings in this regard (see especially notes 70–79, 104, 105, and 107).

Posner's statement, typical of authoritative attempts to affect interpretive communities by rhetoric rather than reality, will not permit the possibility—which I would now call the probability—that the French were more zealous than their German conquerors in pursuing a deadly racial policy through French law. Posner's only support for his incredulous attitude is that "three-fourths of the Jews in France (many of them refugees from Nazism rather than French nationals) survived the war and that the Vichy government tried to protect at least French Jews from the Nazis, and, more generally, to dissociate itself from the 'Final Solution'."[137]

This is a curious piece of rhetoric. First, Posner's fractional estimates do not square with those of, say, Xavier Vallat himself (see above, note 44). Still, Posner's view that three-fourths of the French Jews "survived the war" is generally held to be true.[138] But no inference of admirable governmental conduct flows from any such cold fraction. In countries with far less autonomy than France, far fewer Jews (proportionately) were lost. Then there is Posner's parenthetical phrase, which, like Vichy itself, seems to distinguish between French and foreign Jews. Yet, finally, the French regime proved ready even to sacrifice "its own."[139]

As for deportations, "the first convoy consisting of French Jews only left on 13 February 1943."[140] Posner also misrepresents French behavior insofar as he claims it even tried to dissociate itself from the "Final Solution."[141] French law brought about, and French lawyers actively bargained for, deportations "to the East" (see notes 104 and 105). It can no longer credibly be maintained that the government, at least Laval and the CGQJ, did not suspect the fate of those deported.[142] Marrus and Paxton hedge, in the general diplomatic spirit of their fine book, but seem to conclude that, at least once deportations began from Vichy itself, Laval knew the horrid outcome.[143] And, unofficially, many contemporary diarists of the period knew from their own eyes the plight and foreseeable destiny of Jews deported from Vichy soil.[144]

But even if the French lawyers had not *deliberately* sought to aggravate the condition of Jews on their soil, even if they managed to remain blissfully ignorant of the deportations, we might still seek an explanation for their merely abiding the anti-Semitic innovations of 1940-1944. The constitutional and egalitarian assumptions of one hundred and fifty years would as little point to "neutral" tolerance,[145] as to zealous advocacy for such grotesque laws and policies. Posner is too anxious to be "taken seriously" himself to disregard the issues raised by French wartime legalism.

I turn to Posner's related critique of my earlier approach to what by now might be called "Haennig's Choice."[146] I observe centrally that an allegiance to French constitutional text and tradition was possible even under the eyes of the occupiers,[147] and that Haennig could have mounted a "jugular" attack on the system if he had so desired without risking life or limb. I further suggest that French lawyers, as a minimal position, always retained the option of remaining silent, and that Haennig's very decision to publish equivocal words seems careerist at best, immoral at worst.

Through a challenge to the now influential claims of Stanley Fish, I proceed in this section to suggest that it may be possible to abstract from the everyday practice of law a series of norms that might constrain French (or, someday, American) lawyers from again violating egalitarian traditions as the Vichy lawyers clearly did. By making a modest move in the direction of Owen Fiss and his "disciplining rules,"[148] I thus confirm that constitutional norms deserved to be used as a standard by French lawyers apart from the situational discourse that led them to accept, debate, and, in effect, further the anticonstitutional racial laws.

More strongly, perhaps, I then move to my second corollary: that interpretive theory must at least *allow for* the positing of such norms as absolute constraints upon the day-to-day practice of law. However difficult the distinction may be between disciplining rules and everyday rhetoric, the example of Vichy mandates a theoretical posture recognizing the difference. For theory *does* affect practice; the abandonment of textural standards behind the momentary needs of the Vichy legal interpretive community resulted from a long-standing theoretical posture of text-avoidance or even text-denial within that community. If postmodern theories such as Fish's prevail, they will create an atmosphere in the practice that risks replication of the Vichy experience.

## Richard Posner on "Haennig's Choice"

Richard Posner has come to the defense of Joseph Haennig. As to my finding grotesque Haennig's reasoning, his benign view of Nazi authorities, and his basic acceptance of the racial scheme adopted by Vichy lawyers, Posner says:

> I am unwilling to accept Weisberg's verdict. Although Haennig's article contains no hint of disapproval of the racial laws, it would not have been published if it had. It does not praise the laws. The only thing praised is a German decision that saved a woman who was half-Jewish from the gas chamber. The article may have saved some French half-Jews. Indeed, it may have saved more lives than if Haennig had thrown up his law practice and joined the Resistance. . . . Maybe he thought the racial laws grotesque but knew it would not help to let his feelings show in the article. What would Weisberg have Haennig *do*?
>
> It is true that if most Frenchmen had refused to collaborate with the Nazis, the Jews of France would have been better off than they were by receiving small crumbs of assistance from the likes of Haennig. But the problem with mass defiance . . . is, who shall step forward first?[149]

Posner observes, speculatively, that the Haennig piece "would not have been published" if it were overtly resistant to the racial laws. The statement ignores far more explosive public declarations already known to the bar, by such eminent lawyers as Léon Blum and his own attorneys during the political trials at Riom.[150] True, Blum was already imprisoned when he made his subversive remarks (although they could not have endeared him to the court or to the Vichy and German leaders who were in attendance), but his lawyers challenged the very constitutionality of the Vichy regime, of its legislation, of the trial, and so forth, and went totally unpunished. Indeed, Justice Minister Barthélemy later dined and drank with the defense counsel, feeling powerless to stop the antigovernment rhetoric of Blum, the "Jew" to whom the formally "liberal" minister of justice refers in the handwritten contemporaneous scribbling I append here (see appendix 14.7).

Blum and his lawyers were not unique in "publishing" far more controversial language than Haennig might have risked for his article. The head of the Paris Bar Association, Jacques Charpentier, twice petitioned Pétain directly and unambiguously, at some risk to himself and to his organization.[151] He was demanding, first of all, that separation of powers and right to counsel be observed in the very trial of Blum I have just mentioned; second, he protested with vigor the government's attempt to pass upon membership applications for the Paris bar. The outcome he sought was achieved in both cases.

These protesting lawyers, whose views constituted direct attacks on the government and were publicly known, suffered no losses. Haennig, writing analytically about a body of laws already strongly disputed, might well have had "published" at least *some* language implicitly attacking the very soundness—the "Frenchness," so to speak—of the racial laws. But he chose not to. Here we must seek explanation not in a simplistic and anachronistic view of the Nazis in France as an all-terrorizing or all-censoring authority. *Everything* was in flux in Vichy France, always. Haennig's refusal to challenge the laws at their corrupt heart was typical and collegial, but it was not absolutely mandated.

If he did not go that route, we need to ask why. Perhaps the answer lies somewhere in the following remarkable passage from Charpentier. The head of the Paris bar, so courageous when his vital interests were attacked, said this—*after the war*—about the racial statutes' ostracism of newly admitted Jewish lawyers:

> At the Paris Bar, there had always been a Jewish problem. A number of refugees had a conception of justice very different from our own. . . . Since 1940, a law excluded the sons of such refugees from the profession of law. For several prior years, this type of measure was strongly desired by the Paris Bar. . . . Before the war, we were invaded by those recently naturalized, almost all of eastern origin, whose language was ridiculed by the Press, thus covering us with shame. They brought to the conduct of their practice the customs of their bazaars. In this respect, the Vichy policies comported with our own professional interests, but I only envisioned their application after the fact.[152]

Charpentier and his bar association—unlike their colleagues in Belgium who uniformly protested to a far less independent government the ostracism of their Jewish colleagues[153]—went along with the Vichy statutes. Only rarely were there even mild protests, for example in 1941 when forty Jewish lawyers, some quite prominent, were randomly arrested in Paris.[154] For reasons clear from Charpentier's postwar prose (but having nothing to do with Posner's theory of enforced restrictions on debate), Charpentier chose to criticize not the laws themselves but only their ex post facto application. His choice of discursive center, like Haennig's, was benignly unthreatening to the system's bloodstream.

The example of Charpentier indicates that French lawyers felt empowered to challenge directly some Vichy laws and procedures, but that they almost always fell short of focusing their discourse on the jugular of the corrupt new legislation.[155] Yet the example of Blum and his lawyers at Riom demonstrates the availability—without sanction—of jugular protest.[156] Thus Posner is naive in asserting that Haennig "would not have been published" if he had protested the laws themselves. More troublingly still, Posner reveals his beliefs about professionalism by implying—without reflection—that *publication* should have been a goal of Haennig's in any event. The phrase endorses axiomatically the drive to get published, whatever the context and the other rhetorical or ethical options available to a lawyer acting within it. Posner thus slips in *as an assumption* what is in fact most controversial in Haennig's choice.

Suppose, against the evidence but in line with Posner's declaration, that Haennig indeed could not have been published if he had chosen to attack the jugular? Then why did he choose to publish at all? There are only four possible answers. First, Haennig may have been delighted with, or indifferent to, the racist aspects of Vichy law. Second, even if discomfited by the latter, he may have decided to enhance his career by whatever pragmatic means were available. (Indeed, Haennig's views became authoritative in magisterial circles.)[157]

Yet if either of these was Haennig's position, we surely cannot condone his drive to see his name in print, however benign his analysis seems on first blush. But his decision seems no more edifying if we assume the third possibility: that he strongly opposed the laws but decided to publish a conciliatory analysis that largely accepted their premises. If this were true, he appears to have either lacked some of his colleagues' courage in denying the validity itself of the racial legislation or (less likely) to have been unaware of such collegial precedents. But even here, Haennig had a better option, the one assumed away by Posner's sense of professionalism.

Surely Haennig, faced with these latter feelings, might have adopted what I would call the "rhetoric of silence"—the eloquent refusal to pour additional verbal fuel onto a flamingly corrupt discursive mass. Posner fails even to consider silence as a professional option in Vichy-type situations. I will forgo the urge to see here a careerist program unmindful of ethical considerations, or to elaborate at this time on the risks for lawyers of needing constantly to talk. Instead, I will come to the fourth and most edifying explanation for Haennig's choice: he detested the legislation but thought that his specific analysis might do some good to some unfortunates already subject to it.

This proves at least as problematic as the earlier explanations for Haennig's choice. For what Posner himself calls the article's mere "crumbs," thrown by Haennig to a starving community of oppressed people, turn out to be poisoned. Like all legalistic rhetoric situating itself at the then-prevalent discursive center (such as the landlord-tenant cases previously discussed in this essay), Haennig's seemingly benign rhetoric immediately implicated if not condemned thousands of similarly situated individuals who *could not carry* the new burden of proof proposed by his analysis.

In other words, each legalistic piece that played the game of "drawing the line" (i.e., "interpreting" the Vichy racial laws), in effect tightened the noose around the majority of oppressed people, for such rhetoric further legitimated the overall scheme of victimization. One person, say, can prove that going to the synagogue did not imply real Jewish faith; the next dozen cannot. If the line had not been drawn to protect the first, some other line might have been drawn to protect the dozen. Or lawyers might have resisted the temptation to draw *any* lines, thus bringing the system to a complete halt. Analogously, one tenant, say, in the 20th arrondissement, can show that her husband was arrested prior to June 2, 1941; so she gains a rent reduction and is not thrown out on the street. But if the next tenant was (like most Jews) arrested *after* that date, then no relief is afforded—indeed no defense is available and the courts are not used at all. But if the *first* piece of legal rhetoric had drawn the line more favorably to *all* potential claimants of rent reductions, or if magistrates had quickly begun to express disapproval of the racial scheme altogether, the "crumbs" would have immediately changed into a fuller meal for Vichy's famished Jews.

## Stanley Fish and the Denial of "Text"

Stanley Fish has not as yet commented on the nexus between his well-known interpretive theories and the events described generally as the

Holocaust (and discussed in their French legalistic guise throughout this essay). But his powerful endorsement of the view that professional norms cannot exist apart from the practices of the community allegedly bound by those norms must eventually run up against holocaustic barriers. For Fish, only the situation constrains the professional, and never any set of beliefs "objectively" available to that person or his colleagues. For him, there is simply no recourse to anything but the situation:

> [C]ommunication occurs within situations. . . . [T]o be in a situation is already to be in possession of (or possessed by) a structure of assumptions, or practices understood to be relevant in relation to purposes and goals that are already in place; and it is within the assumption of these purposes and goals that any utterance is *immediately* heard.[158]

This passage, which might serve as an ex post facto apology for Joseph Haennig's essay, establishes on a theoretical level the notion that ideals, norms, beliefs, can *never* constrain professional behavior. In a sense, for Fish, these latter elements simply have no independent existence, for they are naught but a function of the practice—at any given moment—of the community ostensibly bound by them. This community is always free to incorporate into its practice—or to eject from it—earlier understandings of normative conduct.

Nor, for Fish, can any *text* ever bind a practitioner, because no text exists apart from that practitioner and the community to which he belongs:

> Strictly speaking, getting "back to the text" is not a move one can perform, because the text one gets back to will be the text demanded by some other interpretation and that interpretation will be presiding over its production.[159]

The text, like the norm or foundational belief, exists not separately from the community employing it but instead *within* that community. For Fish, it never stands apart from us—rather, it *is* us. Our very sense of what the text is arises from the latest interpretation of the text rather than from anything "within it"; nothing is "within it" except that interpretation.

In a well-known debate with Fish, Owen Fiss argues for the existence of texts and beliefs apart from the interpretive community.[160] A judge, for example, deciding a case under our Constitution, is bound by norms of interpretive conduct that discipline behavior at the time of decision making. And the Constitution, for Fiss, yields meanings (i.e., constrains the reader or interpretive community from purely self-generated or subjective conduct). For Fish, there is no such extrinsic discipline, no way to etch into stone either an interpretive strategy or a set of professional ethics. Instead the standards of professional conduct are determined at any moment by solely internal, situational factors, not by any "objective" or foundational definitions. More recently, and most portentously, Fish has put it this way: "[I]t is the conditions currently obtaining in the profession rather than any set of independent and abiding criteria that determine what is significant and meritorious."[161]

Were it not for the example of Vichy law, I might find myself in substantial theoretical agreement with Fish.[162] It is very difficult to "prove" the existence of any entity sufficiently outside a practice to constrain (objectively) those situated within it. The constraints, as Fish argues, are inside the practice. But, however difficult the task, I am inclined to move toward Fiss' position, because I am convinced that Vichy constrains us, so to speak, to *seek* the constraint of disciplining rules. Were French lawyers culturally attuned to reverence for text instead of textual manipulation (another point I will consider at greater length in a later book), I am convinced they would have sought in larger numbers to reject as outside the bounds of constitutional and procedural French norms these strange racial laws.[163]

Thus, although Fish always consoles his audiences by saying that there is no causal connection between his theory and anyone's practice (he must, of course, because to say otherwise would be to contradict the theoretical premise that there are no norms apart from practice, including *his* norms), I contend that such a connection always exists. If practitioners have been trained to see text as nothing but themselves, they will so act in times of crisis. If they are trained to see texts as apart, they will more likely insist on the primacy of such texts above their own contextual needs and impulses. And since the constitutive French texts would have yielded principled opposition to the jugular vein of Vichy racism, the dreadful results of 1940–1944 might have been avoided.[164]

So the example of Vichy rhetoric knocks out Fish's contention that the "significant and meritorious" can ever be exclusively determined by "conditions currently obtaining in the profession."[165] For there is little of the "meritorious" in the practice of Vichy law, and the only "significant" aspect of it was its demonstration that we must seek—however difficult the task—"independent and abiding criteria" to guide us as legal professionals. Vichy lawyers, as we have seen, were themselves capable of applying their foundational ethics to a critique of the new regime; so it is not merely my analysis that rejects Vichy behavior as nonmeritorious. But most Vichy lawyers, like most Fishian professionals, rested easy with the *theoretical* assumption that their legal rhetoric was situationally, and in no other way, constrained. This is what we must now avoid.

Vichy teaches that practice normatively unconstrained from the notion of "text" is only as good as the values of its most articulate practitioner. Liberated from the smallest allegiance to textual concepts held dear for one hundred fifty years until the moment of Vichy's collaboration with the victorious Germans, Vichy lawyers were able to foster radical change, not the incremental type with which Fish consoles us. The radical move once made—that racial legislation was interpretively acceptable—lawyers went about their business splitting hairs, or, to shift to Posner's metaphor about Haennig, throwing crumbs.

The lesson of Vichy is that professional communities *cannot* accept theories denying the objective existence of texts. They must resist such theories, yet fight to understand what is meant by textuality as something apart from any reader or group of readers, and then substantively learn to evaluate the motives and subjective biases from which all texts are generated. The battleground for us now is the battleground of texts, not of situationalist theory.

Vichy lawyers generated rhetoric that directly led to the concentration camps "in the East." Their willingness to draft laws in a manner often exceeding the German conquerors' demands set precedents even the Nuremberg laws and Nazi courts had not imagined; their subsequent zeal in interpreting that legislation, unconstrained by traditional (textual) French notions of egalitarianism and personal freedom, exemplifies the risks to professional communities of theories privileging situation over standards.

Law of 2 June, 1941, Journal Officiel de la République Française [J.O.] (June 14, 1941).

1. A Jew is: He or she, of whatever faith, who is an issue of at least three grandparents of the Jewish race, or of simply two if his/her spouse is an issue herself/himself of two grandparents of the Jewish race.

A grandparent having belonged to the Jewish religion is considered to be of the Jewish race;

2. He or she who belongs to the Jewish religion, or who belonged to it on June 25, 1940, and who is the issue of two grandparents of the Jewish race.

Non-affiliation with the Jewish religion is established by proof of belonging to one of the other faiths recognized by the State before the law of 9 December 1905. The disavowal or annulment of recognition of a child considered to be Jewish is without effect as regards the preceding sections. [There follows the prohibitions for such people on property ownership and some employment; sanctions—including imprisonment—are then declared for engaging in proscribed activities.]

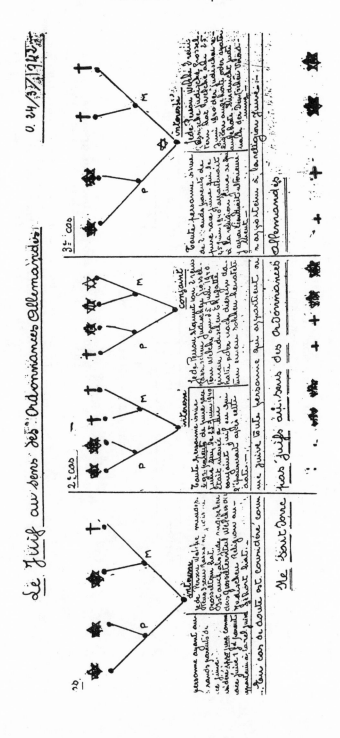

Toulouse, 18 November, 1941

[CDJC, XVII-38 (157)]

M E M O R A N D U M
- - - - - - - - - - -

For the Director of the (CGQJ) Service
on the Racial Laws

S. P.   447
JL/LC

The LEBOUCHER case, with which you are familiar, has drawn
my interest on the following question:

```
Aryan          Aryan         Jewish         Jewish       Aryan          Aryan
Grandfather  Grandmother   Grandfather   Grandmother  Grandfather   Grandmother
    |_____|             |_____|            |_____|
          |                          |                           |
       Father                 Mother  Father                   Mother
          |_____|                            |
                     |                                            |
           Husband — (first cousins) — Wife
```

Each of these spouses has two grandparents of
the Jewish race, but those are identical.

It strikes me as logical to avoid counting
these identical grand-parents twice to reach
the conclusion that these grandchildren are
both Jewish just because they decided to marry
each other.

Please advise if this conclusion is a sound
interpretation.

[Facsimile translated by author]

COMMISSARIAT GÉNÉRAL AUX QUESTIONS JUIVES

## CERTIFICAT

1,508

## DE NON-APPARTENANCE A LA RACE JUIVE

Sur le vu des pièces produites par l'intéressée le Commissaire Général

aux Questions Juives constate que M ᵐᵉ *Langer née Veysset Jeanne*

née le *16 août 1910* à *Bromont-Lamothe (P. de D.)*

ne doit pas être regardée comme juive aux termes de la loi du 2 Juin 1941.

Paris, le *10 septembre 1942*

*Darquier de Pellepoix*

Imp. Chaix (R). — 8726-41.

CERTIFICATE

OF NON-AFFILIATION TO THE JEWISH RACE

On presentation by the party to the CGQJ of various documents, we have decided that _____, born _____ at _____ should not be considered a Jew(ess) on the terms of the law of 2 June 1941.

Paris, _____

Darquier de Pellepoix

*Une pert de 2*
*1. la jurisprudence vi la grosse*

S.P.
H.A.H./U.H.

Monsieur Arnold CROQUEZ $\overline{XXIII}$ -*19*
Avocat à la Cour
82, rue de Varenne
PARIS (7ème)

H.E.

Affaire : ~~ELINA Henri, 44~~, Avenue de Suffren
PARIS.

Mon Cher Maître,

  Afin de régler définitivement
la situation de l'intéressé qui est
en instance depuis le 4 Février
1943, je vous serais obligé de bien
vouloir me faire parvenir un certificat établi par membre du Conseil
de l'Ordre les Médecins attestant que
votre client jouit de toute son
intégrité préoutiale.

  Veuillez agréer, Mon Cher
Maître, l'expression de mes sentiments distingués.

    Sign : E.B.

# APPENDIX 14.6

Commissariat Général
aux Questions Juives

Direction du Statut
des personnes et
des affaires juridiques

———

S.P.
JR. R.

24II P

II. 211

ETAT FRANÇAIS

Paris, le 10 Mars 1944

Le Directeur du Statut des Personnes

à Monsieur le Directeur Régional

8, Rue Ozenne

TOULOUSE

Objet: Statut racial des Géorgiens de confession mosaïque

J'ai l'honneur de vous informer que le Statut des Géorgiens de confession mosaïque a fait l'objet d'une demande spéciale auprès des autorités occupantes.

Pourtant, je crois devoir attirer votre attention sur le fait de la décision qui fut prise en Janvier 1943 par le Statut des Personnes à Vichy, décision qui conférait la qualité de non-juifs à tous ressortissants géorgiens de confession mosaïque, doit être considérée comme nulle et non avenue.

A l'heure actuelle, il est apparu qu'au sens de la loi française, les ressortissants géorgiens de confession mosaïque doivent être regardés comme étant issus de trois grands-parents de religion juive, et soumis au Statut des Juifs. Cette décision résulte du fait que la loi précitée est fondée essentiellement pour déterminer la race des intéressés, sur la religion professée par leurs grands-parents.

Les autorités allemandes exemptent du port de l'étoile les géorgiens de confession mosaïque, parce qu'elles les considèrent comme n'étant pas de pure race juive.

Néanmoins, il n'apparaît pas que cette exemption du port de l'étoile doit entraîner ipso-facto la levée des administrateurs provisoires que vous auriez cru devoir faire placer aux biens des Géorgiens de confession mosaïque. Bien mieux, je crois devoir décider que, dans tous les cas, les Géorgiens de confession mosaïque doivent faire l'objet d'une mesure d'aryanisation.

Le Directeur du Statut des Personnes
signé: ILLISIBLE

Toulouse, N° 2533

The Germans are shocked to see a Jew hold forth against the Marshal.

No Jew could raise his voice against Hitler where they came from.

CABINET
DU
PROCUREUR
DE LA RÉPUBLIQUE

*La compétence des tribunaux militaires allemands et les effets de leurs Décisions sur l'action publique devant les Tribunaux Français par Mᵉ J. Haennig.*

*J. Palais 10-12 Fevrier 1943-*

Office of the Public Prosecutor

On the competence of German military tribunals and the collateral effect of their decisions for French courts, see J. Haennig.

Gaz Palais 10-12 February, 1943

Headline: I have seen them, these Jewish Millionaires: Former Celebrities of the Paris Bar, Interned in a Camp near our Capital

# Paris-soir

VENDREDI 12 SEPTEMBRE 1941

ABONNEMENTS
France-Colonies
Etranger Tarif A.

6° DERNIÈRE
1 franc

ème Année. — N° 428       37, rue du Louvre, Paris (2°)

## ...LOTTE SOVIETIQUE
### bloquée
### DANS LE GOLFE DE FINLANDE

**PETROZADOVSK encerclée par les Finnois**

De gauche à droite : les avocats Weill, Théodore Valensi et Assolay.

## JE LES AI VUS, CES JUIFS
### MILLIONNAIRES...
### EX-CÉLÉBRITÉS DU BARREAU PARISIEN

De gauche à droite : les avocats Ulmo, Crémieux, Bloch et Pierre Masse. (Photos Paris-soir)

### PETROZADOVSK
### encerclée

## internés dans un camp
### proche de notre capitale

### Plus une seule place
## POUR LE GALA
### de demain soir
## AUX AMBASSADEURS

### Quand, dans un décor d'opérette
### à deux pas de la Foire de Leipzig

## ...la foule communie
### DANS LE FOLKLORE GERMANIQUE

(De notre envoyé spécial Jacques MARCY)

# JE LES AI VUS, CES JUIFS
## millionnaires...
## INTERNÉS PRÈS DE PARIS

(SUITE DE LA PREMIÈRE PAGE)

— *Pour l'instant, je leur apprends la discipline de la vie militaire,* nous confie le sympathique capitaine de gendarmerie qui commande le camp. Au début il y a bien eu quelques pleurs et grincements de dents, mais maintenant, ça se tasse, ils ont compris.

— *Compris !* Espérons-le. C'est à quoi nous songeons en croisant les regards sournois des « prisonniers », tout en parcourant les chambrées.

Chambrées de caserne du type de celles où nous étions empilés, nous les « goïms ». Il y a deux ans, en attendant de monter au front, pendant que tous ces « messieurs » faisaient de jolis coups dans les cafés de la capitale en « guerre ». La vie pratique est très simple au camp. Tous les matins réveil en fanfare à 7 heures. Le jus. Les ablutions si pénibles à tout bon Juif qui se respecte. Et la journée commence, rompue par quelques corvées. La préfecture de la Seine assure le ravitaillement. A 11 heures du matin, la soupe, 360 grammes de légumes frais, 275 grammes de pain, 10 grammes de matières grasses par jour. Et 90 grammes de viande une fois par semaine.

Il nous saut naturellement une question :

— *La viande est-elle abattue rituellement selon les principes de la loi juive, c'est-à-dire égorgée ?*

— *Pensez-vous,* nous répondent les responsables du camp en riant, *et croyez bien cependant que nos lascars ne la laissent pas dans leur assiette !...*

L'hygiène règne au camp. Dix-

sept médecins juifs internés aussi ont été promus aux soins des malades, sous la surveillance générale du Dr Tisné, médecin-chef français qui a organisé d'ores et déjà deux infirmeries modèles.

Tout est donc parfait ici. Même l'organisation du courrier qui comporte pour chacun deux cartes du type familial par semaine. Et personne ne souffre d'aucun sévice. Le sort des Juifs internés n'est pas plus tragique que celui de nos chers prisonniers. Avec cette différence que ceux-ci sont innocents, alors que les autres formaient la vaste armée des agitateurs et apéculateurs à la solde de l'étranger.

Mais que voyons-nous ? Ma parole, ce sont les huiles. Qui donc disait que les Juifs misérables faisaient les frais de l'opération ?

Alignés là, devant nous nous les reconnaissons. Ce sont les célébrités du barreau enjuivé d'hier : Me Théodore Valensi, Me Maurice Weill-Reynald Me Edmond Bloch, Me Pierre Masse, Me Ulmo, qui tenta de soudoyer un gendarme, entraînant ainsi de graves sanctions, Me Azoulay, Me Crémieux... tous avocats, politiciens puissants et respectés.

Quel juste retour des choses !

— *Vous allez une activité politique intense ces derniers temps ?* demandons-nous à Pierre Masse.

— *En effet, monsieur, j'étais sénateur en exercice et je le suis encore, répond-il en plissant un œil malin.*

— *Mais oui, très cher vénérable, nous n'en doutons pas...*

— *Et vous, maître Valensi, que pensez-vous de votre séjour ici ?*

— *Je ne puis dire qu'une seule chose : c'est que nous ne sommes nullement maltraités ici.*

Jamais vérité plus certaine n'est tombée de lèvres hébraïques.

Enfin, il faut prendre congé de ces augustes personnages qui vivent comme leurs congénères, la vie du camp : faisant ainsi disparaître la légende du Juif pauvre persécuté et du Juif riche protégé miraculeusement.

Tous égaux devant la répression, comme ils le furent dans leurs besognes néfastes aux intérêts du pays, voilà la solution qui s'impose en attendant le règlement d'ensemble du problème juif.

Mais— et c'est sur cette suggestion que nous terminerons — ne pourrait-on pas occuper sur place ces hommes à quelques travaux utiles tels que : réparation des vêtements usagés, confections, remise en état des objets confiés à la charité aux œuvres du Secours national.

Israël au travail pour la communauté !...

Croyez-nous, c'est encore comme cela qu'ils seront le plus châtiés.

**André CHAUMET.**

GAZOGÈNES
BRANDT

Vous ingérez ainsi par vous-même pourquoi les GAZOGÈNES de QUALITÉ sont bien les GAZOGÈNES de QUALITÉ

Établissements BRANDT, 32 E. de Hanovre et 254, R. de Vaugirard, PARIS (15e)
(Métro : Porte de Versailles)

## LA SEMAINE
### le grand hebdomadaire illustré FRANÇAIS
### parait aujourd'hui
**3 F**

=== RESTAURANT ===

## REOUVERTURE CE SOIR

# MAXIM'S

3, RUE ROYALE — ANJOU 27-94

Direction : ALBERT

NEW-YORK, 11 septembre.
— Le ministère de la Marine rend publique la nomination de John Roosevelt, fils cadet du président, qui a rang d'aspirant, au poste de chef-adjoint de la commission navale à la base aéronautique de San Diégo, en Californie.

## NEW-YORK
— Un gigantesque incendie s'est déclaré la nuit dernière, à Chicago, dans un dépôt de pétrole et de munitions. Toute la nuit, des pompes ont combattu le sinistre qui a été pas maîtrisé à plusieurs lieues de distance.

— Le président Roosevelt a chargé les commissions extraordinaires, composée de cinq membres, d'enquêter au sujet d'une menace de grève chômage de fer américains. Grâce à cette mesure, la grève a été automatiquement reculée de soixante jours.

## BOURSE DU 11 SEPTEMBRE 1941

| VALEURS | Cours précédent | Cours du jour | VALEURS | Cours précédent | Cours du jour |
|---|---|---|---|---|---|
| **Valeurs du Trésor** | | | **Départ. Seine** | | |
| **Rentes** | | | 5 % 1935 | 1000 | 1005 |
| 3 % | 94 20 | 94 35 | 5 1/2 % 1936 | 1099 | 1091 |
| 3 % amortissable | 94 30 | 94 50 | 5 % 1937 | | |
| — 1917 | 108 10 | 108 30 | **Crédit National** | | |
| 4 % 1918 | 100 30 | 100 30 | 5 % 1919 | 513 | 513 |
| — 1925 | 176 10 | 177 10 | 5 % 1920 | 535 | 535 |
| 5 % 1920 | 136 | 136 | 5 % 1931 | 1101 | 1102 |
| 4 1/2 % 1932 A | 101 60 | 101 75 | 5 % 1932 | 1079 | 1079 |
| 4 1/2 % 1932 B | 106 50 | 106 75 | **Crédit Foncier** | | |
| 4 1/2 % 1937 | 203 30 | 203 50 | Commun. 1920 | 1009 | 990 |
| 5 % 1938 | 105 15 | 105 50 | Fonc. 1930 4 1/2 % | 981 | 982 |
| **Obligations** | | | 5 % 1933 | 1025 | 1026 |
| 4 1/2 % 1932 | 1260 | 1267 | 5 1/2 % 1934 | 1050 | 1054 |
| 5 % 1934 | 1100 | 1179 | **P. T. T.** | | |
| 5 % 1935 | 1036 | 1042 | 5 % 1928 | 516 | 513 |
| 5 1/2 % 1932 | 1014 | 1015 | 4 1/2 % 1929-32 | 513 | 513 |
| 6 % 1938 | 136 65 | 136 60 | 5 % 1934-33 | 1024 | 1017 |
| **Bons du Trésor** | | | 5 % 1935 | 1033 | 1038 |
| 4 1/2 % 1933 | 1112 | 1111 | 5 % 1938 | 1040 | 1040 |
| 4 1/2 % 1934 | 1070 | 1070 | **Actions** | | |
| 4 1/2 % 1935 | 1061 | 1060 | | | |
| 5 % 1935 | 1060 | 1048 | **Banques** | | |
| 5 % septemb. 1937 | 1024 | 1032 | Banque de France | 14900 | 14900 |
| 5 1/2 décemb. 1937 | 1036 | 1020 | — de Paris | 1385 | 1382 |
| **Caisse Autonome** | | | Crédit Lyonnais | 3600 | 3600 |
| 4 1/2 % 1929 | 1031 | 1030 | Société Générale | | |
| 4 % 1929 | 121 70 | 121 80 | Électricité, Gaz | | |
| **Obligations** | | | Lyon. des Eaux | 2234 | 2235 |
| **Ville de Paris** | | | C. P. D. E. | 1679 D | 1690 |
| 1930 4 % | 971 | 971 | C. G. d'Électricité | 600 | 601 |
| 1934 5 1/2 % | 1011 | 1008 | Énergie Électrique | 3130 | 3130 |
| 1938 6 % | | 1051 | Union d'Électricité | 1190 | 1186 |
| | | | Écl. Chauf. F. M | 2195 | 2210 |
| | | | Gaz de Paris | 438 | 460 |

### Marché plus calme. — Ferm

Les charbonnages et les valeurs de service public : Électricité, Gaz, Transports, accentuent leur progression dans les limites permises. Le restant de la cote est irrégulier.

Les rentes françaises accusent pour la plupart des gains de quelques fractions.

Aucun changement dans le groupe bancaire. La Banque de Paris est plus résistante à 1.380.

Les chemins de fer s'améliorent : le Nord à 1.650, l'Orléans à 1.465. Les

Métropolitain passe de 2.140 à 2.108. On recherche les valeurs d'Électricité, particulièrement le Littoral-Méditerranéen à 2.020 contre 2.108 ; l'Énergie Industrielle à 3.130 contre 2.108 ; le Gaz pour la France à l'Étranger s'avance de 2.165 à l'Éclairage, Chauffage et Force, trice de 2.195 à 2.210.

Les Houillères poursuivent progrès : Courrières à 525 ; Liévin 695 ; Anzin à 1.205 ; Blanzy à 3 ; Béthune à 1.410 ; Carvin à 1.470.

PERT: OF C.D.J.C

R. F. SS
Sicherheits=Dienst
Nachrichten-Uebermittlung

XLIA-3.
09/23-2

| genommen | | | Befördert | | | | Raum für Eingangsstempel |
|---|---|---|---|---|---|---|---|
| Monat | Jahr | Zeit | Tag | Monat | Jahr | Zeit | |
| | | | -6 JUL 1942 | | | | |
| durch | | | an | | durch | | |

Verzögerung

Nr.

Telegram — Funkspruch — Fernschreiben — Fernspruch

IV J SA 24    dringend ! sofort vorlegen !
Dan/Bir                    Paris, den 6.7.1942

An das
Reichssicherheitshauptamt
- IV B 4 -
Berlin

Betr.: Judenabschub aus Frankreich.
Vorg.: Besprechung zwischen SS-Obersturmbannführer Eichmann und
SS-Hauptsturmführer Dannecker am 1.7.1942 in Paris.

Die Verhandlungen mit der französischen Regierung haben inzwischen zu folgendem Ergebnis geführt :
Sämtliche staatenlose Juden der besetzten und unbesetzten Zone werden für den Abschub bereit gestellt.
Präsident LAVAL hat vorgeschlagen, beim Abschub jüdischer Familien aus dem unbesetzten Gebiet, auch die unter 16 Jahre alten Kinder mitzunehmen. Die Frage von im besetzten Gebiet zurückbleibenden Judenkindern interessiert ihn nicht.
Ich bitte deshalb um dringende FS Entscheidung darüber, ob, etwa beginnend mit dem 15. Judentransport aus Frankreich, auch Kinder unter 16 Jahren mit abgeschoben werden können.

POLICE D'ISRAEL
QUARTIER GENERAL  6 eme BUREAU

משטרת ישראל
המטה. הארצי   לשנה 66

09/

65

IV J SA 225 a               Paris, den 21.7.1942
Dan/Bir


Betr.: Judenabschub.

1.) Vermerk :

Am 20.7.1942 rief SS-Obersturmbannführer EICHMANN und
SS-Obersturmführer NOWAK vom RSHA IV B 4 hier an.

Mit SS-Obersturmbannführer Eichmann wurde die Frage
des Kinderabschubes besprochen. Er entschied, daß, sobald
der Abtransport in das Generalgouvernement wieder möglich
ist, Kindertransporte rollen können. SS-Obersturmführer Nowak
sicherte zu, Ende August/Anfang September etwa 6 Transporte
nach dem Generalgouvernement zu ermöglichen, die Juden aller
Art (auch arbeitsunfähige und alte Juden) enthalten können.

Es wurde SS-Obersturmbannführer Eichmann ferner mitge-
teilt, daß vorläufig lediglich noch 1o Transporte möglich
wären und daß wegen der Festnahme weiterer Juden Verhandlungen
mit der französischen Regierung schwebten.

Wegen des ausgefallenen Transporte aus Bordeaux wurde
erklärt, daß, infolge der durch SS-Standartenführer Dr. Knochen
dem französischen Polizeichef Bousquet gemachten Zusage, vorläufig nur staatenlose Juden zu nehmen, ohne hiesig e Zutun,
eine völlig neue Lage entstanden sei, die das ganze Konzept
umgeworfen hätte.

2.) SS-Obersturmbannführer Hagen zur Kenntnis.

3.) SS-Unterscharführer Heinrichsohn zur Kenntnis und zu den
Judenlagern.

# Lawtalk in America:
# Recent Developments in the Rhetorics
# of the Legal Marketplace

MY FINAL chapter returns to these shores to examine the state of American legal letters in the late twentieth century. I begin with an analysis of one of our most prominent judges, Richard A. Posner, a man whose sheer verbal output cannot fail to impress, and who has recently chosen to direct his attention to Law and Literature. I close by expressing disappointment with the recent writings of another prominent writer in the field of Law and Literature, James Boyd White. Sandwiched in between, and indeed arguably meatier because of its scope of interest, is an essay recounting the lamentable falling off among lawyers in verbal mastery and communicative power. Although Law and Literature—inclusive of the efforts of Posner and White—now seeks to restore American legal rhetoric to its traditionally powerful place, we will see in that essay how much work remains to be done before lawyers again recapture their verbal dominance.

## 15. Thoughts on Judge Richard Posner's Literary Performance

Richard Posner's 1988 book, *Law and Literature: A Misunderstood Relation*, has pleased a large segment of the nonspecialized literary community, fascinated the jurisprudential world, and distracted other specialists in the field of Law and Literature. It has filled the generalist's need for traditional analyses of literary texts unencumbered by postmodernist complexity, deconstructionist jargon, or significant reliance on those corrupters of rationalist thought, the late nineteenth- and twentieth-century continental philosophers. Even a section of the academic literary world, newly mobilized by the scandal surrounding Paul de Man,[1] has been crying for a return to "moral criticism,"[2] a return, really, to the kind of social and political commentary derived from literature that we associate with Lionel Trilling or Irving Howe or (in translation) Georg Lukács, a kind of criticism absent from our shores for almost forty years. *Law and Literature* offers the reader a comprehensive look not only at the many theoretical links between the two narrative fields but also at countless examples of law-related fiction. Wonderfully elaborating upon earlier scholarship, Posner here seems to have tracked down for some mention or other virtually every text in Western literature that looks more than passingly at the law. Although trying always to prove the coincidental nature of this literary infatuation with lawyers' seemingly practical and boring endeavors, Posner unwittingly demonstrates the dynamism of Law and Literature studies. With so much material so delightfully presented by such talented wordsmiths, how can we exile this fund of jurisprudence? How long can we ignore, especially in light of Posner's findings, the obvious: literary art about law is richer, if not necessarily more important, than most other jurisprudential sources.

I welcome, therefore, this return to a criticism that is text-centered, that has a wealth of bibliographical data for all levels of its readership, and that has been accomplished without recourse to insular jargon or convoluted phraseology. Posner seems to recognize in his choice of a direct style—though perhaps only in that choice—that the works he treats create enough ambiguity and difficulty in their own right. He thus enlists himself in the diminishing corps of critics who prefer everyday language. But this (unfortunately for a self-proclaimed "amateur"[3] in literature) is where the modesty ends. For Posner's book does have a clear political bias, and it is unremittingly polemical. It is not a "mature" work, despite its author's implicit assertion of maturity in the face of other scholars' "romanticism."[4] Written to serve a jurisprudential end not always forthrightly communicated, the book finally displays what we might expect, given its author's relatively recent entrance into literary thinking and method—that is, not a reasonably well-attuned literary sensitivity, but instead a defensive attitude over his own anterior jurisprudence. Never, it seems, have so many of the world's most distinguished imaginative works left so apparently bright a reader so unmoved; rarely has mere assertion so prevailed over goodly demonstration in so well-researched a scholarly endeavor.

Given these flaws, it seems to me that the book's major accomplishment is the light it sheds on Posner himself and thus the values of one of our generation's most prominent legal figures. This is no mean feat, and in the elaboration of what I think the book says about Posner's own approach to law, we will find much that relates profoundly to the link between law and literature he seems so intent on trivializing.

Because I believe the book to be important as a display of Posner's legal philosophy and of his literary jurisprudence as well, I will proceed as follows. The first section of this chapter analyzes Posner's normative approach to legal reasoning, as spelled out in an article he wrote contemporaneously with his book, and then associates that approach with his critical methodology in *Law and Literature*. The next section reviews the thematic assertions of the book, again in light of the normative Posnerian vision. And the last section, by reintroducing Posner's theory and practice of the "revenge motif," asserts that literature's ultimately positive (if demanding) view of law survives Posner's revisionism and sets a jurisprudential agenda for the near future.

Four other caveats at the outset: First, in *Law and Literature* Posner pervasively attacks my positions, but he does accord me throughout the respect of comprehensive (if not always comprehending) reflection on my writings; I hope, given that reality, to have maintained some "objectivity" here. Second, my analyses of Posner's jurisprudence (as opposed to his literary techniques) remain tentative, partly because his jurisprudence is still evolving. Third, the discussion here, as in Posner's work, is of course largely normative: having seen many of his actual opinions, and publicly admired them for certain qualities, I do not contend that the somewhat extreme picture of the Posnerian judge that I find in his 1988 article (to be discussed) in any way reflects his own behavior on the bench. Fourth, because of the richness of the material and my own particular interest in it, I focus here almost exclusively on the law-in-literature portions of his book, chapters 1 through 4 (although my section on "Posner's Literary Premises" converses with that book's chapters 5 and 6 as well). I do not cover his chapter 7 ("The Regulation of Literature By Law"), partly because I cannot add much to what I deem to be the best-argued chapter in the book, and partly because, as others have noted,[5] chapter 7 exists almost independently from the book's other parts.

## POSNER'S JURISPRUDENCE

### The Rejection of Cardozo:
### Authority, Arbitrariness, and Impersonality

A 1988 Posnerian text helps us to structure our understanding of the values underlying *Law and Literature*. In his article "The Jurisprudence of Skepticism," written as he was developing his book, Posner sets forth a supposedly skeptical view of legal reasoning, but one that explicitly privileges authority figures in law and permits them to do whatever the occasion and their settled beliefs permit.[6] The life of the law for Posner emerges neither as traditional inductive logic nor as Holmesian experience; rather it resides in the declarations of people who have come to hierarchical power. Indeed, this approach takes on an epistemological tone relevant to Posner's understanding of all narrative disciplines when he writes, "In an age not only of science but of hostility to almost all forms of authority, we tend not to realize how many of our beliefs, including scientific ones, are the product of authority rather than observation" (841), and continues, "Judicial authority is essentially political: Decisions are authoritative because they emanate from a politically authorized source rather than because they are agreed to be correct by persons in whom the community reposes an absolute epistemic trust" (842–43).

Nothing in *Law and Literature* departs from these contemporaneous jurisprudential thoughts; to a large extent the book wishes to reconfirm them. Thus, Posner's interpretation of fictional works always endorses, when dealing with conflicts between individuals and the state, the utterances and the actions of those who have achieved governmental power.[7] There are, as far as I can recall, no exceptions to this rule among the scores of literary examples he cites or discusses here. Even Angelo's obvious abuse of power in *Measure for Measure* is blamed (with considerable insight in the bargain) on the Duke's "anarchic" behavior;[8] Angelo's formalism is "the abuse of a good thing" (110) and not in itself objectionable. Too, it "would be a mistake . . . to think Creon a monster who gets his just deserts, though this is a common view. There is a case to be made for him" (110).

For Posner, it is a mark of "maturity" (another of his books principal "leitmotifs") to accept authoritative declarations both at face value and as innately good. The "maturity" theme is but another form of the authoritarian jurisprudence fashioned by Posner in his 1988 article. *Law and Literature* borrows, in its theory and its practice, from his jurisprudence, the former an explicit part of it.

Thus literature—even the truly skeptical texts he must address because they are most obviously about law—cannot, for Posner, undermine law as an actual social phenomenon. Posner believes that an exegetical stance stressing fiction's darker view of modern law would be too costly, too upsetting. Whatever benefits there are in detecting through literary works the potential corruption of law in the hands of spiritually sick individuals, Posner (like Melville's Captain Vere, whom he passionately defends) gladly forgoes these benefits to avoid the costs of upsetting the populace, to preserve order whatever its underlying nature.

Posner's respect for authority as the main, perhaps the sole, arbiter of meaning leads him to distrust any systematic constraint on the authoritative adjudicator. Hence, in his 1988 law review piece, after throwing a bone at Wittgensteinian (or Fiss–Fishian)[9] "consensus" (855), Posner quickly returns to the power of the single judge, working within a predetermined set of beliefs: "A judge who has a powerful intuition that it would be an outrage to decide a particular case a particular way should not feel compelled to decide it that way merely because a comparison of the reasons pro and con shows the pros with a slight preponderance" (859). And again, he writes: "We should hesitate to take at face value descriptions of judges as striving always to find the correct answer rather than exercising discretion or enacting their personal values and preferences" (872).

Posner's invocation of "intuition" and his candid declaration that judges often act in a discretionary way sound like a move in the direction of Law and Literature jurisprudence. So too does the notion that the audience to the judge's pronouncement must be constantly on its guard to detect the inevitable subjectivism of the decision and the bases in the judge's values for that private urge. But many things still separate Posner from a true literary sensitivity. First, literature is alien to the blanket acceptance of judicial authority apparent in Posner whenever the stakes are high for his notion of social efficiency or order. Thus, as our "debate" on *Billy Budd* has already indicated (see note 7), Posner will not "hesitate to take at face value" Captain Vere's overt assertion of nondiscretionary judicial behavior during Billy's trial.

Furthermore, Posnerian "intuition" in his 1988 article has little to do with the experientially alive, culturally trained intuition with which most of us are familiar. Posner wants an authoritative judge, free to assert not an inductively generated intuition, but rather a program (861) grounded in fixed rules of social scientific "behaviorism" (871). No Solomon (whose trained intuition merged the specific humanity of the litigants with a sense of social policy), Posner's judge floats free to implement a preconceived ideology.

Earlier Law and Literature scholarship has espoused quite a different notion of "intuition." This notion goes back several decades to the jurisprudential essays of another influential judge to write explicitly about the interdisciplinary field, Benjamin N. Cardozo.[10] Those essays, unavoidable to Posner now that he has joined the literary interdisciplinarians, provide such keen insight that they should constantly be kept in mind when one tries to assess the irrational elements in law.

Thus it is a prevailing irony in Posner's supposedly literary view of things that his "powerful intuition"—surely among his most potentially "literary" notions—has nothing to do with the case-specific, culturally attuned adjudication associated with Cardozo. Instead, having conjured "intuition," Posner immediately reasserts the antiexperiential, antiexistential base of his judge's fixed passion: "Of course this [intuition] may make it extremely difficult to know whether a legal decision is correct or incorrect, since, as noted earlier, the judge's intuition will probably not be confirmable (or refutable) by experience" (859).

But why not? Cardozo, after all, uses the phrase "trained intuition,"[11] meaning the judge's inevitable mainstay in difficult moments, private as all intuitions are but fully confirmable because of a common training shared with the legal community as a whole. Two representative passages from Cardozo place Posner's jurisprudence in an odd light. First, Cardozo writes about the difference between pure subjectivism and judicial intuition:

> The important thing, however, is to rid our prepossessions, so far as may be, of what is merely individual or personal, to detach them in a measure from ourselves, to build them, not upon instinctive or intuitive likes and dislikes, but upon an informed and liberal culture, a knowledge (as [Matthew] Arnold would have said) of the best that has been thought and said in the world, so far as that best has relation to the social problem to be solved. Of course, when our utmost effort has been put forth, we shall be far from freeing ourselves from the empire of inarticulate emotion, of beliefs so ingrained and inveterate as to be a portion of our very nature. "I must paint what I see in front of me," said the elder Yeats to his son, the poet. "Of course, I shall really paint something different because my own nature will come in unconsciously."[12]

Second, and (unlike Posner's judge) only because of a broadly literary culture, Cardozo's judge then is empowered to make authoritative decisions where technical legal methods may fail; but even these decisions are bounded by the judge's sense of how finely attuned his culture is to that of other lawyers and judges:

> Now, personally I prefer to give the label law to a much larger assembly of social facts than would have that label affixed to them by many of the neo-realists. I find lying around loose, and ready to be embodied into a judge, a vast conglomeration of principles and rules and customs and usages and mor-alities. If these are so established as to justify a prediction with reasonable certainty that they will have the backing of the courts in the event that their authority is challenged, I say that they are law.[13]

While Posner's judge sits somewhat like a central computer churning out decisions in private dialogue with himself, relatively uninfluenced by the unique factual situation before him and certainly skeptical of or uninterested in the "customs," "usages," and "moralities" that form his surrounding culture, Cardozo's authority figure embraces his own intu-itions as inevitable but as refined and ultimately constrained by the best beliefs of an acquired culture. For Posner, that culture, if it exists at all, will be neither legal nor literary but instead economic, a point he makes in his 1988 article in an attack on Ronald Dworkin's brand of literary jurisprudence:

> The power of legal reasoning to generate determinate outcomes could be saved by turning law into something else—economics perhaps.... But the arguments for the transformation could not be based on legal reasoning.... [A] fragmented political and ethical discourse will no more yield determinative outcomes than legal reasoning will. Ronald Dworkin may be seen in this light as jumping the gun: treating law as the embodiment of his brand of moral and political philosophy before that brand has won enough support to be entitled to dictate which legal outcomes are correct, which incorrect. (859–60)

But if Posner is right to accuse Dworkin of "gun-jumping," it is largely because (as I have suggested elsewhere)[14] Dworkin falls into the trap of using literature for its theoretical or interpretive side before he has as-similated literature for itself, by reading the literary texts themselves. Paradoxically—or really, polemically—Posner in *Law and Literature* gath-ers up the texts that could define an "ethical discourse" and then declares them largely irrelevant to the lawyer and judge:

> I shall argue that the frequency of legal subjects in literature is partly a statistical artifact and that law figures in literature more often as metaphor than as an object of interest in itself; even when the author is a lawyer (like Kafka) or law "buff" (like Melville). (71)

And again:

[I]n order to be read as literature, a work must deal with aspects of culture that are universal. Law is one of them; yet it might, of course, appear in a work of literature as a metaphor for something else. Moreover, only limited aspects of law are apt to have the breadth of appeal that literature demands, and they may not be the aspects of greatest interest to lawyers, or within their special competence. (75)

Posner's jurisprudence, unlike that of his predecessors in the ranks of Law and Literature, appeals to literature only to denigrate its value for law. Posner's vague description of literature as being, at best, metaphorically connected to law effectively takes literature out of the competition with other factors that could influence contemporary law. He adopts this view of literature, I believe, for two reasons. First, Posner must avoid the hard lessons that literature holds for lawyers, because these lessons violate his jurisprudence. Too many works of fiction end in judicial error, for example, to permit a banal ratification of authority figures. Too many depict law as an instrument of terror. Many allow that law is normatively just but instead locate problems in the values of the lawgiver or the law interpreter. So the thing to do is to insist that those works are not really about law at all.

Second, Posner's urge to universalize and marginalize literature is of a piece with what I am calling here the larger, "impersonal" strand of his overall legal vision. Although he professes to be skeptical of logical reasoning in law, Posner's 1988 law review article suggests this impersonal jurisprudence by featuring deductive logic almost throughout. The inductive, case-specific tradition is debunked: "I am led to wonder whether the highly inductive, case-oriented, analogy-saturated 'Socratic' method actually teaches legal *reasoning* at all" (71). Posner continues:

> Most judicial opinions even in the toughest cases depict the process of reasoning as a logical deduction (syllogistic or enthymematic) from previous decisions or from statutes viewed as transparent sources of rules, and consistent with the logical form, imply that even the very toughest case has a right and a wrong answer and only a fool would doubt that the author of the opinion had hit on the right one.[15] (865)

But—skeptical or not—this is hardly an accurate picture of most judicial pronouncements! Even Posner's own opinions usually begin with the facts, the unique, individualizing elements that characterize our system's approach to law.[16] From the statement of facts, and only from that, there arises a sense of the inevitability of the legal rule then chosen (not commanded from on high) to dictate an outcome that looks reasonable. Posner's depiction of the deductive approach to adjudication is understandable in his authority-centered jurisprudence, but it is foreign to the way most judges act.

Impersonal in its approach, Posner's thoroughgoing anti-inductiveness denies to law what he even more inappropriately denies to literature: its origin in the specifics of the matter at hand. If something universal follows, whether in law or literature, it is because of both the appropriateness of those facts to a universal claim and the craft of the narrator in structuring and describing the matter.

One need only contrast Posner's impersonality to the approach, once again, of the more literary Judge Cardozo. For Cardozo, the act of adjudication is constantly inductive, and based on a process of growth and existential change within the judge: "[Q]ueries that are ultimate," he writes, "are slumbering within many a common lawsuit, which can be lifted from meanness up to dignity if the great judge is by to see what is within."[17] In addition, he writes, "But as a system of case law develops, the sordid controversies of litigants are the stuff out of which great and shining truths will ultimately be shaped."[18] In legal and literary culture, as traditionally analyzed, there can be no understanding and no universalizing apart from a base of specific, accurately observed data. These cultures do not take well to reversing that process, no matter how strong the deductive premises of the critic or judge.

Contrary to Cardozo, however, Posner seems to want to avoid the specificity and uniqueness of particular cases, and his jurisprudential preferences naturally spill over onto his literary method. Cardozo's "intuition" is inductive, culturally open, and constantly seeking refinement. Posner's is fixed, uninterested in most cultural emanations, and strongly self-confident. In its impersonality, it manages to reduce even the specifically law-oriented texts of world literature, and certainly the modest uniqueness of any litigant, to a function of its preconceived beliefs.

Affinity is lacking, then, between two distinguished jurists who have chosen literature as a fitting medium in which to develop their notions of jurisprudence.[19] The present generation finds itself, for better or worse, in the process of deciding between the two visions.

## Posner's Way with the Literary Text

When we turn to Posner's hermeneutics—his way of detecting meaning in his literary texts—we find a combination of authority, arbitrariness, and impersonality that would be peculiar in a critical debut if we did not have the contemporaneous jurisprudential work to help us understand it. After 350 pages of polemics against most earlier Law and Literature scholarship, Posner finally reveals this methodology. In his book's "Conclusion" he says: "But I hope I have explained, and not merely asserted, my grounds for disagreement with these scholars" (357). No reader, however, could fail to discern the book's assertiveness, which is in keeping with Posner's view that authority, more than reason, must prevail in law. But this assertive method is less damning to the book when directed against other critics than it is when imposed upon the literary masterpieces themselves.

Thus in no respect is Posner the "New Critic" he claims to be in dealing with literature.[20] He is as uninterested in what the fictional text literally says, if it negates his own "powerful intuition," as he is in what the critical text says. The "intentionalism" to which he subscribes in his capacity as a judge instead carries over to his interpretive method.[21] Where the thorniest problems he faces seem to work against him textually, Posner falls back on what the text's author *must have* or *could not have* meant. For example:

> Neither the apostrophe to Nelson in Chapter 4 of *Billy Budd*, nor the reference in Chapter 5 to Nelson's having prevented a possible mutiny on the *Theseus* by his mere presence, is intended to pull Vere down. There is no mention of any acts of violence on the *Theseus*, and we can be sure that, if there had been violence, Nelson would have responded with the utmost firmness. The purpose of the references to Nelson is to lend verisimilitude to the novella. (160)

And:

> [I]t is difficult to shake off the impression that Camus is inviting the reader to take Meursault's part.... No reader would believe that Meursault would be sentenced to death for not crying at his mother's funeral, so he must commit a capital offense. (89–90)

And:

> *The Trial* is a remarkable work, and full of legal detail from start to finish, yet again its heart seems to lie elsewhere than with law....
> Granted, the "trial" itself—*Prozess*, better translated as "case" or "proceeding" because what is depicted in parodic form is the stretched-out, nonadversarial Continental criminal proceeding, which progresses through a series of interrogations—is full of authentic details of Austro-Hungarian criminal procedure.... But the point is not to show how awful it is to be arrested and charged with an unspecified offense by a secret court whose proceedings drag on interminably.... The legal proceeding that provides the novel's framework is a huge, typically Kafkaesque "sick joke" on the protagonist. (119, 123–24; footnote omitted)

And finally:

> Dmitri's conviction and sentencing are presented as stations on the way to his salvation. . . .
>
> Although he [Dmitri Karamazov] is the victim of a judicial error, his conviction and sentencing may be just in a larger sense. Dostoevski does not regard him simply as a victim of persecution, as Camus appears to regard Meursault.[22]

This nonexhaustive sampling suggests that Posner, in the spirit of most critics writing polemically, claims a private line to Melville, Kafka, Dostoevski, and Camus that the rest of us lack. Although frequently accusing other critics of imposing their views upon the law-related texts he treats,[23] Posner cannot avoid the same pitfall; yet he constantly assumes the tone of one who has dispassionately discovered the real meaning of these stories. Like the constitutional originalist, or statutory intentionalist, Posner in his book methodically avoids the most difficult questions of textual meaning by finding the answer apart from the text: Kafka *could not have* been criticizing free-market economics (182, 186); Melville *could not have* intended his villain John Claggart to be a Christ figure (158, 166); Dostoevski *could not have* wanted us to criticize law by depicting an innocent man found guilty in *The Brothers Karamazov* (166–69). History and philosophy receive the same treatment: France *could not have* embraced the task of genocide more fervently than demanded by their Nazi masters (171–75);[24] Nietzsche, despite his constant pronouncements to the contrary, *had to be* a "Romantic" in some sense (146). On yet a higher level of generalization, prosecutors and judges *must* be sound, and anyone brought to the bar of justice *must* somehow or another be guilty of something.

Posner's hermeneutics, replicating the impersonality of his jurisprudence, works from the general down to the individual case. His method is deductive, relying on the preconceived beliefs of some authoritative reader, not on any new experience, such as that of the literary text itself.

If an authoritative reader of these intensely questioning literary works should decide that a literary upsetting of the applecart would wreak havoc with law, then he or she need only maintain this generalization in case after case, no matter how counterintuitive the application. Thus Posner's Captain Vere is correct in trying and executing Billy Budd (155–65). But on what authority? Not the Articles of War. They do not compel such a result, and they would constrain Vere to leave the matter to the fleet admirals. Then what about the potential mutiny if Billy is left alive? But Billy is the most popular man on board, and surely no mutineer; and anyway this crew is obviously completely disinclined to mutiny. Ironically, it is the sight of Billy hanging from the yardarm, through Vere's edict, that moves these men to near-rebellion. So what is left to justify Vere's act? Billy's life is cheap; he might at any moment have his head lopped off by the next cannonball. Why not execute him against the smallest fear that keeping him alive would undermine discipline and authority (162, 163).

Posner's Billy, shorn of his specific place as the representative of spontaneous, zestful life, legitimately faces the rope because the benefits to Vere marginally outweigh the costs of keeping Billy alive. Like the Posnerian judge discussed earlier,[25] Vere is not constrained by the various "pros and cons" from following his "powerful intuition." But as with that judge, so here we are not permitted to explore the bases of his strange predilections.

The arbitrariness of Posner's jurisprudence allows him to overlook even the texts of the law—unless they serve his purpose—just as it ignores in case after case the evidence of the literary texts under analysis. This selective methodology takes two forms. Where a fictional use of law leaves some questions unanswered, Posner fudges on whether "extrinsic" legal research is justifiable. In discussing *Billy Budd*, for example, Posner examines legal materials for one scant paragraph in determining whether Vere is disobeying the law (156). Yet elsewhere, he imports such extrinsic materials without qualification (e.g., 93–94, 98, 168). Second, Posner simply jettisons the applicable law (even when clear within the story) if it violates the needs of the authority figure. So, on the *Merchant of Venice*, Posner comments, "Whatever the law might say, the enforcement of [Shylock's] bond would be absurd and Portia does what is necessary to prevent it" (96). But if Portia rightly avoids the law to work a higher good, why should not Vere (who had the procedures of the Articles of War to fall back on if he had wished to save Billy) have done the same to save a moral innocent? Posner's treatment of the wrongfully convicted Dmitri, as I have discussed, similarly casts aside the law in favor of an abstract support of authority:

> [T]he conviction of Dmitri [Karamazov], though a judicial error, is consistent with a higher justice, is part of the divine plan. . . .
> To call him innocent and leave it at that . . . is to oversimplify. . . . Although he is the victim of judicial error, his conviction and sentencing may be just in a larger sense. (167, 169)

But if Dmitri Karamazov should be convicted of homicide even though someone else killed the victim, then why not condemn anyone who has thought bad thoughts? Or who has the wrong color eyes? Or who refuses to worship at the prevailing altars?

Posner's jurisprudence is intensely efficient, but his notion of efficiency has something, well, Kafkaesque about it. Portia's extralegal tricks destroy the exogenous Shylock; the tsarist prosecutor's resentful mistake eliminates the sensuous and nonconforming Dmitri; Camus' examining magistrate brings about the guillotining of Meursault, who is a kind of "Romantic" anti-Christ to Posner (151–54). Outsiders can and must be eliminated for the good of the insiders.

But how do we choose who is inside and who is outside? Melville's *Billy Budd*, of course, is asking that precise question. When the unsailorlike Captain Vere contrives to executive the popular Billy, Vere becomes the outsider. Never comfortable among sailors, the bookish and complex Vere is as out of his element as the clearly alienated villain, John Claggart. They are both painted as covert men better suited to the worldly lives of men on land.

When Vere seizes upon Billy's act of striking down the usurping Claggart and decides to destroy Billy in his turn, Melville depicts a crucial moment of change. Culture "veers," fatally, as the essence (not the excrescence) of humanity is hanged. The destruction of the innocent is not inevitable, as Posner's "mature" values would force us to believe. It is the perverse work of "certain men of the world."[26] This insight is hardly "romantic." It is the sophisticated, if disturbing, observation of most law-interested modern novelists.

In sum, Posner's jurisprudence, predicated on authority, arbitrariness, and impersonality, all amplified in his approach to literature, at one and the same time:

1. Ignores the texts of the law;
2. Favors the declarations and actions of persons of authority, taken at face value and even when in opposition to the texts they are sworn to uphold;
3. Privileges cost-efficient judicial decisions;
4. Defines efficiency elliptically, in terms of the authority figures's subjective views, even when (as often happens in literature) those views are demonstrably bizarre and exogenous; and
5. Is deductive, not from traditional interpretive premises but instead from a firmly held set of convictions impervious to traditional argumentation.

Anyone who has gasped at the power exercised by one or two economic theorems over otherwise intelligent and reflective lawyers and judges will recognize Posner's Law and Literature jurisprudence as fully congruent with the underpinnings of his earlier writings: reliance on a handful of generalizations; reliance on people in power to implement them, not necessarily on a sound legalistic basis; establishment of a class of "pariahs," as he calls them (really those unlucky enough to be called upon to be sacrificed to the new faith);[27] zeal for the merely metaphysical notion of marketplace efficiency as opposed to specific, real patterns of human behavior; faith in overt pronouncements; and a disinclination to explore fully the nature of human motivation.

But however forceful his approach has seemed in a contextual vacuum of competing justifications for law, he is now in a domain of literary language too refined and too complex for such a methodology. The virtue of literary stories about law is that they force us to grapple with the unique elements that often come to the fore when law acts on people. No lawyer fully conversant with the literary approach to law can ever again rely on the demand curve to solve pressing problems of policy or adjudication. No reader of these texts can emerge unaware of the immense and often distorting role of language—of narrative—in law.

It is entirely to Posner's credit that his devotion to his book-length study compels a comparison of the literary and economic approaches to law. But the patronizing tone of *Law and Literature* makes one wonder whether he was himself fully ready to consider the consequences of his own readings. Perhaps delaying that extended comparison for another time, Posner instead adopts the dialectical mode, programmatically denying any special place to fiction for law or lawyers. This denial is upsetting, because Posner's choice of subject matter, coupled with his superb intelligence and increasing rhetorical awareness, situated him well to reject polemics and embrace the implications of world literature for his own anterior jurisprudence. We are left to ponder how and why a cost-efficient scholar-judge who chose to devote hundreds of hours to writing about fiction would go about proving that it is of no special value to lawyers. I attempt an explanation in the next section, with the hope that the analysis will address not only the specialist but also will illuminate for other readers the fundamental contribution of literature to law.

## POSNER'S LITERARY PREMISES AS LINKED TO HIS JURISPRUDENCE

### The Universality of Fiction (Impersonality)

Posner, in his book *Law and Literature*, defines "great literature"—accurately in my opinion—as those stories that have been passed (in one form or another) from generation to generation and continue to be told in our own time (71–74). This marketplace explanation—that greatness is defined by constant demand over long periods of time—has relevance for recent debates about what factors create the literary "canon,"[28] that is, how some stories gain acceptance while others are never widely transmitted. But Posner, in attempting to explain why so much fiction relates explicitly to law (74–79), fails to note that both storyteller and audience are receptive to narratives dealing with authority, particularly insular and potentially terrorizing forms of authority (nature, deities, parents, and so on).

In those generations in which law is perceived as particularly influential or in flux, but *only* in those generations, judges and prosecutors join this group of potential terrorizers. It is not happenstance that law gains prominence in literature in several specific times and places (e.g., fifth-century Greece, twelfth- to fourteenth-century Europe, Elizabethan and Jacobean England, and Europe and America from the Industrial Revolution to our own day). Posner ignores or rejects this specificity, although it has already been worked through in the scholarship.[29] Posner wants great fiction to "float free" of its genealogy (76). He wants it to be amorphous. He would rather not face its bounded, contingent reality.

Just as Posner's impersonal method declines to see law-related literature's special place for readers, so he refuses to grapple with its relevance for the authors who delve so deeply into its substance. In genres such as the modern novel, storytellers find in law a precise duplication of their own narrative techniques. When Flaubert and Dostoevski and Trollope and Melville and Twain and Faulkner and so many others—Barth and Doctorow and C. P. Snow and Malamud and Solzhenitzyn in recent decades—write exhaustively (and for some readers exhaustingly) about lawyers and legal proceedings, they are writing about themselves: about the long and difficult process of describing things articulately—of putting a narrative structure around an otherwise inchoate reality.

So, we have great fiction about the law in certain generations, and we have this fiction for specific reasons worthy of explanation. Instead, for Posner, great fiction exists because of some universal element within it (74). As we would expect from his jurisprudential scheme, Posner rigorously expunges the particular from his analysis of literature. Law is there not to be talked about in any precise or useful way but only as one of the many themes from which these writers choose; love, death, war, ambition, and so on. Law is "metaphoric" (71, 75), yet Posner never reveals what the *other* element in the metaphor is.

In fact, these writers doggedly pursue law far more intensively than any other human activity in their works. Indeed, among the authors I have just listed, detailed descriptions of law and lawyers occur far more frequently than do descriptions of other writers or even those of imaginative writing itself! Less prevalent still are literary depictions of medical, business, architectural, or agricultural activities in narrative fiction (though you will of course find the occasional doctor, businessman, architect, or farmer). Yet in mainstream modern fiction, as in several earlier literary epochs, you will find time and again minute examinations not only of criminal procedures but also of cases involving torts, trusts and estates, securities, or real property.[30] The novelist wants to find out, often at the expense of sheer drama, how lawyers go about recreating reality.[31] In this sense, finally, the storyteller finds in the techniques of law a fitting "metaphor" for his or her own manner of talking about things.

But what a metaphor! For, rather than diluting their detailed use of law, these writers sustain every specific description of law as a metaphoric comment on their own endeavors. Captain Vere's resentful destruction of Billy is Melville's equivocal denial of the heroic in favor of the repressed and the complex; Dmitri Karamazov's wrongful conviction stands for the failure of Dostoevski's vision, equally as warped and egocentric as that of Dmitri's articulate prosecutors, depicted with such intensity. The Christian characters' "victory" over Shylock represents the casual, comedic ascendancy of elegance and music over ethics and legal substance in Shakespeare's work. But when Portia reinvokes the themes of oaths, suretyships, and rings at the very end of the play, she ironically challenges the value of such an ephemeral, irresponsible approach as that taken by her oath-breaking husband and his friend, the merchant of Venice himself; Shakespeare is questioning, perhaps, the relative importance of the comedic and the tragic in his writings. (A fuller analysis of *The Merchant of Venice* as Posner treats it will follow shortly.)

For Posner, in law and in literature, the "truths" are there first, to be applied according to the authoritative reader's edict; for most judges and critics, the specific comes first. Blindness to what makes a matter unique (or potentially so) is fatal to understanding. This is particularly true for some literary genres—the epic and the novel—which gain marketplace acceptance largely because of their mimetic, not their normative, power.[32] Philosophers speak in universals; storytellers appeal to the omnipresent factors by being specific. Posner's jurisprudence is as inapt to literature as it is to non-social-scientific legal analysis.

## The "Mature" Reader (Authority)

Early in one of Posner's central chapters ("The Literary Indictment of Legal Injustice"), the author inserts a rather strange and not fully relevant digression on "Romantic Values in Literature and Law" (137–55). The idea seems to be that any rebelliousness in the face of authority represents at best a failed return to Jean Jacques Rousseau's naturalism and at worst "the boundless egoism of early childhood and the sense of loss that accompanies growing up" (140–41; footnote omitted). This section would benefit from considerable rethinking. On every level, from a profound misperception of Nietzsche and the central concept of ressentiment to an unsupported linkage of Romanticism with radicalism (145–46) to ad hominem suggestions that the present writer condones criminality or attacks law (151–52), these pages contain many surprises.

I will leave to a more objective future the decision as to whether my readings of Dostoevski, Melville, Camus (whom Posner at least admits wrote in the spirit of my analysis; he just will not tolerate Camus' vision!),[33] and Flaubert reflect those authors well. But Posner's notion that a sustained questioning of authority is in itself immature cannot be left unanswered.

Let us begin with our own revolutionary forefathers. What would Posner have done with the Declaration of Independence? Perhaps something like this (from his book):

> The Romantic outlook has a tendency to encourage radicalism, whether of the left or of the right. . . . To most Romantics the political, legal, and religious restraints that have evolved to tame the beast in man and create peace and prosperity are a fraud, their actual purpose and effect being to promote selfishness and exploitation, to thwart community, to poison mankind's natural goodness. (145–46)

This reductive prose sweeps under one rug all critiques of any established order. Perhaps that rug—shaggy edges and all—is meant to be attractive, since Posner weaves into it Blake, Wordsworth, Rousseau, Shelley, and—strangely—Gide, Genet, Camus, and unnamed others whose association with what is usually meant by Romanticism would shock literary historians. But even if Posner is allowing for some literary recourse to the unabashed ego and to man in the state of nature, many revolutionaries in recent memory were in fact neoclassicists, not Romantics. Our founding fathers and their French counterparts of circa two hundred years ago, steeped in eighteenth-century political and aesthetic theory, soberly decided that the *kinds* of government they were faced with were unacceptably corrupt.[34]

The political and literary tradition teaches us, in fact, that the romantic state of mind is the most likely to endure the most depraved of tyrannies without rebellion. The writers Posner magically associates with Romanticism make this point often: an example is Nietzsche in his recognition that ressentiment—the clinical inability to strike out at real incursions and insults on one's well-being—is the dominant Romantic mode.[35] These writers consistently urged their readers to abjure various romanticisms, to get a grip on reality as it is, and to rebel when and if necessary against actual injustice.

Posner is out of his element here. Romanticism is a tough nut to crack, and it is a concept he has not yet mastered. Witness, for example, the following confused utterance: "Although the word 'Romanticism,' if it is to be used with any precision, should be reserved for a cluster of particular (and actually quite diverse) movements in the social, political, and artistic thought of the late eighteenth and early nineteenth centuries, the 'Romantic' temperament is one of humankind's fundamental moods" (140; footnote omitted).

In other words, "I'd like to be precise, but it might undermine my thesis, so I'll be diffuse." Romanticism, "used with any precision," ties into Law and Literature in only one regard. It is true that a literary group not discussed by Posner—the German Romantic movement of Kleist, Novalis, the Brothers Schlegel, and others—believed that all knowledge is one. This became a fundamental Romantic tenet, and it explains early nineteenth-century literature's fascination with the merger of genres: prose poems, novellas mixing poetic and dramatic elements, etc.[36] So, to that extent, the interdisciplinary urge is itself "Romantic," and I (if not Posner himself) would accept that accurate and nonpejorative sobriquet. But it is vital to recognize that, whereas the dissatisfaction with artistic or even scholarly structures gives rise to universalist leanings that might be called "Romantic," rebellion against political structures has been of late largely a neoclassical venture.

Thus it is not coincidental that the French "philosophe" and revolutionary, Voltaire, was among the most conservative literary artists and critics who ever lived. The man who helped bring down a monarchy always detested Shakespeare as a barbaric genius because he did not stick to the Aristotelian rules in his plays.[37] But the German Romantics, who were literary revolutionaries, helped instill a political fascination for national myth that would unwittingly feed into the disasters of the Nazi period.[38] It was, of course, against the stupidities of German nationalism and its special progeny, the German anti-Semite, that Nietzsche directed half of his anti-Romantic attack. The other half was directed at what he thought of as the greatest of all Romanticisms, Christianity itself.[39]

Anyone who can link Nietzsche's concept of ressentiment—in all its antidelusionary, antibookish, antifeverish forcefulness—with "Romanticism" is very far afield indeed. Surely the modern writers Posner tries to label as "Romantics" were all attacking the systems of authority that they felt were leading (or, in the case of Camus, had already led) to massive injustice. But true Romantics, with their perennial hope that things will get better and their special gift of articulateness, would have tolerated or contributed to that injustice.

## *"A more flexible or equitable jurisprudence" (Arbitrariness)*

A major theme running through *Law and Literature* is that legal systems, somewhat like people, "mature" as they reject certain values in favor of others. For Posner, the casting off of strict liability in favor of negligence constitutes one of those moves and is reflected in literature through a pervasive critique of the single avenger, who would inflict without further analysis injury or death upon all those associated with his loss: "[R]evenge is associated with a particularly uncompromising form of strict liability for harms inflicted however justifiably. So one is not surprised to find that early legal systems, in which the roots of law in revenge still show, rely on strict liability more heavily than modern legal systems do" (35). While we will return to my titular theme of Posner's revenge in the next section, I would like to deal here with only one example of legal and literary vengefulness treated by Posner: Shylock's behavior in *The Merchant of Venice*.

This rich comedy, in my view second only to *Billy Budd* in importance for Law and Literature studies, has received relatively light treatment by some interdisciplinarians.[40] Again, Posner's attention to the text is welcome. Again, his analysis proves to be substantively reductionist, methodologically curious, and totally subservient to his jurisprudential vision.

Briefly to recapitulate a plot lovingly recounted earlier in this volume: Shylock, seeking satisfaction from a merchant (Antonio) on a bond that obliged the latter to repay a debt at forfeit of a pound of his flesh, comes to court in Venice. Apparently unattackable on the law, Shylock refuses to explain his urge to exact the penalty and is about to kill the debtor-defendant when the beautiful Portia (disguised as a male legal expert) saves the day. (S)he warns Shylock to cut "just a pound of flesh" (IV.i.322), no more nor less. If the measure is inexact, or if anything not "denominated" in the bond—such as "one drop of Christian blood" (IV.i.307)—is extracted, Shylock's life and property fall to the mercy of the state. Shylock accepts the argument and would leave the court, defeated and unrecompensed. But Portia requires more, citing a little-known statute that finally, in ascending order of repugnance to him, forces Shylock to his knees, to the loss of legal control of his property, and to the acceptance of Christianity.

For Posner, Shylock's defeat is also the defeat of an outmoded ethical and legal system:

> In rejecting Old Testament vengefulness and Judaic preoccupation with formal, law-like observances, Antonio rejects Shylock's dominant characteristics.... In legal terms, one might say that strict rules of law, however necessary to a well-ordered society, must be applied with sensitivity and tact so that the spirit of law is not sacrificed unnecessarily to the letter. One is reminded that in the evolution of a legal system the first stage after revenge is law in the sense of fixed rules, formally or as one might say technically interpreted; strict liability, of which Shylock is an exponent, looms large at this stage. (95-96; footnote omitted)

From this point, the argument becomes a little devious. Posner inserts a paragraph indicating that Portia's ploy in fact is hardly equitable at all; rather, she, too, is "forced to argue in the legalistic terms that are the only ones available in the legal culture depicted in the play" (97). Although Posner attempts to maintain that Portia is still acting in the "spirit" of equity, he must admit that she turns to legal argument, and to one "stronger than it first appears" (97). Quickly thereafter, though, he returns to the assertion that the play's "mature values ... imply a view of law in which the primitive impulse of revenge and the earliest, formalistic stage of law are rejected in favor of a more flexible or equitable jurisprudence" (98-99). In essence, Posner wants it, and thus gets it, both ways. While most Law and Literature critics have had to choose whether Portia is out-lawyering Shylock[41] or using equitable remedies,[42] Posner tries to avoid the choice altogether.

Posner's traditionalist defense of Portia's courtroom tactics assumes that her legalistic techniques carry the day for her. But it strikes me that she is a mere legal technician only once, in the contract law quibble, and that her citing the alien statute at the end of the trial scene essentially constitutes a move to equity.[43]

As a mere technician, Portia is none too effective. Her argument opens itself to the oft-stated critique, noted by Posner (94), that the pound of flesh *had* to include blood in the extraction. Land sales include trees, soil, and other objects without specific mention, and the forfeiture of the bond should be similarly construed. Since Shylock says eloquently, "I stay here on my bond" (IV.i.239)—not on any revenge principle— Portia's lone contract law argument should hardly defeat him. It does so only because Shylock is in fact not a lawyer, not represented by one, and disinclined to argue in his own behalf if he thinks a fair reading of the law has been delivered. Surely, if he knew who Portia really was, he—like most modern litigants—would reject the interpretation of a thoroughly self-interested interloper.[44] Her legal acuity alone cannot account for Portia's success.

Whether out of a sense of amazement that Shylock has so easily surrendered (the most benign explanation), or because she is so caught up in her creative lawyering that she craves more of the role, or because she really is the racist implied in an earlier pronouncement,[45] Portia unnecessarily pursues her attack. Some twenty-five lines after the matter has been decided successfully, Portia conjures a statute vital only if her aim is to bring Shylock totally down as an individual:

> Tarry, Jew!
> The law hath yet another hold on you.
> It is enacted in the laws of Venice.
> If it be proved against an alien,
> That by direct or indirect attempts
> He seek the life of any citizen,
> The party 'gainst the which he doth contrive
> Shall seize one half his goods; the other half
> Comes to the privy coffer of the state;
> And the offender's life lies in the mercy
> Of the Duke only, 'gainst all other voice. (IV.i.342–52)

Her purely legalistic, contractual quibble already had won. But Portia needs a different—shall we say a more vengeful?—victory. As some literary scholars have begun to observe, Portia's statutory argument teaches us more about revenge than anything Shylock has hitherto tried.[46] Posner does not clearly see this for what it is; his blindness toward Vere's subjective use of the courtroom in *Billy Budd* afflicts him here as well:

> The additional rabbit that Portia pulls out of her hat ... is dramatically necessary in order to complete Shylock's defeat. If he merely could not enforce the bond he would be disappointed but would have his wealth intact (except maybe for the money loaned Bassanio) and would not have to convert to Christianity. Here as elsewhere Shakespeare sacrifices plausibility to dramatic effect.[47]

Recall, first, that Posner seems to believe that Portia's reference to the superannuated statute is but a legalistic technique; if so, there is nothing really "implausible" about her citing it, since it does on its terms apply to Shylock's case. But Posner's argument is more seriously flawed: he assumes that the dramatic necessity of this comedy compels the extreme remedy that Portia produces by using the statute. Yet nothing about the Elizabethan audience required such great misery, even for villains far worse than Shylock. The comedic knot has been delightfully untied by Portia's first, contractual argument. So Posner's parenthetical analysis misses the most logical view of Portia's behavior: she, and not anything dramatically compelled, wants more from this situation. Despite having her husband's mind set at ease, his friend's life saved (and, not so parenthetically, his pocketbook enriched), and the quality of mercy sustained in open court against a harsh legalism, she wants the rest of Shylock's wealth, at least as an equitable remainder, and she wants his soul in fee simple absolute.

Portia, liberated by equity to take charge of this matter in its broadest sense, wants *her* pound of flesh. As wondrous and attractive a comic heroine as e'er graced the stage, she is also playing to her immediate audience within the play, not really to Shakespeare's larger audience. Her verbal mastery, and her ability to use power, will not be lost later upon Bassanio when the disguise is lifted. Her vindication of the worst Christian instincts, epitomized by Gratiano's hysterical anti-Semitism, will only endear her to the kinds of people Bassanio has chosen as friends. More damning still, she reinvigorates her own earlier racism, directed against the failed Moroccan suitor in Act II. She has come to court solely to appease her husband's anxiety about Antonio, and she will leave having taught her husband about her own verbal power, a lesson continued on a far more ironic level, as we shall see, in the play's still legalistic final Act V.

Portia's statutory argument, mere surplusage if Portia's sole aim was to save a life and end a lawsuit, portrays graphically not so much an excess of law as an extraordinary example of what happens to law when it falls into the hands of self-interested and articulate authority figures. Portia mimics the cruel values of her friends and colleagues, epitomized in the humiliation of the traditional *bouc émissaire*, or scapegoat, the Jew. The Jew, with his peculiar allegiance to clan, to oaths, to marriage vows,[48] must be destroyed, not simply defeated. So, as Shakespeare knew, it had always been when Christian values were put to the test by the older ethical system.

Posner is right, therefore, when he turns to equity to justify Portia's behavior, and he is right when he says

> In recognition of the subtlety and generosity, by sixteenth-century standards, of Shakespeare's characterization of the Jew, it should be noted that Shylock's insistence on the principle of literal interpretation need not be viewed merely

as the product of a primitive and vengeful spirit. As an unpopular alien (a point that Shylock harps on and the Christians do not deny), naturally he would mistrust a jurisprudence that gave judges a broad dicretion to mitigate the rigors of legal rules, for he could expect any discretion to be exercised against him. (97)

The statement, Posner's finest about the play, undermines not only the rest of his interpretation but also his arbitrary jurisprudence. Where insensitive judges, blessed with rhetorical force, are allowed to lose sight of law, we get not "equity," as Posner would have it, but raw power, usually mustered against society's least powerful members. The cerebral Posnerian judge, shorn of any commitment to law, to life, or to literature, can hand down edicts that, Portia-like, have elegance but, in the words of Lorenzo just before the trial scene, "defy the matter" (III.v.65).

As I demonstrated earlier in this volume, by her return to Belmont in Act V, Portia's tolerance for equitable jurisprudence, and Christian metaphysics has been exhausted. Posner thus is quite right that "Shakespeare was not the kind of Christian who thinks it possible to manage society using the Sermon on the Mount as one's blueprint of social engineering" (98). But the implications of this insight Posner refuses to contemplate.

People need law, at least decent systems of law, implemented fairly and not by recourse to self-interest or arbitrary declaration. If Shylock's reliance on promise and oaths seems "primitive," we must understand that this reliance is his only protection—and it may be ours as well. So, when Posner states later that "Shylock exemplifies ressentiment" (133), he is being arbitrary, and he is dead wrong.[49] Shylock's passion is extreme, but it is adequately motivated and directed against the unique source of enmity, Antonio. Rightly, and comedically, Shylock pays for his lack of moderation, but he pays in excess currency.

Posner's "more flexible and equitable jurisprudence" requires from its practitioners a serious and constant self-examination. It requires from the public the most careful scrutiny to guarantee that the flexibility will not be used arbitrarily and at the expense of unpopular and powerless others. In periods such as our own, when there is no binding culture or prevailing sense of rightness, flexibility is risky.

Literature can bind us and help us to define a personal and communal voice. Posner's rejection of the literary nature of law is itself arbitrary and defensive. With Portia, as with Vere, he is unwilling to explore the values literature reveals as covertly underlying the "flexible" jurisprudence of the authoritative adjudicator.

## CONCLUSION: THE REVENGE THEME

This essay's title has a double meaning that by now may be evident. First, of course, I am referring to the theme of revenge that Posner treats pervasively in the law-in-literature part of his book. Second, I make reference to the polemical, often extreme tone he uses in referring to the work of earlier scholars in this interdisciplinary field. The first of these meanings I have treated in the preceding section—and it has also been dealt with extensively in other analyses of Posner's book.[50] All have noted the irony that, in an attempt to prove that literature has little to say to lawyers, Posner instead demonstrates in his opening chapter that it can be a unique source of learning about key jurisprudential topics. The second vengeful aspect of Posner's book I have to some extent resisted answering, since many of his more extreme remarks are directed at me. However, I will suggest—as does the literature I treat, most notably Dostoevski's *Notes From the Underground*[51]—that verbal excesses usually demarcate vengeful states of mind. Nothing in Posner's earlier work presages the tone of *Law and Literature*. A sensitive chord has apparently been struck.

But the revenge theme can also help introduce a more forward-looking aspect to the ongoing debates. Is private revenge inevitably a weaker, or even less efficient, path to order than that provided by a legal system, no matter of what type?[52] And within legal systems, is the move from hidebound legalism to flexible fairness inevitably felicitous?

These questions, lucidly raised and discussed by Posner in terms of literature, should be addressed through Law and Literature studies as through no other medium. Indeed, despite Posner's assertions, it has been. At the very outset of *The Failure of the Word*, I write:

> One of the oldest literary paradigms, that of insult and revenge, structures all of these highly modern texts. But, beginning with *Notes From Underground*, the "insult" has been reduced to a figment of the protagonist's overheated verbal imagination. Harking back to Hamlet, but lacking the need for vengeance revealed to that protagonist, these seminal characters use words not only to avoid disturbing realities but also to create them.[53]

The modern revenge theme emphasizes the purely imaginary vengeance of people bereft of any ordering system by which to make judgments about themselves and others. It is not a marginal aspect, but rather almost a defining feature of contemporary intellectuals. Literature reveals that such people, if kept out of power, do little harm except to themselves and a handful of victimized others who fall prey to their negative vision.

But fiction also indicates that, on many occasions, such people achieve institutional power.

The kind of power novelists focus upon is, quite naturally, of a piece with their own power, because it is grounded in the narrative acts that define literary art. It is the socially more forceful, but still essentially literary field of law that fascinates them.

Mainstream modern fiction cannot look benignly upon law, not (as Posner insists, in rebutting what he wrongly sees as an attack on law by earlier scholars) because it rejects law per se, but rather because it fears those who have come to control law. A cycle of "insult-and-revenge" pervades this literature, and it is insufficiently recognized as the chief threat to just dispositions of so many of today's basic issues. To mention just a few of those issues: Can women be treated fairly in our legal system? If not, why not? If so, how? Can minorities ever achieve fair treatment under law? Like women, as this fiction forcefully demonstrates, their "otherness" is perceived as a threat to many institutional legal figures, covertly or overtly. The system's modernistic show of vengeance is, as Robert Cover has eloquently demonstrated, just as "violent" as that of primitive epic warriors.[54] Can vitalistic values—love of environment, sexual and artistic expression, individual eccentricity, personal privacy meshed with public responsibility—survive a predominantly verbal and often repressed and antivitalistic legal power structure? Can the perspective of children, so wonderfully conveyed by great fiction, be appreciated by modern legal institutions? Or the plight of the poor and the homeless?

At a higher level of generality, one that might satisfy even Posner's demand that Law and Literature propose both an approach and a solution to social problems, I would suggest that literature provides the best jurisprudential chance for fathoming the complex effects of theoretical equality upon hierarchically nonequal citizens of a bourgeois democracy. Most modern law-related fiction, as we have seen, notes that the insult-and-revenge phenomenon is transformed in modern society to imagined insults and impersonal (usually verbal) lashings out at innocent victims. Equality unmatched by economic parity is a tough concept to frame one's life by and appears to breed resentments in many hierarchically influential people. (Garry Wills' brilliant portrait of Richard Nixon gives us our best nonfictional glimpse at this pervasive problem.[55]) But this phenomenon has been ignored, even by our foremost traditional jurisprudential thinkers (like John Rawls),[56] who treat insult-and-revenge almost as an afterthought, instead of as a destructive corollary, of theoretical equality.

We are bereft, as a legal culture, when we have no sense of values to

connect us. The social sciences have not shown the way to a more coherent, fair, or just legal environment, although they try to address some
of these problems. Traditional jurisprudence has not touched the lives
of most academics, much less of most practicing lawyers and judges.
Literary jurisprudence provides a method to understand the values both
of the institutionally powerful and of those whose lives they come to
adjudicate. We must move beyond insult-and-revenge, not only in our
private but also in our public behavior. This is the work, through the
discipline of literature, of the next decade of Law and Literature studies.
I believe that Richard Posner has greatly helped to move us in that direction.

# 16. From Jefferson to the Gulf War: How Lawyers Have Lost Their Golden Tongue

I need not remind this audience[57] of the traditional linkage of law and
literature since the early days of the Republic. Perhaps our greatest Revolutionary thinker—Thomas Jefferson—laid claim to the unifying virtues
of law and letters. Perennially fascinated by the classics,[58] Jefferson once
took the time to produce quite an effective essay on English prosody.[59]
As a writer, he achieved greatness by recalling (as he did in every genial
act of engineering and inventive brilliance) that form and function, style
and substance, always merge in excellent prose. In his sole full-length
book, *Notes on the State of Virginia*,[60] Jefferson brought a lawyerlike
sense of organization to topics ranging from Virginia's climate and to-
pography to the ambitions of first-decade America. In a sentence aptly
emphasized by Robert A. Ferguson, who redeems Jefferson's book from
its relative obscurity,[61] the author of the *Notes* perfectly articulates the
new land: "Young as we are, and with such a country before us to fill
with people and with happiness, we should point in that direction the
whole generative force of nature, wasting none of it in efforts of mutual
destruction."[62]

This sentence stands as a model for my remarks here. Its force comes
from the unity of idealism and practical duty, of nature and reason, of
the spiritual and the material—unities that continue to characterize (however great the changes that have occurred) the late twentieth-century
practitioner of American law. But beyond this, and in a manner more
remote from today's legal climate, the sentence *speaks its meaning*. The
words *are* the meaning, nothing less. We find in passages such as this, as
Ferguson puts it, "the association of voice with action and control, the

assertion of solution within the context of speech, and the glorification of a dialectic or argumentative intellect."[63]

As with those other lawyer-writers of our Republic's founding program—the authors of the Federalist Papers—Jefferson recognized in the 1780s that his prose needed not only to describe but actually to *become* the vision of the new nation. "Young as we are," he begins, in an introductory clause that anticipates the sentence's forcefully personal subject, "we"—*we* must do the work both of the sentence and of the fledgling nation. We find here none of the impersonality of today's legal prose. The writer takes full responsibility for his program, makes it also his reader's, and, in the process, associates "nature" with himself, his reader, and "such a country" as together they will "fill with people and with happiness."

The southern lawyer in particular perhaps proceeded across the next seventy-five years—even while the North began to pursue a more impersonal and gradually alienated voice—to unify his program and his words. Amid such prominent lawyer-writers as John Pendleton Kennedy, Sidney Lanier, George Fitzhugh, A. B. Longstreet, and many others, Edgar Allen Poe stands almost anomalously as one of the few great southern writers who never studied law.[64]

In the early nineteenth century, of course, one would not contemplate letters without lawyers, or law without the ally of strongly expressive words. Lawyers like Daniel Webster and Richard Henry Dana carried our national vision from one generation to the next, burnishing it with the fire of strong subjects and verbs, of disequilibrating metaphor, of stunning imagery. Yet today, at least until the recent reawakening that takes the name "Law and Literature," the lawyer may think of language as a barrier to thought rather than a carrier of it; he may denigrate rhetoric, style, and narrative to a status of strangeness or even artificiality in legal prose.

On the syntactical level, in sentence after legalistic sentence, the twentieth-century lawyer metamorphoses Jefferson's "we should point" into "it might be said," or "the conclusion may be warranted," or "the effort might be made." Vibrant thoughts and arguments disappear into impersonal constructions and nonresponsible agencies.[65] Jefferson's thought, these days, would be transmogrified as follows: "It is to be hoped that, in view of the youthful qualities of this country, which needs to be filled with people and with happiness, that nature in its various aspects will be permitted to be utilized to those ends, avoiding if and when possible, costly wars." But this unhappy translation of Jefferson leaves us altogether bereft of his original thought.

For Robert Ferguson—as for Oliver Wendell Holmes much earlier in the century[66]—the falling off of legal communication can be directly explained by the increased specialization of modern legal practice. But surely the Jeffersonian lawyer, too, reveled in a sense of high competence and professional expertise. Nor need we assume, even if today's lawyers *are* indeed more specialized, an inevitable gap between expertise and expression. The specialized lawyer needs, as much as the generalist, to write well. Specialized language—"stripped technical discourse," as Karl Llewellyn's esthetics most forcefully puts it[67]—is the law's most beautiful language, and it was not for nothing that the French novelist Stendhal (seeking inspiration) read three pages of the *Code Napoléon* every night.[68]

If increased specialization alone cannot explain the profession's recently degraded use of language, neither can the more cynical view that greedy lawyers deliberately obfuscate so that only they can decipher the law's mysteries. I will return to that heresy shortly. History more than greed explains the bizarre quality of lawtalk, and history also proves that legalese is not always a bar to inclusive communication. Jefferson himself could trace the redundancies "null and void" or "last will and testament" to that day some seven hundred years before his time when the Normans reached England and brought their native tongue's equivalents to the words English lawyers already had carved in stone.[69] Yet there was beauty to those mellifluous phrases, as to their alliterative cousin, "release, relinquish, and remit." As a practitioner, Jefferson surely did not fear the use of such other strange creatures of our legal language, the *fee tail male* and the *estate pur autre vie*; he had protected more than one child *en ventre sa mere*. He seized legal language at its most technical, and he made the language live. Not against the historical grain but fully toward it, he became the powerful protector of "life, liberty, and the pursuit of happiness" for all.

Today, the practitioner's language mystifies and alienates—it does not protect or attract—the laity. But this is due neither to specialization nor to the inevitable obscurity of technical discourse. Rather, the fault lies in the *everyday* use of language. Not in their jargon but in their commonplace syntax do contemporary lawyers lose their audience and surrender their historical place at the center of the nation's discourse. And the costs of this impoverished professional speech have begun to outweigh greatly whatever meager benefits may come from strangeness.

Until law and literature, like Plato's Androgyne, strive to recouple, until the Jeffersonian unities reemerge in legal language, the profession runs at least four considerable risks. Two of these threaten law's relationship with the public; two perhaps more portentously involve the law's sense of itself. These risks are:

1. the risk of ridicule and even rebellion among the laity;
2. the risk of surrendering the law's dominance in American politics and culture;
3. the risk of severe professional dissatisfaction; and
4. the risk of professional ethical relativism.

As a window to the profession's values, the writings of the law have been scrutinized more of late than in the past. People peer at what lawyers write, seeking an index of the profession's goals and beliefs. But if heightened recently, this scrutiny comes from a long and distinguished tradition.

For years, lawyers have been aware of the public's unhappiness with their professional writing. Despite their acute ability to listen carefully and speak well, lawyers found fewer incentives to transcribe such communication skills onto parchment. They came to understand their own prose, and the public suffered through it. But the laity started complaining very early on about legal writing—and, unfortunately for lawyers, the complainants numbered among them our culture's best-known writers.

This criticism, loudest over the past 150 years, finds its modern origins in Shakespeare. It was Dick the Butcher, in the second part of *Henry VI*, who uttered the line that the profession itself seems masochistically to like best: "The first thing we do, let's kill all the lawyers" (IV.ii.73); what we often forget is that the remark refers specifically to the way lawyers write, which the rebel Jack Cade insists can "undo a man" in and of itself. Later, Jonathan Swift would detect in lawyers "a peculiar cant and jargon of their own that no other mortal can understand."

Not coincidentally, however, the upsurge of lay criticism about legal language begins around the time that law was losing its ascendancy over cultural discourse. Thus Charles Dickens, in novel after novel, pillories the legal speech he knew so well. In *Bleak House*, examined earlier in this volume,[70] a host of otherwise dissimilar lawyers manage as a group to startle their lay listeners into reactions of amazement, distaste, even madness and self-destruction. And our own century has (with the exception of the horrific continental worlds of Kafka, Camus, and Solzhenitsyn—where terror and legal language are inexorably linked) produced scathing satire on the writing of lawyers. Notable examples can be found in the very literature of the South that once exalted law and unified it with letters; William Faulkner's lawyers in such novels as *Sanctuary* or *Light in August* distort justice as they speak cleverly but to no ethical purpose.

To one extent or another, these artists share Carl Sandburg's view that "in the heels of higgling lawyers, Bob, / Too many slippery ifs and buts and howevers / Too much hereinbefore provided whereas, Too many doors to go in and out of." Sandburg poetically replicates Keats' pithier remark that "[he] would classify lawyers in the natural history of monsters," and later associates the lawyer's anarchic verbosity, as had Dickens before him, with the lawyer's greed: "When a lawyer is through, what is left? Enough for a mouse to nibble on?"

Such views of lawyers we all know, and they are not lost on the profession either. Lawyers read, often voraciously, and they positively devour satires about themselves. (This self-critical taste in reading comes in part from the lawyer's innate modesty, which I will discuss further on.) Even in popular culture, legal writing is raked over the coals. The sleazy lawyer in the film *Body Heat* (1981) falls not because of his questionable morality; it is ultimately his poorly drafted perpetuities clause that gives him away. A certain knee-jerk formalism and boilerplate mentality defeats the hapless Hamilton Burger time after time as he vies with the more creative and verbally forceful Perry Mason. Formalism and archaism have provided grist for the cartoon writers, too: Motley Crew once portrayed a lawyer hurling Latin phrases at his flabbergasted clients who, upon examining the bill he hands them as they leave, conclude that "Latin lessons must be expensive."

Leave it to that sensitive barometer of cultural pressure, the *New York Times*, to reveal in a 1977 headline that attorneys could no longer even understand one another; as the *Times* put it, "Lawyers Now Confuse Even the Same Aforementioned." By then, change was in the air, for around that time pioneering states were passing the first Plain English statutes,[71] and the federal government was also trying to sweep clean the thick and musty world of regulations, tax advisory opinions, and even briefs to the Supreme Court. The laity was beginning to make itself felt.

If lawyers have, by their words, alienated the individual nonlawyer; if the threat of litigation now must coerce the straightforward discourse that Jefferson always used when addressing a lay audience; if potential clients now think twice before retaining a clumsy wordsmith to verbalize the sensitive moments in their lives—yet the profession faces even a greater risk regarding the outside world. The lawyer's place as the arbiter and the rhetorician of the nation's values may have been permanently surrendered. No longer does a James Madison or a Daniel Webster or an Abraham Lincoln fashion the Republic's aspirations by linking them to simple but elegant speech.

No. For, as a result of a pitched battle across a decade and before television audiences of millions, the verbal struggle has been lost. And who now dominates the discursive center? Not the creative writers; their voices are dispersed and idiosyncratic. Surely not the preachers; they are in disarray or in jail. Not even the journalists, who have sacrificed whatever prose power they once had to the twenty-second sound bite and the pretty face. The winners and at least temporary rhetorical champions are . . . the military.

Think for a moment of the Iran-Contra hearings. Against an army of brilliant lawyers, it was the Army that emerged victorious. Oliver North became a national hero, his interlocutors forgotten (despite the nobility of their purpose), because of the drabness of their speech! North's snappy "Disobey orders? Not this lieutenant colonel! I saluted smartly, turned on my heels, and did my bidding!" easily prevailed over such dreary, verbose lawyers' interrogatories as "At what point in time?" "Did there come a time when . . . ," "At such a time as . . . ," and "On the basis of the above." These preposition sandwiches, which studiously delay the meat of the inquiry, bowed to the strong, active subjects and verbs of the military. This trend continued during the Persian Gulf crisis. A general responded to a question about the usefulness of American airpower with the crisply rendered "Our planes will at least interdict Saddam's tanks." And General Schwartzkopf's direct speech, characterized by pithiness and syntactical force, easily outpaced the puffy self-promotion of Congress as it verbosely debated the wisdom of the military action. Most of those wordy legislators were, of course, trained in the nation's law schools. But whoever (or whatever) is teaching the military to communicate, he, she, or it should be hired by lawyers. Whereas lawyers habitually change nice short verbs into nouns and then make those long abstractions the subjects of their sentences, these colonels and generals reverse the process, making verbs out of nouns, shortening their sentences, and winning the hearts and minds of the American people. Consider the following sentence at the close of a brief: "The ultimate termination of this litigation would be materially advanced by correction, at this stage, of the deprivation of due process resulting from denial to X of access to information at issue." No profession so encumbered can long endure. We can learn from the military to avoid lengthening verbs into nouns, such as the *five* abstract nouns ending in "-tion" contained in the sentence. Let us interdict abstractions, wherever possible.

While lawyers risk alienating the lay reader and listener, their poor communication strategies also directly threaten their own inner peace. Poor writing, in my opinion, has produced unhappy lawyers. And here I refer not to the dismal daily task of trying to understand another lawyer's prose; instead, I make the claim that the individual writer's *own* habits produce depression on the job.

Workplace unhappiness pervades all corners of our society, in a way that would have shocked Jefferson and his effusively industrious compatriots. A recent survey reports that 68 percent of American corporate executives dislike their jobs and that 99 percent of that sad group see no possibility of job satisfaction any time in the future! But the American Bar Association has brought this point home to lawyers. Citing a 1990 ABA paper, the *New York Times* revealed that "job dissatisfaction among lawyers is widespread, profound, and growing worse." David Margolick's column continues: "The increased stress of dissatisfaction and billable hours have disturbing and important implications for the profession. . . . These lie in the area of increasing social dysfunction or destructive behavior by lawyers and the impact of this behavior on themselves, their families, their quality of work and productivity, their firms and their clients."

While draconian, this rhetoric rings true. Given their salaries and their respected place in society, lawyers are not as happy as they should be. Yet in explaining this "dysfunction," the ABA report wrongly substitutes effect for cause. The profession's way of practicing (including the way it communicates) is the cause of the depression, not the reverse. Once the legal profession reclaims its natural birthright and resumes forceful communication both within its own ranks and when it speaks to the laity, I believe that lawyers will regain a Jeffersonian enthusiasm for their craft.

The first step to professional bliss lies, once again, on the path to strong syntax. The lesson is brief and deceptively simple: choose the best subject, grammatically speaking, for the sentence. My experience with hundreds of lawyers has taught me that almost every ill, every sense of powerlessness before the blank page or anger when that page is filled with weak prose, will disappear as soon as this lesson is learned. The lawyer's so-called dysfunction is probably nothing more than a *fear of naming.* When our elementary school teachers taught us not to say, "The cat was eaten by the dog," but rather, "The dog ate the cat," they revealed the key to strong expository writing. By making the subject *dog* (the most active thing present to our thought), we produce a syntactically wonderful sentence. The various faults of the alternative—"The cat was eaten by the dog"—are all eliminated. First, strong verbs follow from strong subjects: *ate* is a good transitive verb, not *was eaten*—a paltry passive that adds flab to the verbiage and nothing to the sense. Five words suffice where seven otherwise afflict us. The reader has a vivid, not just a thorough, reflection of the writer's thought. And the writer has fully expressed his or her own verbal power, without superfluous language, without burning the midnight oil to find the apt phrase. The writer is happier; the reader is ecstatic.

Instead, here are several all-too-typical sentences from the profession:

1. Claimants in this action would be benefited by the Price-Anderson waiver of defenses clause.
2. The Senate-passed version of the bill is not said to be retroactive.
3. Borrowing from the reasoning in the cases, and applying the time worn canons of construction, it may be concluded that the interpretation accorded the predecessor of Section 6511 has been accepted by Congress.
4. The purpose of this memorandum is to determine whether an excise tax may be levied by the Legislature.

In each of these sentences, the writer pushes the true subject off by choosing a false subject, often one that is really the object of the original action. When "claimants," instead of "Price Anderson waiver," become the first sentence's subject, the awkward and wordy "would be benefited" must be inserted. In the second sentence, the Senate-passed version of the bill "is not said to be retroactive"—here the subject disappears altogether; neither the cat nor the dog shows up. The reader is left to ponder *who* failed to discuss retroactivity, although we have a vague hunch that the Senate itself is the actor. Instead, the writer has chosen an abstraction—"version"—as the subject, creating verbiage and confusion and diminishing the writer's own sense of mastery over the thought that needs expression.

The third sentence exemplifies the legal writer's compulsion to avoid the first person singular. "It may be concluded" trots out four words for the simple "I conclude" that the vertical pronoun allows. How clean! How direct! And how likely to cure that dysfunction conjured by the ABA report. Most lawyers, of course, would almost kill to avoid saying "I." But when, on rare occasions, the writer *is* the subject of his thought, he should be the subject of the written phrase as well.

The fourth example exerts a double-bind passivity: "The purpose of this memorandum" keeps the writer from actually beginning to work; this is called "throat clearing." But while a nervous speaker may be permitted this tick at the outset of a speech, a writer does not enjoy such latitude. Instead, throat clearing becomes fatal, because the writer loses the reader at exactly the moment of fullest attention—the beginning of the sentence, the paragraph, or the document as a whole. And finally, "an excise tax may be levied by the Legislature" parrots the unacceptable "cat was eaten by the dog" paradigm. The final sentence should read simply, "This memorandum determines whether the Legislature may levy an excise tax."

Syntactical weakness does not mean analytical weakness. But lawyers must relearn the essential lesson that thoroughness and effectiveness *need not compete* in the domain of legal communication. Only this will lead to renewed job satisfaction. Why do lawyers habitually push the strong, the real, the active, to the end of their sentences, even sometimes to the end of their paragraphs or entire documents? While two recent experts have asserted fourteen reasons for this phenomenon, thus in part also exemplifying it, I would answer with the "three Ms": modesty, market, and models. Before turning to the last risk of bad professional prose (ethical relativism), I will elaborate briefly on the three Ms:

*Modesty.* Unlike their public image, exacerbated by such egocentric television shows as "L.A. Law," or by such glamour-ridden celluloid legal protagonists as Al Pacino, Robert Redford, and Harrison Ford, lawyers are in truth a modest lot. I contend that they take this admirable trait one step too far by transporting it into almost every sentence they write. True, the law itself often eludes facile restatement. But, surely, at the end of a memorandum, the writer has earned the right to say, "I conclude," or even "I believe," instead of the more typical "It might be concluded," or "There is reason to state in closing that . . . ," or sundry other depressingly wordy alternatives. Judges need not bury their hard-earned judgments—for which they are, after all, paid—behind passive prose. Lawyers need not deliberately structure first lines of letters or first paragraphs of documents to hide their salient points. The reader cries out for direct information; the lawyer demurs. Such excessive modesty betrays not only the individual practitioner's right to speak up forcefully but also his reader's desire for him to do so.

*Market.* Three related market factors contribute to poor expository prose. First, and most cynically, some say that lawyers deliberately obfuscate to increase their revenues. In this view, hiding the subject and using abstractions are deliberate ploys, designed to extend each matter and justify higher fees. As Dickens opined, "The soul vocation of English law is to make money for itself"—a sentiment echoed by Will Rogers, who once said, "Every time a lawyer writes something, he is not writing for posterity, he is writing so that endless others of his craft can make a living out of trying to figure out what he said." This market explanation for weak writing will not withstand scrutiny. If lawyers knew how to write simply and strongly, they would do so, not only for other lawyers or judges, but also for increasingly demanding clients. Effective writing enhances the lawyer's reputation, the client's satisfaction, and the judge's willingness to see it his or her way.

Next, and almost as cynically, a second market-based assertion posits that the public actually *craves* the mystery and majesty of the law's obscure prose. Without a special language of its own, the law would lose its veneer, its very status. After all, doctors cure real illnesses, architects design real structures, and the military (again!) fights real battles. Lawyers create, or so it is said, a web of words to order and then mask reality, to master it and keep it from the uninitiated, who thenceforth yearn to enter its mysteries. I think there is much to this view, at least historically, but we have already seen this Kafkaesque vision overcome by an activist laity intolerant of legal gobbledygook. The costs of writing obscurely have begun to outweigh the market benefits. Clients have demystified the law; they no longer quake in their boots as they demand from counsel prose they can understand in one reading.

So it is the third market-based explanation, and the least cynical, that strikes me as most accurate. Lawyers spend their professional lives seeking the respect of their colleagues, of those who judge them throughout their careers. These respected insiders base such judgments in large part on the lawyer's written work product. So younger lawyers in particular strive to determine what this most important "market" demands. To the extent that lawyers continue to feel that they *must* provide their colleagues with passive, unassuming, wordy prose, they will in all good faith continue to write poorly. If lawyers believe that they must give judges colorless prose, if they believe that their firm or department demands passive self-effacement, if the whole climate of legal writing reinforces the weakest habits of the profession's prose, lawyers will continue for no economic reason at all to write poorly. But only lawyers truly control the marketplace of legal language, and they are beginning to fortify it. Lawyers are learning that they should not anticipate market rejection when they assert themselves through prose. They have renewed their kinship with Jefferson and his colleagues, who imbibed with their mothers' milk the understanding that thoroughness and forcefulness are allies, not competitors, when lawyers speak and write. They perceive anew that career emoluments follow the salutary turn to strong subject choice. The market demands that the profession redeem its heritage of excellent writing. And this brings us to the third M that helps explain our era's disjunction of law and literature.

*Models.* From the moment the novice enters law school, he is pushed toward the flat prose he will use once past the bar. Appellate opinions, the stuff of his first-year training, might inspire—think of this volume's focus upon Cardozo[72]—but few teachers these days stress the link between style and substance that is essential to a knowledge of our system of justice. If the student does well enough to "make law review," he paradoxically will lose whatever good writing skills he might have preserved through that first year. I recall vividly my first staff meeting on an East Coast law journal that shall remain nameless. I received a circular on law review writing; one of its early paragraphs began, "Since the mechanics of writing will vary enormously with the scope and content of the note and with the style and approach of the author." With that sentence fragment proposed as my model, I chose not to read further. Many students today, less passive perhaps than I was, are choosing not to join the law journals. Some start their own. Many of these students retain their native or imbued facility with the written word. So do some who proceed to clerk for judges, thus increasing the chances that the judicial opinion will also serve once again to inspire. But many others regenerate the passive prose that has for so long infected our profession.

When the kind of models proposed in this volume gain ascendancy, when lawyers read at least one novel a month, when senior attorneys again take a personal interest in *how the law means* within their firms, then the third risk of legal communication will be sharply diminished. Lawyers will be happy, exhilarated by the prospects of strong and compelling prose afforded by their profession. And if, too, the stories that lawyers read challenge them to understand their place within the profession and to see that the way lawyers talk affects the potential for justice within every legal situation, then the fourth risk of poor professional communication may also be alleviated. I turn now to that most important of risks.

Poor subject choice, as we have seen, permits the lawyer to hide the true nature of his thought; often it permits the masking of the legal writer himself, as though he were not really responsible for his words. Stories about law reveal the outermost risks of impersonal communication. Such brilliant storytellers as Shakespeare, Melville, Dickens, Twain, and those moderns, William Faulkner, Joyce Carol Oates, John Barth, Toni Morrison, Bernard Malamud, and E. L. Doctorow, link their frequent legal themes to the way lawyers talk and write. When stories talk about law, therefore, a sense of ethics as well as of style emerges (if the two can really be separated).

Storytellers seem to be challenging lawyers to recall the human dimension that remains at the core of their seemingly "technical" discourse.

No lawyer who has read *The Bluest Eye* can misperceive the aspirations of those different from himself, those who might not talk or even feel the way a lawyer does; none who has opened himself to *Billy Budd, Sailor* can be insensitive to the pitfalls of deceptive professional speech; none who has read *Bleak House* can ever again blithely mislead a client; all who have read *Intruder in the Dust* will recall that the pursuit of justice in law requires a forged link between words *and* actions.

So the four risks of our contemporary legal world can be alleviated by a return to the early American fusion of law and letters. The discipline of the 1990s for lawyers will be macronarrative, not microeconomic, in nature. Literature will make the practice of law once again not only enjoyable but fully persuasive, one in which lawyers help—as Jefferson once said—to create a candid world "for the truth of which we pledge a faith yet unsullied by falsehood."

# 17. Notes on Three Works by James Boyd White

Since the publication in 1973 of *The Legal Imagination*, James Boyd White has rightfully claimed a leading position in what has since been declared the "field of Law and Literature." In those early years, but decreasingly since, White would have eschewed such an interdisciplinary label for his works. To some extent, his first work presented itself simply as a law school casebook, and specifically an upper-class writing book; later works can be perceived as lengthy, ongoing attempts to redeem law as a rhetorical discipline, and to battle the emerging tendency to see it as one of the social sciences.

Yet, from the beginning, White's evident fascination was for the parallels he saw between law and literature. White portrays the judge as at once a literary critic and a poet—reading the precedents and statutes with an eye toward the new text that inevitably changes both those and the universe of legal language as a whole. That new text, rendered by the judge as poet, would be informed by the fullest vision available to the adjudicator, and while White never says so explicitly, he clearly feels that the reading of fiction "a certain way" would perhaps best serve the judge's ability to create effectively.

Later White began to speak of "communities." Law is not a set of rules, nor an arena for implementing any political or social program. It remains solely a rhetorical art form; yet the rhetoric of the legal actor must always strive to encompass if not all then at least the best of the complexities raised by the given dispute. The art of the judge demands a use of past authorities (the statutes or cases) to create new effects through language. Somehow in this very process, what White likes to call a "reconstitution of communities" will occur. Not every community will be served, far less pleased, but if the opinion grapples with the evoked complexities—and makes that struggle overt—it will likely advance the global rhetoric of the law.

White never denies—indeed he exults in—the ambiguous nature of language. He insists on the value of "speaking two ways"; yet somehow, community can be served if the judge strives to fathom the rhetorical potential of each factual situation. Words may be imprecise and tricky, but even when they "lose their meaning" (the very title of one of White's books), the excellent judge can redirect a discourse to create a new community.

In his latest work (at this writing), *Justice as Translation*, White continues the themes of the past seventeen years. The pitfalls he seems to find in almost all judicial discourse may be overcome if the judge understands that everything is language and that almost anything can be done with language. Communities are formed and reformed by language, not by an intuitive sense of justice or a specific program of social transformation. Instead, the "translation" inherent in good judicial writing for White always begins with the already established *discourse* of the matter at hand. The good judge manages to hear all the sides of that talk and then to create a new text. The text differs from the earlier discourse, just as a translation differs from its "original," yet it is always responsive to it.

Readers have been finding White's work both inspiring and frustrating, almost from the beginning. I share that reaction, as the following discussions of three of his books demonstrate. The first two sections of this essay appeared (in somewhat different form), in 1974 and 1987, respectively, and the third appears here for the first time. Throughout this period I have waited for White to explain how his purely rhetorical system can have any ethical affect. Or, asked differently (as I did in 1973), *should* law aspire to complex rhetoric instead of poetic correctness, to wit instead of judgment, to endless argument instead of culturally informed justice? For, if the essence of law is (merely) the creation of communities between rhetorical actors, what distinguishes good courts from bad? As the essays in this book (chapter 5) relating to Vichy France indicate, rhetoric and even community play central roles in the most totalitarian of legal systems. If lawyers and judges need only guarantee that everyone who comes under their sway will be allowed to talk, but that the *nature* of that talk need be neither straightforward nor thorough (premises asserted consistently in White), what helps the legal actor to understand the rightness of his or her "translation"? Where, finally, do we find in James Boyd White some direction about the goal, and not merely the process, of legal discourse?

If White disparaged such an inquiry, I might be content (with others) to leave him to a rhetorics of law. But, in his latest text, he insists on using the term "ethical" to describe his vision, uses it at least thirty times to describe the process of "speaking two ways" that he so admires. He does not thereby disprove, however, that the slipperiness of legal discourse may produce elegant translations in the service of the legal rhetorician's power and at the expense of all those who cannot—or choose not to—speak the required language. Oppressive systems of law need not shut the mouths of legal actors to enact tyranny. To believe White—but how can we really?—the grant of opportunity to all to speak (however circumscribed the formality) satisfies the prerequisite of establishing the anterior texts that the judge then translates. But he offers no account of the dimension of the problem of guaranteeing that each actor will be able to produce and communicate an *accurate* "text." Always of more importance to White than an honest act of communication is *any* act, for it is the absence of words and that alone that his system cannot abide.

To this extent, White also disregards the probability that the ensconced "translator" (the authoritative lawyer or judge) simply has no interest whatsoever in inviting disempowered outsiders into the discursive arena. As in the police officer's parroting of the *Miranda* warning (applauded by White), formalism replaces the disempowered outsider. Nor should we expect those who control the law's verbal apparatus to exceed other groups in their desire to share rhetorical power. On this aspect, too, and as early as in *The Legal Imagination*, White refuses to contemplate literature's own recognition that the cleverest among us are often our least ethical. Those who "speak two ways" in literature—from Homer's Thersites to Melville's Captain Vere—are normatively portrayed as dishonest, or elitist, or manipulative. They are rarely "ethical," in White's sense, and if they are, it is usually despite their verbal abilities. But White, who sometimes asserts that language is all we have, has seemed disinterested in communities who have been stripped of *their own* language (often by lawyers), but who still have needs and even beliefs that the legal system must somehow serve. Denying the claim that law is merely political rhetoric, White nonetheless fails to inform his reader of any standard by which the rhetoric of judgment should otherwise be evaluated.

Each of the following sections responds to one of White's books. The progression in his writing is reflected in the varying texts and metaphors he emphasized as the years went by. More importantly, the similarities among White's works—and the issues I believe he still needs to face—are evoked by the dominant concerns of all three responses.

## Notes (1974) on *The Legal Imagination*

As one trained in the humanities but involved in the law school environment, I have had occasion to notice both the strengths and the weaknesses of the contrasting pedagogical approaches of these two disciplines. While law professors are often reluctant to go beyond a narrow set of rules into the wider area of self-critical perception, humanists tend to resist contact with any methodology extrinsic to their own aesthetic perceptions. Yet I firmly believe that an expansive view of any discipline may well lead to the truest expression of its essence and potential. To anyone sharing these notions, and to many others who may be skeptical of them, the appearance of James B. White's *The Legal Imagination* should be a welcome event. The final word of the title of this textbook for law students immediately suggests the area of similarity between two seemingly disparate "cultures."[73] Those interested in the relationship of law to the other humanistic disciplines[74] will greatly benefit from Professor White's efforts.

I have encountered no other book in which the "case method," that traditional staple of American legal education, has been so effectively used. One reason for this may be that White does not exclude selections whose sources are other than the federal or state reporters. Thus, while the average casebook more or less compels the student to restrict his vision of legal situations to one narrow set of facts and one procedural setting, *The Legal Imagination* encourages the reader to expand his or her view of a case beyond the legal language that is that situation's microcosm.

One of the author's central observations is that lawyers should recognize that their craft is inevitably associated with the most profound of human experiences. Chapter 2, which contains a section entitled "A Comparative Anthology on Death," is characteristic of this focus and serves to demonstrate White's effective handling of both legal and nonlegal sources. As he does in each chapter, the author begins the discussion by commenting in his own voice on the relationship of the law to the subject under consideration:

> [T]o speak in an inherited and formal language is a dangerous enterprise, and ... for one who engages in it, as the lawyer does, the management of just the right relationship with that language is critical to his success, both in the exercise of his art and in the claims he makes for the meaning of what he does.[75]

The author demonstrates his point by presenting Application of the President and Directors of Georgetown College, Inc. (84)[76] where a dissenting judge argued that the lower court had been powerless to order transfusions to be given to a woman who was otherwise about to die because the ad hoc proceeding had not presented a "case or controversy." Following this case, and indeed most of the others in the book, the author asks a comprehensive series of questions designed to stimulate the kinds of thinking that rarely surface in the law school classrooms. These "Questions" are among the consistent strengths of the text, invariably shaping independent analysis of the legal issues presented. The final questions on the Georgetown College case relates to the role of the attorney:

> Is the lawyer defined procedurally—by the rules and practices of an institution of which he is a part—or is he a free and independent soul? Is he ever told by forces outside of himself that he may not speak to certain matters or, if he is to speak, how he must do so? (89)

The "anthology on death" also includes literary and historical selections on the subject, cases and statutes exemplifying the laws of wrongful death, intestacy and wills, and a moving and effective piece by a psychoanalyst on "The Treatment of a Dying Patient" (174–80). Already made alive to this last excerpt's relevance by the thrust and direction of prior questions and comments, the reader is asked to consider this query:

> Can you think of any analog to this passage in the lawyer's life, any moment where your legal education and your mastery of legal language will enable you to do what no one else can? You are asked to search for the unique, for the heroic, in your profession. What can you bear that another cannot? (180)

Here, as in each section, the author concludes with several "writing assignments" that also encourage an expansion of legal and imaginative consciousness, demonstrating that the two need not unalterably be separated. For example, the student is asked to devise a nonlegal account of a death, and then to assume he is "the lawyer to whom the spouse, child, or parent of the person who died has come" (186). The task here is to express the conversations that the lawyer might have in this instance with the client, an opposing lawyer, a judge, or a jury: "Does the law add to your possibilities here as well as limiting them—is it a valuable resource for speech and thought?" (187).

Although the law is clearly being tested here as an effective instrument of communication, the idea is not to find it failing, but rather to emphasize its creative potential. If this broadening can occur, the individual student will recognize the choice open to him as a working professional.

White returns indirectly to this point later in the text, observing that in our judicial system, "[t]he facts determine what law is relevant; the law, what facts are relevant" (820). Under this peculiar logic, we must preserve the particular reality that inspires every case. Thus, in determining the basis of the "rule" of a case, the student must remain alive to the infinite fascination of each unique litigable circumstance. These human situations, however, doggedly resist formulation, consistently test (and frequently undermine) the rule's validity.[77] Observing the legal pretense that "all people or events similarly labeled are in all respects similar" (234), White therefore emphasizes what most other casebooks minimize—the living event that inspires, but is often forgotten in, the appellate rule.

Small wonder then that literary art plays a role in this textbook. In chapter 3 ("How the Law Talks About People—Who Is This Man?"), literature is especially vital in elucidating and exemplifying the latter point. The author effectively employs two short stories of Saki, essays of Lamb and Forster, and selections from Shakespeare, Tolstoy, Chaucer, and others to demonstrate the difference between "character" and "caricature," and to apply this distinction to the legal experience:

> Character is true to life; caricature, false to it. The obvious suggestion is that the law—especially in its basic form, the rule—is a literature of caricature; it pares away all that can be said about a person's life until nothing is left except the rule and the label. (248)

In addition to using numerous excerpts from literary authors, White suggests from time to time that the law student read a work in its entirety. These "assignments" stem from a recognition that mere excerpts from great literature may not always suffice to convey the meaning of a full-fledged theme; often, a work must be seen as a structural whole. Surely a few paragraphs from Proust or Melville (as cited by White) may leave the student of law (or literature) more confused than enlightened as to what the full text means and why the author-editor is using a particular passage. In the same way, of course, legal opinions in more typical casebooks are often brutally edited; but when the method is used on a work of art, the necessary failures of the abridgment process, even when done as intelligently as in *The Legal Imagination*, become even more evident.

The instructor who uses this book may wish to consider structuring his class more strictly around completed works. An example taken from a seminar that I once cotaught[78] may allow a comparison between the two methods of presenting literature in a legal framework. The class read, among other texts, *The Brothers Karamazov*, focusing on the lengthy trial of Dmitri for the murder of his father (a section called "A Judicial Error").[79] Only within the framework of the entire novel does the trial acquire its own significance for the lawyer and the layman alike. In the courtroom's reconstruction of the events narrated in the earlier two-thirds of the book, the legal process seems to arrive at an incorrect judgment. The erroneous conviction of Dmitri is a critique par excellence of the way the law twists reality into a false codified form. Yet the enormity of the error can only be comprehended in light of the full narration of the events as they occurred. Through this process, culminating in a wonderful Dostoevskian portrait, exact in its descriptions of the courtroom, attorneys, evidentiary techniques and legal tricks, the morality of a whole culture is called into question, and the culture is peculiarly ours as men and women of law and literature.

The excerpt method, then, even when used as competently as in White's book, often cannot compare with the majestic effectiveness of the entire work of art, especially where, as is true of a surprising number of masterpieces, the law forms the thematic core of the play or novel.[80] This may indeed be the reason that White assigns the occasional complete work. To be sure, the interspersing of totality with segmentation has the advantage of creating a most interesting "case method." And even where White's choice of selections or his approach may not duplicate my own,[81] his breadth of learning is evident. Indeed, the book is a kind of marvelous personal bibliography of a lifetime of reading, annotated suggestively and with unblemished correctness by appositive questions and comments.

Sometimes—but very rarely—the voice of the author is not sufficiently amplified by leading inquiries or cogent prefaces. For example, it is unclear to me why Emily Post's regimented view of the relationship between divorced parents (660–63) is any more of a waste of the reader's time than H. W. Fowler's essay on the split infinitive (656–59); the author, however, takes this as self-evident (663). Similarly, White's statement (in the section on "How A Statute Works") that "conversations will simply fail" if they "never take any shape at all" (216) seems partially to contradict one of the most stimulating suggestions of the rest of his book:

that "shape" (or form) in itself can be the element that leads inevitably to falsification and, thus, to failure.

Similarly, even where the author (as he so frequently does) draws the reader's attention to the most interesting literary portrayals of legal activities, he occasionally does not give them adequate editorial attention. This criticism cannot wholly be answered by the perennial problem of space limitation, since the text contains several quite lengthy and excellent analyses of other, arguably less germane works (see, for example, pp. 274–78, on the *Alcestis* of Euripedes). For another example, White (818) draws the reader's attention to Book Two of the *Iliad*, observing that the speeches of the noble Agamemnon, Odysseus, and Nestor are Homeric examples of good lawyerlike arguments, but he omits mention of the ignoble Thersites, the Greek who is most "lawyerlike" in a modern sense, and whose negative depiction is a prototype of many nineteenth- and twentieth-century literary characters:

> Now the rest had sat down, and were orderly in their places, but one man, Thersites of the endless speech, still scolded, who knew within his head many words, but disorderly; vain, and without decency, to quarrel with the princes with any word he thought might be amusing to the Argives. . . . This was the ugliest man who came beneath Ilion. . . .
> So he spoke, Thersites, abusing Agamemnon the shepherd of the people. But brilliant Odysseus swiftly came beside him scowling and laid a harsh word upon him: "Fluent orator though you be, Thersites, your words are ill-considered. Stop, nor stand up alone against princes. Out of all those who came beneath Ilion with Atreides I assert there is no worse man than you are. Therefore you shall not lift up your mouth to argue with princes, cast reproaches into their teeth, nor sustain the homegoing."[82]

After making his brief for abandoning the battle, Thersites is summarily expelled from the Greek camp, not to be tolerated by those heroes whose primary task is action rather than verbosity. In this respect, White might also have noted the fact that Odysseus himself is transformed into a sophistic lawyer figure in a passage of Ovid's *Metamorphoses*, Book 12, that sets the activity of argument in an interesting and antagonistic juxtaposition to heroic action.[83]

Such comments, however, prove more the excellence of the whole of this book than they do any slight deficiency in parts of it. White, in his selections, editorial appendages, and analyses, has offered to the law student what he describes as "an attempt to connect different sides of my own intellectual life" (967). In the imaginative diversity of that life, he has found ample resources to enrich our own perceptions, both legal and literary.

Turning now to the more theoretical issues raised in the book, the author seeks in chapters 5 ("Judgment and Explanation: The Legal Mind at Work") and 6 ("The Imagination of the Lawyer") to associate the judicial act (an opinion) with the literary critic. So, in part A of chapter 6 (a section called "Is the Judge Really a Poet?," 761–806), the author suggests a common answer to a dual question: "Why do poets and judges write, then, and why do we read?" (762). In these chapters of elaboration, White speaks at considerably greater length in his own voice than he does earlier in the text.[84]

My own reaction to the efficacy of White's ultimate comparison is a mixture of admiration and skepticism. The latter reaction is due to the author's failure to make a distinction between two modes of thought, which I believe to be vital to an understanding of the relationship between the legal and the artistic process (i.e., the distinction between wit and judgment). John Locke made this crucial comparison[85] in his *Essay Concerning Human Understanding*:

> And hence perhaps may be given some reason of that common observation,—that men who have a great deal of wit, and prompt memories, have not always the clearest judgment or deepest reason. For wit lying most in the assemblage of ideas, and putting those together with quickness and variety, wherein can be found any resemblance or congruity, thereby to make up pleasant pictures and agreeable visions in the fancy; judgment, on the contrary, lies quite on the other side, in separating carefully, one from another, ideas wherein for the most part lies that entertainment and pleasantry of wit, which strikes so lively on the fancy.[86]

White himself alludes to this distinction from time to time in his text (238, 853), without precisely pinning it down. Indeed, at various places the author repeats the following illuminating passage from Alexander Pope's *Essay on Criticism*, written 1711, some twenty years after the publication of Locke's essay:

> Some Beauties yet, no precepts can declare,
> For there's a Happiness as well as Care.
> Musick resembles Poetry, in each
> Are nameless Graces which no Methods teach,
> And which a Master-Hand alone can reach
> If, where the Rules not far enough extend,
> (Since Rules were made but to promote their End)
> Some Lucky LICENCE answers to the full
> Th'Intent propos'd, that Licence is a Rule.
> Thus Pegasus, a nearer way to take,
> May boldly deviate from the common Track.

Great Wits sometimes may gloriously offend,
And rise to Faults true Criticks dare not mend;
From vulgar Bounds with brave Disorder part,
And snatch a Grace beyond the Reach of Art,
Which, without passing thro' the Judgment, gains
The Heart, and all its End at once attains.[87]

White's attraction to these lines should be explicable in terms that I
have already set forth—the desire to free the lawyer's imagination and to
allow the student and future practitioner to see that there is more to his
life and work than can ever be codified in any rules of law. When he
asks, after citing the passage in full a second time, "Would you ever speak
in such a way of the judge's job?" I take White to imply that the judge,
like the poet, should nurture the capacity to recognize those situations
in which a creative approach is needed. Surely he means his legal reader
to listen to Pope's advice as a poet might; the foremost achievements of
either enterprise may occur in precisely those situations that "gloriously
offend" against the cold and unimaginative rule.

Thus is the issue joined. Is the judge's role indeed one of "Great Wit"?
If a poet should be allowed his license, should the judge, too, depart
from "vulgar bounds with brave Disorder"? If White's answer is implicitly
an affirmative one, Pope's is not. For in the penultimate line, the poet
says that an act of genius takes place "without passing thro' the Judgment." The act of artistic "grace" or wit, although not necessarily greater
than an act of judgment, is clearly different from one.

In a sense, White's association of these two contrasting modes of
thought is, as he of course realizes, an outgrowth of the most modern
of human outlooks, little noticed in the neoclassical age of Locke and
Pope, namely, the problem of relativism. Locke roughly defines wit as
the capacity to find the general in the particular, and judgment as the
quality of working to the particular from the general.[88] Yet he might not
so have defined the two had he not felt that man's "judgments of probability are rooted in our faith in the ultimate rationality and morality of
the universe."[89] Only with this absolute sense of values can the judge
best do his work of applying those general principles of reason and
morality to each particular case that comes before him, and, if he is a
good judge, of reaching the correct conclusion. Wit, perhaps the higher
faculty,[90] has absolutely no place in this phenomenon of judgment unless
there simply are no absolute standards on which to judge.

Granting the modern possibility of confusing two so theoretically an-
tithetical modes of perception, one need not conclude that they should
be interrelated. Indeed, White raises some of the troubling implications

of associating the judge with the poet. Continuing an analysis of legal metaphor begun somewhat tenuously earlier in the book (57–64), he observed, in Robert Frost's words, that "every opinion is a 'new metaphor inside or it is nothing'" (773). But in the very selection from Frost to which White refers, the poet states that a poem "begins in delight and ends in wisdom" (771). Once it is noted that the judgmental process at its best is precisely the reverse of this,[91] then the attempt to link the activities linguistically may be questioned; the judge's metaphor must be based on a first principle that, unlike the poet's, is impersonal and immutable, namely, the wisdom of his society.

Similarly, I think White stretches Sir Philip Sidney's description of the poetic process ("he coupleth the general notion with the particular example" (761) when he suggests that both poet and judge "usually address particular events or experiences, and each does so in a way that is meant to give them a general significance, a representative meaning" (777). Again, ideally the judge's function is to apply impartially the "general notion" that precedes any particular case, and is called "justice," to every "particular example" that comes before him, regardless of the aesthetic result of the decision.

To start with the general, there must of course be a set of values that, in Plato's terms, define "absolute justice" (692). But it is one thing to admit that, in the twentieth-century Western world, there may be no such standards, and quite another to imply that judgment should then seek to be a form of wit (even at its highest) rather than an outgrowth of absolute truth. For the latter tendency surely is to value the argument, or the process, more than the aim that they serve.[92] In the case of wit (or poetry) this priority is fine, precisely because the object of that enterprise is often nothing more than the imaginative process itself. The laugh or the delight that is wit's effect can disappear into thin air, whereas the act of judgment may have ramifications that never cease. In this sense, White's following comparison of poem and law might be strongly challenged:

> Much of the same can be said of the judicial opinion; its "rule" . . . is not the meaning of that opinion or the opinion would have consisted of that rule without more. Where the rule is statutory, where the message is given us, the judicial activity would remain wholly unexpressed: the opinion would consist merely of the statement of the rule and the declaration of the judgment. I daresay you know opinions that could be described this way, but we know that at its best the judicial mind does more than this, that its expression defines and exemplifies an education. (765)

"[T]he opinion would consist merely of the . . . declaration of the judgment"? But is not this supremely significant act the sole and sublime purpose of the entire judicial process? Is the opinion, the manner in which judgment is reached, really more important than the ultimate decisive act, the moment of truth? And, although I do agree that a "correct" judgment *must exhibit this correctness* in every word it uses, does this mean that the single legal rule can never be perfectly expressed with extensive argument? At least mention must be made of the fact that the civil law countries still resist such a concept even in their official practice; in France only the Cour de Cassation,[93] and in Germany only the Bundesverfassungsgericht[94] regularly hand down extensive opinions, while the function of the European lower courts is generally to declare a judgment and to articulate little more than the precise law on which the judgment is based. While recent European history surely calls into question this relative judicial passivity, even common-law jurists may nevertheless find arguments in favor of such an approach, especially where judges rigorously defend basic notions of civil and political liberty.

In the final analysis, the issue must be whether the aim of the judicial opinion should be to invite the kind of interpretation that a poem requires. If so, does not the risk arise that a complete system of law, whose function it is to end in judgment, will erroneously attain to the mode of wit?

These are hardly new issues, but it is immensely to White's credit that his rich book refuses to skirt them. And while I might not agree that everyone would "be willing to say that the lawyer is always arguing" (806) (which "lawyer" aspires to truth, the taciturn Shylock who "stands for judgment" or the tricky and argumentative Portia?; does Oedipus *argue* during his own trial, or does he relentlessly seek truth?; how is it that the aesthetically perfect arguments of prosecutor and defense attorney in *The Brothers Karamazov* inevitably end in total error?), I can also only express admiration for the way White presents arguments on these crucial matters. I personally am in his debt, significantly richer for having been exposed to his creative and highly informed imagination.

## Notes (1987) on *Heracles' Bow*

Since the publication of his book *The Legal Imagination*,[95] James Boyd White has been the foremost rhetorician of law in our academic culture. With a consistency approaching self-confessed repetitiveness,[96] White has sought to save law from science, bureaucracy, and, particularly in his latest book, from the social sciences. Law is, for him, neither a knowable series of rules available for application to any given case, nor a governmental power base, nor a mechanism designed to fulfill particular ends such as economic efficiency or even the betterment of the general welfare. It is nothing more nor less than rhetoric, "The art of establishing the probable by arguing from our sense of the probable" (31). For White, law consists of the eternally shifting relationships of speaker to audience; he believes less in the power of the individualized speech act (say, of the poem or judicial opinion) than of the relationship, the dialogue itself. Ours is "a culture of argument, perpetually remade by its participants" (35)

In *Heracles' Bow*, White attempts to redeem rhetoric not only for its central place in law but also in its own right. Admitting that rhetoric suffers both from purely contemporary and considerably more longer-standing disaffection (Plato attacked it as "a false art"),[97] White nonetheless affirms his admiration for all rhetoricians:

> This means that the rhetorician—that is, each of us when we speak to persuade or to establish community in other ways—must accept the double fact that there are real and important differences between cultures and that one is in substantial part the product of one's own culture. The rhetorician, like the lawyer, is thus engaged in a process of meaning-making and community-building of which he or she is in part the subject. To do this requires him or her to face and to accept the condition of radical uncertainty in which we live: uncertainty as to their effect on others, uncertainty even as to our own motivations. (39–40)

For White, the rhetorician positively reflects, rather than negatively emphasizes, the "radical uncertainties" (40) of human existence. The predominant metaphors in *Heracles' Bow* evoke the fluidity both of life and language; to survive the unpredictable swells of our relativistic culture, what better protection than the equally slippery, swampy medium of words? It is as though we are to picture a system less concerned with mastering or resisting our elemental doubts than with replication and furthering them through rhetoric.

Where can one situate such a worldview in the context of late twentieth-century thought? How can a belief in words, and their power both to validate an institution (law) and to ennoble the individual, make sense to us at the end of a century in which, to many minds anyway, words have been hideously debased, employed more to distort and destroy than to coexist with or improve their listeners? White, who himself suggested the antinomy between "rhetoric" and ethics in the section on American slavery laws in *The Legal Imagination* (432–85), still struggles to answer this question in *Heracles' Bow*. Like Jürgen Habermas for philosophy,[98] like some left-wing reformist thinkers for religion,[99] White here tries to provide for lawyers a validation of the pursuit of intersubjective language in a world correctly skeptical of words and doubtful that their institutional purveyors truly seek dialogue more than domination.[100]

White thus makes a controversial claim that, as it is defended, becomes increasingly instead of decreasingly problematic. His assertion that law is rhetoric seems more intuitively accurate than, say, the view that law is science or economics. But his defense of legal rhetoric finally lacks the two elements provided by both traditional jurisprudence and the social sciences: a normative scale on which to judge legal behavior and a forthright analysis of such behavior as it is in fact practiced.

The absence of prescriptive knowledge in White's writings seems at first harmonious with most Law and Literature theory. Since Cardozo's famous essay "Law and Literature,"[101] American proponents of that interrelation have taken it as axiomatic that law can never be reduced to norms; along with the neorealists, but with more of an interest in narrative, Law and Literature expounded the complete individuality of all legal players. Much less bound to rules or theory than was elsewhere suggested, the legal actor was perceived as consistently in the business of expressing his or her own interests or values through narrative. Sometimes the narrative act inspired and transformed the actor (Cardozo's belief),[102] at other times it merely couched self-interest in acceptable or even overwhelming narrative structures (my own, more pessimistic view),[103] but in no difficult case was the actor assumed in fact to be significantly more constrained than by the power of his or her own rhetorical talent.[104]

Often White assumes the posture of the narrative realist, albeit in the guise of several long footnotes directed at various modern legal theoreticians.[105] But predominantly he breaks from this Law and Literature tradition, promising his reader norms, not realities:

> I should perhaps also make explicit, although it should be obvious enough, that my account of law is not meant to be a description of the way it is actually practiced by most judges and lawyers but a representation of the possibilities I see in this form of life both for its practitioners and for the community at large. My apology for the possibilities of the life of the law should thus not be misread as a defense of existing arrangements; rather, it should be taken as an elaboration of the hopes I think we can and should have for the law and for ourselves as lawyers, which may in fact serve as a ground upon which a criticism of law at once idealistic and realistic can rest.

Yet White never manages to convey systematically what these "hopes" are. Or perhaps they are too simple to need systematic elaboration. As another reviewer of *Heracles' Bow* has suggested, there may be little more to White prescriptively than the wish that we shall all continue to talk to each other, and the hope that in so speaking we shall change minds while keeping our own open to counterargument.[106]. These are fine sentiments, but I am not sure that even in today's still antiliterary legal climate,[107] we need three books and a dozen essays to make the point.

Instead, White's strengths appear to be descriptive. He quite accurately, and I think extremely clearly,[108] describes the way law has always been practiced. Far from identifying the "ideal possibilities of the forms of speech and life we call the law" (242), White elaborates an apologia for the way it actually is done. But his descriptive analysis also stumbles, not only because he denies its presence, but also because he often seems not to notice (or at least unwilling to articulate overtly) the implications of his data.

Although one should, one need not go beyond the first chapter of *Heracles' Bow* to seize the paradox of White's rhetorical mode. This chapter, "Persuasion and Community in *Philoctetes*" (3–27), furthers the reputation of its author as a knowledgeable and insightful critic of classical texts.[109] Sophocles' *Philoctetes*, which also provides the book's title, tells the story of Heracles' bow, a magical weapon possessed by Philoctetes but sought by Odysseus on behalf of the Greek warriors. They need the bow to defeat the Trojans, but to get it they must convince the exiled Philoctetes to hand it over. Since Odysseus partially brought about that exile, he realizes that he would stand little chance of success, so he convinces Achilles' son Neoptolemus to confront Philoctetes. Reluctant at first to do so, since the task involves either lying or force, Neoptolemus fairly quickly[110] accedes to Odysseus' arguments that the bow is a necessity both for his own honor and for the greater glory of the Greeks. Neoptolemus thus approaches the exiled Philoctetes, woos him falsely, undergoes the reversal of empathizing with him, and finally succeeds only in having him agree to return to Greece with the bow. That remedy will not do, however; the majestic Heracles himself has to appear to remind both Philoctetes and Neoptolemus that their heroic destiny requires bringing the bow immediately into battle against the Trojans.

Like King Hamlet's ghost in Act III of *Hamlet*, Heracles encourages others to action more by the rhetoric of his presence than by words: he requires a scant forty lines to convince Philoctetes and Neoptolemus to join the battle. This powerful, essentially nonverbal rhetoric of presence

White chooses not to recognize (or at least not to analyze), but it is unanswerable. The play ends with Philoctetes stirred to the very action that Odysseus desired at its beginning.

I do not argue with White's original position regarding this play, namely that it well describes the kinds of rhetoric available to lawyers. As Odysseus persuades Neoptolemus, and then the latter alternatively conquers and is conquered by Philoctetes, the viewer does see several models of lawyerlike rhetoric. Furthermore, White forthrightly states that Odysseus' (and for that matter Heracles') goal-oriented forms of persuasion succeed pithily, whereas Neoptolemus' (and in a sense Philoctetes') more empathetic and variable rhetoric fails to convince or finally to affect the outcome of events. But White professes a lack of concern with mere "ends." Here, and throughout the book, he claims to be interested in the *means* used by a speaker, means that must comprehend both the humanity of others and "the conditions of uncertainty that render [ends-means] 'rationality' worse than useless" (20).

By this test, according to White, Odysseus utterly fails. White says this of him:

> Odysseus is not a mode of the crafty lawyer after all, unscrupulous but effective, rational but base, but an example of a lawyer who is bad in both senses of the term. At just the level where his claims for himself are most seriously made, that he is a pragmatic success, he is in fact a total failure.
>
> What Odysseus misses is the reality of the social world, and its power. His cast of mind, which itemizes the world into a chain of desiderata and mechanisms, is incapable of understanding the reality and force of shared understandings and confidences . . . or, in terms of this play, [of deriving] confidence and pleasure in those activities by which Neoptolemus and Philoctetes create a world of action and significance. (20)

White sees Odysseus as the poorest sort of lawyer (at one point he calls him a corporatist, or worse yet, a "fascist" [9n1]), a man "whose whole being is spent in the service of ends he cannot examine" (21). On the other hand, "Neoptolemus' position, by contrast, is based upon his own character or identity. . . . His initial response to Odysseus' suggestion is a kind of instinctive reaction, learned but not wholly understood: for him force and persuasion are both acceptable but deceit is not" (9).

The claim that Odysseus loses himself and sacrifices others through a deceitful and all-consuming quest for ends, and that Neoptolemus preserves his sense of self by treating others honestly and as complete "persons" cannot withstand scrutiny, however. First, the play itself is much kinder to Odysseus; as the chorus proclaims, "Odysseus was one man, appointed by many, by their command he has done this, a service to his friends."[111] He seeks no personal gain, and he may (for all we are told) have fully examined the merits of his task. After all, Heracles himself finally proclaims the rightness of Odysseus' goals, and the audience simply cannot doubt their justness.

What is more, Odysseus' *means* are always communicated overtly. He never hides from Neoptolemus the sordid side of dealing with Philoctetes and frankly advises him to forgo his own sense of virtue temporarily for the greater welfare of the Greek community. (To condemn this would be to condemn, in Shakespeare's *Measure for Measure*, the doomed Claudio's plea to his virtuous sister, Isabella: "Sweet sister, let me live. / What sin you do to save a brother's life, / Nature dispenses with the deed so far / That it becomes a virtue" [III.i.134–37]. These situations cannot be treated as unambiguous or morally clear.)

As for Neoptolemus, his failure to resist Odysseus' argument speaks more to his own weakness than to any fault in Odysseus. Far from embodying honesty, he goes on to employ pure deceit on the pathetic Philoctetes, lying to him over a dramatic space more than ten times greater than Odysseus' frank seventy-line dialogue with him. When the dismayed title hero finally learns of Neoptolemus' deceit, the play's most terrifying moment of cruelty and catharsis arises. The viewer cannot deny the emotional effect of Neoptolemus' deliberate and long-lasting mistreatment of Philoctetes.

Yet, as to Neoptolemus' tactics, White has this to say:

> Despite his conscious intentions, Neoptolemus is at the most basic level in fact not dishonest: both his own story and his responses to Philoctetes' story are in a deep sense true. The false surface version of his story, that Odysseus has deprived him of the arms of his father, has its deeper true version (to which we have just been witness) in the scene in which Odysseus does deprive Neoptolemus of himself—"give me yourself for just a shameless part of a single day." In thus disintegrating him Odysseus has deprived Neoptolemus of his capacity as a man, of his nature and inheritance as a coherent and virtuous self speaking a coherent language—of his "arms" indeed. What Neoptolemus pretends is in fact true: he and Philoctetes are bound together by similar injuries at the same hands. (31)

Here White the rhetorician gets the better of White the moralist. Apparently he wants his reader to reject Odysseus' mere quest for ends (however meritorious) and at the same time endorse Neoptolemus' means (which are dishonest) while preserving the right to interpret falsehood as truth, down as up, wrong as right. Odysseus' grimy directness is thereby devalued as somehow inhumane and Neoptolemus' long-winded lies re-valued as "in fact not dishonest."

If White means this to be normative—and we are dealing with his most important chapter—the lesson is hardly edifying. Apparently the rhetorically sound lawyer should be neither effective as to goals nor totally honest as to means. Neoptolemus' cruel lies to Philoctetes, if rationalized as truths, proffer a norm that seems to condone hypocrisy. Perhaps we should lie, expecting our falsehoods to be interpreted later as truths. Or perhaps White hopes that we ourselves, like Neoptolemus, will renounce our deceit. Yet only the sight of Philoctetes' agony from the wounds he has been suffering in exile moved Neoptolemus (after seven hundred lines!) to such sympathetic honesty. How many lawyers, caught in the web of lies, will be saved by this kind of Sophoclean reversal? Neoptolemus' wordy equivocation, taken as a norm, might preclude more deception and cruelty than Odysseus' forthright commitment to a re-spectable goal.[112]

Yet prescriptively, and I think without so intending it, White here accurately portrays the lawyer's rhetorical enterprise. Once a client im-poses a task on a lawyer, the latter must often replicate Neoptolemus' prevarication in the face of Odysseus' demand. Quite a few matters in every career contain distasteful elements; no lawyer has the lifelong op-portunity to pick and choose his tasks. (Some clients, like Odysseus in my reading at least, have probably reflected on the merits of their position before retaining counsel.) The role of lawyer then usually compels the already doubtful practitioner to create rhetoric in the service of those goals. In almost every case, the lawyer falsifies, or at least grossly exag-gerates, some aspect of the existing facts or law. (White euphemizes this by saying, throughout *Heracles' Bow*, that the lawyer acts upon a received body of wisdom and rhetoric and in so doing changes it.) Rarely if ever does the object of this falsification (the Philoctetes-figure), whether op-posing party and counsel, judge or jury, inspire in a workaday lawyer sufficient sympathy to reverse himself. Instead exaggerations expand until checked by an adversarial act of power (symbolized in the play by Her-acles' appearance).

Yet, perhaps by analogy to an almost Dostoevskian irrationality that lies within each of us, legal rhetoric usually produces some resolution acceptable to the client and also to the other parties. And so, until and unless political events (as they often have) raise the moral stakes im-measurably,[113] the systematic use of questionable rhetoric seems attuned to our culture's desires.

If Neoptolemus stands as the model of a good lawyer, it can only be within a system as just described. But in fact Sophocles leaves open the question of whether Odysseus and Heracles, in their frank espousal of a single, reflected goal, may not offer us a less deceptive, more efficient,[114] and I would be tempted to say more Judaeo-classical model for law.[115] Admittedly, such a model requires us to do what White attempts only occasionally in his book: *to analyze the ends themselves* before proceeding, to make certain that our own fundamental values are sound (not, as in White's terraqueous world, always in flux) and then to proceed forthrightly with others in the service of those values. To put it in White's own terms, Odysseus becomes a "fascist" only if the ends he is serving are rotten and vicious (as they here are not); Neoptolemus risks becoming a fascist every time he willingly places his mouth at the service of anyone who has rhetorical force (or the capital) to induce him to speak up at length and without conviction.

In the final chapter of *Heracles' Bow*, White continues his apology for legal rhetoric by creating a dialogue in the manner of Plato's *Gorgias*. His aim is to respond to that dialogue's attack on rhetoric by having two modern lawyers converse with Socrates on the merits of their position. The first of these, Euerges, seems wholeheartedly pleased with acquisition and power (all his *urges* are fulfilled by the system as it is). But the second, like White himself, tries to rationalize the law as a noble rhetorical enterprise. His name, aptly chosen, is Euphemes. This idealist perceives the lawyer as consistently enriching the lives of all around him (or her), beginning with the client: "I will not treat you shabbily; do not expect me to treat others so. I will not be your mouthpiece, but your lawyer" (225–26).

Saving the case of a lawyer in an utterly corrupt system (but nonetheless suggesting that, as in modern-day South Africa, it might be better to persevere within the system), Euphemes rationalizes the lies and distortions endemic to the lawyer's rhetorical workplace. To White's credit, he has Socrates challenge Euphemes in some of the most difficult areas of rhetorical behavior: cross-examination of the truthful witness, arguments to convince a judge, etc. As to the latter, Euphemes observes:

> What this view of the law means about the ethics of legal argument is this. First, while I am in a sense "insincere" when I say to a judge, for example, that "justice requires" or the "law requires" such and such result, this insincerity is a highly artificial one, for no one is deceived by it. No one in the courtroom would be surprised to learn that this is a form of argument and not a statement of personal belief. But at the same time I am implicitly saying something else, with respect to which I am by any standard being sincere: that

the argument I make is the best one that my capacities and resources permit me to make on this side of the case. This is a statement made by performance rather than in explicit conceptual terms, and it is a statement not about the nature of "justice," but about the nature of the resources our legal culture affords for defending or attacking a particular result. But is is a statement honestly made.

In making this statement the lawyer's audience is the judge, and we serve her directly not by telling her what we actually think she ought to do, but by showing her something about the nature of her own situation in our culture. Together, the arguments of the two lawyers define the boundaries within which the judge operates by showing what even these parties, opposed as they are, must agree to, and they tell her what topics the culture requires her to face and deal with. Our arguments also provide her with a testing ground for her own thoughts. (37)

Given this description, there are few situations, however morally in-tolerable, that a lawyer could not rationalize and even further through rhetoric. The last sentence particularly brings us back to Neoptolemus and his relationship with Philoctetes. For, as the former deceives and injures the latter, he also cedes to Philoctetes his moral integrity as surely as he had surrendered it to Odysseus. Philoctetes plays the White-ian judge to Neoptolemus' legalistic distortions. "Listen to my lies but per-ceive them as honest. Show me by your own potential forthrightness the path I should follow!" If this is the program White intends (through Eupheme, and perhaps with some sense of irony) for law, he has created an apologetically descriptive, not a normative, manual for what goes on anyway. And this is fine if, as in Stanley Fish, it is intended; I do not think White intended such complacency.

If I have stressed the first and last chapters of *Heracles' Bow*, it is because they (like chapter 2, from which I have already extensively cited) represent the rhetorical body of the book. But there is also the book's "soul." It is the soul of White the literary critic. When he moves in on the specific text—legal, literary, or other—White is superb. Thus chapters 7 and 8 strike me as the strongest in the book, covering quite astutely Gibbon's *History of the Decline and Fall of the Roman Empire* (which White includes to demonstrate both that history is also poetic and that writing often transforms the project of the writer), Aeschylus' *Oresteia*, and Katherine Anne Porter's "Noon Wine." These chapters, together with chapter 5 ("Reading Law and Reading Literature: Law as Language") convincingly further White's view that "the life of the lawyer is at its heart a literary one" (77).

It is in the waters between rhetoric and poetics that White seems to founder. And if *Heracles' Bow* has not succeeded in the formidable task of justifying rhetoric (either generally or as its author would like it practiced), the book surely extends admirably his once equally ambitious project (now, in part thanks to him, fully acceptable) of emphasizing the imaginative, narrative, and fictive elements that pervade the lawyer's life.

## Notes (1991) on *Justice as Translation*

In his latest book (1990), White progresses to the point where his constant themes take on an imagistic aura. The slipperiness of language, the inconstancy or nonexistence of the underlying "concepts" that words are somehow supposed to seize, the insufficiency of legal economics—in part because it has too naive a view of language—and the notion that law is primarily the linguistic constitution of communities, these themes are associated here with the act (almost the metaphor) of translation. Just as the translator takes up sounds and signs and relocates them in a new linguistic form (knowing that the latter can never really replicate the earlier language), so the lawyer and the judge work from a variety of inherited or given languages to a new discourse that will inevitably differ from the old but that seeks to resonate with it as it establishes a new reality.

The metaphor of translation moves us not only to look at justice a new way but also to understand that White's own enterprise cannot be reduced to bare conceptual language. Thus toward the end of the book (with some foreshadowing in a rather mean-spirited early section on the bankruptcy of all other academic languages), White dictates the terms of an ideal reading of his book:

> So I want to say: Do not look for propositions here, for conceptual elaborations and extended analogies, for anything stated, but for movement, for shifts in the meanings of words. Listen to the voices: my voices and your own, as you hear yourself respond in different ways to what I say. There, in the music the voices make, whether beautiful or harmonious or raw and ugly, is where the meaning lies; it is to that music that our attention and judgement should above all be directed.[116]

I am tempted here to underscore the antitranslation aspects of this *Diktat*: the originator of the text here sets up some requirements for the translator-reader, instead of permitting the kind of open-ended and comprehensive reading that White otherwise always seems to seek. The reader is asked to listen to "yourself respond," but the groundrules are laid down by the author. Responses that fall outside the dictated mode are ruled out, a form of colonialism that White's readers sometimes see him exercising over other people's texts.[117] Yet the program, if hardly new,[118] is attractive. The justice of a reading—whether of White's work, or of a legal text—stands or falls on its alertness to the musicality, the nuanced tonality, of the original communication. So no text should be reduced to its merely conceptual denominator, for such a reduction impoverishes the text and reflects more on the translator, who mistakenly believes that words are mirrors of ideas instead of signposts to the reality of the speaker.

White's evocation deserves to be taken up. Although I risk perfidy, in his terms, for "conceptualizing" his program, it is hard to see any other way to discuss the validity of White's claims. Of course, one could read White to mean that the sole importance of his enterprise lies in the sensitivity to his signs and sounds of the private, individual reader. On a larger level of generalization, White has implied this in his early rejection of any Law and Literature movement or "manifesto."[119] He seemed at first to resist the notion that his work fit in to any pattern or had any other aim but the personal enrichment of his reader. Yet eventually, as the opportunities (one might cynically say the "market") grew for Law and Literature, White gradually adjusted his position (his "translation"?).[120] He knows how to play the academic game and seems by his method of reading others to value his own place in the hierarchy.[121] So, both on its merits and in the terms of his own practice—his own ways of translating—my efforts seem valid both to hear his words my own way and then to situate them in a larger discursive field.

My translation of White is bounded by the book's own choice of signs. For example, the word "ethical" is used almost endlessly here. There is even a (brief) section on "ethics" (41–42), in which White seems to define the term as "respect for the other." But this translation shifts as we recognize the misanthropic state of White's own contemporary vision, with its wholesale dismissal of all other academic discourse (encapsulated, ironically, as "an insistent assertiveness" (9) or in terms of "relative deadness" (12), or of most other human perspectives ("living in the world . . . with disturbed and feeble imaginations" (158). If one thing emerges clearly from this text, it is that White has precious little respect for others.[122]

Instead, White uses pervasively the compound adjectival phrase "ethical and political," or occasionally "ethical and intellectual." Otherwise undefined, these usages probably do stand for no more than their sound-sense. I think that White wants us to translate this leitmotif into a perception that his rhetorically based, slippery system is somehow also "ethical," somehow thus markedly different from the allegedly value-free economic analysis that he yearns so hard to defeat or at least to deflate.

The location of a space, a "difference," between the sound-sense of words and their potential link to some underlying conception, fascinates White. Although he never mentions Derrida, never sees himself as a deconstructionist, White stands with the postmoderns in denying the view that a word can (or should) seek to capture some idea or thing. White's attack on "concepts" (25–33, but especially 35) replicates Nietzsche's[123]—another unnamed postmodernist—and his desire to be heard as a composer of sounds situates him in an arena he has hitherto avoided.

But just as the deconstructionists are running aground as their theory of language meets the sound-group of ethical discourse,[124] so White falls apart as he at one and the same time asserts the musicality of justice and also its ethics. Compare these two "movements" of his jurisprudential "dance":

> We all know what it is like to be patronized, flattered, manipulated, or, on the other hand, spoken to directly and honestly—in a way that recognizes our autonomy and freedom—and we know that the relations we create in our talking can be analyzed and judged. (19)
>
> The art of expression is the art of talking two ways at once, the art of many-voicedness. (27)

How can direct and honest discourse also be fork-tongued? White's whole enterprise stands or falls on his giving us an answer to this question, but he never does. As I "translate" this dilemma, I think of Dickens' Pip, begging the lawyer Mr. Jaggers (in chapter 51 of *Great Expectations*) "to be more frank and manly with me." Jaggers goes part of the way, but by the end of the chapter he rigorously regains the lawyerlike posture of professional indirectness. So, with White, there is a struggle to engage the honest, but it always yields to the artful.

And the twain—if they someday might—do not meet in this book. White's examples of talking two ways also never ring true as aspiring toward honesty. Thus, in his "translation" of the *Miranda* rule and other formal speech acts as being part of the Fourth Amendment's yearning for a community of citizens even and especially when the state's police power is engaged, White says:

> This language is artificial, in the sense that it is made by the Court, not the parties; its terms are not those in which either the officer or the citizen would naturally talk, say to their friends or family. But it is possible that the officer, the suspect, and those who readily identify with either, can find in their language an expression or recognition of what they regard as their important and legitimate concerns. To the extent this is so, the discourse functions as an

important force of social definition and cohesion, placing the individual or the official in a comprehensible public world in ways that she can respect. (178)

White goes on to admit that the actor here "need not mean what he says," but that being "forced to participate in a rhetorical process designed to express certain clearly articulated values, whether or not he agrees with them" somehow "seems essential" to the kind of law White evokes and admires.

The passage, the whole idea, is fraught with so much inconsistency that we can only credit it as worth our time if we view it as just so much sound. As such, it gives forth a sensuous blast of coercion (the sound-sense "force" pervades): there is something good, something "cohesive" in compelling the suspect and the police officer to adopt a certain rhetoric. Like Lord Dedlock in *Bleak House*, who finds the mysterious workings of English chancery somehow to be "essential" to his own well-being, who has "a stately liking for the legal repetitions and prolixities" that for him become "national bulwarks," White here suggests that a formalistically imposed rhetoric does us all some good. But in the space between the phrase "comprehensible public world" and "that she can respect," White has left open all the ethical questions he has promised to answer.

*Why*, exactly, should *either* player in the *Miranda* scenario feel that the mouthing of a scripted phrase deserves respect? Or is it really that we who have power, we who might someday author such words and can at present control their meaning, that *we* feel better because, rather than being forced (ourselves) to think that physical violence underlies the relationship between state and suspect, we now have the satisfaction of perceiving it as a verbally regulated translation of each actor's needs.

This verbal "dance," White has told us in this passage, is "designed to express more or less clearly articulated values." But what does that mean? If a criminal suspect could even approach verbally the "values" of the implicated individual, one whose autonomy has been violated (for better or worse) by the State, would they be *Miranda* or even Fourth Amendment values? So far do "we" make the opposite assumption that we beg the individual to say nothing, to be dishonest, to forgo asserting even his own innocence or shock or outrage, until "we" (meaning one who knows how to dance verbally) are called in to mediate those "values," to make them not "clearly articulated" but instead, again, double-edged, slippery, pleasing to the ear of the authority whose translation ultimately is the only one that counts.

So, in a revealing footnote about the lawyer as translator, White earlier has said:

> [T]hink of the lawyer interviewing a client: the story she has just been told makes sense of a kind, no doubt, it may even be compelling and vivid; yet the lawyer never accepts it in its first form but goes on to ask questions the function of which is to make explicit the language behind the language, the context that gives the utterances the meaning they have for the client. She tries to retrieve and make conscious as much of the context as she can in order to discover the range of ways the story can be told, its array of potential meanings. (36*n*)

Here, too, the client—the outsider to the rhetorical expectations of the system—is not so much silenced as forced to be understood a certain way. Like the Jewish litigant in Vichy France I discuss elsewhere in this volume, the criminal suspect—indeed, every "client" of the system—must speak and be heard a certain way. White's rhetoric in this passage has the merit of crystallizing this process, for it *assumes* that the client has entered with a "compelling and vivid" discursive opener; yet the lawyer "never accepts" even such rhetoric but must move on to divine "the language behind the language." But this obviously means *not* the inchoate and perhaps not fully expressed values of the client, but rather the linguistic necessities of the formalized legal act of adversarial representation. The lawyer, in White's system, is true only to what the law requires. Should it require reformulation beyond even the first "language behind the language," the lawyer will press to find the pathway into the client's case that might bring about success, or the lawyer will probably not serve as translator (i.e., will drop the case) if such discourse cannot be elicited from the client.

White's duplicitous scenario is softened by the disingenuous ending to the passage, which tells us that the lawyer seeks "the range of ways the story can be told." Were this the typical act of translation, it would have the ethical merit at least of broadening the client's needs to those (potentially) of the fuller society. Of course, the lawyer seeks not every possible retelling, but only the one that best will serve the client's winning chances. (A good lawyer will also retell the story to replicate her adversary's likely retelling, but these two outer discursive limits represent the professional's sole narrative responsibility throughout most of the adversary process.) The "ethical and political" dimension of the lawyer's conversational stance does not readily appear, unless (as White's earlier writings seem to deny)[125] adversarial zeal itself is an ethical expression.

Ultimately, we are left with a familiar question, but one that has little to do with ethics, at least not in White's sense. What "language behind the language" are we lawyers to feel comfortable with? To the extent that we normatively place words in people's mouths, or use their words as mere springboards to our own professional exigencies, it is unlikely that we are really translating. Instead, the rhetoric of the nonlegal actor in our system is coerced by the legal actor; it will never do, on its own.

Put somewhat differently, if there is nothing to law but linguistic constitution and reconstitution, and if the lawyer is always seeking the metalanguage of the nonlawyer's rhetoric, what constrains the legal actor from ignoring the discourse of the other altogether? Too much emphasis placed on language as the end of law threatens to silence (or to puppetize) the other, to bring about an elegant "translation" of a text that has been ignored. We may thus have a complex law, even a purely rhetorical one, but it is hardly a vision of law that can be called "ethical."

That White distrusts any external referent as a firm guide to ethical legal conduct becomes clear here in two ways. First, he pervasively attacks law and economics as reductive to an extrinsic model of good or bad, efficient or inefficient conduct. But on a larger epistemological plane, White sees all experience as being rhetorical:

> Nothing human is free of language. (xi)

Yet White fails to hew to this line. The contradiction between his yearning for translation and his lip-service to ethics finally emerges in his grudging admission that something about law, something about people, precedes or even overcomes language:

> This means that our performances with language are ethical and political performances, whether we know it or not, and that they can be analyzed as such. Thus to speak and act "like a lawyer," as one learns to do in law school, is to commit oneself to a certain community and discourse, to enact a view of language *and the world* that entails an ethics and a politics of its own, even to give oneself a certain character, and these things can be studied and judged. (215, emphasis added)

But as a blueprint for an ethos of "the world," White's book utterly fails. If we are to find, to study, and to teach that part of our professional experience that stands (as it does graphically in this passage) apart from language, we will have to turn elsewhere. For in White we find at best fleeting glimpses of the ethical referents that guide professional conduct. And why should we expect more from a thinker who abjures "concepts" and who thinks of law as a rhetorically enriching system the delights of which are there for the attuned practitioner, irrespective of his or her underlying values?

At one point, in discussing Chief Justice Roger B. Taney's opinion in *Dred Scott*, White—torn between recognizing the rhetorical force of much of Taney's reprehensible racism and justifying a critique of the opinion on rhetorical grounds—confides that we must finally be moved by "the simple truth, that we are all people, all one species, and that 'race' itself is not a natural category" (128). Our hearts yearn to comprehend, for we surely agree with, this sentiment. But in a system fully privileging language, we are hard pressed to find the tools to discern what is "natural," what is prelinguistic (or even conceptual?). Small wonder lawyers in varied Western cultures have almost always been able to integrate racist premises into smoothly functioning and rhetorically satisfying systems of law.[126]

Why not recognize that police authority is not "natural," or that capital punishment excludes from "the species" the condemned man, or that it is a "simple truth" to allow a woman the reproductive control over her own body? But we know that in these as yet unsettled areas, White would be satisfied with a well-crafted, complex opinion, unmindful of such ultimate "ethical" questions.

Although little that White says is objectionable (because he deals conservatively only with assumptions shared by the vast majority of his readers), little helps us to mold an ethics of law. We are left with an often moving, and almost always engaging confession, a translation of White's earlier work into a new and more personalized idiom.

# Conclusion

EACH ESSAY has carried with it the unifying message of this volume: in law and literature, style and substance combine. More clearly true perhaps when applied to the poem or the novel, this insight needs special emphasis today regarding legal discourse. There can be no Pascalian duality when it comes to the language of the law; we cannot abstract from the legal utterance a scintilla of "meaning" that is not itself conveyed through the linguistic medium itself. We have seen applicable, moreover, to our understanding of "disinterested" legal analysts like Joseph Haennig in Vichy, France, the primacy of *how* a document speaks. And the probative value of linking form and content has even been demonstrated as we perused the literary criticism of scholars ranging from Shakespearians to Faulknerians, from the new critical Law and Literature writers to the postmoderns.

Flowing from this premise were several major currents. The "canon" cannot be demolished until its radical premises are discovered amidst its traditionalist-*seeming* foundations. Stories about law—whether or not from the established canon—provide a unique source of understanding, likely to bring a greater ethical awareness to late twentieth-century legal communication. No bad judicial opinion can be "well written." No seemingly just opinion will endure unless its discursive form matches its quest for fairness. "Objective" treatment of corrupt legal materials is itself corrupt, however seemingly benign. Good writing ennobles, and—in the case of legal writers—it brings great professional satisfaction and the restoration of law to our culture's center stage. And finally: law and literature, for all their disparities, are one.

# Notes

## Preface

1. See C.R.B. Dunlop, "Literature Studies in Law Schools," *Cardozo Studies in Law and Literature* (1991), 3:1; see also Elizabeth Gemmette, "Law and Literature: An Unnecessarily Suspect Class in the Liberal Arts Component of the Law School Curriculum," *Valparaiso Law Review* (1989), 23:267.

2. The articles are far too many to itemize: for a good listing of bibliographical data, see James Elkins, "A Bibliography of Narrative," *Journal of Legal Education* (1990), 40:203. As for book-length studies, a partial list includes: Milner Ball, *Lying Down Together: Law, Metaphor, and Theology* (Madison: University of Wisconsin Press, 1985); Robert Ferguson, *Law and Letters in American Culture* (Cambridge: Harvard University Press, 1984); Sanford Levinson and Steven Mailloux, *Interpreting Law and Literature* (Evanston, Ill.: Northwestern University Press, 1988); David Papke, *Narrative and the Legal Discourse* (Liverpool: Deborah Charles, 1991); Richard A. Posner, *Law and Literature: A Misunderstood Relation* (Cambridge: Harvard University Press, 1988); Brook Thomas, *Cross-Examinations of Law and Literature* (New York: Cambridge University Press, 1987); Richard H. Weisberg, *The Failure of the Word: The Protagonist as Lawyer in Modern Fiction* (New Haven: Yale University Press, 1984), and *When Lawyers Write* (Boston: Little, Brown, 1987); James Boyd White, *Heracles' Bow* (Madison: University of Wisconsin Press, 1985), and *Justice as Translation* (Chicago: University of Chicago Press, 1990).

3. These are the *Cardozo Studies in Law and Literature* and the *Yale Journal of Law and the Humanities*.

4. See, as just one excellent example, Drucilla Cornell, "Post-Structuralism, the Ethical Relation, and the Law," *Cardozo Law Review* (1988), 9:1587.

5. Current examples have been E. L. Doctorow, *Billy Bathgate* (New York: Random House, 1989); Scott Turow, *Presumed Innocent* (New York: Farrar, Straus and Giroux, 1988); Tom Wolfe, *The Bonfire of the Vanities* (New York: Farrar, Straus and Giroux, 1987).

6. See, for example, John Gardner, *On Moral Fiction* (New York: Basic Books, 1977); Eugene Goodheart, *The Failure of Criticism* (Cambridge: Harvard University Press, 1978).

7. For further data on the observation that younger people do not read, see Roger Cohen, "The Lost Book Generation," *New York Times Education Supplement*, January 6, 1991, p. 34. Although the standard reasons for what Cohen calls "aliteracy" range from television to diet, Cohen and most other careful observers also include trends in educational practice. I believe (as one who was trained by, and continues to revere, some of our better known "deconstructionists") that postmodernist influences on the teaching of fiction in colleges and secondary schools share part of the blame. At their best, postmodernists continue to provide dazzling and close readings of wonderful texts, but as their theories trickle down, there is significant impoverishment both in the techniques of teaching literature and in the choice of texts to be taught. Many college students, for example, are introduced to "theory" before—and often to the exclusion of—the great stories and myths of our heritage. It is surely no coincidence that at one Law and Literature conference on Melville's *Billy Budd, Sailor*, only the law professors brought their texts in every day, while some of the literature professors appeared to feel uncomfortable discussing the actual text, and others even professed proudly that they had never read some of Melville's masterpieces at all.

8. Richard A. Posner, *Cardozo: A Study in Reputation* (Chicago: University of Chicago Press, 1990). One surprising aspect of this interesting endeavor is that Posner has chosen a well-worked Cardozo opinion for lengthy stylistic analysis, *Hynes v. New York Central Railroad Co.*, 231 N.Y. 229 (1921). I hasten to observe that my considerable attention to *Hynes*, in the present volume (see essay 3) and elsewhere, actually predates Posner's evaluation of the case, sometimes by a full decade or more. While Posner does cite some of my earlier published work on *Hynes*, he continues (as he did in parts of his *Law and Literature*) to rely much more heavily on other writers than he feels comfortable admitting. Still, the book on Cardozo evinces a broadening of Posner's perspective on Law and Literature, and I believe we can look forward to an increasing sensitivity in this basically nonliterary judge to matters stylistic and even ethical.

9. *Miller v. Civil City of South Bend*, 904 F. 2d 1081 (U.S. Court of Appeals for the Seventh Circuit), 1990, certiorari granted by the Supreme Court, *sub nom. Barnes v. Glen Theatre*, 111 S. Ct. 38 (1990).

10. For a comparable reaction to White, see David Trubeck, "Translation as Argument," *William and Mary Law Review* (1990), 32:105.

# 1. *Poethics*: Toward a Literary Jurisprudence

1. Among the pioneering volumes that introduced Law and Literature as a *jurisprudential* project was "Law and Literature: A Symposium," *Rutgers Law Review* (1976), 29:223–330 (see especially J. Allen Smith, "Law and the Humanities: A Preface," p. 223).

2. See John H. Wigmore, "A List of 100 Legal Novels," *Illinois Law Review* (1908), 2:574, reprinted and revised in *Illinois Law Review* (1922), 17:26; see also Richard H. Weisberg, "Wigmore's 'Legal Novels' Revisited: New Resources for the Expansive Lawyer," *Northwestern Law Review* (1976), 71:17; and Richard H. Weis-

berg and Doris Kretschman, "Wigmore's 'Legal Novels' Expanded: A Collaborative Effort," *New York State Bar Journal* (1978), 50:122.

For Cardozo, see especially Benjamin N. Cardozo, "Law and Literature," *Yale Review* (1924-25), 14:699, reprinted in Cardozo, *Selected Writings of Benjamin Nathan Cardozo*, ed. M. Hall (1947; reprint, New York: Matthew Bender, 1975 ed.), pp. 339-56.

3. See Robert Ferguson, *Law and Letters in American Culture* (Cambridge: Harvard University Press, 1984); and this volume's essay 16.

4. See John Rawls, *A Theory of Justice* (Cambridge: Harvard University Press, 1971); and Ronald Dworkin, *Law's Empire* (Cambridge: Harvard University Press, 1986).

5. See John Ciardi, *How Does A Poem Mean?* (Boston: Houghton, Mifflin, 1960).

6. Roland Barthes, "An Introduction to the Structural Analysis of Narrative," *New Literary History*, (1975), 6:237.

7. Richard H. Weisberg, *The Failure of the Word: The Protagonist as Lawyer in Modern Fiction* (New Haven: Yale University Press, 1984), p. 6 and passim.

8. Cardozo, "Law and Literature," in *Selected Writings*, p. 340.

9. Compare in this respect the *Billy Budd* debate of recent years, which has fascinated not only academics but also practitioners (see, for example, Tom Goldstein, "Once Again, 'Billy Budd' Is Standing Trial," *New York Times, June 10, 1988*, B6). All groups have been interested in the move from the standard positivism-naturalism approach to Captain Vere's arguments in that tale to an analysis of the subjective motivations for the character's actions. The latter has provided an alternative framework of understanding for the story, but both approaches uniquely convey a jurisprudential perspective. For one example, see Robert Cover, "Prelude: Of Creon and Captain Vere," in his *Justice Accused* (New Haven: Yale University Press, 1975), pp. 1-7.

10. Thoughtful traditionalists such as Owen Fiss, however, continue to express their anxieties about the onslaught of "nihilism" on all levels of legal behavior. See Fiss, "The Death of the Law?" *Cornell Law Review* (1986), 72:1. However, Fiss seems less unsettled recently; see "The Law Regained," *Cornell Law Review* (1989), 74:245.

11. *Palsgraf v. Long Island Railroad Co.*, 248 N.Y. 339, 172 N.E. 99 (Court of Appeals, New York, 1928), per Judge Cardozo. See also note 37 and attached appendix 3.1.

12. *Brown v. Board of Education*, 347 U.S. 483 (1954).

13. *McCulloch v. Maryland*, 17 U.S. (4 Wheat.) 316 (1819).

14. *Buck v. Bell*, 274 U.S. 200 (1927).

15. Cardozo, "The Growth of the Law" (1924), in *Selected Writings*, p. 225.

16. Cardozo, "Faith and a Doubting World," (Address to the New York County Lawyers Association, 1931), *Selected Writings*, pp. 105-6.

17. *Meinhard v. Salmon*, 249 N.Y. 458 (Court of Appeals, New York, 1928). The quoted phrase has become one of the most cited passages in the law, covering an infinitude of situations well beyond the contemplation of the parties (or the judges) in *Meinhard* itself.

18. Cardozo, "Law and Literature," in *Selected Essays*, p. 342.

19. See essay 3 in this volume.

20. *Plessy v. Ferguson*, 163 U.S. 537 (1896).
21. *National League of Cities v. Ussery*, 426 U.S. 833 (1976).
22. *Garcia v. San Antonio Metropolitan Transit Authority*, 469 U.S. 528 (1985).
23. *Craig v. Boren*, 429 U.S. 190 (1976). *Boren*'s holding—that legislative gender-based distinctions must be subject to significant Fourteenth Amendment scrutiny—has not been altered by the conservative Court.
24. *New York Times v. Sullivan*, 403 U.S. 713 (1971), cited with unanimous and enduring praise in *Falwell v. Hustler*, 485 U.S. 46 (1988).
25. See note 12. Evidence for the view that *Brown* is losing ground can be seen, for example, in *Oklahoma City v. Dowell*, 111 Supreme Court 630 (1991), an opinion that chips at the very core of school desegregation progress.
26. *Roe v. Wade*, 410 U.S. 113 (1973). Some observers already believe that *Webster v. Reproductive Health Services*, 1492 U.S. 490 (1989), has done away with *Roe*.
27. *Meinhard v. Salmon*, 249 N.Y. at 458 (Court of Appeals, New York, 1928).
28. *Osterlind v. Hill*, 263 Mass. 73, 160 N.E. 301 (Supreme Judicial Court of Massachusetts, 1928).
29. Cardozo, *The Paradoxes of Legal Science 127* (New York: Columbia University Press, 1930), pp. 25–6.
30. Karl Llewellyn, "On the Good, the True, the Beautiful in Law," *Jurisprudence* (Chicago: University of Chicago Press, 1962), pp. 167, 181n14.
31. Oscar Cox, "Review: Cardozo's *Law and Literature*," *Cornell Law Quarterly* (1931), 17:189.
32. Jerome Frank, "The Speech of Judges: A Dissenting Opinion," *Virginia Law Review* (1943) 29:625–30. The article was published under the name Anon E. Mous.
33. Cardozo, "Law and Literature," reprinted in Cardozo, *Selected Writings*, p. 352.
34. Cardozo, "Law and Literature."
35. Cardozo, *The Nature of the Judicial Process* (New Haven: Yale University Press, 1921), p. 12.
36. *Hynes v. New York Central Railroad*, 231 N.Y. 229, 131 N.E. 898, 17 A.L.R. 803 (Court of Appeals, New York, 1921).
37. *Palsgraf v. Long Island Railroad*, 248 N.Y. 339, 172 N.E. 99 (Court of Appeals, New York, 1928).
38. *Hollaris v. Jankowski*, 315 Ill. App. 154, 42 N.E. 2d 859 (Court of Appeals, Illinois, 1942).
39. Cardozo, "Law and Literature," reprinted in *Selected Writings*, p. 342.
40. Wigmore, "A list of 100 Legal Novels"; see also note 2.
41. Charles Dickens, *Bleak House*, 2 vols. (New York: Collier, 1911), 1:9. All subsequent citations refer to this edition.
42. See also Richard H. Weisberg, *When Lawyers Write* (Boston: Little, Brown, 1987).
43. See, for example, the description of a recent securities offering, with alleged constructive knowledge by the dealmakers (and their lawyers) that the costs of the deal might bankrupt the company whose shares were being offered. *New York Times*, January 3, 1991, p. 1D.
44. For a detailed treatment of communication in *Billy Budd*, see essay 11 in this

volume; see also Weisberg, *The Failure of the Word*, chapters 8 and 9.

45. John Barth, *The Floating Opera* (1956; reprint, New York: Bantam, 1972), chapter 10, "The Law".

46. See especially, Dostoevski's portrait of Porfiry Petrovich in *Crime and Punishment*, discussed in Weisberg, *The Failure of the Word*, chapter 3. Porfiry stunningly employs long silences (sometimes ten minutes in length!) to evoke Raskolnikov's complete confession. How few unpoethical lawyers ever learn that the interstices between words usually reveal more than the words themselves—or that one's own silence often elicits from others valuable language that would otherwise not be forthcoming.

47. See the mention of legalistic wrongdoing in *Sanctuary*, in essay 9 in this volume.

48. See, for example, Oral Argument *Pennzoil v. Texaco, U.S. Law Week* 55:3487, January 20, 1987.

49. For a more detailed treatment of Meursault's difficulties with the law, see Weisberg, *The Failure of the Word*, chapter 7, pp. 119–23.

50. I am greatly indebted to Frances Olsen for her insights about this story.

51. Toni Morrison, *The Bluest Eye* (New York: Washington Square Press, 1970), pp. 41–2.

## 2. Let's Not Kill *All* the Lawyers: Anglo-American Fiction's Equivocal Approach to the Lawyer Figure

1. Richard H. Weisberg, *The Failure of the Word: The Protagonist as Lawyer in Modern Fiction* (New Haven: Yale University Press, 1984).

2. Weisberg, *The Failure of the Word*, chapters 8 and 9.

3. Mark Twain, *Pudd'nhead Wilson* (New York: Harper, 1922). Pudd'nhead stands as the *sole* sympathetic lawyer in mainstream fiction to win his case; however, the long wait before he even gets a client marks him more typically among the group of nice guy legal losers.

4. See, for example, the special Faulkner issue, "The Law and Southern Literature Symposium," of the *Mississippi College Law Review* (1984), 4:165–330.

5. The Beiliss case involved a Jew arrested in the last days of the tsars for the "ritual murder" of a Christian child. One of tens of thousands of such cases on the continent of Europe since at least the eleventh century, the classically trumped-up charge accused Beiliss of drawing out the child's blood for use in the preparation of the Passover matzoh. Beiliss courageously refused to confess during a long and hard Russian imprisonment; finally the public outcry over the absurd charges resulted in an open trial and acquittal. For a description see S. Kucherov, *Courts, Lawyers and Trials Under the Last Three Tsars* (New York: Praeger, 1953). The Beiliss affair seems to have captured the imagination of another novelist attracted to the law; see A. Band, "Kafka and the 'Beiliss Affair,'" *Hasifrut* (1976), 22:38–45.

6. The tsarist system of criminal procedure is as faithfully portrayed in Malamud as it was in Dostoevski. See Weisberg, *The Failure of the Word*, chapter 3.

7. See Weisberg, *The Failure of the Word*, chapter 7, for an analysis of Camus' *La Chute (The Fall*, 1956).

8. For some superb passages comparing the two, see Donald Fanger, *Dostoevski and Romantic Realism* (New York: Cambridge University Press, 1965).

9. Edgar Johnson, in one of the longer appraisals, disposes of Jaggers in two paragraphs; Johnson, *Charles Dickens: His Tragedy and Triumph*, 2 vols (New York: Simon and Schuster, 1952), 2:900–901. There are considerably more intensive surveys in the journals. The two closest in spirit to the analysis here (though disagreeing in many respects) are Stanley Tick, "Toward Jaggers," *Dickens Studies Annual* (1976), 5:133–49, and Ronald Baughman, "Dickens and His Lawyers," *Drury College Alumni Review* (1967), pp. 19–29. Tick's piece superbly recognizes the mixed quality of Jaggers' ethics; Baughman's is the best I have read on equating the figure of the lawyer with the artist who created him.

10. J. Hillis Miller, *Charles Dickens: The World of His Novels* (Cambridge: Harvard University Press, 1958). Miller seems more interested in Wemmick, "himself a victim of the great legal organization," p. 254; Jaggers relates rather parenthetically to Miller's themes of master-slave and guilt-innocence as one being "surely 'master' rather than 'slave' in the world of the novel" (p. 254).

11. Humphrey House, *The Dickens World* (London: Oxford University Press, 1941), p. 15. *Quaere.*

12. As with another principal text analyzed later in this chapter (*The Floating Opera*, in essay 8), *Great Expectations* was given alternate endings by an author sensitive to critical and editorial reception. In the earlier version, no hope was offered that Pip and Estella would someday marry; the second ending permits such a hope. While I do not want to follow what William H. Marshall has called the tendency to see Dickens' variations "as somewhat incidental," it does seem far less significant to novelistic meaning than *The Floating Opera*'s variations; see Marshall, "The Conclusion of *Great Expectations* as the Fulfillment of Myth," *The Personalist* (1963), 44:338.

13. Charles Dickens, *Great Expectations* (1860–1861; reprint, New York: Signet, 1963). Here pp. 94–95. Subsequent citations are to this edition.

14. Recall Clamence, Camus' criminal lawyer in *The Fall* (who will more aptly be compared with Barth's Todd Andrews in essay 8.) Tom Wolfe's marvelous portrait of Sherman McCoy's defense lawyer in *The Bonfire of the Vanities* also comes to mind.

15. Johnson, *Charles Dickens*, 2:990–91.

16. Miller (note 10, above) recognizes, for different reasons, that Jaggers and Wemmick are figures in opposition. So, ultimately, does Lawrence Jay Dressner in a fine article, "Great Expectations: The Tragic Comedy of John Wemmick," *Ariel* (1975), pp. 65–80. It might surprise some (but not me) that Dressner perceives Jaggers as far the more idealistic, ethical, and even sensitive professional, (pp. 70–71).

17. John H. Hagan, Jr., "The Poor Labrynth: The Theme of Social Injustice in Dickens' *Great Expectations*," *Nineteenth Century Fiction* (1955), 7:178.

18. Johnson still sees the Dickens of 1860 as almost totally rebellious (e.g., *Charles Dickens*, p. 990). Also, see generally, T. A. Jackson, *Charles Dickens: The Progress of a Radical* (London: Lawrence and Wishart, 1937).

19. From early childhood, Dickens knew the most mortifying aspects of nine-teenth-century English society, and his early novels in particular express what we might

call a left-wing reformer's perspective. He surely felt no differently about law, and particularly criminal law. Indeed the catalogue of capital crimes in Dickensian England included *all* felonies as late as the 1840s, when reform reduced the list to murder, treason, and property crimes accompanied by crimes against the person. Public hanging, an abomination to Dickens, was a commonplace until abolished in 1868 and is alluded to by Jaggers in chapter 51. Yet Dickens demonstrates a conviction in *Great Expectations* that he does not doubt most defendants to be guilty. He seems by 1861 to retain "little sympathy for the individual criminal. He favored the continued use of the tread-wheel, defended the 'silent system' and thought that to spend money on model prisons . . . was a useless waste." Patrick J. Rooke, *The Age of Dickens* (London: Wayward Publishers, 1970), p. 59.

Criminal justice and the penal system (both in England and America) were a continuing but perhaps a gradually conservative preoccupation of Dickens. See Phillip Collins, *Dickens and Crime* (Bloomington: Indiana University Press, 1968), particularly at p. 22, where he effectively refutes Edgar Johnson on this point.

20. See *Great Expectations*, pp. 185, 224, 233, and 261.

21. In one of my "Law and Literature" seminars, several students tested Jaggers' professional behavior (and that of Barth's Todd Andrews) against the standards of the Professional Code of Ethics. The findings, narrowly, indicated no clear breach of ethics.

22. Baughman, noting that Carton shares the Dickensian tendency to leave his lawyer figures unmarried, regards Carton and Jaggers as "each representing the extreme pole of personality. Carton exhibits in a greater degree the Romantic qualities of the lawyers—their tender, inner nature—while Jaggers manifests the neo-Romantic, the man who has grown wise to the world, forcing his inner nature behind a toughened protective covering" ("Dickens and His Lawyers," p. 24).

23. Dickens' brief but unforgotten career in the law began at age sixteen when he went to work for a solicitor. He quickly moved to the firm of Ellis and Blackmore. Within six months, finding "the law slow and irksome" (Johnson, *Charles Dickens*, 1:52), he took up the job of shorthand reporter in the Court of Doctors' Commons. This employment in what Dickens later called "A little out-of-the-way place" (Steerforth's description in *David Copperfield*) was also brief. But the adolescent impressions remained imbedded.

In addition to his aborted youthful legal ambitions, Dickens maintained friendships with lawyers at the highest level. One was Mr. Sergeant Thomas Noon Talfourd, the renowned copyright lawyer who had represented Dickens in the equitably successful but financially unrenumerative Chancery prosecutions of literary pirates during the 1840s. Yet another was Chief Justice Lord Campbell, who created something of a cause célèbre in 1855 by stating publicly how he would have preferred to have been author of *Pickwick Papers* than Her Majesty's highest-ranking officer of the Courts. Furthermore, Dickens' intimate friend and official biographer and executor, John Forster, was a barrister of independent means who had chosen acting as the novelist's Boswell over practicing law. Nor can the author's sixth son, Henry Fielding Dickens, who ultimately was to be knighted and made Queen's Counsel, be left out of the analysis.

24. *Great Expectations*, pp. 313 and 359 provide several examples of this.

25. *Bleak House* first appeared in twenty serialized monthly numbers and was published in book form in 1853.

26. Dickens' journal, *Household Words*, frequently published violent attacks on Chancery. See "The Martyrs of Chancery [I]" in the December 7, 1850, number, anonymously accounting the grim histories of several people imprisoned by Chancery, without any legal recourse, and lost to the world for decades though they had done no wrong. That piece occasioned a response by Sir Edward Sugden (later Lord Chancellor, St. Leonards), published a month later; Sugden claimed—and in large part proved—that the legal analysis in the "Martyrs" piece was quite flawed. This defense of Chancery, at least as it had been reformed by Sugden's own 1830 statute, drew in its turn the rejoinder "Martyrs of Chancery [II]" on February 11, 1851, which again emphasized pathetic individual cases. It is unclear whether Dickens himself wrote either of the two "Martyrs." See, generally, Allen Boyer, "The Antiquarian and the Utilitarian: Charles Dickens vs. James Fitzjames Stephen," *Tennessee Law Review* (1989), 56:595.

27. Both Boythorn's suit against Sir Leicester and Bucket's ability to exonerate George Rouncewell indicate that Dickens may have admired aspects of English law, once they were separated from Chancery. His own tribulations with the law were largely associated with Chancery (e.g., his costly and unsuccessful suit to retain copyright to *A Christmas Carol*). Dickens otherwise may have retained a respect for the common-law system, which (as in the case of Boythorn) permits the redirection of violent energies while not repressing the adversarial urge to justice of the individual participant. As to Rouncewell, he benefits from the presumption of innocence (so passionately defended by Mr. Jaggers in *Great Expectations*, as quoted in essay 6).

28. Recall, too, that Esther Somerson's early perspective on the Lord Chancellor is glowing (chapter 3) and that she never is fully convinced that Chancery—as opposed to those who choose to deal with it—is itself to blame for all the harm done in its precincts.

29. I will note for the present only that the third-person narrator shares Tulkinghorn's secrecy, cynicism, and obfuscating tendencies. Chapter 2 exemplifies this, as the narrator, seriatim, refuses to give us Sir Leicester's exact age, darkly compares the aristocracy to the deadening forces of Chancery, and lies about Lady Dedlock's having no children. Could it be that the third-person narrator is, in fact, a lawyer? (My text elaborates on this suggestion toward the close of this essay, as Tulkinghorn and the narrator are increasingly linked in their fascination for Lady Dedlock.)

30. The pertinent chapters in *Bleak House* are 2, 10, 12, 16, 29, 41, and 48.

31. Vere's "Struck dead by an angel of God! Yet the angel must hang!" in Herman Melville, *Billy Budd, Sailor*, ed. H. Hayford and M. Sealts (Chicago: University of Chicago Press, 1962), chapter 19.

32. Charles Dickens, *Bleak House*, 2 vols. (New York: Collier, 1911) 1:16. All references in the text continue to be to this edition, by volume and chapter.

33. Barth, *The Floating Opera* (1956; reprint, New York: Bantam, 1972). All subsequent citations to the novel, unless otherwise indicated, refer to this edition, which incorporates the revisions made by Barth in 1967. These include restoration of the original, equivocal ending (excised by Barth in the 1956 version, apparently on the advice of his first publisher, in favor of "a happy ending"). See David Morrell,

*John Barth: An Introduction* (University Park: Pennsylvania State Press, 1976), pp. 5–12.

34. Michiko Kakutani, "John Barth, in Search of Simplicity," *New York Times*, June 28, 1982, p. C11.

35. The leading article to this effect is Richard W. Noland, "John Barth and the Novel of Comic Nihilism," *Wisconsin Studies in Contemporary Literature*, (1966), 7:239–57, particularly striking since Noland based his analysis on the 1956 version of the novel, with its "happy" ending. Also worth reading is Evelyn Glaser-Wohrer, *An Analysis of John Barth's Weltanschauung* (Salzburg: Institut fuer Englische Sprache und Literatur, 1977), chapter 2, "Between Nihilism and Existentialism."

That my view here disagrees with the emphasis of these studies does not detract from their earnest endeavor to place Todd Andrews in the philosophical traditions of Jaspers, Schopenhauer (whom Barth, after all, admired, but not so much as the American pragmatists like William James), and Sartre.

36. As was suggested (see note 14, above) and as will be elaborated throughout this essay, Todd is both comparable to, and clearly distinguishable from, such continental lawyer figures as Clamence. The similarity is most apparent in their clever use of language to mask inner truths; the main differences lie in Clamence's prototypically European absence of absolute values (as compared with Todd's buried, but discoverable, "less than absolutes") and Todd's American legalistic inductivism (as contrasted with Clamence's European deductivism).

37. See my discussion of the tricky notion of novelistic "plot" in Weisberg, *The Failure of the Word*, chapters 1 and 4, and in Weisberg, "Law and Literature: Self-Generated Meaning in the 'Procedural Novel,' " in Clayton Koelb and Sosan Noakes, eds., *The Comparative Perspective on Literature* (Ithaca, N.Y.: Cornell University Press, 1988).

38. This feigned lapse of memory is nicely associated by Stephen L. Tanner with Todd's professed "deliberate inconsistency" (p. 348); see Tanner, "John Barth's Hamlet," *Southwest Review* (1971), 56:347–54. Perhaps to prove his point, Tanner himself confuses the dates as "June 22 or 23."

39. Barth's conversations with Evelyn Wohrer indicate his nonelitist theories of novel-writing: "I don't like it to be charged against me that my fictions have no relation to the world that we experience. I would find that meaningless, I don't like fictions like that." Glaser-Wohrer, *John Barth's Weltanschauung*, p. 214n26.

40. Morrell points out that "Barth is not a very biographical writer," but that "Just as Todd is writing in 1954 about 1937, so in 1954 Barth got his idea for *The Floating Opera* because he was reminded of an old showboat he had seen in 1937" Morrell, *John Barth*, p. 5n24. Thus while Barth is, of course, much younger than Todd, the novel's time frame and setting are graphically familiar to the author.

41. Todd generally associates sex with monetary payment and outbursts of laughter. The violent incident at the brothel with Betty June prefigures the "payment" of $5,000 to Col. Morton, which ends in Todd's New Year's Eve intimacy with Mrs. Morton. The teenage laughter when Todd sees himself and Betty June in the mirror while copulating, like the monetary aspect, symbolizes his absence of spontaneous enjoyment, a self-conscious, agonized laugh typical of intellectual novelistic protagonists (one thinks of Mann's Adrian Leverkuhn, in *Doktor Faustus*, for whom the

"Auflachen" is the surest symbol of intense despair, as well as Dostoevski's Underground Man and Ivan Karamazov).

42. Todd says once that "Most people ... regarded me as rather eccentric" (185); yet this seems true only in regard to his lawyerlike traits; for generally he fits in comfortably with the surrounding bourgeois culture.

43. Glaser-Wohrer, *John Barth's Weltanschauung*, p. 218.

44. Thus the many details surrounding Harrison Mack Senior's estate are assimilated by Todd, and he works from that data to a theory of the litigation. As I have been suggesting, Todd's obsession with Hamlet derives in part from his emulation of the prince's similar inductive methodology.

45. In the 1956 "happy" ending, Todd discovers that little Jeannine may have had a convulsion while watching the show; this dissuades him from suicide. Critic Stanley Edgar Hyman (among others) called this "sentimentality"; see Hyman, "John Barth's First Novel," *The New Leader* (April 12, 1965), p. 21. Barth thus went back to his original ending.

46. One of modern fiction's unique contributions, the connection between lawyer and criminal, epitomizes postmodern instability. Camus' lawyer Clamence has stolen the valuable altarpiece, "the Just Judges"; Todd almost commits mass homicide. Dostoevski's Porfiry and Dickens' Jaggers consistently probe the limits of legality while still doing their jobs well. Fiction reveals what many moderns feel: law has fallen so far that it is indistinguishable from criminality. These same texts, however, beg us to see that the distinction must be restored.

47. Lawrence Jay Dressner, "Great Expectations," p. 79.

48. The first example comes from *Intruder in the Dust*; the rest from the Snopes trilogy. Significantly, Jason Compson is the only potential client Gavin always rejects; see William Faulkner, *The Mansion* (New York: Random House, 1955), p. 327. My predominant text here is Faulkner's novel *The Town* (New York: Random House, 1957), and all subsequent citations are to this edition.

49. Cleanth Brooks, *William Faulkner: The Yoknapatawpha Country* (New Haven: Yale University Press, 1963), p. 216.

50. Irving Howe, *William Faulkner: A Critical Study*, 3d ed. (Chicago: University of Chicago Press, 1975), p. 284.

51. "*The Town* is good to read. . . . Faulkner is getting at something new here"; but the equation of Gavin with Faulkner, "while hard to escape" is a "less attractive speculation." Joseph Reed, Jr., *Faulkner's Narrative* (New Haven: Yale University Press, 1973), p. 243.

52. Steven Marcus, "Snopes Revisited" (1957), reprinted in Fredrick J. Hoffman and Olga W. Vickery, eds., *William Faulkner: Three Decades of Criticism* (New York: Harcourt Brace, 1963), p. 382.

53. Marcus, "Snopes Revisited," in *William Faulkner: Three Decades*, p. 390.

54. Brooks, *Faulkner: The Yoknapatawpha Country*, p. 228.

55. Concerning Gavin's abilities as a detective, particularly in the stories of *Knight's Gambit*, see Mick Gidley, "Elements of the Detective Story in William Faulkner's Fiction," *Journal of Popular Culture* (1973), pp. 97–124. As for Gavin as Faulkner's spokesman, the controversy centers on *Intruder in the Dust*; but, eventually, critics had some difficulty dissociating Gavin from Faulkner (even where they disagreed

with Gavin's lengthy statements in the novel). One attempt (which also reviews the critical debate) is David M. Monaghan, "Faulkner's Relationship to Gavin Stevens in *Intruder in the Dust,*" *Dalhousie Review* (1972), 52:449–57.

56. Warren Beck, *Faulkner* (Madison: University of Wisconsin Press, 1976), p. 8.

57. And, perceiving Benbow as "Gavin's prototype"; see Warren Beck, *Man in Motion: Faulkner's Trilogy* (Madison: University of Wisconsin Press, 1963), p. 110. Beck could not be more eloquent, in this book, in defending Gavin, whom he sees as a disinterested, compassionate voice. But Beck's inaccurate vision of Gavin as a weak, fading flower in the Benbow tradition ultimately does less justice to the character (and to Faulkner's use of him) than would a direct attack on Stevens' actions and words.

Lawrence Thompson was among the first critics in this mold—that is, to sympathize somewhat with Gavin but also to find him "quixotic"; see Thompson, *William Faulkner: An Introduction and Interpretation,* 2d ed. (New York: Barnes and Noble, 1963), p. 158. On balance, as we shall see, Gavin's pragmatic qualities outweigh his occasional adolescent excesses and ultimately come to direct them toward effective action.

58. See, for example, William Doster, "The Several Faces of Gavin Stevens," *Mississippi Quarterly* (1958), 11:191, where he speaks of "an almost perfect picture of the use of pure reason" in the story "Smoke," and of Stevens "as a clever [not quixotic or abstractly idealistic!] intellectual," but in *The Town* hits him with the derogatory "egghead" label (p. 195).

59. Brooks, *Faulkner: The Yoknapatawpha Country,* p. 194; Howe, *Faulkner: A Critical Study,* p. 146.

60. The phrase, of course, is the headnote to Faulkner's *The Town.*

61. Brooks finds Flem to be "a kind of monster" (*Faulkner: Yoknapatawpha Country,* p. 228), worse than Jason Compson, whom he judges to be "at least recognizably human" (p. 229). And Marcus, more accepting of Flem's humanity than Brooks, can still say that Linda "inexplicably" loves her father ("Snopes Revisited," p. 383), despite ample textual justification for such filial affection. More than one speaker in the novel itself attests to Flem's admittedly peculiar, but nonetheless human paternal generosity (*The Town,* pp. 323–25); courage (p. 300); and capacity for silence (p. 297), the last a trait that Gavin (as well as Ratliff) comes to admire and even emulate, as we shall see.

62. See Joseph Blotner, *Faulkner: A Biography* (New York: Random House, 1974); S. Snell, "Phil Stone and William Faulkner: The Lawyer and the Poet," *Mississippi College Law Review* (Spring 1984), 4:169; and many other sources about the importance of law to the Faulkner family and to the author throughout his life.

As to literary influences, Faulkner knew Balzac and Dostoevski, as well of course as Dickens and Twain, and particularly perhaps the legal and detective-story aspects of their fiction. On Faulkner's knowledge of the first two, see Gidley, "Elements of the Detective Story," pp. 98–99; Peter J. Rabinowitz, "The Click of the Spring: The Detective Story as Parallel Structure in Dostoevski and Faulkner," *Modern Philology* (1979), 76:355; Scherer, "La contestation du jugement sur pièces chez Dostoevski et Faulkner," *Delta: Revue du Centre d'Études et de Recherche* (1976), 3:47; Jean Weisgerber, "Faulkner's Monomaniacs: Their Indebtedness to Raskolnikov," *Comparative Literature Studies* (1968), 5:181.

63. Not all critics would agree to the characterization. Myles Hurd, for example, speaks of Benbow's "chastity neurosis" but blames Horace's weakness not so much on Freud's categories as on Faulkner's indecisiveness. See Hurd, "Faulkner's Horace Benbow: The Burden of Characterization and The Confusion of Meaning in *Sanctuary*," *College Language Association Journal* (1980), 23:416.

64. On Pudd'nhead's ability to advance his career through the traditional tactics of the successful literary lawyer, see Alsen, "Pudd'nhead Wilson's Fight for Popularity and Power," *Western American Literature* (1972), 7:135; D. M. McKeithan, "Trial of Luigi Capeelo," in *Court Trials in Mark Twain and Other Essays* (New York: Nijhoff, 1958), p. 26. Also, see our discussion of *Pudd'nhead Wilson* earlier in this chapter.

65. For a cogent comparison of Pudd'nhead with Gavin Stevens, see Arthur Mizener, "The Thin, Intelligent Face of American Fiction," *The Kenyon Review* (Autumn 1955), 17:507 and 518-24.

66. As we argue further on, Gavin can only settle into the mature pleasures of marriage (as background to Faulkner's *The Mansion*) after he has integrated his professional use of silence into his personal life at the end of *The Town*.

67. See Reed, Jr., *Faulkner's Narrative*; see also Michael Millgate, "William Faulkner: The Problem of Point of View," in Linda W. Wagner, ed., *William Faulkner: Four Decades of Criticism*, (East Lansing: Michigan State University Press, 1973). Millgate states that *The Town* "deserves greater recognition as a novel in which Faulkner seems finally to have come to terms with the problem of point of view with which he had wrestled so long" and proceeds to characterize Stevens as "refusing, grandly but foolishly to recognize" the limitations or a "highly imperfect world" (p. 189).

68. Marcus, "Snopes Revisited,"in *William Faulkner: Three Decades*, p. 389.

69. Beck, *Man in Motion*, p. 110. The identical fallacy appears in Peter Swiggart, *The Art of Faulkner's Novels* (Austin: University of Texas Press, 1962): "Both are idealistic Jefferson lawyers, and both lack a full understanding of the evil they seek to combat" (p. 198). As we argue further on, Gavin is not an idealist and justly doubts that what he is fighting (i.e., Flem Snopes) represents pure "evil."

70. The former phrase resounds in the criticism. See, for example, Edmund Volpe, *A Reader's Guide to William Faulkner* (New York: Farrar, Straus and Giroux, 1964), p. 326 (for both phrases).

71. As the usually modest Gavin says to Chick Mallison of a case he tries in the story "Tomorrow," "it was the only case, either as a private defender or a public prosecutor, in which he was convinced that right and justice were on his side, that he ever lost." William Faulkner, "Tomorrow," *Knight's Gambit* (New York: Random House, 1939), p. 85; all subsequent citations refer to this edition. No litigator lacking the keenest pragmatic skills could have mounted such a record. And even in "Tomorrow," Gavin winds up unraveling the mystery of the losing case.

72. See Richard Weisberg, "Comparative Law in Comparative Literature: The Figure of the 'Examining Magistrate' in Dostoevski and Camus," *Rutgers Law Review* (1976), 29:237-58.

73. Vere, I argue elsewhere, uses the "forms, measured forms" of the law to mask a purely subjective desire for vengeance. See Richard Weisberg, "How Judges Speak:

Some Lessons on Adjudication in *Billy Budd, Sailor* with an Application to Justice Rehnquist," *New York University Law Review* (1982), 57:1. The text of that article and the one previously cited (note 72, above) were expanded in Weisberg, *The Failure of the Word.*

74. Volpe, *A Reader's Guide,* pp. 328 and 330.

75. As late as *The Town* (and certainly in the earliest story, "Smoke"), Gavin frequently employs dubious methods to achieve just ends. Thus he allows Montgomery Ward Snopes to be arrested for violating the otherwise rarely enforced Jefferson Automobile Law (first legislated by old Bayard Sartoris). When Montgomery Ward exclaims that everyone present also owns a car, Gavin replies, "We've passed the H's. We're in S now, and S-n comes before S-t. Take him on, Hub" (*The Town,* p. 164).

76. Dostoevski, like Faulkner, was fascinated with sets of three. Thus, in *The Brothers Karamazov,* there are three interviews with Smerdyakov that change Ivan's life; three judicial inquests of Dmitri; and a consuming tripartite structure of narrative exposition, preliminary investigation, and trial. See Weisberg, *The Failure of the Word,* p. 52.

77. The exception is a single moment in the story "Knight's Gambit," in which Gavin suddenly comes to appreciate his nephew, Chick: "Then he discovered that his uncle was looking at him, steady and speculative and quite hard. 'Well,' his uncle said. 'Well well'—looking at him while he found out that he hadn't forgotten how to blush either" (*Knight's Gambit,* p. 174).

78. On Eula's ("Helen's") silence, see Faulkner, *The Mansion,* p. 133.

# 3. Christianity's Ends

1. See John T. Doyle, "Shakespeare's Law—The Case of Shylock," *The Overland Monthly* (July 1886) for the concept of the "jurisconsult" as used in actual cases.

2. In an interesting twist (discussed further on in terms of "mediation"), Portia in essence delegates to Antonio the unsavory job of dictating Shylock's punishment under the Alien Statute. Her delegating offer ("What mercy can you render him, Antonio?") probably marks the beginning of the ironic tone she takes towards her husband's friend until the end of the play. I doubt that she expects any "mercy" from the merchant for Shylock, and decidedly none is forthcoming.

Antonio is empowered to dispose of one-half of Shylock's estate (the Duke having just reduced the other half to a "fine"), but he winds up disposing of even more. For he not only devolves upon Shylock's hated son-in-law Lorenzo the principal of this half of Shylock's *present* wealth (after seemingly taking the income from that portion for his own use during Shylock's life, what lawyers today would still call an estate in Antonio *pur autre vie*) but also imposes an arrangement that in effect commits Shylock to bequeath to that same Lorenzo and his wife any wealth left at Shylock's death that he might otherwise still have or accrue *in the future*. And this undoubtedly would include the other half of his present estate that may not be reduced to the "fine" suggested by the Duke! Shylock retains, after all this, the highly limited right to dispose during his lifetime of half of his present wealth (less the Duke's "fine," the amount of which we do not know) and any new earnings from his business; but he is stripped by Antonio of all control over the other half and of all right to bequeath anything left in his name to anyone else but the new Christian couple.

3. See, for example, the summary of lawyers' descriptions of the bond in O. Hood Phillips, *Shakespeare and the Lawyers* (London: Methuen, 1972), pp. 102–16.

4. See, for example, George W. Keeton, *Shakespeare's Legal and Political Background* (London: Pitman, 1967), p. 136.

5. Rudolf von Ihering was one of the first authoritative commentators to write an unequivocal defense of Shylock. See his *Der Kampf um's Recht* (Vienna, 1886), translated in pertinent part in H. H. Furness, ed., *The Merchant of Venice: A New Variorum Edition of Shakespeare* (1888; reprint, New York: Dover, 1964).

6. Von Ihering's antagonist, Joseph Kohler, felt that whatever the strict legalities of Rome, Venice, or England, the play must be understood as Shakespeare's plea (through Portia) for a higher level, a "refined consciousness of law and right"; see Furness, ed., *The Merchant of Venice*.

7. See an especially interesting book-length effort to this effect by Mark Edwin Andrews, *Law Versus Equity in "The Merchant of Venice"* (Boulder: University of Colorado Press, 1965). And see above, essay 15, p. 206.

8. Since the word surety is, as used by Portia in Act V, central to this essay, I would remind readers that *Black's Law Dictionary* defines the word as an "original, primary, and direct" assumption of liability on a debt; that is, unlike a "guarantor," the surety can be sued by the disappointed creditor even before the latter goes after the debtor. Antonio fits the legal description, as his single money bond permits Shylock to attack him in court the moment the repayment date passes, and to ignore Bassanio. Such a triangular relation also fits the metaphysics of the play (as I shall argue). Constantly, the mediator takes a more prominent role toward the directly obliged parties than either does to each other. Portia, I claim, finally puts an end to the suretyship in Act V by bringing it out in the open, explicitly labeling it, and rendering it suspect.

9. René Girard, "To Entrap the Wisest: A Reading of *The Merchant of Venice*," in *Literature and Society: Selected Papers from the English Institute* (Baltimore: Johns Hopkins University Press, 1980), p. 100.

10. See, for example, Peter Jack Alscher, "Shakespeare's *Merchant of Venice*: Toward a Radical Reconciliation and a 'Final Solution' to Venice's Jewish Problem" (Ph.D. diss., Washington University, 1990), pp. 105–6. Alscher eloquently and convincingly compares the Alien Statute to the most heinous of real laws, including those that were designed to bring about the "final solution" of the "Jewish question" in our own century.

11. An exception seems to be the blissfully traditional Lawrence Danson, whose approach (on the present reading) is nonsensical. Danson fails to see the obvious: from the end of Act IV on, Portia exhibits at best an ironic disdain for Antonio, and at her keenest a complete distaste for the mediated values of the Venetians generally. Yet Danson, somewhat unmindful even of the weirdly bittersweet atmosphere of Act V, sees it as a conciliatory "dance" among Portia, Bassanio, and Antonio. Poor Portia! Will everything she has learned about Antonio's incursions on her marriage still fail to gain her a few moments of unmediated romance with her husband? See Danson, *The Harmonies of "The Merchant of Venice"* (New Haven: Yale University Press, 1978).

12. The Blakeian phrase was applied to Vere's dilemma by Robert Cover in *Justice*

*Accused: Antislavery and the Judicial Process* (New Haven: Yale University Press, 1975), p. 3. For my appreciation of Cover's approach to the tale, see Richard H. Weisberg, *The Failure of the Word: The Protagonist as Lawyer in Modern Fiction* (New Haven: Yale University Press, 1984), p. 142.

13. See Merlin Bowen, *The Long Encounter* (Chicago: University of Chicago Press, 1960); C. B. Ives, "*Billy Budd* and the Articles of War," *American Literature* (1962), 34:31–38.

14. Barbara Johnson, "Melville's Fist: The Execution of *Billy Budd*," *Studies in Romanticism* (1979), 18:567–92.

15. Cover, *Justice Accused*, p. 4.

16. See Weisberg, *The Failure of the Word*, chapters 8 and 9.

17. See, for example, A.W.B. Simpson, "Disagreeable Rhetoric" (a review of *The Failure of the Word*), the *Times Literary Supplement*, March 29, 1985: "The mechanisms of legalistic reasoning employed by such characters as Melville's Captain Vere . . . entail divorcing the lawyerly skill of a fluent and ingenious analytical use of language from the central idea of legalism, which is the pursuit of justice"; S. Heinzelman and S. Levinson, "Words and Wordiness: Reflections on Richard Weisberg's *The Failure of the Word*," *Cardozo Law Review* (1986), 7:453: "Weisberg shows beyond serious question that Vere systematically distorted the existing understandings of British maritime law"; W. W. Holdheim (a review of *The Failure of the Word*), *Arcadia* (1986), 21:324: "An authoritative rereading of Melville's *Billy Budd, Sailor* . . . decides (definitively, I think) the ongoing conflict between pro-Vere and anti-Vere interpreters. . . . The heroic interpretation of Vere has become untenable after this analysis"; and Ronald Baughman (a review of *The Failure of the Word*), *Legal Studies Forum* (1985), 9:233: a "most persuasive discussion . . . to show that Captain Vere is the primary destroyer of Billy Budd."

18. See Richard Posner, "From *Billy Budd* to Buchenwald" (a review of *The Failure of the Word*), *Yale Law Journal* (1987), 96:1173–83.

19. See Herman Melville, "Editors' Introduction," *Billy Budd, Sailor*, ed. H. Hayford and M. Sealts (Chicago: University of Chicago Press, 1962), pp. 34–35 (emphasis added). All subsequent citations refer to this edition.

20. For a complete legal analysis of Melville's use of the Articles of War, see Weisberg, *The Failure of the Word*, pp. 145–48.

21. Brook Thomas, *Cross-Examinations of Law and Literature* (New York: Cambridge University Press, 1987), p. 211.

22. Thomas, *Cross-Examinations*, p. 212. Both Thomas and Posner seem to feel that the port captains and the admiralty, who should have adjudicated this matter, would have treated Billy just as harshly as Vere has. There is no evidence for this. Although Posner ("From *Billy Budd* to Buchenwald," p. 1183*n*36) cites the case of seaman John Cumming, tried and executed in 1784 for striking an officer (Billy's offense), twice as many contemporary cases under Article II, Section 22 resulted in leniency.

Thus, a George Hudson, convicted in 1800 of striking an officer and using reproachful language to him on the *Beaver*, was sentenced to death, "but from circumstances the Court recommended him for mercy." And in the other reported case that year under the relevant section, a man convicted of assaulting and throwing a cup of

# NOTES

tea at an officer on the *Arethusa* was merely dismissed from the service. Of ten cases involving the more serious crimes of mutiny or homicide during the five years preceding and following the story's setting, only six were sentenced to death, and of these, two were pardoned. Taking all twelve reported cases together, then, only four sailors *convicted* of capital crimes similar to Billy's were actually hanged. And this, of course, only after trial by port captains (not the ship's own captain) and full appeal to the admiralty! See John MacArthur, *Principles and Practices of Naval and Military Court Martials*, 4th ed. (1813), "Appendix: A Chronological List of Trials."

Thomas makes another point about my approach. In Brook Thomas, "*Billy Budd* and the Untold Story of the Law," *Cardozo Studies in Law and Literature* (1989), 1:53, he suggests an "important shift" within a model of legal interpretation I had used throughout *The Failure of the Word*. Thomas claims that, whereas I say the real-life lawyer trying to work with a rotten set of laws in Vichy France (see *The Failure of the Word*, pp. 1–9 and the essays on Vichy in this volume) is "clearly not a villain," yet I proclaim Vere a villain, a reading that for Thomas "implicitly legitimates [British naval] laws whose foundation needs questioning" ("*Billy Budd* and the Untold Story," p. 212). Hence Thomas claims to see a movement, which he does not like, from a pure critique of "the Law" (Vichy France) to a critique of the adjudicator of the law (Vere).

If there is a "shift" here, it is fully intended. Both Vere and the real-life French lawyer, it is true, lend rhetoric to a corrupt environment. Both are wrong to do so. But Vere goes further: he *creates* the corruption. The actual French lawyer felt (wrongly, in my opinion) that he had to work with legislation that, on its face, was hideous—the French racial laws against the Jews. (See chapter 5 of this volume.) Thus he is no villain, although I ask readers to question strongly his willingness to contribute to such a grotesque system of law. But Vere works with a set of laws that—at least in this case—might have treated Billy benignly. We do not know how Billy's case would have ended if, as those laws required, Vere had brought it back to the fleet captains instead of conducting his own drumhead court. Vere, then, imposes corruption. He is like the actual statute-writers in Vichy, not merely a statute-reader like the conjectural but real-life French lawyer I discuss in *The Failure of the Word*. Vere's position of absolute authority on the ship, emphasized by Melville during the trial scene, allows him to substitute his "story of the law" for the narrative provided by the actual Articles of War. Melville wants us to judge Vere, not the Articles.

23. See Richard H. Weisberg, "Law In and As Literature: Self-Generated Meaning in the 'Procedural Novel,' " in C. Koelb and S. Noakes, eds., *The Comparative Perspective on Literature* (Ithaca: Cornell University Press, 1988), p. 224.

24. See Richard A. Posner, "Law and Literature: A Relation Reargued," *Virginia Law Review* (1986), 72:1361.

25. See, for example, John Gross, *New York Times*, November 22, 1988, favorably reviewing Richard A. Posner, *Law and Literature: A Misunderstood Relation* (Cambridge: Harvard University Press, 1988). For a more balanced journalistic account of our debate, see Tom Goldstein, "Once Again, 'Billy Budd' Is Standing Trial," *New York Times*, June 10, 1988.

26. While Posner and Thomas throw brickbats at my "legalisms," the more gentle and sympathetic Robin West describes my book as "anarchical and idiosyncratic";

see West, "Communities, Texts, and Law: Reflections on the Law and Literature Movement," *Yale Journal of Law and the Humanities* (1988), 1:129n3. Professor West, of course, is not specifically referring there to the debate on *Billy Budd*, but I pause to note the irony that the same basic approach can lead to two such differing descriptions. Could it be that the very "legalism" that urges us to look closely at the utterances of others finally produces understandings that are radically discomfiting?

But if this is so, then the predilection of postmodern interpreters to deny the relevance or even the existence of a text separate from the reader is revealed as not only egocentric but also unnecessary to the concomitant aim of undermining prevalent "truths." Nietzsche, wrongly associated with postmodernist hermeneutics, believed both in careful—even legalistic—readings of texts and in the downfall of Christian culture and all it represented. We might take his hint and recognize that the rebuilding of a sound Western culture begins with the reestablishment of texts worthy of legalistic readings, the texts of justice originally undermined by that early Christian deconstructionist, Saint Paul. See my "De Man Missing Nietzsche: 'Hinzugedichtet' Revisited," in C. Koelb, ed., *Nietzsche as Postmodernist* (Albany: SUNY Press, 1990), p. 111.

27. Of course, the "story" consists as much of these "digressions" as of the so-called tragedy of Captain Vere!

28. Professor Mailloux's antipathy to what he calls "foundationalism" is itself, of course, a mere foundationalism, although a "post-modern" obsession. See Steven Mailloux, "Judging the Judge: *Billy Budd* and 'Proof to All Sophistries,' " *Cardozo Studies in Law and Literature* (1989), 1:87. See also Richard H. Weisberg,"On the Use and Abuse of Nietzsche for Constitutional Theory," in Sanford Levinson and Steven Mailloux, eds., *Interpreting Law and Literature* (Evanston, Ill.: Northwestern University Press, 1988), 181–83.

29. Professor Mailloux correctly recalls that the narrator, in one specific context, dissociates Vere from the "considerate" mode. See Mailloux, "Judging the Judge," p. 85. But that context, early in the tale, is not (as we shall see) analogous to the extraordinary political and personal pressures upon Vere during Billy's trial. And we should also bear in mind that the very root of the word *considerate* is "sidereus"—"star"—very likely an allusion to Vere's nickname, "Starry."

30. Perhaps the most lucid expression of what is meant by "innocence" here is W. H. Auden's. Melville, for Auden, believed that "innocence and sinlessness are identical" and that "once a man becomes conscious he becomes a sinner." See William T. Stafford, ed., *Billy Budd and the Critics* (Berkeley: University of California Press, 1969), p. 216. Billy, certainly not "sinless" in a traditional, Christian sense, may well be "innocent" in his utter lack of self-reflection. Otherwise, he is hardly naive and surely no saint.

31. Billy's heterosexuality is surely no vice but a natural, sailorlike characteristic. Despite the textual evidence, Kingsley Widmer is typical of critics who find an "antisexuality" in the foretopman and then conclude that he is "innocent." See Widmer, *The Ways of Nihilism* (Berkeley: University of California Press, 1970), p. 25.

32. Bowen, *The Long Encounter*, pp. 217–22.

33. See Weisberg, *The Failure of the Word*, chapter 9.

34. See Merton M. Sealts, "Innocence and Infamy: *Billy Budd, Sailor*," in John Bryant, ed., *A Companion to Melville Studies* (New York: Greenwood Press, 1986),

NOTES

pp. 416–419: "With regard to Vere's conduct of Billy's trial and execution, Hayford and Sealts [in their 1962 "generic text"] concluded—perhaps somewhat hastily—that Melville 'simply had not familiarized himself with [naval] statutes of the period. ...' 'Melville's expertise in naval law and history' must be *assumed*, according to Richard H. Weisberg, a man trained both in literature and in jurisprudence. ... [However,] Melville is inviting his reader to examine Vere's actions in the context of the story as he himself conceived it, *not* with strict reference to naval law and history."

35. I am puzzled by Judge Posner's treatment of Admiral Nelson in Richard A. Posner, "Comment on Richard Weisberg's Interpretation of *Billy Budd*," *Cardozo Studies in Law and Literature* (1989), p. 75 and n. 13. Judge Posner reduces the Nelson presence in the tale (which is extensive, and precedes structurally the introduction of Vere and Claggart!) to this: "The purpose of the references to Nelson is to lend verisimilitude to the novella and maybe even to suggest what Vere might have become had he not fallen in action shortly after the trial and execution of Billy Budd" (p. 75).

But surely Melville did not wish to gain "verisimilitude" at the cost of so delaying (as he does) the introduction of two of his central characters. No, Nelson is in fact a major character himself in the story. As such, too, he is constantly opposed to Vere, by nature, by accomplishment, and—most important—by his innate understanding of sailors. It is not likely that Vere would ever have "become" even the shadow of his glorious colleague; thus, the incident on the *Theseus* (59)—drawn from history, yes, but designed to color our view of how Vere later handles a far less mutinous situation. Posner sees "no suggestion that there had been any acts of violence on the *Theseus*," but after all "danger was apprehended from the temper of the men," and Nelson would hardly have been called to pacify them (which he does, shedding no blood) if the possibility of violence had been absent from the scene. Vere needs Billy's neck to put down a nonexistent mutiny; Nelson sacrificed no one to remoralize a nascently rebellious crew.

In his footnote on Nelson, Judge Posner suggests that "far from being a free spirit, [Nelson] apotheosized duty." This phrase reveals a misunderstanding of my entire thesis. Freedom is never unconstrained. Billy's spontaneity is bounded by his innate sense of justice; Nelson's empathy with his sailors abides their straightforwardness and also regulates itself through an idea of duty. Billy and Nelson are both heroic, free spirits who serve the King. (Similarly, as I am suggesting throughout this essay, the freest, most liberating readings of texts are first constrained by a kind of "legalistic" attention to the *critic's* "duty": attention to the text as something apart from the reader.)

36. See Weisberg, *The Failure of the Word*, chapter 9.

37. To my knowledge, the only critic to mention, before 1984, the association of Claggart and Christ, citing the initials and the "man of sorrows" epithet (from Isaiah 53:3 and adopted in the New Testament to apply to Christ), is Martin Leonard Pops, *The Melville Archetype* (Kent, Ohio: Kent State University Press, 1970), p. 241; but he concludes that Claggart is a kind of "anti-Christ" and hence shares some of Billy's qualities. With this conclusion compare Leslie Fiedler, *Love and Death in the American Novel* (New York: Criterion Press, 1960), p. 435.

The symbol X has stood for Christ's name at least since the time of Constantine, and in modern American parlance, too. The symbol derives from the pictorial combination of the first two letters of the name in Greek, chi and rho. (Cf. H. Leclerc, *Dictionnaire d'archéologie Chrétienne et de liturgie* (Paris: Letougey et Ané, 1913), pp. 1481–1534, and the *New Catholic Encyclopedia* (New York: McGraw-Hill, 1967–1979), 4:473–79).

## 4. The Self-Imploding Canon

1. Carolyn Heilbrun and Judith Resnik, "Convergences: Law, Literature, and Feminism," *Yale Law Journal* (1990), 99:1913.

2. J. M. Cohen, "The Arrival of the Bee Box: Feminism, Law, and Literature," *Harvard Women's Law Journal* (1990), 13:345.

3. Milner Ball, "Confessions," *Cardozo Studies in Law and Literature* (1989), 2:185; the quotation, citing Mari Matsuda, another superb innovator in the field, is from p. 192.

4. See Robert Weisberg (a respected namesake), "The Law-Literature Enterprise," *Yale Journal on Law and the Humanities* (1988), 1:1; the quotation is from p. 5.

5. See, for example, Judith S. Koffler, "The Feminine Presence in *Billy Budd*," *Cardozo Studies in Law and Literature* (1989), 1:1; and Koffler, "Terror and Mutilation," *Human Rights Quarterly* (1983), 5:116.

Robin West is at one and the same time a leading feminist lawyer and a central player in Law and Literature, roles that she sees as unified, not binary. See, e.g., West, "The Feminine Silence: A Response to Koffler," *Cardozo Studies in Law and Literature* (1989), 1:15, "Economic Man and Literary Woman: One Contrast," *Mercer Law Review* (1988), 39:867, and "Jurisprudence and Gender," *University of Chicago Law Review* (1988), 55:1.

6. See the *Texas Law Review* symposium, "Law and Literature" (1982). More recently, see Sanford Levinson and Steven Mailloux, *Interpreting Law and Literature* (Evanston, Ill.: Northwestern University Press, 1988), a work casually attacked by Heilbrun as insufficiently feminist. On this score, she cites approvingly Judith Koffler (Heilbrun, "Convergences," p. 1926n57), but elsewhere in the same piece she attacks Koffler herself for stressing literature instead of "the conditions of women." For Heilbrun, not to *be* Heilbrun is apparently unforgivable, although she likes Stanley Fish when he has "allowed feminist contributions in literary studies to affect his writing and thinking."

7. The Law and Humanities Institute (LHI) has long been a well-known presence in the field. See, for example, "Literature Touches a Lawyer's Task," *Insight*, October 3, 1988, and "Literature and the Law: A Perfect Fit," *The National Law Journal*, July 18, 1988 (by Marcia Chambers). The LHI is *not* noted for being behind the critical times.

8. For descriptions of some forty Law and Literature classroom approaches, see Elizabeth Gemmette, "Law and Literature: An Unnecessarily Suspect Class in the Liberal Arts Component of the Law School Curriculum," *Valparaiso Law Review* (1989), 23:267.

9. See, e.g., Tony Chase, "On Teaching Law and Popular Culture," *Focus on Law Studies* (1988), 3:1.

10. Richard H. Weisberg, *The Failure of the Word: The Protagonist as Lawyer*

*in Modern Fiction* (New Haven: Yale University Press, 1984), chapters 8 and 9; see also Ball, "Confessions," p. 194.

## 5. Lawtalk in France

1. Michael R. Marrus and Robert O. Paxton, *Vichy France and the Jews* (New York: Basic Books, 1981); and Herbert R. Lottman, *The Left Bank* (Boston and New York: Houghton Mifflin, 1982).

2. Marrus and Paxton, *Vichy France and the Jews*, p. 355.

3. Günter Grass, *The Tin Drum*, trans. Ralph Manheim (London: Secker and Warburg, 1962), p. 194.

4. Marrus and Paxton, *Vichy France and the Jews*, p. 353.

5. See Lee T. Lemon and Marion J. Reis, eds., *Russian Formalist Criticism: Four Essays* (Lincoln: University of Nebraska Press, 1965), p. 12.

6. Anonymous ballad.

7. See, for example, Wolfgang Kayser, *The Grotesque in Art and Literature*, trans. Ulrich Weisstein (Bloomington: Indiana University Press, 1963), p. 186–87.

> And does the ridiculous still form part of the grotesque? With slight modifications we subscribed to Wieland's analysis of its reception. But in what structural element of the grotesque does its justification lie? The possibility of such a view is most easily grasped in connection with the grotesque that emerges from a satiric world view. Laughter originates on the comic and caricatural fringe of the grotesque. Filled with bitterness, it takes on characteristics of the mocking, cynical, and ultimately satanic laughter while turning into the grotesque. Wieland felt the urge to laugh even in the presence of the Hell Bruegel's "fantastic" grotesques. Did he mean the kind of laughter that is an involuntary response to situations which cannot be handled in any other way? The laughter which, in Minna von Barnhelm's opinion, sounds more horrible than the most terrible curses?

For further readings on *the laugh* as the grotesque sign *par excellence*, see the line of essays in France from Baudelaire to Bergson to Valéry, and see Thomas Mann's epic novel, *Doktor Faustus*.

8. Nikolai Gogol, "The Nose" (1836), in Leonard J. Kent, ed., *The Collected Tales and Plays of Nikolai Gogol* (New York: Modern Library, 1969), p. 475. All subsequent citations refer to this edition.

9. Vladimir Nabokov, *Lectures on Russian Literature*, ed. Fredson Bowers (New York: Harcourt Brace, 1981), p. 44. Nabokov warns us to avoid Gogol if we are interested in "ideas" and "facts" and "message"; in this vein Nabokov, following Eikenbaum, responds to a whole school of Gogol critics who somberly and wrongly ascribe to him a predominant motive of Russian social reform. Eikenbaum's 1919 essay, "Kak sdelana 'Shinel' " (How "The Overcoat" was made), placed the understanding of Gogol on the level of narrative (through the introduction of narrative style, or "skaz," to such analyses) and not on more impressionistic, sociological grounds. See also Lemon and Reis, *Russian Formalist Criticism*, p. 122.

My approach, through the mediation of Nabokov, equates narrative style with fundamental, "social" meanings. Nabokov, in *Lectures on Russian Literature*, carefully points out in his inquiry into *Dead Souls* and "The Overcoat," that what he calls "the sudden slanting of the rational plane of life" in Gogol (p. 54), the "irrelevant" details and deliberate masking of the "most important information" (p. 60) do offer hints about basic *human* realities in modern culture. "The gaps and black holes in the texture of Gogol's style," Nabokov tells, us, "imply flaws in the texture of life itself" (p. 57).

10. Franz Kafka, *The Trial*, trans. Willa and Edwin Muir (1916–17, published 1925; reprint, New York: Knopf, 1957), p. 278. All subsequent citations refer to this edition.

We experience Kafka always this way, whether as a creature scurrying in an intricate underground home ("Der Bau," "The Burrow") alternately avoiding and approaching its central meaning (the castle keep) as the premonition of a large beast urges him to give up everything; or a son so hungry for definition ("Das Urteil," "The Judgment") that, after cowering like the burrow's inhabitant before the beast of his own father, dashes off to execute the latter's sentence upon him: death by drowning. We almost long for the certainty, albeit a grotesque one, of Gregor Samsa, transformed, in the story's first line, with his full fate upon him, into a hideous cockroach ("Die Ver-wandlung," or *The Metamorphosis*).

11. For an analysis of "The Judgment" highly relevant to the topic of terror and the relationship of literature, law, and history, see Band, "Kafka and the 'Beiliss Affair'," *Hasifrut* (1976), 22:38–45. Band argues that Kafka's story (and *The Trial*, among other works) was influenced by the infamous Russian blood-libel case that later formed the basis of Malamud's *The Fixer*, which I have discussed earlier in this volume.

12. Richard Pearce, "Grotesque Vision and Revolutionary Consciousness" (Paper delivered at a seminar on "The Grotesque" for the annual meeting of the Modern Language Association, December 1974), p. 5.

13. Kafka learned the technique of defamiliarization in a way that would have pleased the Russian formalist critics—while he was horseback riding. See Ronald Hayman, *Kafka* (New York: Oxford University Press, 1982), for an example of Kafka's sense of defamiliarization: "if the view is considered from the saddle of a horse leaping the hurdle the experience is defamiliarized" (p. 77). Shklovski's favorite examples of alienation are descriptions by Tolstoy of reality from the horse's viewpoint (see Lemon and Reis, *Russian Formalist Criticism*, p. 14).

14. Hayman, *Kafka*, p. 81. Kafka was employed as a lawyer in the Worker's Accident Insurance Institute in Prague for fourteen years.

15. See for example Hayman, *Kafka*, p. 108. Elias Canetti also notes "the richness of his memory for concrete detail", see Elias Canetti, *Kafka's Other Trial*, trans. Christopher Middleton (New York: Schocken, 1974), p. 8. This trait is indigenous to most novelists of the period who employ narrative terror.

16. Similarly, when Edmund lies dying amidst the carnage of *King Lear*'s final scenes, a messenger calls that fact to Albany's attention; he remarks "That's but a trifle here." The majestic Lear, his daughter Cordelia dead in his arms, dominates Albany's observations. Edmund is, at that point, a mere detail.

17. Marrus and Paxton, *Vichy France and the Jews*, p. 41, quoting "La police des étrangers," *Le Temps*, November 9, 1938; "Surveillance et controle des étrangers," *Le Temps*, November 14, 1938.

18. Marrus and Paxton *Vichy France and the Jews*, p. 39.

19. *Vichy France and the Jews*, p. 75.

20. *Vichy France and the Jews*, p. 203. The work of various French agencies in fighting "Jewish influence" was placed under the control of a new bureau, the infamous Commissariat général aux questions juives (CGQJ), created by a Vichy statute of March 29, 1941. Virtually all the ensuing dirty work of identifying and rounding up Jews and their property emanated from this office; under the successively virulent anti-Semitism of its two principal leaders, Xavier Vallat and Darquier de Pellepoix, the CGQJ actually had to be tempered, on occasion, by its German overseers. German police presence and even bureaucratic influence was often minimal—the French could be counted on to eliminate Jewish influence without such help. See the comprehensive study by Joseph Billig, *Le Commissariat général aux questions juives*, 3 vols. (Paris: CDJC, 1955), available from the CDJC, the Centre de documentation juive contemporaine, 17 rue Geoffroy Asniers, Paris 4e; and Jean Laloum, *La France antisémite de Darquier de Pellepoix* (Paris: Syros, 1979). The CGQJ is discussed in greater detail in the next essay of this volume.

21. Marrus and Paxton, *Vichy France and the Jews*, p. 94. The best compilation of all French and German racial statutes and *ordonnances* applicable to occupied and Vichy France is R. Sarraute and P. Tager, eds., *Les Juifs sous l'Occupation: Recueil des textes officiels français et allemands 1940-1944* (Paris: CDJC, 1982); see also below, note 53. The French statute of June 2, 1941, is also, of course, published in the traditional reporter, the *Gazette du Palais* (1941, 2d sem.), pp. 592–94.

22. See Billig, *Le Commissariat général*, 1:89–93; and Marrus and Paxton, *Vichy France and the Jews*, p. 94. The even more virulent Darquier also was displeased with the statute; see Laloum, *La France antisémite*, pp. 45–51.

23. I hope to expand on this and the next essay in a later, book-length study of the French legal profession and its behavior in 1940-1944. Academia, religion, and medicine seem also to have largely accommodated to the racial beast in their midst.

24. Marrus and Paxton observe with much justice, "Vichy's aryanization provisions were even more severe than the German ones" (*Vichy France and the Jews*, p. 205). An example contrasts the French-authored statute of June 2, 1941, with the German *ordonnance* it effectively replaced. The latter, reflecting the Nuremberg statute-writers' view that no one with fewer than two Jewish grandparents would ever choose to be a Jew (nonsense from the viewpoint of Jewish law with its emphasis on the maternal grandmother), absolutely excludes from the label "Jew" anyone with three Aryan grandparents or with two but who is not a member of the Jewish religion. The French statute required more from a person with two Jewish grandparents: affirmative adherence to a Christian religion. And further, the German *ordonnance* looked to an individual's religious adherence as of the date of the *ordonnance* (April 26, 1941); the French dated the analysis to June 1940, thus excluding from admissibility any act of conversion during those ten crucial months. See also Robert Aron, *Histoire de Vichy 1940-44* (Fayard, 1954), agreeing at pp. 227–33 with the basic premise.

In all kinds of legalistic ways, the French showed themselves to be more rigorous on racial issues than the Nazis. At one point, for example, as documented at the Centre de documentation juive contemporaine, the head of the Parisian SS, Roethke, had to write CGQJ to advise them that the testimony of a Catholic priest on the question of whether an individual had been baptized was considered by the Germans to be authoritative; Roethke expressed his surprise that the French seemed to view such testimony as merely private and nondispositive. The SS chief found himself urging the CGQJ to adopt the more lenient German position. Centre de documentation juive contemporaine (hereafter, CDJC) no. CXV-83. See this chapter's notes 71–80 for other such examples.

25. For example, Vallat continued his efforts to have Jews' identity cards stamped "Juif" against the opposition of René Bousquet, head of the French police, who observed that even the Germans had not gone so far. Marrus and Paxton, *Vichy France and the Jews*, pp. 105–6.

26. For a searching analysis of the role of the French academy in the enthusiastic furthering of the racial laws, see Georges Wellers, André Kaspi, and Serge Klarsfeld, eds., *La France et la question juive, 1940–1944* (Paris: Sylvie Messenger, 1981), pp. 79–94. See also this chapter's note 59.

27. Marrus and Paxton, *Vichy France and the Jews*, pp. 125–26. Darquier, too (and as late as the end of 1942), was planning an even more rigorous statute—one that, for example, would have prohibited marriage between Aryan and Jew. See Laloum, *La France antisemite*, p. 50; see also CDJC nos. CXV-8a, CXIV-24, CXIV-80, CXIV-82, CXV-22a, and CXV-49.

28. Marrus and Paxton, *Vichy France and the Jews*, pp. 94, 140. Perhaps the most casuistic and excited debate in the French courts of this period concerned the question of whether the individual or the state had the burden of proof as to adherence to a Christian religion when there were two Jewish grandparents. The jurisprudence is complex; fuller analysis is to be found in the next essay. However, at one extreme, it can be briefly observed, was a court like the one proudly cited by the CGQJ, which declared a certain Michel Benaim to be a Jew; the court of Rabat placed the burden on Benaim,

> an individual, issued from two Jewish grandparents and two non-Jewish grand-parents, who is both baptized according to the Catholic faith and circumcised according to the rites of the Hebraic law, but who has never really belonged to the Catholic religion [and who] must, by reference to Article One section two, be declared Jewish as not having proved his nonadherence to the Jewish religion by an actual membership in one of the other religions recognized by the French state before the law of December 9, 1905. (CDJC no. CXV-20)

In fairness, it must be observed that the preponderant approach of the French courts (who examined the issue in legalistic detail, and this is really the main point here) was to place the burden on the prosecution to prove the individual's nonadherence to a Christian faith. See, for example, judgments by the courts of Bergerac, Aix, and Nice (CDJC nos. CXV-61 and CXV-119).

29. Joseph Haennig, "Doctrine," in *Gazette du Palais* (1943, 1st sem.), p. 31 (my translation). The *Gazette du Palais* was the traditional reporter of French statutes and cases. The Haennig piece is briefly mentioned by Marrus and Paxton, *Vichy France and the Jews*, p. 143. Joseph Haennig was fairly prominent during the period. His name appears on a document as one who, on at least another occasion, attempted

to assist a Jew through the legalisms of the racial statute; see CDJC no. III–14 and appendix 8 to the next essay.

30. See Marrus and Paxton, *Vichy France and the Jews*, p. 142. Further study is needed, and I do not mean here to suggest that lawyers like Haennig were necessarily at fault from a moral perspective. Yet I believe that the response to a version of this essay that I delivered at Brandeis University on this point by Professor Dietrich Orlow overly emphasized the possibility that Haennig's analysis "at least attempted to save the woman's life." See Orlow, "Comments on Weisberg's 'Avoiding Central Realities' and Richards' 'Terror and the Law'," *Human Rights Quarterly* (1983), 5:190. See also my debate with Judge Richard A. Posner on this point in the next essay. There may have been—or there may not have been—a benign intent in Haennig's writings and also in the judicial opinions already cited that placed the burden of proof on the prosecutor. But that question is of little significance to my point. The mere willingness of the vast majority of the legal profession in France even to participate in such analyses eventually cost the lives of thousands of individuals unable to deny their Jewishness (even under these "benign" analyses!) and who were thus destroyed by a system that had been fully validated by the very fact of such benignities. Certainly by 1943, after thousands of Jews had already been rounded up for deportation, the judicial system and its lawyers knew full well that such hair-splitting was welcomed by those who aimed to eliminate vast numbers of Jews on French soil.

31. Marrus and Paxton, *Vichy France and the Jews*, p. 252.

32. Lottman, *The Left Bank*, p. 168.

33. See Richard Weisberg, "How Judges Speak: 'Considerate Communication' in *Billy Budd*, with an Application to Justice Rehnquist," *New York University Law Review* (1982), 57:1.

34. Robert Cover, *Justice Accused: Antislavery and the Judicial Process* (New Haven: Yale University Press, 1975), p. 4.

35. Marrus and Paxton, *Vichy France and the Jews*, p. 142.

36. For a fine critique of American law's coexistence with slavery, see James Boyd White, *The Legal Imagination* (Boston: Little Brown, 1973), pp. 430–89.

37. Henry Sussman, "The Court as Text: Inversion, Supplanting, and Derangement in Kafka's *Der Prozess*," *Publications of the Modern Language Association* (1977), 92:50.

38. In Sussman's terms the defendant Block is "both the reader who is entirely at the mercy of the Court's fictions and the law's most sensitive exegete. Block straddles the violent gulf between a labored faith and the cynicism of an accomplished reader" ("The Court as Text," p. 53).

39. Günter Grass, *The Tin Drum*, p. 194. For a moving, poetic approach to this subject see Elie Wiesel, "Art and Culture after the Holocaust," in E. Fleischner, ed., *Auschwitz: Beginning of a New Era* (New York: Ktav, 1974), pp. 403–15.

40. See John F. Morley, *Vatican Diplomacy and the Jews During the Holocaust* (New York: Ktav, 1980), pp. 49–51, 64–71 See also Robert O. Paxton, *Vichy France: Old Guard and New Order 1940–44* (Norwich, Conn.: Fawcett Crest, 1972), pp. 149–51.

It must be further observed that Marshal Philippe Pétain actually wrote to his ambassador in the Vatican in 1941 to ask his advice about the *morality* of some of the French racial statutes. His ambassador, Léon Bérard, was able to respond to Pétain some weeks later that "I can affirm that no pontifical authority has been concerned or preoccupied in any way with this part of French politics." The Catholic Pétain, considered by many Frenchmen to be a religious as well as a political savior, must have gained solace from Bérard's twelve-page letter, tending to indicate that racial statutes would not in any way be tampered with by the Vatican (CDJC no. CIX-102). On this correspondence and its "beneficial" effect on Pétain, see Wellers, Kaspi, and Klarsfeld, eds., *La France et la question juive*, pp. 154–55. See also CGQJ's consoling correspondence with Monseigneur Valerio Valery (CDJC no. CXIV-30a).

In his response at Brandeis, Professor Orlow tended to minimize the specificity of my suggestion that French religious authorities contributed to the phenomenon of cultural distraction discussed throughout the present essay. Professor Orlow may have thought that the comment represented a traditional modern assessment of all religions in a time of decaying moral values; quite the contrary—to view the suggestion that way is to avoid the central reality of the analysis. The prevalent religion in France *at that time* is being scrutinized here, not religion generally. What was it about the French practice of Catholicism itself that allowed the French mainstream to find a kind of special enjoyment in the racial laws? This subject deserves significant attention now that documentation permits us to study it with the historical specificity it deserves.

41. Franklin H. Littell, *The Crucifixion of the Jews* (New York: Harper and Row, 1975), p. 35.

42. Marrus and Paxton, *Vichy France and the Jews*, pp. 30–31, 197–203. Despite certain data, these authors seem reluctant to consider the religious climate (generally or specifically) as an important factor in explaining French behavior.

43. Littell, *Crucifixion*, p. 95.

44. Estimates of the number of Jews deported from France between 1940 and 1944 vary greatly. Robert Paxton's original research placed the number between 60,000 and 65,000 (*Vichy France*, p. 183). This statistic, he speculated, included 6,000 French citizens (p. 183). Later, working with Michael Marrus, Paxton modified his figure and placed the number closer to 75,000 (Marrus and Paxton, *Vichy France and the Jews*, p. 343). This latter figure coincides with Serge Klarsfeld's estimate in Klarsfeld, *Vichy Auschwitz* (Paris: Fayard, 1983), p. 7; Klarsfeld estimated a prewar population of 360,000 (p. 344). Joseph Billig, however, concluded that as many as 120,000 Jews were deported from France during that time (Le Commissariat général, p. 253).

Xavier Vallat, the first head of the infamous agency in charge of Jewish questions, the Commissariat général aux questions juives (CGQJ), writing from prison just after the war, said this: "France counted 330,000 Jews in 1939, of whom 50 percent were foreigners. In 1946, the number was 180,000, of whom 160,000 were of French nationality." Vallat, "Affaires Juives," in *La Vie de France sous l'Occupation*, 2 vols. (Stanford: Hoover Institute, 1947), 2:672. Vallat's figures, even factoring in some prearmistice migration or postarmistice flight, are quite different from the currently accepted ones. Vallat ostensibly had no reason to lie, since he was already in prison and had good reason to know the figures. Other comments made by Vallat about wartime racial policy, however, cast everything he says into some doubt; thus, in this same document he imposes one of the more amazing bits of rhetoric about the Vichy years: "One decidedly cannot reproach French officials for not having known of the abominations that even those who were the victims did not suspect" (2:677). For more of Vallat's rhetoric on related issues, see below, note 67.

45. See, for example, Stanley Fish, *Is There a Text in This Class? The Authority of Interpretive Communities* (Cambridge: Harvard University Press, 1980). Fish maintains that every person speaks "from within a set of interests and concerns," and it is "in relation to those interests and concerns" that a person's words are understood. If communication or understanding occurs, it will not be because the two people speaking "share a language, in the sense of knowing the meanings of individual words and the rules for combining them, but because a way of thinking, a form of life, shares [them] and implicates [them] in a world of already-in-place objects, purposes, goals, procedures, values, and so on; and it is to the features of that world that any words [they] utter will be heard as necessarily referring" (pp. 303–4). Fish insists that "communication occurs only within such a system (or context, or situation, or interpretive community) and that the understanding achieved by two or more persons is specific to that system and determinate only within its confines" (p. 304). See also below, note 47 and accompanying text (summary of the Fish–Fiss debate).

46. Richard H. Weisberg, *The Failure of the Word: The Protagonist as Lawyer in Modern Fiction* (New Haven: Yale University Press, 1984).

47. See Owen M. Fiss, "Objectivity and Interpretation," *Stanford Law Review* (1982), 34:739; Stanley Fish, "Fish v. Fiss," *Stanford Law Review* (1984), 36:1325.

48. This school of thought, often labeled "deconstructionist," has been thrown into disarray by revelations about the wartime activities in Belgium of one of its outstanding figures, literary critic Paul de Man. De Man is strongly identified with this school, and his writings are highly influential within it. No less a figure than Jacques Derrida said, in eulogy: "As we know already but as we shall also come to realize more and more, he transformed the field of literary theory, revitalizing all the channels that irrigate it both inside and outside the university, in the United States and Europe." See Lehman, "The Fall of Paul de Man," *New York Forward*, January 11, 1991, p. 11.

In 1987, four years after de Man's death, details surfaced about his wartime activities. He had written facially collaborationist pieces for the pro-Nazi newspaper *Le Soir*. This revelation tarred de Man, his later critical works, and, by association, the deconstructionist school. Many words, much energy, and some intellectual capital has been spent in vilifying, defending, and explaining Paul de Man (Lehman, "The Fall of Paul de Man"). For a critique of de Man's theory, see W.W. Holdheim, "On Jacques Derrida's 'Paul de Man's War'," *Critical Inquiry* (1989), 15:784; for a defense, see Shoshana Felman, "Paul de Man's Silence," *Critical Inquiry* (1989), 15:704.

For my part, as one of de Man's former graduate students, I believe that the relationship of deconstructionism to post-Holocaust intellectual developments deserves study apart from the unfortunate hysteria of anecdotes about any one thinker. See Richard H. Weisberg, "Text into Theory: A Literary Approach to the Constitution," *Georgia Law Review* (1986), 20:939, 942–62 (discussing Heidegger and de Man), and "De Man Missing Nietzsche: 'Hinzugedichtet' Revisited," in Clayton Koelb, ed., *Nietzsche as Postmodernist* (Albany: S.U.N.Y. Press, 1990).

49. Paxton, *Vichy France*, p. 32.

# 5. Lawtalk in France

50. Philippe Serre, interview with author, Paris, December 21, 1988.

51. Serre interview, quoted in Richard H. Weisberg, "France: From Vichy to Carpentras," *Wall Street Journal*, October 12–13, 1990, op. ed. page, col. 3, international edition.

52. Marrus and Paxton, in their necessarily brief section on Vichy law, list another half-dozen, with one on their list tangential to the landlord-tenant problem discussed in this essay. See Marrus and Paxton, *Vichy France and the Jews*, p. 143.

53. "Loi portant statut des juifs, 3 October 1940," *Journal Officiel la République Française* (hereafter, JO), October 18, 1940), 4:312, reprinted in Sarraute and Tager, eds., *Les Juifs sous l'Occupation*, p. 19. This statute, the first to define who is a Jew under Vichy law, was reputedly written by Joseph Barthélemy's predecessor, Justice Minister Raphaël Alibert, a known anti-Semite. Although it differed in certain ways from the June 2, 1941, statute, which replaced it, both have been considered "Vichy" statutes by most authoritative French sources (and certainly by wartime German sources): "Le 3 octobre [1940], le gouvernement de Vichy promulguait le statut des Juifs en y introduisant la notion de race" (On October 3, the Vichy government promulgated the Jewish laws by introducing to them the notion of race), per "Inventaire:" File AJ 38," at the Archives Nationales (hereinafter, AN), Paris, 1st cahier; see also Michèle Cointet, "Le Conseil national de Vichy" (Ph.D. diss., University of Paris X 1984), p. 135 (on file with author). The Germans always split their analyses of racial legislation into clear categories—their own and Vichy's. (As I explore below in note 70, they wound up frequently adopting the Vichy racial laws for the occupied zone as well.)

Vichy Justice Minister Joseph Barthélemy has offered a self-interested minority view from his perspective as one who, after all, signed the June 2, 1941, law: "Cette législation n'est pas d'initiative française: elle est toute entière d'origine allemande" (These laws are not a French creation, but entirely originated by the Germans). See Joseph Barthélemy, *Ministre de la Justice: Mémoires* (Paris: Pygmalion, 1989), p. 311; see also below, notes 104 and 105 and accompanying text (describing independent statutory activity by Vichy).

54. Sarraute and Tager, eds., *Les Juifs sous l'Occupation*, pp. 185–92 (giving a full list of these laws).

55. "Loi du 2 juin 1941 remplaçant la loi du 3 octobre 1940 portant statut des juifs," JO (June 14, 1941), p. 300, reprinted in Sarraute and Tager, eds., *Les Juifs sous l'Occupation*, p. 49. See also appendix one, at the end of the chapter.

56. Hannah Arendt, *The Origins of Totalitarianism* (New York: Harcourt, Brace 1951; 1979, pp. 295–96.

57. The French government under Marshal Pétain had its seat of operations in Vichy and was part of the "zone non-occupée" that enjoyed at least nominal independence from the German authorities. But the Germans increasingly allowed Vichy law and Vichy policy to extend to the "zone occupée" as well. See below, note 70.

58. The court system remained, structurally, substantially unchanged, although there was at least one major new court created—the "Cour suprême"—and there were new, summary jurisdictions of existing courts, e.g., the infamous "sections spéciales" which tried and executed political prisoners, agitators, randomly selected hostages, etc., without right of appeal and in complete secrecy and undue haste. But the Jewish

laws were worked out largely by the traditional dual system of French adjudication: the civil courts, with their appeals courts culminating in the "Cour de cassation"; and the administrative courts, commencing here often with decrees of the minister of justice or, later, decisions of the Commissariat général aux questions juives, created by the law of March 29, 1941, *JO* (March 31, 1941), reprinted in Sarraute and Tager, eds., *Jes Juifs sous l'Occupation*, p. 39., reviewable by the chief administrative court, the Conseil d'État.

The Conseil d'État received increased power under Vichy, and had within it specific sections and committees charged with examining all racial legislation. For example, the Conseil's "Section du statut des juifs," consisting of members from each of its major standing sections, issued the opinion on "What Means of Proof . . ." that Joseph Haennig commented on in his 1943 article (see above, note 29 and accompanying text). See also Commission du statut des juifs, "Avis du Conseil d'État du Décembre 1942, Législation de l'Occupation, January–March, 1943," p. 29, reprinted in Sarraute and Tager, eds., *Les Juifs sous l'Occupation*, p. 172.

59. These include *avocats* and *avoués* (the former pleading before courts and agencies; the latter, with their cousins, the *notaires*, handling land transfers and other transactions), and formal groupings of private lawyers such as the Paris Bar Association, under the leadership of Jacques Charpentier, of whom more later (see below, note 131 and accompanying text). Law professors in France, unlike here, are better considered government functionaries than private attorneys. They too played a significant role in furthering the racial rhetoric innovated by Vichy. Joseph Barthélemy himself was drawn from the academy to the seat of ministerial power. For the participation of other law professors, see, e.g., Danièle Lochak, "La Doctrine sous Vichy, ou les mésaventures du positivisme," in *Les Usages sociaux du droit* (Paris: P.U.F., 1989), pp. 252, 252–53; also, see below, notes 96 and 130.

60. Constitutional issues were raised most publicly in the prolonged and much discussed "Riom trial." See, generally, Henri Michel, *Le Procès de Riom* (Paris: Albin Michel, 1979), pp. 107–13. At Riom, the Vichy government brought criminal charges against various Third Republic leaders deemed responsible for the French defeat. Defense counsel for some of these accused consistently raised "foundational," constitutional arguments against the appropriateness of the proceedings, and in the case against Léon Blum the defendant's Jewishness itself emerged as an issue. See below, notes 92 and 147; and appendix 14.7, at the end of the chapter (discussing the trial of Léon Blum).

As another example here, Vichy undertook a major constitutional reform project that envisioned, but never achieved, basic changes unrelated to the racial laws. See, e.g., Barthélemy, *Ministre de la Justice*, p. 123, discussing Jacques Bardoux, a leading member of the Vichy-originated Constitutional Commission. Nonetheless, the regime's racial policy affected both the makeup of the committee charged with that reform (no Jews were allowed), and its specific proposed provisions about freedom of religion, ex-post facto laws, foreign treaties, property ownership, denaturalization, and so on. I will treat this slice of Vichy legal life at greater length in another book devoted entirely to Vichy law.

61. Questions of burden of proof arose in a variety of legal areas not necessarily racial in nature. One notable justice ministry official, Jean-Armand Camboulives—

soon to be a key figure in the *cour de cassation*—effectively protested against a proposed law that would have required all French to "justify their means of existence and the source of their property since 1 September 1939." Camboulives felt that such a law would unjustly shift the burden of proof, traditionally on the state, to the individual. Letter from Camboulives to Barthélemy (October 15, 1941), AN 72AJ-412, dossier 6. No such argument as to principle was ever raised, in or out of government, on the shifting of the burden of proof to the purported Jew under the racial laws. Instead, as we shall see, that debate had to develop gradually, through the subtle rhetoric of judicial decisions and learned articles. Legal discourse took a similar tack on matters of penalties of internment or even deportation, and on the relationship of the new racial legislation to preceding or concurrent French laws that did not on their terms apply to race.

62. The Riom political trial posed a threat to this privilege and provided open discussion of the issue by defense counsel. See notes 60 and 151 (Charpentier's protests to Pétain).

63. The explosion of statutory material during the Vichy years is noted often and from many perspectives. Some of the increase, of course, derived from the several hundred or so new racial statutes, ordinances, decrees, and major cases. Dalloz, "Jurisprudence générale" for 1937-1941, and then 1942-1946, gives six full pages of statutes and cases under "Juifs." In a memo of March 15, 1942, to the CGQJ, the then principal Vichy minister, Admiral François Darlan rejects the latter's call for yet another change in racial definition by citing some *eighty thousand* specific matters that had *already* been filed under the existing statute by that date (see CDJC no. CXIV-24). But this litigious aspect of Vichy culture was more generalized. Thus, on February 17, 1943, a Vichy memo argued for the hiring of many new judges on all levels:

> The complexity of recent legislation, the increase in the small number of crimes and misdemeanors, have considerably raised the number of matters brought before various jurisdictions. For example, the criminal court of Montpellier, which decided 966 matters in 1938, took on 2,980 in 1942; the Limoges court saw its caseload increase from 696 to 2,502; Bordeaux's from 2,557 to 4,601; Quimper's from 398 to 990. (AN BB30-1715) To remedy the situation, this internal Vichy memorandum went on to suggest not the calling up of Jewish judges who had been fired, but instead the immediate repatriation of French judges still held as prisoners of war in Germany.

64. For a representative diagram, see appendix 14.2 at the end of the chapter (CDJC no. XVIIa-38 [166 and 167]).

65. From an article entitled "Qu'est-ce qu'un juif?" (CDJC no. CDXXIX-1), *Bulletin quotidien d'études et d'informations économiques* (Paris, August 19, 1942), no. 380.

66. Letter from CGQJ to its regional director in Toulouse (CDJC no. XVIIa-38 [156]). The context of the correspondence is interesting, too. The Toulouse director was inquiring about the case of two first cousins who had married, thus having common Jewish grandparents—the *Leboucher* case. See appendix three at the end of the chapter (CDJC no. XVII-38 [157]). He felt that the common grandparents "should not be counted twice to conclude that the grandchildren become Jewish because they have married." After all, absent the first-cousin relationship, a discrete total of four *separate*

Jewish grandparents (not two!) would be necessary to consider the couple Jewish. The central CGQJ bureaucrat was willing to agree, because, as we just saw, he felt the June 2 statute should be read to insist on the *Jewishness* of the spouse; thus, each cousin had to be treated individually to determine his/her Jewishness, and the marriage of one to the other would be irrelevant.

67. Vallat, "Affaires Juives," 2:659–60. Vallat goes on to assert, among other things, that the Vichy racial laws helped to save "95 percent of French Jews," while admitting that, of the 330,000 Jews he counted on French soil before the war, only 180,000 remained in 1946 (2:672). He blames only a few "sordid" individuals or groups for the spoliation of Jewish property, amounting to many millions of francs, without reimbursement or eventual return of the property in most cases (2:659). Vallat, whose legislative abilities and anti-Semitic attack on Léon Blum while both were in the National Assembly commended him (Vallat) to the Germans for the post on the CGQJ, was charged with developing the Jewish legislation (see e.g., Billig, *Le Commissariat général*, 1:59). As to spoliation, Vallat himself described one of his main tasks at the CGQJ to be "de pourchasser la fortune anonyme et vagabonde d'Israel" (to pursue the anonymous and roving fortune of Israel). Billig, *Le Commissariat général*, 1:7.

68. Letter from CGQJ to the regional prefect of Toulouse, complaining of the prosecutor's approach to the burden-of-proof question in the *Dorfman* case (CDJC no. XVIIa–45 [2501]).

69. Not that the story of the French literary community is altogether a happy one, as regards the new racial situation. See, e.g., Lottman, *The Left Bank*; see also essay 13 of this volume.

70. René Gillouin, quoted in Cointet, "Le Conseil national de Vichy," p. 960.

71. See Aron, *Histoire de Vichy*, p. 227; see also Marrus and Paxton, *Vichy France and the Jews*, pp. 205, 232, 241–245, 263, 334.

72. CDJC no. CXV–83. See note 92 and accompanying text (discussing the *Weiller* case). On baptism, see notes 82 and 96 and accompanying text.

73. See CDJC no. XVIIa–45.

74. CDJC no. XXVI–36.

75. Letter (dated "Paris, le 10 Mars 1944") from the "Directeur du Statut des Personnes" to the CGQJ regional director in Toulouse (the CDJC archival reference number is missing, but see appendix six at the end of the chapter for the full document).

76. See appendix ten at the end of the chapter (correspondence between Paris and Berlin advising Adolph Eichmann that Laval was insisting—against German wishes—that Jewish children sixteen years old and under be deported with their parents; it took Eichmann several weeks to condone Laval's innovation). See also Marrus and Paxton, Vichy France and the Jews, p. 263; a top police official, René Bousquet, pleaded with them to allow deportations from the *unoccupied* zone (p. 241).

Bousquet, in his eighties at this writing, was recently ordered to stand trial for crimes against humanity, based in part on information uncovered by Parisian lawyer Serge Klarsfeld. See Eytan, "Mitterand Accused of Hiding Vichy Ties," *Jewish Week*, December 28, 1990, p. 10, col. 1

77. Telegram from the head of the French gestapo in Paris to Dr. Knochen, marked

"Endlösung der Judenfrage in Frankreich," July 2, 1943 (CDJC no. XXVII–23). Bousquet's police provided all that was needed for the massive roundups of 1942 and 1943.

78. Marrus and Paxton, *Vichy France and the Jews*, p. 5.

79. Note from Dr. Knochen to the German Military High Command in Paris (January 28, 1941), Yad Vashem 0–9/4–1 (CDJC no. V–64). For further discussion of this infamous law of October 4, 1940, see below, note 105; see also, e.g., Billig, *Le Commissariat général*, 3:314.

As French plans to extend denaturalization to persons receiving citizenship after 1932 (and even 1928) progressed, the Germans permitted the French to go their own way, planning again to capitalize on the Vichy legal initiative for their late-war deportation drive. See, e.g., "Memorandum to all police precincts in Paris from the Parisian Obersturmbannführer" (July 16, 1943), referring to this statute as the basis for the Parisian roundups of July 23–24, 1943 (CDJC no. XXVI–76).

80. Judgment of January 15, 1942, Tribunal de première instance, Rabat (CDJC no. CXV–20).

81. Reported in J. Lubetzki, *La Condition des juifs en France sous l'Occupation allemande* 1940–44 (Paris: CDJC, 1945). But, in an expert opinion rendered on a similar matter in 1944, law professor Jacques Maury indicates that this case was ultimately reversed by the Court of Appeals of Limoges; *see* Opinion of Jacques Maury, March 6, 1944 (CDJC no. XVIIa–44 [240]).

82. Mosse (CDJC no. XVIIa–38 [165]). Dr. Mosse's view renders irrelevant the personal beliefs of the grandparents, as long as they were nominally Jewish; the principal case renders highly relevant the personal beliefs of infants being baptized. The only way to harmonize the opinions is to see that both made life more difficult for individuals trying to show their non-Jewishness.

Ironically, the notorious CGQJ took a more "liberal" approach to baptized babies. In an advisory opinion, the agency declared that war babies born of mixed parentage, although not in fact belonging to a recognized faith "before June 25, 1940," would be viewed (if baptized immediately) as non-Jewish. Why? "Obviously it could not have been baptized before June 25, 1940, because it was not yet born." Letter from the CGQJ to its regional director in Toulouse (Vichy), August 18, 1942 (CDJC no. XVIIa–38 [158]).

83. See Judgment of June 12, 1940, Tribunal correctional, Bergerac, extract from *Gazette du Palais*, August 1–4, 1942 (CDJC no. CXV–61), and Judgment of April 12, 1943, Tribunal civil, Nice (CXV–119). See also, generally, essay 13 of the present volume.

84. Judgment of April 2, 1943, Conseil d'État, extract from *Gazette du Palais*, April 29–30, 1943 (CDJC no. XVIIa–45 [242]).

85. Communication from the CGQJ to the "Préfet Délegué" in Montpellier, dated "Vichy, September 9, 1943" (CDJC no. XVIIa–38 [163]).

86. Decision of April 30, 1943, Conseil d'État (CDJC no. XVIIa–45 [252]).

87. Letter, dated February 12, 1942, from the Justice Ministry to the CGQJ (CDJC no. CXV–8a).

88. See appendix 14.4 at the end of the chapter (CDJC no. XXXII–123).

89. Session of February 12, 1943, Tribunal civil de la Seine (1ere Chambre), Paris. (Report of court decision in this case on file with the author.)

90. See a CGQJ internal memorandum (undated) reporting the incident as it progressed through June 22, 1944, and describing the February 9, 1944, decision of the Conseil d'État as "surprising" and "contrary to the law of 2 June 1941" (CDJC no. XVII-36 [154a]).

91. See appendix five at the end of the chapter. Letter to M. Arnold Crochez, *Avocat d'la Cour*, from CGQJ (CDJC no. XXIII-19).

92. See above, note 72. The *Weiller* case is to be found at CDJC no. XVII-45 (254).

93. Weisberg, *The Failure of the Word*, Introduction and Appendix.

94. Nonetheless, thoughts of the still-existing constitutional guarantees were not gone for everyone. Léon Blum, in his opening speech to the court at Riom (see note 60), called the trial itself a "legal monstrosity," since he and others were appearing as men already condemned, at least by the head of state. The audience listened "with growing interest to this legal discussion which little by little was transformed into an appeal for true justice and then reached the heights of a protest in defense of the French republican ideal." Joel Colton, *Leon Blum: Humanist in Politics* (Durham: Duke University Press, 1987), pp. 407–8.

Blum's defense counsel at the Riom trial, André Le Troquer, demonstrated a similar belief in constitutional protection when he "moved to have the court declare itself illegal on the ground that the constitutional act establishing it had not been ratified by the nation" (p. 408). Le Troquer also "launched a diatribe against the Vichy regime—its suppression of representative institutions, its curbing of free speech, its arbitrary arrest, and imprisonment practices" (p. 408).

Daladier's attorney—Edouard Daladier had been premier in the year the war commenced and was on trial with Blum—vociferously protested the Vichy courts' use of ex post facto laws, invoking the *Declaration of the Rights of Man* as his authority and remarking, "Our children will read the jurisprudence of the year 1942 and will not understand it" (p. 411). Altogether during the trial, an understanding was exhibited that the norms of French law ought to continue through this trying period. Even some Vichy functionaries expressed their uneasiness in the face of what they considered very persuasive foundational arguments.

Had no lawyers ever voiced foundational, principled objections, the vast professional majority's willingness to collaborate through the elasticity of their rhetoric possibly could be understood as politically inevitable. But this was not what happened. Therefore, Haennig's slippery, liberal-seeming discourse perfectly exhibits his profession's fatal, but fully voluntary, participation in dreadful, legalistic violence.

95. For my view of the professional's compulsion to publish even when the subject matter is grotesque, see pages 169–72.

96. Marrus and Paxton have accurately described Joseph Haennig's article as a suggestion to French courts to refer to German law "objectively and broad-mindedly." They opine that "this suggestion was not, to our knowledge, taken seriously by any French jurisdiction." Marrus and Paxton, *Vichy France and the Jews*, p. 143.

The authors misunderstood, in that passage, that Haennig was trying to convince French courts that had *already* exceeded German jurisprudence on the burden of proof-evidentiary standard issue discussed in this essay. Indeed, Haennig's superficially bizarre rhetoric continued to be necessary throughout the war to French lawyers urging more benign interpretations on their courts and colleagues. For example, note in the extract below the expert analysis of law professor Jacques Maury, who was asked as late as March 6, 1944—only three months before the Normandy invasion—to argue the same issues. Called upon to advise on the Jewishness of three young children of mixed parentage (two baptized before June 25, 1940, and one afterwards), Maury cites Haennig on the still problematic case of the youngest child, who could not necessarily prove his non-Jewishness solely through the baptism:

> One can take it today as certain [despite conflicting earlier cases in the civil courts as well as the Conseil d'État] that an individual can demonstrate by any means, even by presumptions, that he did not belong to the Jewish race on 25 June 1940. This is, indeed, the German solution, whether by ordinances of the occupying authorities of 1940, 1941, and 1942, or by application of the laws of the Reich of 15 September 1935 (*see* articles by M. [Joseph] Haennig, *Gaz*[*ette du*] *Pal*[*ais*] 7–9 October 1942, and 27–30 March 1943).

Opinion of Jacques Maury, March 6, 1944 (CDJC no. XVIIa-44 [240]). See also appendix eight (at the end of the chapter), where Haennig is cited by a government lawyer as being prominent at the bar.

97. *Gazette des Tribuneaux*, October 20, 1939.

98. See, e.g., Judgment of April 2, 1942, J.P., Paris—20th Arrondissement, *Gazette des Tribuneaux*, no. 50, December 6–12, 1942 (CDJC no. CDXXIX-2).

99. Judgment of December 12, 1942, J.P., Paris—20th Arrondissement (CDJC no. CDXXIX-2).

100. Judgment of June 19, 1941, J.P., Paris—20th Arrondissement (CDJC no. CDXXIX-2); see also, Judgment of October 22, 1941 (*Reiner*), J.P., Paris—20th Arrondissement (CDJC no. CDXXIX-1); Judgment of January 7, 1943, J.P., Paris—20th Arrondissement (CDJC no. CDXXIX-2).

101. The June 2 statute did not, on its terms, forbid Jews from being tailors.

102. Judgment of July 30, 1942, J.P., Paris—20th Arrondissement (CDJC no. CDXXIX-2).

103. See above, note 53.

104. That there was such French-authored statutory activity prior to June 2, 1941, was irrefutable (see, especially note 105 below for further discussion of the incarceration law of October 4, 1940, on which see also note 79 and accompanying text). In addition, legal analysts should have been aware of denaturalization laws of September and October 1940 that permitted the summary rounding up and detention of denaturalized or foreign residents. The legal profession itself was stigmatized; lawyers falling into the "foreign" category numbered in the hundreds and they were barred (under the law of September 11, 1940) from practice and then (by the law of October 1, 1940) subject to detention "s'ils sont en surnombre dans l'économie française et si ayant cherché refuge en France, ils se trouvent dans l'impossibilité de regagner leur pays d'origine" (if they are too numerous in the French economy and if having sought refuge in France, they now cannot get back to their native country). Each magistrate undoubtedly knew by late 1942 of dozens of former lawyers

either arrested or thrown out of work. My analysis of the reaction of non-Jewish lawyers to these events must await another forum (although part of my present subject), but there surely was a long history of French arrests prior to June 2, 1941, and these would have been known to these magistrates.

105. "Loi sur les ressortissants étrangers de race juive, 4 octobre 1940," *JO* (October 18, 1940), no. 3481, reprinted in Sarraute and Tager, eds., *Les Juifs sous l'Occupation*, p. 22.

By all accounts, First Justice Minister Alibert not only signed the law, but also authored it (as suggested, for example, by a Vichy functionary close to the authorship of the law, Gilbert LeSage, in an interview with the author, Paris, December 13, 1988). Obersturmführer Dannecker consistently described it as a Vichy law: "I notice that, in the unoccupied zone, three concentration camps for stateless Jews have already been established, legitimated under the *Vichy law* of 3 October [sic] 1940." Note from Obersturmführer Dannecker to Sturmbannführer Zeitschel (Paris, February 28, 1941), Yad Vashem V–63. Emphasis added.

Although Dannecker wrote "3.10.40 [October 3, 1940]," he must have been referring to the law of October 4, 1940. The Germans relied on this law throughout the war. Without doubt, the concentration camp reality in France originated as one of Vichy law's earliest innovations (see note 79 and accompanying text).

106. Marrus and Paxton, *Vichy France and the Jews*, pp. 42, 263–64, 271; see also note 77 and accompanying text.

107. See sources cited in note 106. Maurice Rajsfus tells of his own experiences during this two-day "grande rafle," referred to by Vichy with the sinister euphemism "Vent printanier" (spring wind). He and his family were among the almost 13,000 Jews arrested in the "round-up." Rajsfus stresses the central role of Parisian police, whom he describes as almost entirely without sympathy for those they were rounding up. When it was announced by the police some hours after the arrests that children under sixteen would not be further detained, parents were forced to decide whether to send their children back into the street alone, or to keep their family together. The parents of the fourteen-year-old Maurice and his sixteen-year-old sister reluctantly decided to let them go. The two children thus escaped deportation and death, but thousands did not, including an eleven-year-old cousin to whom he dedicates the book. See Maurice Rajsfus, *Jeudi Noir, 16 juillet 1942: L'honneur perdu de la France profonde* (Paris: L'Harmattan, 1988).

108. The formula frustrated a stingy landlord in the late 1942 *Neyman* case. Sometime in July 1942, probably during the "grande rafle," Neyman was arrested. His arrest left his wife unsupported; earlier, their business had been snatched and, ever since May 1941, run by an "administrateur provisoire." Nonetheless, Neyman had been able to pay the rent until his arrest. Even before they lost their business, an earlier decision of April 6, 1940, had reduced their rent in response to Neyman's military service. But the landlord now argued that "the new diminution in resources resulted not from a Circumstance of War but instead from rules and decrees currently in force against the Jews." The court would not (rather than could not) accept that reasoning, choosing to fall back upon the established formula that Neyman "a été arreté par les Autorités d'Occupation." Again, the court ignored the fact that the French police acting under Vichy law had arrested Neyman in July 1942. Although

the court ignored Vichy involvement, it did allow a 50 percent rent reduction, retroactive to the July arrest. Judgment of December 8, 1942, Tribunal civil de la Seine (CDJC no. CDXXIX-2).

109. See Weisberg, *The Failure of the Word*, chapters 8 and 9.

110. A minority of lawyers did publicly raise foundational concerns about the development of wartime French law. (See note 94—discussion of the Riom trial, with its defense lawyers' jugular foundational attacks on the Vichy legal system; and pages 169-71—further accounts of Riom and other public arguments by lawyers against the Vichy laws; also, see below, note 153, noting a letter from Belgian lawyers expressing outrage at racial laws introduced in their country. French lawyers felt more comfortable avoiding such higher levels of generalization when discussing race-related issues. The fact that a spectrum of rhetorical choice existed in Vichy, however, casts into a shadowy corner even the seemingly benign jurisprudence of the landlord-tenant cases.

111. See, e.g., *Les Loyers de guerre* (Paris, 1943), 3:56 (in CDJC no. CDXXIX-2), a treatise accepting the distinction.

112. See notes 104 and 105 and accompanying text.

113. Judgment of February 1, 1943, J.P., Paris—11th Arrondissement (CDJC no. CDXXIX-2).

114. This law, overtaken by the law of October 4, 1940 (see note 105), stated that "certain individuals may be interned in specially designated camps."

115. See above, note 80; see also notes 104 and 105 and accompanying text (discussing the detention laws, especially that of October 4, 1940, and the 1942 roundups in Paris of almost 13,000 Jews in a two-day period).

116. A few months earlier, the 11th arrondissement had followed basically the same logic in the *Chmoulovski* case. Judgment of November 2, 1942, J.P., Paris—11th Arrondissement (CDJC no. CDXXIX-2). The court there gave a 30 percent rent reduction to an unemployed and stateless Jewish war veteran.

117. For two references on the work of the UGIF during the Vichy years, see Cynthia J. Haft, *The Bargain and the Bridle* (Chicago: Dialog, 1983), and G. Wellers and I. Schneerson, eds., *L'Activité des organisations juives en France* (1947; reprint, Paris: CDJC, 1983).

118. Letter from the UGIF, October 30, 1942 (CDJC no. CDXXIX-1).

119. Judgment of July 23, 1942, J.P., Boulogne-Billancourt (CDJC no. CDXXIX-2).

120. Judgment of February 25, 1943, J.P., Paris—3d Arrondissement (CDJC no. CDXXIX-2).

121. Judgment of May 5, 1942, J.P., Paris—13th Arrondissement (CDJC no. CDXXIX-2).

122. For the basic Vichy text creating a *numerus clausus* and other restrictions on the practice of medicine by Jews, see the decree of August 11, 1941, *JO*, September 6, 1941, p. 450, reprinted in Sarraute and Tager, eds., *Les Juifs sous l'Occupation*, p. 69.

123. Also a fiction, although frequently used: the only "legislator" in Vichy was Pétain, assisted by his ministers.

124. Judgment of September 29, 1941, Chambre des Référés, Cour de Paris (CDJC no. CDXXIX-2).

125. See the discussions above, in notes 98 through 121 and accompanying text.

126. See above, notes 70 through 79 and accompanying text.

127. See above, note 104, regarding the Vichy detention law of October 4, 1940, whose origin the writer of this memo, like so many of his profession, disregards. Furthermore, by the time of the UGIF analysis, the mass roundups in Paris had already taken place, making obvious even to a nonlawyer that detention was a Vichy policy, implemented with no or little German urging or assistance. See above, note 105 and accompanying text.

128. The number of these German ordinances was not to grow much larger, whereas the French law regarding Jews was to number almost two hundred statutes, decrees, rulings, etc. See Sarraute and Tager, eds., *Les Juifs sous l'Occupation*, pp. 185–92; also, see above, note 63.

129. There is very little in the German ordinances about detention (see above, notes 53, 70–79, and 104). The Sixth Ordinance, it is true, imposed a curfew on Jews from 8 P.M. to 6 A.M., and forbade them from moving their residence (see the Sixth Ordinance of February 7, 1942, published February 11, 1942, reprinted in Sarraute and Tager, eds., *Les Juifs sous l'Occupation*, p. 139); and the Ninth (July 8, 1942, published July 15, 1942, reprinted in *Les Juifs sous l'Occupation*, p. 161) forbade them entry into certain movie houses and restricted their shopping in department stores and smaller establishments to just one hour a day (3 to 4 P.M.), the hour during which, as one writer put it, "most shops were closed." See H. Amoureux, *La France et les Français de 1939 à 1945* (Paris: Colin, 1970), p. 67. The Germans first capitalized on the (October 4, 1940) statute that Vichy had promulgated long before the occupiers were even prepared to address detention issues in France, and then they permitted Vichy to write and implement the additional legislation dealing with detention.

130. It was not until the eighth German ordinance, on May 29, 1942, that Jews in the occupied zone were forced to wear the yellow Star of David (see Lubetzki, *La Condition des juifs en France*, p. 155). The Vichy debates about the Star were colorful and complex; Vichy's legalistic debates about Jews, including learned treatises by law professors suggesting special insignia and other means of isolating Jews, make up an unfortunate part of this history. See, e.g., A. Broc, *La Qualité de juif: Une notion juridique nouvelle* (Paris: Press of the University of France, 1943), pp. 14–20, beginning his legal treatise on the Jewish laws with a "learned analysis" of the religious history of the Jews, one that sets them apart from all other religions and is deserving of being segregated.

See also H. Baudry and J. Ambre, *La Condition publique et privée du juif en France* (Lyon: Desvigne, 1942) a treatise promising practitioners a better understanding of the vital part of "la France nouvelle." The authors state, "For those in whom some liberalism brings out a distaste for what they think of as [these laws'] show of sectarianism, we will respond that anti-Semitism has never been inspired by anything except the nonsociability and nonassimilability of the Jew" (pp. 11–12). The authors' analysis commences with the traditional anti-Semitic history of "the wandering Jew."

131. Part of a forthcoming study, as I indicated earlier, will be the treatment of lawyers specially, both by the legislation and by their non-Jewish colleagues. The UGIF text refers to the beginning of the focus on arrests of lawyers, which continued

throughout the war and eventually touched thousands of private lawyers and mag- istrates alike. See appendix 14.9 at the end of the chapter (*Paris-Soir* article of Sep- tember 12, 1941). The number of lawyers arrested was not "all," of course, but forty. Among the forty lawyers arrested and interned in Drancy on August 21, 1941, many of whom were deported thereafter and never returned, was the distinguished Parisian lawyer, Pierre Masse, and others of his rank. Among the eloquent postwar accolades to the memory of Pierre Masse, see the "Discours prononcé par M. Marcel Poignard" (July 11, 1946), in a publication of the Association of the Bar of Paris (Paris: Imprimerie du Palais, 1946), pp. 25–28. Poignard's predecessor as the "Batonnier" of the Order of Lawyers of the Bar, Jacques Charpentier, also treats Masse and some other Jewish colleagues at the wartime Paris bar with reverence in his memoirs of the Vichy period, throughout which he served as leader of the Paris Bar Association. See Jacques Char- pentier, *Au Service de la liberté* (Paris: Fayard, 1949), pp. 156–57 (on file at the Bibliothèque des Avocats, Palais de Justice, Paris). Charpentier protested to Jacques Bardoux, a Vichy lawyer who was in charge of the Constitutional reform project then under way, about the arrest of the forty, but in vain. On Charpentier's equivocal rhetoric in his book about Jewish lawyers at the bar generally, see below, note 151 and accompanying text.

The Nazis themselves took an interest in the arrests of Jewish lawyers, although they do not appear to have originated them. See Memorandum (dated October 5, 1941) of Von Bose, himself a lawyer and Legal Counsel to the German Ambassador in Paris (CDJC no. VI [138]). In that memo, Von Bose reports to the Gestapo that he had been visited by three Parisian lawyers (Aulois, Vallier, and Mettetal) asking that some of the more prominent of the forty arrested lawyers be released from Drancy, "in the interests of anti-Semitism." The French lawyers' reasoning appears to have been that, with so many mediocre, "undesirable" Jewish lawyers still free, the average French lawyer might be disgusted to see these prominent ones imprisoned, and the arrests might "inspire pity in a segment of their anti-Semitic colleagues." (Pierre Masse's name was apparently *not* raised by the group.) In fact, of the "prominent" group, Ulmo, Frank, and Kahn were temporarily released. On these points, see Memorandum from Von Bose dated November 4, 1941 (CDJC no. VI [138]). All three lawyers, however, eventually perished during the Occupation. The case of Jacques Frank is movingly told by Maurice Alléhaud after the war (document in the Bibliothèque des Avocats, Palais de Justice, Paris, pp. 229–34). Frank, released from Drancy on No- vember 2 (according to Alléhaud, however, less due to pressure than to horrible health), never regained his former spirit and, several months later, committed suicide by throw- ing himself out a window (p. 234).

132. The writer continues to disregard Vichy's independent statutory and deten- tion activity (see above, notes 53, 104, and 105).

133. The UGIF confusion, real or feigned, about certain grim realities of war, must be understood in the context of sheer terror pervading that organization, which tried to help Jews but was officially beholden to German and French overlords. As just an example (relating to landlord-tenant law) of the Kafkaesque nature of the UGIF's tasks, consider that they were instructed by the Germans and the Parisian police, in mid-1944, to reimburse out of the UGIF's limited treasure those Aryan landlords whose apartment doors had been forced open by the police and damaged

in the search for Jews. See UGIF document, "Extrait du Registre des Déliberations: Déliberation du 30 Mai 1944" (May 30, 1944), Yad Vashem 09/27.

134. See, e.g., notes 70 through 79 and accompanying text.

135. Richard Posner, *Law and Literature: A Misunderstood Relation* (Cambridge: Harvard University Press, 1988), p. 172.

136. See above, note 51 and accompanying text..

137. Posner, *Law and Literature*, p. 172.

138, See, for example, Marrus and Paxton, *Vichy France and the Jews*, p. 344.

139. See, e.g., Doris Bensimon, *Les Grandes Rafles* (Paris: Editions Privat, 1987): "3,000 of the 4,051 children arrested on 16 July 1942 were French-born" (p. 14); see also Marrus and Paxton, *Vichy France and the Jews*: "The Vichy regime set out to reduce the Jews—all Jews, not merely immigrants or refugees—to a subservient role, ... and to subject them to humiliating restrictions" (pp. 365–66).

140. J. Adler, *The Jews of Paris and the Final Solution* (New York: Oxford University Press, 1985), p. 45.

141. Adler, *The Jews of Paris*, p. 45.

142. See, e.g., Billig, *Le Commissariat général*, p. 229.

143. Marrus and Paxton, *Vichy France and the Jews*, pp. 354–56.

144. See, e.g., Pierre-André Guastalla, *Journal (1940–44)* (Paris: Plon, 1951), entry for September 2, 1942: "Horrible things are happening in the camp of Milles near Aix and also in all the camps of France. Jews of German, Austrian, Czech, and other backgrounds are being herded there, whether they're 20 or 60 years old, then crammed into cattle cars and sent to Poland in sealed trains" (p. 178).

145. See Marrus and Paxton, *Vichy France and the Jews*, p. 145. As Marrus and Paxton put it, on their more modest claim: "It is hard today not to be surprised at the routine fashion with which this new legal order was explained and applied" (p. 144). Marrus and Paxton recognize, of course, that in areas they studied more closely— government behavior, such as that of Laval's—the French outperformed their conquerors' wishes and even desires (see pp. 232, 263, and 364).

146. See David Margolick, "At the Bar," *New York Times*, May 17, 1991, p. B18 (centrally discussing the Haennig dilemma); Posner, *Law and Literature*, pp. 173–74; and Richard Posner, "Review of Weisberg's *The Failure of the Word*," *Yale Law Journal* (1987), 96:1173, 1188–89. See also Milner Ball, "Confessions," *Cardozo Studies in Law and Literature* (1989), 1:185, 189 (referring to the Haennig parable as a revealing warning "on giving succor to monstrous causes by making them—wordily, academically, lawyerly—debatable"); John Ayer, "Review of Weisberg's *The Failure of the Word*," *Michigan Law Review* (1987), 85:895, 908–10 (disagreeing with char- acterization of Haennig as "villain," and also with concepts that " 'wordiness' leads to vice" or that the "wordless are by nature any purer than the wordy"); and Robert Weisberg, "The Law-Literature Enterprise," *Yale Journal of Law and the Humanities* (1988), 1:1, 32–33 (referring to *The Failure of the Word*'s use of Haennig as evidence of the "continuing significance of [the] intellectual effort which is Law and Literature").

147. I have referred throughout this essay to the example of Léon Blum and of others (see, e.g., note 94, above; the discussion of Blum will continue shortly).

148. See Fiss, "Objectivity and Interpretation," and Fish, "Fish v. Fiss" (response to Fiss), note 47, and note 160 and accompanying text (summarizing the debate).

149. Posner, *Law and Literature*, pp. 173–74.

150. See, for example, AN file 72 AJ–411 (Barthélemy's own detailed notes—a mixture of admiration and concern in the face of foundational arguments courageously mounted by the Riom defense against the Vichy government and the legitimacy of the trials), passim; see also Michel, *Le Procès de Riom*, and Barthélemy, *Ministre de la Justice*.

151. Charpentier wrote directly to Pétain demanding that the defendants at Riom be adequately represented by counsel. He himself defended Paul Reynaud at that trial. But his proudest moment, according to his own description, was his second protest to Pétain over the reinstatement by the French government of a lawyer who had been disbarred by Charpentier's association. That passionate protest, which succeeded, indicates the willingness of leading French lawyers to stand up for certain principles (in Charpentier's case, the right to counsel and the right of the Paris bar to administer itself without governmental interference). However, Charpentier's record in other areas implicating foundational French beliefs, including the racial laws, is far more spotty. On all these points, see Charpentier, *Au Service de la liberté*, and the text accompanying note 152 (discussion of Charpentier's actions and rhetoric on the "Jewish problem" at the Paris bar); see also AN file 72 AJ–411.

152. Charpentier, *Au Service de la liberté*, p. 127.

153. See the four-page handwritten letter (dated November 19, 1940) from three leading Brussels lawyers, expressing outrage at the racial legislation there, to General von Folkenhausen, Military Commander for Belgium (Yad Vashem IV–203).

154. See appendix 14.9, at the end of the chapter, and a discussion of these arrests at note 131.

155. Vichy landlord-tenant law, even in decisions *most* favorable to Jewish litigants, illustrates this failure (as discussed in the previous section of this essay).

156. To be distinguished, however, is the Philippe Serre method of attack (see above, note 50). Those who challenged the authority of the regime ab initio, as opposed to the constitutionality of its eventual laws and procedures, were often harshly victimized.

157. See appendix 14.8 (at the end of the chapter), an anonymous reference to Haennig on the official government stationery of a public prosecutor.

158. Fish, *Is There a Text in This Class?*, p. 149.

159. Ibid.

160. See Fiss, "Objectivity and Interpretation," and Fish, "Fish v. Fiss."

161. Stanley Fish, *Doing What Comes Naturally: Change, Rhetoric, and the Practice of Theory in Literary and Legal Studies* (Durham: Duke University Press, 1988), p. 177.

162. See Richard H. Weisberg, "A Response to Fish and White," *Mississippi College Law Review* (1984), 5:57.

163. Vichy lawyers were content to avoid constitutional norms not because they conceived of no reality apart from their practice; instead, they avoided them because their cultural and professional environment condoned text-avoidance and encouraged pragmatic interpretive flexibility *as* a professional, hermeneutic norm. For French lawyers, the avoidance of central realities was part of their professional and cultural training. See essay 13. In other words, (most) Vichy lawyers felt unconstrained by the

constitutive texts of their tradition because their professional culture fully empowered them to avoid textualism when other concerns had been brought into competition. (This assertion will require an analysis in my Vichy book-length study of traditional French anti-Talmudism and of the relationship of legal to Catholic interpretive theory that the Vichy years expressly brought forth through learned legalistic discussions of the anti-Jewish racial laws.) For present purposes, this observation may serve to alert the reader that preponderant cultural (and theoretical) beliefs *do affect* professional practice.

164. See above, note 51 and accompanying text (statement by Philippe Serre that "the Germans would not have insisted on a racial policy if the French had refused").

165. Fish, *Doing What Comes Naturally*, p. 177.

## 6. Lawtalk in America

1. See, e.g., *Paul de Man, Wartime Journalism, 1939-1943*, in *Paul de Man*, eds. Werner Hamacher, Neil Hertz, and Thomas Keenan (Lincoln: University of Nebraska Press, 1988). Stanley Corngold, "Paul de Man," *Times Literary Supplement*, August 26–September 1, 1988, p. 931 (letter to the editor). For a prescandal analysis of the relationship of deconstruction to repressive political regimes, see Richard H. Weisberg, "Text into Theory: A Literary Approach to the Constitution," *Georgia Law Review* (1986), 20:939, 946–62. For a defense of de Man, see Jacques Derrida, *Mémoires pour Paul de Man* (Paris: Galilée, 1988). For other references, see essay 14, note 48.

2. This tendency has its roots in such excellent works as John Gardner, *On Moral Fiction* (New York: Basic Books, 1977) and Eugene Goodheart, *The Failure of Criticism* (Cambridge: Harvard University Press, 1978). For a more recent example, see Tobin Siebers, *The Ethics of Criticism* (Ithaca: Cornell University Press, 1988).

3. Richard Posner, *Law and Literature: A Misunderstood Relation* (Cambridge: Harvard University Press, 1988), p. xi.

4. See, generally, Posner, *Law and Literature*, pp. 137–71.

5. See, e.g., Louis Auchincloss, "Legal Fictions" (book review), *Journal of the American Bar Association* (October 1, 1988), pp. 124, 126.

6. Richard A. Posner, "The Jurisprudence of Skepticism," *Michigan Law Review* (1988), 86:827 (hereafter cited in text).

7. The most important of these interpretations, and the most widely circulated prior to the publication of his *Law and Literature*, is Posner's defense of Captain Vere in Melville's *Billy Budd, Sailor*. Because that defense, and my attack on Vere as a verbal falsifier, are in the public domain, I will refer periodically to the "debate" in these pages. Readers interested in reviewing and tracking the debate should again refer to this volume's chapter 3.

8. Posner, *Law and Literature*, p. 110 (hereafter cited in text). Posner correctly identifies the theme of delegation, which is of importance to lawyers in this age of specialization and delegation, as emerging from the Duke's behavior at the start of *Measure For Measure*. The play's problems begin, just as they do in *King Lear*, when a still capable and reasonably decent head of state gratuitously surrenders power to less known and less experienced persons. Shakespeare's aversion to figures who avoid power when they could exercise it also comes through in his treatment of *Hamlet*.

For Posner's discussion of the theme of inaction in *Hamlet*, see pp. 54–62. Posner does not, however, give himself enough time to explore fully his insight into the perils of delegation. For a fuller discussion of this insight, see Alexander Leggatt, "Substitution in *Measure for Measure*," *Shakespeare Quarterly* (1988), 39:342.

9. See, e.g., Owen M. Fiss, "Objectivity and Interpretation," *Stanford Law Review* (1982), 34:739; Stanley Fish, "Fish v. Fiss," *Stanford Law Review* (1984), 36:1325. Posner treats Fish skeptically in *Law and Literature*, pp. 263–65. Fish treats Posner skeptically in Stanley Fish, "Don't Know Much About the Middle Ages: Posner on Law and Literature," *Yale Law Journal* (1988), 97:777.

10. See Benjamin N. Cardozo, "Law and Literature", reprinted in Cardozo *Selected Writings of Benjamin Nathan Cardozo*, ed. M. Hall (1947; reprint, New York: Matthew Bender, 1975), p. 338.

11. See, e.g., Benjamin N. Cardozo, "The Growth of the Law" (1924), in *Selected Writings*, p. 226 (quoting Roscoe Pound). In this essay Cardozo also criticizes deductive judges in a discussion of his famous *Hynes* decision (p. 230). For my depiction of Posner's jurisprudence as championing an antiliterary deductivism, see below, notes 16 through 19 and accompanying text.

12. Benjamin N. Cardozo, "The Paradoxes of Legal Science" (1928), in *Selected Writings*, p. 330.

13. Benjamin N. Cardozo, "Address to New York State Bar Association meeting (January 22, 1932)," in *Selected Writings*, p. 18.

14. See Richard H. Weisberg, "Judicial Discretion, or the Self on the Shelf," *Cardozo Law Review* (1988), 10:105, 118n38.

15. The word "fool" in this context reminds one of tactics employed by Posner in his literary pronouncements as well. When attempting to dispose with a stroke of the pen of an earlier scholar's considered argument, he wrote: "One has to belong to the intelligentsia to believe things like that: no ordinary man could be such a fool" (*Law and Literature*, p. 174, quoting George Orwell). Of course, in literary criticism as in law, rhetorical excesses devoid of substantive content eventually bounce back at the rhetorician.

16. I am apparently on a mailing list for the distribution of all Posner's opinions on the Seventh Circuit Court of Appeals. I cannot read each of them, but when I do pick one up I am usually surprised to see a moderate voice, quite different from that of the normative judge discussed in Posner's writings—quite different, indeed, from the often intemperate critical voice he assumes in his book. My favorite opinion of his, one I have offered to professional audiences as an example of clear and concise judicial writing, is *United States v. Holzer*, 848 F.2d 822 (1988). For another well-written opinion, beginning typically with the facts of the case, see *LaSalle National Bank v. General Mills Restaurant Group, Inc.*, 854 F.2d 1050 (1988). And see this volume's part 1 for a very brief discussion of his 1990 opinion in *Miller v. Civil City of South Bend*.

17. Benjamin N. Cardozo, "Mr. Justice Holmes," *Harvard Law Review* (1931), 44:682.

18. Benjamin N. Cardozo, "The Nature of the Judicial Process" (1921), in *Selected Writings*, pp. 118–19.

19. Cardozo and Posner do wind up agreeing, in part, on the importance of style

and rhetoric to the authoritative judicial opinion. Compare Cardozo, "Law and Literature," in *Selected Writings*, pp. 269–316, and Richard A. Posner, "Law and Literature: A Relation Reargued," *Virginia Law Review* (1986), 72:1351, 1375. But whereas Cardozo asserts the inevitable interweaving of style, substance, and the writer's values, Posner seems unwilling to consider the relationship of ethics to aesthetics. Indeed, Posner asserts in his jurisprudential article—again in the spirit of his admired Captain Vere—that "We should not be so naive as to infer the nature of the judicial process from the rhetoric of judicial opinions" ("The Jurisprudence of Skepticism," p. 865).

20. Posner, *Law and Literature*, p. 211. The New Critical School, led by scholars of the 1940s and 1950s such as Cleanth Brooks, John Ciardi, John Crowe Ransom, and Allen Tate, claimed to reassert the primacy of the literary text, rejecting earlier approaches such as Trilling's sociological and psychological criticism, the comparative or philosophical approach, or even the quite traditional method of biographical criticism. They wanted, in Geoffrey Hartman's description, "to purify criticism." Geoffrey H. Hartman, *Criticism in the Wilderness* (New Haven: Yale University Press, 1980), p. 247). The fallacy in the claim that "texts" can be approached without recourse to "extrinsic" ideas or data is evident in Posner's work. But, beyond this, his approach benefits so little from the technical contributions and linguistic understanding of the New Critics, and his approach is so unyieldingly polemical, that one wonders why he associates himself with the school at all.

21. See Posner, *Law and Literature*, p. 211.

22. Posner, *Law and Literature*, pp. 167, 169. This last example demonstrates, if analyzed in some detail, Posner's intentionalist methodology. To the assertion that Dostoevski "meant" us to minimize the consequences of Dmitri's unjust conviction, contrast this text, from the last chapter of *The Brothers Karamazov* (1880; translated by Constance Garnett, 1929):

> At the gate of the house Alyosha [Dmitri's younger brother, and a saintly voice of truth in the novel] was met by the shouts of the boys, . . . Kolya Krassotkin was the foremost of them.
>
> "How glad I am you've come, Karamazov!" he cried, holding out his hand to Alyosha. . . . "Is your brother innocent or guilty? Was it he killed your father or was it the valet? As you say, so it will be. I haven't slept for the last four nights for thinking of it."
>
> "The valet killed him, my brother is innocent," answered Alyosha. . . . "So he will perish an innocent victim!" exclaimed Kolya; "though he is ruined he is happy! I could envy him!"
>
> "What do you mean? How can you? Why?" cried Alyosha, surprised.
>
> "Oh, if I, too, could sacrifice myself some day for truth!" cried Kolya with enthusiasm.
>
> "But not in such a cause, not with such disgrace and such horror!" said Alyosha.

If Alyosha, whose faith is a mainstay to him and others throughout this masterpiece, cannot accept Dmitri's conviction, how can we? The temporal legal error Dostoevski describes so compellingly and so precisely cannot be deflected by critical legerdemain.

Perhaps, on the other hand, I should welcome Posner's grasp at the immature

Kolya Krassotkin's desperately "romantic" assertion. Any port in a storm, and why not seek out the youthful voices of this novel's literally minor figures to counterbalance the otherwise pervasive horror felt by the main characters in the face of Dmitri's wrongful conviction? But, of course, even Kolya is not pretending, as does Posner, that Dmitri is anything less than fully innocent.

So passionate is Posner's defense of the legal system in *Law and Literature* that it must exceed anything reasonably offered to it by a text such as *The Brothers Karamazov*. Incredibly, and in violation of his rule that "extrinsic" sources should not be used to determine legal meanings Posner concludes: "Not only is the trial basically fair, but Dmitri's sentence (twenty years of penal servitude in Siberia) is lenient for the time, place, and circumstances, which the judge and jury believe to be parricide in the course of theft" (p. 168).

Assuming that we can call a trial "fair" that is tainted by pervasively self-interested prosecutors, finds the wrong person guilty, and sentences him to twenty years in Siberia, there is another fallacy in Posner's statement. First, he is wrong in asserting that Dmitri's sentence is "lenient" (and note again that Posner is having recourse to the "extrinsic" evidence he rejects in others' work). In the Russia of the tsars, capital punishment had not been imposed on convicted murderers for at least a century before the events Dostoevski describes. See Will Adams, "Capital Punishment in Imperial and Soviet Criminal Law," *American Journal of Comparative Law* (1970), 18:575–76; accord Samuel Kucherov, *Courts, Lawyers and Trials Under the Last Three Tsars* (New York: Praeger, 1953), p. 211.

Thus Dostoevski's immediate audience would not have deemed a sentence of twenty years "lenient." It was surely close to the maximum imposed by judges who were not disposed to using capital punishment for murderers. And if we recall that Raskolnikov, who actually commits two murders (one premeditated) in *Crime and Punishment* (1866), receives a sentence of only eight years in exile, we will surely think Dmitri's twenty years to be quite harsh indeed.

Finally, Posner knows, from having read earlier criticism (see Weisberg, *The Failure of the Word*, pp. 45–81, discussed extensively by Posner, *Law and Literature*, pp. 166–71) that Dmitri's trial—apart from its erroneous outcome—is anything but fair: the prosecutor virulently resents Dmitri for having attracted his wife's attentions, and the key prosecution witnesses (the servant Grigory and Dmitri's jilted girlfriend Katarina Ivanovna) vent their spleen against the defendant in open court by distorting the evidence. The text's infinite care in depicting a criminal proceeding that goes astray because of legalistic mistakes and subjectivist distortions is reduced by Posner to yet another "metaphor" of law's benignity.

23. See for example, Posner, *Law and Literature*, pp. 169, 186.

24. In his discussion of the relevance of modern fiction to the Holocaust, Posner's surprising tunnel vision becomes all too apparent. He wishes to demonstrate, but again through mere assertiveness, that (as he emphasizes in his "Conclusion") Law and Literature should not be "political" and cannot solve any major social problems. His own politics aside, Posner demonstrates a paltry knowledge of French legal history and, more particularly, French law under the Occupation and during the Vichy regime. I am struck by the rigidity of his view that the French neither initiated nor implemented a pattern of racial definition, and even deportation, beyond that required by the

Germans. A growing scholarly literature proves this view to be unsupportable. See essays 13 and 14 of this volume.

25. See note 11 above and the discussion on pp. 193–96.

26. Herman Melville, *Billy Budd, Sailor*, ed. H. Hayford and M. Sealts (Chicago: University of Chicago Press, 1962), p. 87.

27. Posner's disdain for outsiders pervades *Law and Literature*; some examples: "[V]oices crying in the wilderness tend to be shrill" (p. 21); "A punctilious legalism is the pariah's protection" (p. 97).

28. See, generally, Robert Hallberg, ed., *Canons* (Chicago: University of Chicago Press, 1984); Frank Kermode, *Forms of Attention* (Chicago: University of Chicago Press, 1985).

29. See Weisberg, *The Failure of the Word*, pp. 1–9. See also John A. Alford, *Literature and Law in the Middle Ages: A Bibliography of Scholarship* (New York: Garland, 1984); R. Howard Bloch, *Medieval French Literature and Law* (Berkeley: University of California Press, 1977); O. Hood Phillips, *Shakespeare and the Lawyers* (London: Methuen, 1972).

30. See, e.g., John Barth, *The Floating Opera*, 1956 (torts, trusts, and estates—see this volume's essay 8); Honoré de Balzac, *Ursule Mirouet*, 1841 (trusts and estates); Samuel Warren, *Ten Thousand a Year*, 1841 (trusts and estates); Arthur Solmssen, *The Comfort Letter*, 1975 (securities); William Faulkner, *The Snopes Trilogy*, 1940–1959 (real property). For an earlier twentieth-century list that leans far more heavily upon noncriminal law than would our post-Holocaust approach, see John H. Wigmore, "A List of 100 Legal Novels," *Illinois Law Review* (1908), 2:574, reprinted and revised in *Illinois Law Review* (1922), 17:26.

31. See Richard H. Weisberg, "Law in and as Literature: Self-Generated Meaning in the 'Procedural Novel,'" in C. Koelb and S. Noakes, eds., *The Comparative Perspective on Literature* (Ithaca: Cornell University Press, 1988), p. 227.

32. For perceptive approaches to the question of market acceptance of fictional works see, for example, George Lukács, *The Theory of The Novel*, trans. A. Bostock (Cambridge: MIT Press, 1971); Ian Watt, *The Rise of the Novel* (Berkeley: University of California Press, 1965).

33. See Posner, *Law and Literature*, pp. 153n34, 154–55.

34. See, e.g., Garry Wills, *Explaining America: The Federalist* (Garden City, N.Y.: Doubleday, 1981), pp. 16, 66, 257.

35. See Weisberg, *The Failure of the Word*, pp. 14–18.

36. "Romantic poetry is a progressive, universal poetry. Its aim isn't merely to reunite all the separate species of poetry and put poetry in touch with philosophy and rhetoric. It tries to and should mix and fuse poetry and prose, inspiration and criticism, the poetry of art and the poetry of nature." Friedrich von Schlegel, "Athenaeum Fragments," in *Friedrich Schlegel's Lucinde and the Fragments*, trans. P. Firchow (Minneapolis: University of Minnesota Press, 1971), p. 161.

37. Voltaire's diatribe against Shakespeare appeared in his *Du théâtre anglais* (1761).

38. See, e.g., Herman Glaser, *The Cultural Roots of National Socialism*, trans. Ernest A. Menze (Austin: University of Texas Press, 1978), pp. 86, 109, 210; Roderick Stackelberg, *Idealism Debased: From Völkisch Ideology to National Socialism* (Kent,

Ohio: Kent State University Press, 1981), pp. 5, 12.

39. See Weisberg, *The Failure of the Word*, pp. 14–16.

40. But as a wonderful counterexample, see Judith S. Koffler, "Terror and Mutilation in the Golden Age," *Human Rights Quarterly* (1983), 5:116, 123–34.

41. See Terry Eagleton, *William Shakespeare* (Oxford and New York: Blackwell, 1986), p. 37. For an argument by a distinguished lawyer that Shylock is correct and that Portia's gimmick is legalistic trickery at its worst, see Rudolf von Ihering, *Der Kampf Um's Recht* (1886), translated in H. H. Furness, ed., *The Merchant of Venice: A New Variorum Edition* (1888; reprint, New York: Dover, 1964), pp. 410–11.

42. See Mark Edwin Andrews, *Law Versus Equity in "The Merchant of Venice"* (Boulder: University of Colorado Press, 1965), pp. 19–72. Agreeing with Andrews and opining that if Portia's courtroom tactics were viewed (as Posner views them) as legalistic, they would be "scarred by grave errors" is E. F. J. Tucker, "The Letter of the Law in *The Merchant of Venice*," *Shakespeare Survey* (1976), 29:93, 98. I have collected the works by Tucker, Andrews, von Ihering, and several others writing on this play in Richard H. Weisberg, "Seminar in Literature and the Law" (Spring 1980), pp. 247–83 (unpublished course materials, available in the main library at Columbia University).

43. For a discussion of the equity in this scene, see Andrews, *Law Versus Equity*, pp. 13–14, 69–70.

44. Portia is saving the life of her husband's best friend and business associate. Her marriage is unconsummated and will remain so until she can dispatch this bad piece of litigious business.

45. See *The Merchant of Venice* (II.vii.78–79): "A gentle riddance. Draw the curtains, go. / Let all of his complexion choose me so."

46. See, e.g., Peter Jack Alscher, "Shakespeare's *Merchant of Venice*: Toward a Radical Reconciliation and a 'Final Solution' of Venice's Jewish Problem" (Ph.D. diss., Washington University, 1990), chapter 2.

47. Posner, *Law and Literature*, p. 94; footnote omitted. Posner proceeds in a manner that opens up another issue worthy of discussion:

> The lack of realism in the play's treatment of law extends to the procedures as well as the substance of law. Portia not only is an imposter but has an undisclosed interest in the outcome of the trial; the parties have no lawyers; Venice has no professional judges; a civil case ends in a criminal conviction. And yet the play is about law in a more profound sense than any other work considered thus far. (p. 94).

Posner's use of the word "yet" in the final sentence of this passage is puzzling. I would have concluded with the words: "*Thus* the play is about law. . . ." When fiction reveals, as no other medium can in such detail and with such sensitivity to language's role in legal behavior, that corrupt procedures are used by fully empowered officials, precisely then fiction is talking "about law."

Posner does of course say that the play is "about" law, but as we have seen, he means that it is about the ratification of law's development from strict liability to flexibility. So in a way his earlier imprecision reappears in the quoted statement, which implies that no literary work, no matter how competently and specifically it depicts a legal case, can be about law if the legal actors commit errors, knowingly or otherwise. No wonder Posner insists that most law-related fiction is basically about something else!

Of course, Posner's strange logic erases in one stroke an essential literary contribution to our jurisprudence. By describing not only a single trial, but all the surrounding human and linguistic elements that inform the legal outcome, literature uniquely positions itself to criticize law. If any criticisms that appear in the form of institutional distortion must be disqualified, then we are left with nothing to learn from these otherwise rich sources of legal knowledge.

48. "These be the Christian husbands!" Shylock remarks with wonder as Bassanio and Gratiano outdo each other in their willingness to sacrifice even their own wives in order to save Antonio's life (*Merchant of Venice*, IV.i.292). Shylock for all his supposed avarice would not have sold his wife's ring "for a wilderness of monkeys" (III.i.115).

49. The statement is, for me, particularly unfortunate since Posner seems, contextually, to associate the view with my own work on ressentiment. Nowhere, of course, do I equate Shylock's hatred of Antonio, which is based on a series of real insults to him "in the Rialto" (see *Merchant of Venice*, I.iii.103–26), with the imaginary spites of a fully ressentient protagonist.

50. See, e.g., Robert Weisberg, "The Law-Literature Enterprise," *Yale Journal of Law and the Humanities* (1988), 1:1, 22–26. Michael L. Richmond, "In Defense of Poesie," *Fordham Law Review* (1989), 57:901.

51. See Fyodor Dostoevski, *Notes From the Underground* (R. E. Matlaw translation, 1960); see also Weisberg, *The Failure of the Word*, pp. xi–xii.

52. Posner joins this issue when he writes, "Hamlet's biggest mistake, the standard revenger's mistake, is to get carried away" (*Law and Literature*, p. 59).

53. Weisberg, *The Failure of the Word*, p. xi.

54. See Robert M. Cover, "The Bonds of Constitutional Interpretation: Of the Word, the Deed, and the Role," *Georgia Law Review* (1985–86), 20:815, and "Violence and the Word," *Yale Law Journal* (1986), 95:1601.

55. See Garry Wills, *Nixon Agonistes* (Boston: Houghton Mifflin, 1970), pp. 55–71. (Ressentiment is explicitly associated with the former president.)

56. See John Rawls, *A Theory of Justice* (Cambridge: Harvard University Press, 1971), pp. 530–41 (touching only briefly upon the implications for personal behavior of normative equality principles unmatched by actual equality).

57. This essay derives from a speech given in Charlottesville in May 1991 as the inaugural lecture of the Friends of the University of Virginia Law Library.

58. See, e.g., Douglas L. Wilson, ed., *Jefferson's Literary Commonplace Book* (Princeton: Princeton University Press, 1989).

59. See "Thoughts on English Prosody," in Merrill D. Peterson, ed., *Thomas Jefferson: Writings* (Washington, D.C.: The Library of America, 1984), pp. 594–622.

60. Ibid., pp. 123–325.

61. See Robert A. Ferguson, *Law and Letters in American Culture*, chapter 2.

62. "Notes on the State of Virginia," in *Thomas Jefferson: Writings*, p. 300.

63. Ferguson, *Law and Letters in American Culture*, p. 242.

64. See Ferguson, ibid., p. 291.

65. See, generally, Richard Weisberg, *When Lawyers Write* (Boston: Little, Brown & Company, 1987).

66. Holmes referred to lawyers as "a little army of specialists." See Ferguson, *Law and Letters in American Culture*," p. 290.

67. See Karl Llewellyn, "On the Good, the True, the Beautiful, in Law," in *University of Chicago Law Review* (1942), 9:224.

68. Stendhal, letter to Balzac, October 28–29, 1840, in H. Martineau, ed., Balzac, *Correspondance* (1968), 3:401, cited in Weisberg, *When Lawyers Write*, p. 4.

69. See David Mellinkoff, *The Language of the Law* (Boston: Little, Brown & Company, 1963), chapter 6.

70. See chapter 2.

71. For its part, Jefferson's home state proclaimed that "English shall be designated as the official language of the Commonwealth." See Virginia Code Annotated 22.1–212.1.

72. See chapter 1.

73. At a lecture given by Professor White in April 1972, at the University of Chicago, he spoke of the work (then in progress) under the title of "Principles and Practice of Legal Expression"; both titles are helpful in defining his approach in this book.

74. One writer and thinker about the law who has referred to it as one of the humanities is Edward Levi, former president of the University of Chicago. See Edward Levi, *Point of View: Talks on Education* (Chicago: University of Chicago Press, 1969), p. 113.

75. James B. White, *The Legal Imagination* (Boston: Little, Brown, 1973), p. 81. All subsequent citations refer to this edition.

76. 331 F.2d 1010 (D.C. Cir. 1964) (Miller, Judge, dissenting).

77. See G. Cohn, *Existentialism and Legal Science*, trans. George Kendal (Dobbs Ferry, N.Y.: Oceana Publications, 1967).

78. With Benno C. Schmidt, at the Columbia University Law School, fall 1973. The seminar was called "Law and Literature."

79. For a brilliant study of this section of *The Brothers Karamazov*, see Wolfgang Holdheim, *Der Justizirrtum als Literarische Problematik* (Berlin: de Gruyter, 1969). Professor Holdheim offers a splendid analysis of various works of art centering on scenes of judicial error.

80. The interest of Western literature in the law borders on fascination, from early epic times to the current best-seller list, in drama as well as the novel. Among several anthologies and lists of such works prepared by lawyers, see Ephraim London, ed., *The World of Law* (New York: Simon & Schuster, 1960) and John H. Wigmore, "A List of 100 Legal Novels," (1908), reprinted and revised in *Illinois Law Review* (1922), 17:26. See also White's own "Bibliographical Note," *The Legal Imagination*, pp. 968–69.

81. A strong point of White's book is that an instructor who uses the book has the option of substituting his own preferences for some of White's selections. For example, *The Merchant of Venice, Measure for Measure* or even *King Lear* might be substituted for White's choice of *Troilus and Cressida* (*The Legal Imagination*, pp. 51–56); a novel by Dickens, Dostoevski or Camus (*The Stranger*, say, or *The Fall*) for

one by Jane Austen; the full text of *Billy Budd* over White's excerpt (pp. 70–73); the long legalistic passages in *Burnt Njal* instead of the short and largely incomprehensible episode from that epic in White (pp. 101–4). More recent novels also come to mind, such as Aleksandr Solzhenitsyn's *The First Circle*. See Richard H. Weisberg, "Solzhenitsyn and the Soviet Law," *University of Chicago Law Review* (1974), 41:417.

82. *The Iliad of Homer*, trans. with an Introduction by Richmond Lattimore (Chicago: University of Chicago Press, 1951), 2:211–16, 2:243–51.

83. In this section, Ovid portrays the judicial battle between Ulysses (Odysseus) and Ajax over who inherits the shield of the dead Achilles. The judges award the honor to the garrulous Ulysses, after which the heroic but less articulate Ajax kills himself in grief. (I am indebted to a student, Peter Kardon, for drawing my attention to this early example of literature and the law.)

84. Some ninety-five of the one-hundred-seventy pages in chapter 6 consist of direct communication from the author as opposed to literary, philosophical, or historical selections, and there are no legal cases whatsoever in this chapter.

85. The German Romantic philosophers then elaborated upon Locke's ideas. See especially various aphorisms of Friedrich von Schlegel, in his works on language and in the journal *Athanaeum*. Also see, generally, Eric A. Blackall, *The Emergence of German as a Literary Language, 1700–1775* (Cambridge [Eng.]: Cambridge University Press, 1959), in which the eighteenth-century thinker Christian Wolff is quoted as defining wit ("Witz") as the ability to see similarities, a quality that is deemed necessary to produce aesthetic pleasure (p. 100); judgment is rather the ability to see differences, a nonaesthetic category.

86. John Locke, *Essay Concerning Human Understanding* (1690; reprint, 1894), 1:203.

87. Quoted in White, *The Legal Imagination*, pp. 625, 730.

88. The witty person is, indeed, he who can pick up virtually any specific reference and make it universally understandable to the minds of his various listeners; he keeps the conversational ball rolling. The person with sound judgment may be an utter bore precisely because his manner is ruled by a considered loyalty to a certain set of firm standards, a general code to guide him in any specific situation.

89. Locke, *Essay Concerning Human Understanding*, 1:121n16.

90. At least according to Friedrich von Schlegel, who was, some years later, to build a poetic system around the concept of wit. However, he considers wit and judgment to be closer faculties than Locke apparently did. As to Schlegel's distinction between the two, the following quotation on judgment seems particularly apropos:

> For in all such cases the decision invariably depends upon an immediate feeling of propriety, which, though first called forth and developed by the social intercourse of life, is in truth original and innate. Such, indeed, it must ever be. For where it does not exist naturally, it can never be learned nor artificially acquired. The original want of this inward feeling can never be replaced by any varnish of external culture, however brilliant. And the case is also the same even in the sphere of science; for instance, in the shrewd, searching glance by which the skillful physician takes his diagnosis of disease; or in the clear, perspicacious sagacity which enables the judge, in some highly complicated suit or doubtful criminal trial, to seize the right point on which truth and justice hinge. For in judicial cases, with

## 6. Lawtalk in America

much that admits of demonstrative proof, or which, as a matter of fact, is un-
questioned, there is still more where nothing but this psychological penetration,
long practiced in such matters, and to which past experience has given confidence
in itself, can immediately see through all the sophistical wiles not only of the
pleadings and the skillful advocate, but also of the litigant parties themselves, or
of the crafty criminal.

Friedrich von Schlegel, *The Philosophy of Life and the Philosophy of Language*,
trans. A. J. Morrison (New York: AMS Press, 1948), p. 440. On the negative aspects
of wit, as opposed to judgment, and on the modern preponderance toward cleverness
instead of justice, see Friedrich Nietzsche, *The Genealogy of Morals*, trans. F. Golffing
(New York: Doubleday, 1956), Essay One, Aphorism 10; Essay Two, Aphorism 11;
Essay Three, Aphorism 14.

91. The judgment must be predicated on wisdom. If the act of judgment is correct,
in the service of truth, it will "delight" in the end.

92. Thus, moved as one is by White's dramatic portrayal of the objective, legal
manner in which the first century of American law turned a class of human beings
into chattel (*The Legal Imagination*, pp. 430–503), one is also puzzled by his open
admiration for the same apparent "objectivity" in Stephen Douglas' insistence that
the "principle" of state sovereignty and fair elections is more important than the
absolute termination of slavery (pp. 840–43).

93. See C. Szladits, *European Legal Systems* (Columbia University, lithograph materials, 1972), p. 190. Note that the highest administrative court, the Conseil d'Etat,
may also hand down an opinion (pp. 191–92).

94. Szladits, *European Legal Systems*, pp. 195–99.

95. James Boyd White, *The Legal Imagination* (1973); see also White, *When
Words Lose Their Meaning* (Chicago: University of Chicago Press, 1984).

96. James Boyd White, *Heracles' Bow* (Madison: University of Wisconsin, 1985).
All subsequent citations refer to this edition. White calls this book "the third in a
series" (p. xiv), and later points out that "[o]ther versions of some of the ideas at
work here can be found" in the two earlier books (p. xviii). Far from criticizing this
repetitive aspect, I applaud it in the practice of this review, for it is the constancy in
White that I most fully address—his views on law as rhetoric and literature. Indeed,
I do not treat at length here the more idiosyncratic chapters in this book, e.g., chapter
4 ("The Invisible Discourse of the Law: Reflections on Legal Literacy and General
Education"), and chapter 9 ("Making Sense of What We Do: The Criminal Law as
a System of Meaning").

97. Plato, quoted in White, *Heracles' Bow*, p. 31.

98. Jürgen Habermas, *The Theory of Communicative Action: Reason and the
Rationalization of Society*, trans. Thomas McCarthy (Boston: Beacon Press, 1984).
The notion of dialogue is critiqued in Jean François Lyotard, *The Post-Modern Con-
dition: A Report on Knowledge*, trans. G. Bennington and B. Massumi (Minneapolis:
University of Minnesota Press, 1984), pp. 65–66.

99. See, e.g., Hans Küng, *Christianity and the World Religions. Paths of Dialogue
With Islam, Hinduism and Buddhism* (Garden City, N.Y.: Doubleday, 1986). Trans.
Peter Heinegg.

100. The foremost modern antirhetorician or, as I might better call him, "dialogue-

skeptic," is of course Friedrich Nietzsche. Nietzsche, himself a brilliant stylist, always warned against writers and institutions primarily centered around the word; he consistently exhorted his readers to distrust the word, to get behind it and to detect the essentially nonverbal will to power that had generated the words themselves. Thus, for example, his lifelong attack on Flaubert, in whose work "life no longer resides in the whole. The Word gets the upper hand and jumps out of the sentence, the sentence stretches too far and obscures the meaning of the page, the page acquires life at the expense of the whole—the whole is no longer a whole. But that is the simile for every style of *décadence*." Nietzsche, "Wagner's Case," Aphorism 7, in *Werke*, (Berlin: de Gruyter, 1968), 6:21, my translation.

Nietzsche believed that rhetoric furthered the negative aims of the resentful institutions that had come to dominate modern Europe (see, e.g., on the perversion of justice by modern German law, Essay Three, Aphorism 14 of *The Genealogy of Morals*, p. 259). For the twentieth-century observer, Nietzsche's skepticism is all the more valid: after Hitler or even (much more benignly) during our own era of political and mass-media "dis-information," we cannot look naively at the notion of "dialogue" or the institutional purveyors of rhetoric.

101. Benjamin N. Cardozo, "Law and Literature" (1924–25), reprinted in Cardozo, *Selected Writings of Benjamin Nathan Cardozo*, ed. M. Hall (1947; reprint, New York: Matthew Bender, 1975), p. 339.

102. Cardozo, "The Growth of the Law" (1924), in *Selected Writings*, p. 89.

103. Richard H. Weisberg, *The Failure of the Word: The Protagonist as Lawyer in Modern Fiction* (New Haven: Yale University Press, 1984), chapter 9.

104. Thus Cardozo: "The [judicial] opinion will need persuasive force, or the impressive virtue of sincerity and fire, or the mnemonic power of alliteration and antithesis, or the terseness and tang of the proverb, and the maxim. Neglect the help of these allies, and it may never win its way." Cardozo, "Law and Literature," in *Selected Writings*, p. 342.

105. See, e.g., *Heracles' Bow*, pp. xn1 and xin2.

106. See L. H. Carter, "Review of White, *Heracles' Bow*," *Georgia Law Review* (1986), 20:793–94.

107. While the characteristic affection of law for literature (see, e.g., Ferguson, *Law and Letters in American Culture*) in this country is again on the upswing, serious scholars such as Frederick Schauer continue to display a dismally undereducated antipathy towards literary expression. See, for example, Schauer, "Liars, Novelists, and the Law of Defamation," *Brooklyn Law Review* (1985), vol. 51 at, e.g., p. 253 (novelists are accurately called "liars") and p. 257 ("it should not be at all surprising that any society would consider truth, in its unadulterated form, as having some primacy over fiction"). Judge Bork also has seemed insensitive to literary art's "higher truths" and pervasive impact on the polity. See Robert Bork, "Neutral Principles," *Indiana Law Journal* (1971), 47:28.

Since Professor Schauer is acknowledged by White for his help in commenting on portions of *Heracles' Bow*, I may be underestimating his potential awareness of the value to our culture of literary expression, which easily surpasses in every generation the only superficially more "truthful" pursuits of scientists and newspaper reporters. Other signs, such as Richard Posner's recent entrance into the Law and Literature debates (see, e.g., Posner, "Law and Literature: A Relation Reargued," *Virginia Law Review* [1986], 72:1351; response by L. H. LaRue, "Posner on Literature," *Michigan Law Review* [1987], 85:325; Posner, "Review of Weisberg's *The Failure of the Word*," *Yale Law Journal* [1986], 96:1173) portend a verification of J. Allen Smith's hopeful remarks in "The Coming Renaissance in Law and Literature," *Maryland Law Forum* (1977), 7:84.

108. I disagree with Posner's characterization of White's recent writings as "pitched at so high a level of abstraction that" one might lose "the thread of his discourse." Posner, "Law and Literature," p. 1392 (Posner is referring to an essay that became chapter 2 of *Heracles' Bow*). I find White's writing to be clear and invariably coherent.

109. See, e.g., Posner, "Law and Literature," p. 1359.

110. It takes Odysseus a mere seventy lines to convince Neoptolemus to assist in the task of seizing Heracles' bow from Philoctetes. See *Philoctetes* (lines 50–120), in David Grene and Richmond Lattimore, eds., *Greek Tragedies*, vols. (Chicago: University of Chicago Press, 1960), 3:49–52.

111. *Philoctetes* (lines 1142–43), in *Greek Tragedies*, 3:91.

112. In the play itself, the bad rhetorician is identified (by Philoctetes) as Thersites, not as Odysseus. I have had occasion in the past to challenge White's view of legal rhetoric with the example of this ignoble, argumentative Greek. See preceding section, "Notes (1974) on *The Legal Imagination*," The relationship of rhetoric to community (means-end?) seems positive in the pithy leader Odysseus, hateful in the wordy coward Thersites.

I think White needs to consider a vital aspect of the Odysseus–Thersites dichotomy. For the Greeks, "community" was an essentially *nonverbal* phenomenon. It fell outside of rhetoric. It was claimed and established almost by group intuition, sometimes buttressed by the sight of great leaders standing for a disputed position and cowards opposing it. In *Philoctetes*, there is simply no doubt that Odysseus' "ends" are just. No rhetoric can change this fact. So Odysseus, essentially honest, does not deign to distort his position through endless verbiage.

113. I am in the process of studying legal behavior during one of those periods when discursive lying of the sort unchallenged here by White contributed to a rotten structure of annihilation and terror. See Richard Weisberg, "Avoiding Central Realities: Narrative Terror and the Failure of French Culture Under the Occupation," *Human Rights Quarterly* (1983), 5:161 (see also essays 13 and 14 of the present volume). White himself sensitively treats an equivalent American period of hideous legal rhetoric in *The Legal Imagination*, pp. 432–85. Surprisingly, there has been little development of the implications for this rhetoric of such historical periods.

114. White denigrates efficiency throughout *Heracles' Bow* (see, e.g., pp. 30–32, 214). I think his theory of language, more perhaps than his anti-"ends" epistemology, explains White's sharp antipathy to law and economics. His rhetoric has always privileged "inconsistency and tension, the openness to ambiguity and uncertainty" (p. 124)—the single writer's "many-voicedness" (p. 124) or "writing two ways." Not all legal rhetorics, of course, need strive for such complexity and absence of directness. I think that White can mislead legal writers by suggesting that the single, clear, harmonious (indeed, "efficient") voice is somehow foreign to law. Indeed, he does so

explicitly in a curious chapter ("Legal Literacy and General Education") of *Heracles'*
*Bow* in which he makes the claim that the recent "plain English" movement in law
will be fruitless, because legal thinking will automatically render any system of words
(even "plain" ones) strange and unfamiliar (see p. 72). While it may seem that White
is being an elitist here, I think not; he means that lawyers *among themselves* will never
be able to simplify their manner of writing. I take a considerably different approach
to legal writing in Weisberg, *When Lawyers Write* (Boston: Little, Brown, 1987).

115. See my *The Failure of the Word*, pp. 15–18.

116. James Boyd White, *Justice as Translation* (Chicago: University of Chicago
Press, 1990), p. 231. All subsequent citations refer to this edition.

117. For an example of White's acquisitive brand of colonialism, see his treatment
of my reading of *Billy Budd, Sailor* in his essay reviewing Richard Posner's *Law and*
*Literature; A Misunderstood Relation*, in *Harvard Law Review* (1989) 102:2014.
There, White adopts a perspective on Captain Vere substantially similar to my own,
but he masks this fact by criticizing my use of so-called extrinsic evidence to show
that Melville was knowledgeable in the law and wished his readers to notice Vere's
errors. White first asserts that the story contains no "intrinsic" indication of Vere's
dubious tactics; but then he turns around and states that, on second reading, one
*does* find such evidence right there in the text (see p. 2041.) One is left to wonder
why any careful reader would not have seen such data the *first* time! But this would
be to endow my reading with more methodological validity than White would want,
since he is at one and the same time adopting parts of that reading as his own and
debunking it wherever possible. In fact, I carefully utilize the "intrinsic" data as a
threshold into the so-called extrinsic naval law that Melville knew so well. See, e.g.,
*The Failure of the Word*, pp. 146 and 165. Of course, there is something subjective
in my response to all this; I probably feel somewhat akin to the reader of the grocery
list that White conjures to question whether authorial intention is always the best
method for seeking meanings: "However sensible this view may be of ordinary com-
munications—where I leave a shopping list on the refrigerator door, for example, which
you might read in light of your knowledge of my feelings about rutabagas, say, or
Bermuda onions—it has a serious defect in principle as applied to a legal or constitutional text" (137). I would prefer White to buy his *own* groceries, or at least not
to subvert those whose shopping lists he is taking to the store.

118. White calls this book a "sequel" to his *When Words Lose Their meaning*
(Chicago: University of Chicago Press, 1984), and many pages reiterate that book's
arguments; see, e.g., pp. 32–35 and 247–48. He thus continues in a tradition perhaps
less of building than of relying on his earlier works. See also note 96 to this chapter.

119. See White, "Law and Literature: No Manifesto," in *Tennessee Law Review*
(1987) 54:161.

120. In this book, White unambiguously associates himself for the first time with
a field called "Law and Literature," although of course not wholeheartedly. (White
has little good to say about any single academic writer in these pages, much less the
work of a whole movement!) See pp. 16–21.

121. In more than one place, White speaks of what he calls "the relative deadness
of much of our professional discourse" (p. 12), against which he poses his project,
which would seek "to integrate, to bring together in interactive life, aspects of our

own minds and beings that we normally separate or divide from each other" (p. 12).

122. White states casually at several points that "it would be easy to mock" (p. 167), or "it is easy to mock" (p. 172) the rhetoric of others. (He is speaking in both cases of Justice William Douglas, a man White can only strive to emulate, even rhetorically.) There is a kind of mean-spiritedness about the writings of others abroad in *Justice as Translation*. See p. 9, where White blanketly accuses other legal academic writing of "thinness"; or pp. 136–37, where the legal realist or economist is seen as "never in favor of a truer grasp of reality, but always in favor of a reductive fiction"; or p. 11, where we professionals are found generally to speak and write "in ways that are false to the character of our own intellectual lives."

123. See Weisberg, "De Man Missing Nietzsche: '*Hinzugedichtet*' Revisited," in Clayton Koelb, ed., *Nietzsche as Postmodernist* (Albany: State University of New York Press, 1990), pp. 116–17.

124. But see the superb efforts of my colleague, Drucilla Cornell, to redeem the ethical within the deconstructive; see, e.g., "Time, Deconstruction, and the Challenge to Legal Positivism: The Call for Judicial Responsibility," in *Yale Journal on Law and the Humanities* (1990), 2:267, pp. 277–86.

125. See my discussion of *Heracles' Bow* in the prior section of this chapter.

126. See Essays 13 and 14 of this volume.

# Index

140, 153–55, 279*n*58; Theodor
Dannecker, 151; deportations, 167–
68, 175, 277*n*44; Louis-Ferdinand
Destouches, (Céline), 139; Drancy
concentration camp, 128; Adolf
Eichmann, 282*n*76; René Gillouin,
150–53; Joseph Haennig, 138–42,
156–57, 169–75, 275*n*29, 276*n*30,
290*n*146; *jurisprudence*, 127, 142–
43, and burden of proof on racial
identity, 146, 151, 156, 280*n*61,
291*nn*150, 151, and circumcision
evidence, 156, and constitutional
first principles, 145–46, 157, 168,
173, 280*n*60, and exceeding Nazi
demands and precedents, 138, 146,
151, 167, 274*n*24, 282*n*76, and
landlord-tenant cases, 146, 158–66,
and law of June 2, 1941, 137–41,
146–64, 166–68, 172, and law of
October 3, 1940, 146–50, 279*n*53,
and magistrates' rhetoric, 161–62,
166, and Mosaic Georgians, 151;
Helmuth Knochen, 152; *lawyers'
rhetorical behavior*, 141–42, 148–
49, 157–58, 168–74, 251, and
"interpretive communities," 144–45,
173–77, and post-Holocaust theory,
145, and postmodernist
hermeneutics, 145; Pierre Laval,
128, 151; *numerus clausus*, 148,
170; Darquier de Pellepoix, 139;
Philippe Pétain, 137, 146, 150;
Protestantism, 143, 149; Riom
political trial, 169–71; Jean-Paul
Sartre, 141; Philippe Serre, 146,
169, 279*n*51; Union générale des
Israélites français, 163–66; Xavier
Vallat, 137–38, 149, 167, 277*n*44,
282*n*67
Freud, Sigmund, 119
Frost, Robert, 234
Fuller, L. L., 4

Garcia v. San Antonio M.T.A., 9
Genet, Jean, 204
Germany, 235; and Nazis, 47, 56, 205;
and Romantic movement, 205; *see*

*also* France: under Nazi occupation
Gibbon, Edward, 243
Gide, André, 204
Girard, René, 100
Gogol, Nikolai, 129, 134, 136–37;
*The Nose*, 130–34
Grass, Gunter, *The Tin Drum*, 128,
142
"Great Books," the, 117–23, 201–2,
254*n*7; feminist criticism of, 118–
23; Law and Literature,
commitment to, 117, 121–23

Habermas, Jürgen, 236
Hagan, John H., 62
Hand, Learned, 15
Hardenberg, Freiherr von, *see* Novalis
Hart, H. L. A., 4
Hartman, Geoffrey, 119–20
Hayman, Harold, 135
Hegel, Friedrich, 4
Heilbrun, Carolyn, 118–19
Hitler, Adolf, 129, 144
Hölderlin, Friedrich, 120
*Hollaris v. Jankowski*, 17–21, 32–34,
and Scanlan, Presiding Justice, 20–
22
Holmes, Oliver Wendell, 6, 15, 214
Holocaust, 128–29, 140–45, 151–52,
167; *see also* Christianity; France:
under Nazi occupation
Homer, *The Iliad*, 231, 303*n*112
Hopkins, Gerard Manley, 5
House, Humphrey, 58
Howe, Irving, 189
*Hynes v. New York Central Railroad*,
17–20, 24–28

Iran-Contra hearings, 218, and Oliver
North, 218
Ives, C. B., 105

Jackson, T. A., 62
James, Henry, *The Ambassadors*, 89
James, William, 17
Jefferson, Thomas, 213–15, 217, 219,
222; *Notes on the State of Virginia*,
213–14